The Millennials

AMERICANS
BORN 1977 to 1994

The Millennials

AMERICANS BORN 1977 to 1994

2nd EDITION

BY THE NEW STRATEGIST EDITORS

New Strategist Publications, Inc.
Ithaca, New York

New Strategist Publications, Inc.
P.O. Box 242, Ithaca, New York 14851
800/848-0842; 607/273-0913
www.newstrategist.com

ISBN 1-885070-53-5

Printed in the United States of America

Table of Contents

Chapter 4. Housing

Chapter 5. Income

Chapter 6. Labor Force

Tables

Chapter 3. Health

Chapter 4. Housing

Chapter 7. Living Arrangements

Chapter 8. Population

Chapter 9. Spending

Illustrations

Chapter 4. Housing

Chapter 5. Income

Chapter 6. Labor Force

Chapter 7. Living Arrangements

Chapter 8. Population

Chapter 9. Spending

Introduction

The Millennial generation—America's children, teens, and youngest adults—is the most mysterious of the five generations of living Americans. Literally the new kids in town, the characteristics of Millennials are only now beginning to emerge as the oldest graduate from college and enter the workforce. *The Millennials: Americans Born 1977 to 1994* provides a demographic and socioeconomic profile of the generation. Because Millennials are the children of Baby Boomers, the generation has attracted the media spotlight. Because of its size, business and government are paying attention to the generation's wants and needs.

The Millennial generation, aged 10 to 27 in 2004, numbers 73 million and accounts for 26 percent of the total population—close to the Baby Boom's 28 percent share. For convenience, children under age 10 are also included in the Millennial profile in this book. The under-10 age group adds another 44 million, for a total of 116 million people under age 28 in the U.S. in 2004—or 40 percent of the population. Millennials aged 18 or older account for a substantial 20 percent of the adult population—a proportion that grows every day.

The Millennial generation follows the small Generation X, also known as the Baby-Bust generation. The oldest Millennials were born in 1977, when the long anticipated echo boom of births began. In that year, the number of births ticked up to 3.3 million. This rise followed a 12-year lull in births that is called Generation X. By 1980, annual births were up to 3.6 million. By 1990, they topped 4 million. Altogether, 68 million babies were born between 1977 and 1994.

As is true with every other generation of Americans, Millennials are defined by their numbers. And like the large Baby Boom before them, the Millennial generation's entrance is making waves. Public schools are straining with enrollments not seen since Boomers filled classrooms. Colleges and universities, which had been competing for scarce Gen Xers, now pick and choose from among the best as applications soar. Millennials are also making their mark in the housing market, with the homeownership rate rising faster among young adults than among Gen Xers or Boomers. In time, Millennials will also make their mark in the labor market and will shape the nation's families with their own lifestyles and values.

Every generation of Americans is unique not only because of its numbrs, but also because of the historical moment. Millennials are no exception. Already, three distinct characteristics are emerging, characteristics that will reshape American society as Millennials mature. One, Millennials are racially and ethnically diverse—so diverse, in fact, that in many parts of the country the term "minority" no longer has meaning for their peer group. Two, they are fiercely independent thanks to divorce, day care, single parents, latchkey lifestyles, and the technological revolution that has put the joy stick squarely in their hands.

Three, Millennials feel powerful. Raised by indulgent parents, they have a sense of security not shared by Gen Xers. Optimistic about the future, Millennials see opportunity where others see problems.

The Millennials: Americans Born 1977 to 1994 examines the youth generation from two perspectives. One, as independent individuals establishing themselves in the household and labor market. Many of the tables in the book examine young adults as workers, householders, parents, and consumers. Because about half the Millennial generation is not yet independent, the second perspective explores children living with their parents. Many tables investigate family activities and lifestyles—household television rules, day care arrangements, stay-at-home mothers and fathers, the labor force participation of parents, and the spending of married couples with children. Together, the two perspectives provide a comprehensive picture of the lifestyles of children, teens, and the youngest adults.

How to use this book

The Millennials: Americans Born 1977 to 1994 is designed for easy use. It is divided into nine chapters, organized alphabetically: Children and Their Families, Education, Health, Housing, Income, Labor Force, Living Arrangements, Population, and Spending.

This edition of *The Millennials* includes statistics on the education, living arrangements, labor force participation, health, incomes, and spending of the youngest generation and its parents. The socioeconomic estimates presented here reflect 2000 census results, which counted 6 million more Americans than demographers had estimated. *The Millennials* presents information on the relationship between children and parents from the Census Bureau's Survey of Income and Program Participation. It includes labor force data for 2003, with the government's updated occupational classifications. It contains the Census Bureau's latest population projections—the first set released by the bureau in years. And because the government now breaks out the Asian population separately in its estimates, most of the all-important racial and ethnic breakdowns include Asians for the first time, along with blacks, Hispanics, and non-Hispanic whites. New to this edition is a chapter on housing, revealing the surge in homeownership among Millennials during the past decade.

Most of the tables in *The Millennials* are based on data collected by the federal government, in particular the Census Bureau, the Bureau of Labor Statistics, the National Center for Education Statistics, the National Center for Health Statistics, and the Centers for Disease Control and Prevention. The federal government is the best source of up-to-date, reliable information on the changing characteristics of Americans. Also included in *The Millennials* are the latest data on alcohol, cigarette, and drug use among teenagers from the University of Michigan's Institute for Social Research.

While most of the tables in this book are based on data collected by the federal government, they are not simply reprints of government spreadsheets—as is the case in many reference books. Instead, each table is individually compiled and created by New Strategist's editors, with calculations designed to reveal the trends. Each chapter of *The Millennials* includes the demographic and lifestyle data most important to researchers. Each table tells a story about Millennials and their families, a story amplified by the accompanying text and chart, which analyze the data and highlight future trends. If you need more information than tables and text provide, you can plumb the original source listed at the bottom of each table.

The book contains a lengthy table list to help you locate the information you need. For a more detailed search, see the index at the back of the book. Also at the back of the book is the glossary, which defines the terms and describes the surveys commonly used in the tables and text. A list of telephone and Internet contacts also appears at the end of the book, allowing you to access government specialists and web sites.

Each new generation of Americans is unique and surprising in its own way. With *The Millennials: Americans Born 1977 to 1994* on your bookshelf, you won't be surprised by the unique characteristics of this exciting generation of Americans.

Children and Their Families

■ Family togetherness is alive and well. The Census Bureau reports that 65 percent of children aged 6 to 17 have dinner with their parents every day.

■ The 73 percent majority of children aged 6 to 17 must follow at least one of three types of television rules—their parents regulate the type of program, the time of day, or the number of hours they watch TV.

■ Only 8 percent of children aged 12 to 17 living in married-couple families have repeated a grade versus 21 percent of their counterparts in never-married single-parent families.

■ When asked whether they have engaged in a variety of risky behaviors, the majority of teens in 9th through 12th grade say no. But a substantial minority of teens are risk takers.

■ Fully 77 percent of 15-to-17-year-olds use the Internet, with 86 percent using it for school assignments and 60 percent using it to play games.

■ Because college costs are high and rising, college students are more likely to come from high-income than low-income families. Nearly half (47 percent) are from families with incomes of $75,000 or more.

■ When asked how concerned they are about their ability to finance their college education, only 34 percent of college freshmen say they have no concerns. The 53 percent majority has "some" concerns, and 13 percent have major concerns.

Parents and Children Eat Together

Most children have dinner with their parents every day.

Although some pundits worry about the state of the American family, a government study shows family togetherness is alive and well. The Census Bureau reports that 76 percent of children under age 6 have dinner with their parents every day. The figure is 65 percent among children aged 6 to 17.

Fully 70 percent of preschoolers are praised by their parents three or more times a day. The figure falls to 41 percent among children aged 6 to 17 as struggles with teenagers take a toll on the parent-child relationship.

More than 90 percent of preschoolers play with or talk to their parents for five or more minutes at least once a day. Among school-aged children, the figure is a substantial 75 percent.

■ Children interact with mothers more than fathers because most fathers have full-time jobs and spend less time at home.

Most school-aged children eat dinner with their parents every day

(percent distribution of children aged 6 to 17 by frequency of eating dinner with parent[s] in a typical week, 2000)

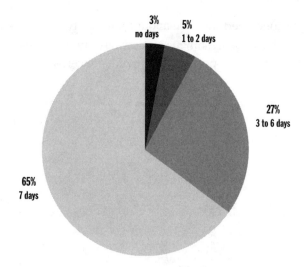

3%
no days

5%
1 to 2 days

27%
3 to 6 days

65%
7 days

Table 1.1 Children's Daily Interactions with Parents, 2000: Children under Age 6

(total number of children under age 6 and percent experiencing selected interactions with parents, by type of family, 2000; numbers in thousands)

	total	living with married parents		living with unmarried parents	
		interaction with		interaction with	
		designated parent	father/ stepfather*	designated parent	father*
Children under age 6	**23,385**	**17,240**	**16,649**	**6,145**	**835**
Parent ate breakfast with child in typical week					
No days	14.2%	12.6%	26.0%	18.5%	34.8%
One to two days	16.5	15.6	33.1	19.1	25.4
Three to six days	16.3	16.7	16.5	15.3	8.8
Seven days	53.0	55.1	24.3	47.2	31.1
Parent ate dinner with child in typical week					
No days	5.3	5.0	7.5	6.2	15.2
One to two days	3.3	2.8	8.5	4.6	7.0
Three to six days	15.1	14.6	24.4	16.4	11.3
Seven days	76.4	77.7	59.7	72.8	66.5
Parent praised chlld					
Never or once a week	1.8	1.5	2.5	2.6	5.8
A few times per week	7.6	6.1	9.7	12.1	17.0
Once or twice per day	20.3	19.3	24.8	23.1	23.0
Three+ times per day	70.3	73.2	63.0	62.3	54.2
Parent talked to/played with child for five minutes or more just for fun					
Never or once a week	1.0	0.4	1.7	2.6	5.8
A few times per week	6.5	5.3	10.6	9.7	17.5
Once or twice per day	21.1	19.3	27.7	26.2	22.3
Three+ times per day	71.4	75.0	60.0	61.5	54.4

* Fathers must be biological, step, or adoptive and must be present in the household.
Note: The designated parent is the mother in married-couple families. The resident parent is the designated parent in single-parent families. If neither parent is present, the guardian is the designated parent.
Source: Bureau of the Census, A Child's Day: 2000 (Selected Indicators of Child Well-Being), *Current Population Reports, Detailed Tables for P70-89, 2003, Internet site http://www.census.gov/population/www/socdemo/00p70-89.html*

(total number of children aged 6 to 17 and percent experiencing selected interactions with parents, by type of family, 2000; numbers in thousands)

		living with married parents		living with unmarried parents	
		interaction with		interaction with	
	total	designated parent	father/ stepfather*	designated parent	father*
Children aged 6 to 17	48,278	34,645	33,114	13,633	636
Parent ate breakfast with child in typical week					
No days	20.5%	18.3%	30.2%	26.1%	38.9%
One to two days	28.7	27.3	33.1	32.3	32.2
Three to six days	21.5	22.1	17.3	19.9	12.8
Seven days	29.3	32.3	19.3	21.7	16.1
Parent ate dinner with child in typical week					
No days	3.2	2.8	5.0	4.4	3.6
One to two days	5.4	4.9	8.9	6.8	8.2
Three to six days	26.8	27.0	32.1	26.5	17.7
Seven days	64.5	65.4	54.0	62.4	70.6
Parent praised chlld					
Never or once a week	5.2	4.6	6.9	6.8	11.8
A few times per week	22.7	21.4	26.5	26.0	24.2
Once or twice per day	31.3	31.3	30.6	31.2	36.2
Three+ times per day	40.9	42.7	36.0	36.1	27.9
Parent talked to/played with child for five minutes or more just for fun					
Never or once a week	5.7	4.9	6.8	7.9	8.5
A few times per week	19.6	18.7	24.2	22.1	28.6
Once or twice per day	33.4	33.0	33.8	34.7	35.0
Three+$ times per day	41.2	43.4	35.2	35.4	27.9

* Fathers must be biological, step, or adoptive and must be present in the household.
Note: The designated parent is the mother in married-couple families. The resident parent is the designated parent in single-parent families. If neither parent is present, the guardian is the designated parent.
Source: Bureau of the Census, A Child's Day: 2000 (Selected Indicators of Child Well-Being), *Current Population Reports, Detailed Tables for P70-89*, 2003, Internet site http://www.census.gov/population/www/socdemo/00p70-89.html

Most Families Control Children's Television Viewing

Even teens are limited in their television use.

Younger children are most likely to have limits on their television viewing. A Census Bureau study reveals that nearly 90 percent of children aged 3 to 5 must follow at least one television rule. The 64 percent majority must follow three types of rules by which their parents regulate the type of program, the time of day, and the number of hours they can watch TV.

The percentage of children whose families have television rules is slightly higher among those aged 6 to 11. But the proportion falls among children aged 12 to 17. In this age group, 73 percent must follow at least one television rule and 42 percent must follow all three rules.

The percentage of children with television rules differs little by income or race and Hispanic origin. But there are differences by parental education level. The more educated the parent, the more likely it is that the child must follow rules regarding television use.

■ From 74 to 78 percent of children under age 12 whose parents have graduate-level degrees must follow all three television rules.

Teens are less likely than younger children to have television rules

(percent of children with at least one television rule in their household, by age, 2000)

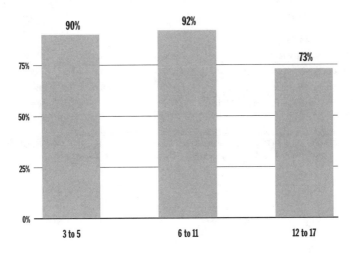

Table 1.3 Family Television Rules, 2000: Children Aged 3 to 5

(total number of children aged 3 to 5 and percent with television rules, by characteristics of child and parent, 2000; numbers in thousands)

	number	percent with at least one television rule	percent with three types of television rules
Children aged 3 to 5	**11,780**	**89.9%**	**64.4%**
Sex of child			
Female	5,808	89.0	63.3
Male	5,971	90.7	65.5
Race and ethnicity of child			
Asian and Pacific Islander	391	86.2	61.3
Black	1,813	88.3	68.3
Hispanic	1,928	83.7	64.2
Non-Hispanic white	7,631	91.8	64.0
Marital status of parent			
Married	8,700	91.0	66.2
Separated, divorced, widowed	1,233	89.9	63.2
Never married	1,846	84.4	56.9
Parent's educational level			
High school or less	5,393	86.2	60.5
Some college	2,083	92.4	64.2
Vocational or associate's degree	1,399	92.2	63.0
Bachelor's degree	2,180	92.9	72.0
Advanced degree	725	96.6	74.0
Poverty status			
Below poverty level	2,006	84.5	59.8
At or above poverty level	9,520	90.6	65.1
100 to 199 percent of poverty	2,968	88.0	64.7
200 percent of poverty or higher	6,552	91.7	65.3

Note: Television rules include type of program watched, time of day, and number of hours watched.
Source: Bureau of the Census, A Child's Day: 2000 (Selected Indicators of Child Well-Being), Current Population Reports, Detailed Tables for P70-89, 2003, Internet site http://www.census.gov/population/www/socdemo/00p70-89.html

Table 1.4 Family Television Rules, 2000: Children Aged 6 to 11

(total number of children aged 6 to 11 and percent with television rules, by characteristics of child and parent, 2000; numbers in thousands)

	number	percent with at least one television rule	percent with three types of television rules
Children aged 6 to 11	**24,581**	**92.0%**	**69.0%**
Sex of child			
Female	11,998	91.8	69.2
Male	12,583	92.3	68.7
Race and ethnicity of child			
Asian and Pacific Islander	846	88.9	69.8
Black	4,061	89.5	69.9
Hispanic	4,520	89.1	70.3
Non-Hispanic white	15,080	93.9	68.5
Marital status of parent			
Married	17,858	92.8	70.5
Separated, divorced, widowed	4,047	90.9	68.1
Never married	2,676	88.4	59.9
Parent's educational level			
High school or less	11,990	89.6	66.8
Some college	4,385	94.1	69.5
Vocational or associate's degree	3,236	92.7	68.0
Bachelor's degree	3,784	95.3	73.3
Advanced degree	1,186	97.1	77.5
Poverty status			
Below poverty level	4,379	87.4	66.0
At or above poverty level	19,663	93.0	69.5
100 to 199 percent of poverty	5,956	89.4	68.0
200 percent of poverty or higher	13,707	94.6	70.1

Note: Television rules include type of program watched, time of day, and number of hours watched.
Source: Bureau of the Census, A Child's Day: 2000 (Selected Indicators of Child Well-Being), *Current Population Reports, Detailed Tables for P70-89, 2003, Internet site http://www.census.gov/population/www/socdemo/00p70-89.html*

Table 1.5 Family Television Rules, 2000: Children Aged 12 to 17

(total number of children aged 12 to 17 and percent with television rules, by characteristics of child and parent, 2000; numbers in thousands)

	number	percent with at least one television rule	percent with three types of television rules
Children aged 12 to 17	**23,697**	**72.6%**	**41.7%**
Sex of child			
Female	11,526	71.5	40.9
Male	12,171	73.6	42.5
Race and ethnicity of child			
Asian and Pacific Islander	834	70.2	44.8
Black	3,745	69.6	45.6
Hispanic	3,683	69.6	44.3
Non-Hispanic white	15,301	74.2	40.3
Marital status of parent			
Married	16,787	75.3	43.8
Separated, divorced, widowed	5,431	65.3	34.5
Never married	1,480	68.5	44.2
Parent's educational level			
High school or less	11,665	70.2	40.0
Some college	4,110	73.9	44.0
Vocational or associate's degree	3,420	75.6	41.5
Bachelor's degree	3,063	76.4	43.9
Advanced degree	1,440	72.6	45.0
Poverty status			
Below poverty level	3,476	71.9	44.4
At or above poverty level	19,861	72.7	41.3
100 to 199 percent of poverty	5,353	71.3	41.5
200 percent of poverty or higher	14,508	73.2	41.2

Note: Television rules include type of program watched, time of day, and number of hours watched.
Source: Bureau of the Census, A Child's Day: 2000 (Selected Indicators of Child Well-Being), Current Population Reports, Detailed Tables for P70-89, 2003, Internet site http://www.census.gov/population/www/socdemo/00p70-89.html

Many Children Participate in Extracurricular Activities

There are sharp differences in participation depending on family characteristics, however.

Among children aged 6 to 11, 31 percent participate in extracurricular sports. The figure rises to 37 percent among children aged 12 to 17. Participation in extracurricular clubs stands at 34 percent in both age groups. Children aged 6 to 11 are more likely to take lessons (32 percent) than those aged 12 to 17 (26 percent).

Children with highly educated parents are most likely to participate in extracurricular activities. Fifty-five percent of children aged 6 to 11 whose parents have graduate-level degrees are involved in lessons, for example, versus just 22 percent of those whose parents have a high school diploma or less education.

Participation in extracurricular activities is also higher for non-Hispanic whites and children in married-couple families. Boys are more likely to be involved in sports, while girls are more likely to be involved in clubs and lessons.

■ Many families cannot afford the cost or time that extracurricular activities demand, particularly the poor, minorities, and single parents.

The percentage of children who participate in sports rises sharply with parental education

(percent of children aged 6 to 11 who participate in extracurricular sports, by parental education, 2000)

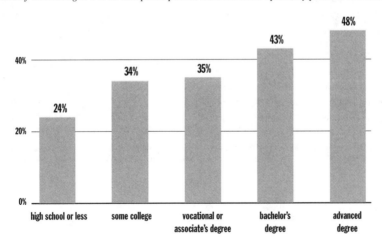

Table 1.6 Extracurricular Activities, 2000: Children Aged 6 to 11

(total number of children aged 6 to 11 and percent participating in extracurricular activities, by characteristics of child and parent, 2000; numbers in thousands)

| | number | percent participating in | | |
		sports	clubs	lessons
Children aged 6 to 11	**24,581**	**30.6%**	**33.8%**	**32.0%**
Sex of child				
Female	11,998	24.4	36.0	36.8
Male	12,583	36.5	31.8	27.5
Race and ethnicity of child				
Asian and Pacific Islander	846	20.4	27.1	36.0
Black	4,061	20.6	27.6	25.4
Hispanic	4,520	21.5	20.2	20.7
Non-Hispanic white	15,080	36.7	39.9	37.1
Marital status of parent				
Married	17,858	34.7	37.2	36.1
Separated, divorced, widowed	4,047	25.1	26.7	22.5
Never married	2,676	18.6	22.1	20.0
Parent's educational level				
High school or less	11,990	23.5	24.9	21.5
Some college	4,385	31.1	36.0	35.1
Vocational or associate's degree	3,236	35.1	40.9	37.6
Bachelor's degree	3,784	42.9	47.9	50.0
Advanced degree	1,186	48.9	52.8	54.6
Poverty status				
Below poverty level	4,379	15.9	22.8	18.6
At or above poverty level	19,663	34.3	36.6	35.3
100 to 199 percent of poverty	5,956	24.1	27.2	23.7
200 percent of poverty or higher	13,707	38.7	40.7	40.3

Source: Bureau of the Census, A Child's Day: 2000 (Selected Indicators of Child Well-Being), *Current Population Reports, Detailed Tables for P70-89, 2003, Internet site http://www.census.gov/population/www/socdemo/00p70-89.html*

Table 1.7 Extracurricular Activities, 2000: Children Aged 12 to 17

(total number of children aged 12 to 17 and percent participating in extracurricular activities, by characteristics of child and parent, 2000; numbers in thousands)

| | number | percent participating in | | |
		sports	clubs	lessons
Children aged 12 to 17	**23,697**	**37.2%**	**34.4%**	**26.2%**
Sex of child				
Female	11,526	32.5	37.5	30.2
Male	12,171	41.6	31.4	22.3
Race and ethnicity of child				
Asian and Pacific Islander	834	25.7	31.5	33.1
Black	3,745	30.5	25.0	19.4
Hispanic	3,683	28.0	22.9	20.3
Non-Hispanic white	15,301	41.7	39.4	29.1
Marital status of parent				
Married	16,787	40.2	37.9	29.3
Separated, divorced, widowed	5,431	30.3	27.7	19.8
Never married	1,480	28.3	19.1	14.2
Parent's educational level				
High school or less	11,665	29.6	26.2	19.6
Some college	4,110	40.1	37.6	28.6
Vocational or associate's degree	3,420	39.6	39.6	29.1
Bachelor's degree	3,063	49.3	46.7	37.7
Advanced degree	1,440	58.4	52.6	41.2
Poverty status				
Below poverty level	3,476	24.9	23.2	17.9
At or above poverty level	19,861	39.6	36.6	27.9
100 to 199 percent of poverty	5,353	30.7	29.5	20.8
200 percent of poverty or higher	14,508	42.9	39.2	30.5

Source: Bureau of the Census, A Child's Day: 2000 (Selected Indicators of Child Well-Being), *Current Population Reports, Detailed Tables for P70-89, 2003, Internet site http://www.census.gov/population/www/socdemo/00p70-89.html*

Children's School Success Depends on Family Characteristics

Those with educated, married parents do the best.

Nearly half of children aged 12 to 17 whose parents are highly educated are in gifted classes, according to a Census Bureau survey. Forty-nine percent of teens whose parents have graduate-level degrees are in gifted classes versus only 14 percent of children whose parents have a high school diploma or less.

Other findings also reveal that children with educated, married parents whose families are well above poverty level do far better in school than those whose parents are poorly educated, single, and living below poverty level. Among children aged 12 to 17, only 8 percent of those living in married-couple families have repeated a grade, for example, versus 21 percent of those in never-married single-parent families. Similarly, 19 percent of children living below poverty level have repeated a grade versus only 9 percent of those at or above poverty level. The percentage of teenagers who have ever been suspended from school is twice as high among those from single-parent than from married-couple families.

■ School performance is unlikely to improve until more children live in stable, two-parent families.

Family stability determines school performance

(percent of children aged 12 to 17 who have ever repeated a grade, by marital status of parent, 2000)

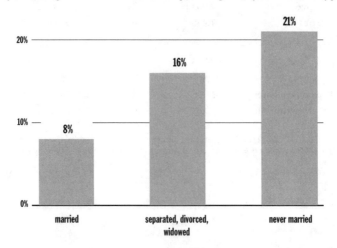

Table 1.8 Children in Gifted Classes, 2000

(total number of children aged 6 to 17 and percent in gifted classes, by characteristics of child and parent, 2000; numbers in thousands)

	children aged 6 to 11		children aged 12 to 17	
	number	percent in gifted classes	number	percent in gifted classes
Children aged 6 to 17	**24,015**	**12.7%**	**23,008**	**21.8%**
Sex of child				
Female	11,685	13.1	11,215	23.5
Male	12,330	12.3	11,793	20.2
Race and ethnicity of child				
Asian and Pacific Islander	818	11.8	817	27.5
Black	4,005	10.0	3,636	18.4
Hispanic	4,466	9.1	3,564	14.3
Non-Hispanic white	14,671	14.7	14,888	24.3
Marital status of parent				
Married	17,393	13.6	16,340	24.1
Separated, divorced, widowed	3,994	10.3	5,250	17.2
Never married	2,628	10.2	1,418	12.4
Parent's educational level				
High school or less	11,741	8.6	11,220	14.4
Some college	4,249	15.4	4,012	22.3
Vocational or associate's degree	3,172	13.4	3,352	23.4
Bachelor's degree	3,684	19.6	2,998	34.2
Advanced degree	1,169	21.2	1,424	48.9
Poverty status				
Below poverty level	4,239	7.6	3,309	13.7
At or above poverty level	19,249	14.0	19,364	23.4
100 to 199 percent of poverty	5,801	10.5	5,199	15.9
200 percent of poverty or higher	13,448	15.5	14,165	26.2

Source: Bureau of the Census, A Child's Day: 2000 (Selected Indicators of Child Well-Being), *Current Population Reports, Detailed Tables for P70-89, 2003, Internet site http://www.census.gov/population/www/socdemo/00p70-89.html*

Table 1.9 Children Who Have Changed Schools, 2000

(total number of children aged 6 to 17 and percent who have changed schools, by characteristics of child and parent, 2000; numbers in thousands)

	children aged 6 to 11		children aged 12 to 17	
	number	percent who have changed schools	number	percent who have changed schools
Children aged 6 to 17	**24,037**	**23.3%**	**23,086**	**40.1%**
Sex of child				
Female	11,702	23.8	11,251	40.5
Male	12,335	22.8	11,834	39.7
Race and ethnicity of child				
Asian and Pacific Islander	818	19.9	821	35.2
Black	4,005	27.9	3,642	39.2
Hispanic	4,466	23.1	3,582	39.4
Non-Hispanic white	14,693	22.1	6,012	40.3
Marital status of parent				
Married	17,410	21.3	16,389	38.6
Separated, divorced, widowed	3,998	29.1	5,280	45.8
Never married	2,628	27.7	1,418	36.0
Parent's educational level				
High school or less	11,746	24.1	11,277	39.0
Some college	4,258	25.0	4,015	44.8
Vocational or associate's degree	3,176	22.4	3,367	41.4
Bachelor's degree	3,689	21.1	3,003	37.7
Advanced degree	1,169	18.2	1,424	37.2
Poverty status				
Below poverty level	4,244	26.6	3,334	41.6
At or above poverty level	19,267	22.4	19,413	39.6
100 to 199 percent of poverty	5,815	24.3	5,217	39.4
200 percent of poverty or higher	13,452	21.6	14,196	39.7

Note: Changing schools does not include normal progression and graduation from elementary and middle schools.
Source: Bureau of the Census, A Child's Day: 2000 (Selected Indicators of Child Well-Being), Current Population Reports, Detailed Tables for P70-89, 2003, Internet site http://www.census.gov/population/www/socdemo/00p70-89.html

Table 1.10 Children Who Have Repeated a Grade, 2000

(total number of children aged 6 to 17 and percent who have ever repeated a grade, by characteristics of child and parent, 2000; numbers in thousands)

	children aged 6 to 11		children aged 12 to 17	
	number	percent who have repeated a grade	number	percent who have repeated a grade
Children aged 6 to 17	**24,214**	**5.3%**	**23,417**	**10.7%**
Sex of child				
Female	11,810	4.3	11,413	8.7
Male	12,404	6.2	12,004	12.7
Race and ethnicity of child				
Asian and Pacific Islander	818	2.6	824	6.4
Black	4,029	7.7	3,710	17.2
Hispanic	4,488	4.6	3,648	11.3
Non-Hispanic white	14,813	4.9	15,123	9.4
Marital status of parent				
Married	17,544	4.4	16,552	8.2
Separated, divorced, widowed	4,020	7.3	5,397	15.9
Never married	2,650	7.7	1,468	20.5
Parent's educational level				
High school or less	11,837	6.4	11,509	13.6
Some college	4,305	4.9	4,076	9.9
Vocational or associate's degree	3,198	4.9	3,390	8.7
Bachelor's degree	3,703	3.5	3,010	5.9
Advanced degree	1,172	1.4	1,431	4.9
Poverty status				
Below poverty level	4,268	8.7	3,416	19.3
At or above poverty level	19,416	4.5	19,653	9.2
100 to 199 percent of poverty	5,883	6.6	5,302	13.7
200 percent of poverty or higher	13,533	3.6	14,351	7.5

Source: Bureau of the Census, A Child's Day: 2000 (Selected Indicators of Child Well-Being), *Current Population Reports, Detailed Tables for P70-89, 2003, Internet site http://www.census.gov/population/www/socdemo/00p70-89.html*

Table 1.11 Children Aged 12 to 17 Who Have Been Suspended, 2000

(total number of children aged 12 to 17 and percent who have ever been suspended, by characteristics of child and parent, 2000; numbers in thousands)

	number	percent who have been suspended
Children aged 12 to 17	**23,008**	**10.4%**
Sex of child		
Female	11,215	7.0
Male	11,793	13.7
Race and ethnicity of child		
Asian and Pacific Islander	817	5.3
Black	3,636	17.9
Hispanic	3,564	8.5
Non-Hispanic white	14,888	9.3
Marital status of parent		
Married	16,340	8.1
Separated, divorced, widowed	5,250	16.2
Never married	1,418	16.6
Parent's educational level		
High school or less	11,220	11.6
Some college	4,012	11.7
Vocational or associate's degree	3,352	9.9
Bachelor's degree	2,998	6.3
Advanced degree	1,424	5.7
Poverty status		
Below poverty level	3,309	14.5
At or above poverty level	19,364	9.5
100 to 199 percent of poverty	5,199	11.9
200 percent of poverty or higher	14,165	8.7

Source: Bureau of the Census, A Child's Day: 2000 (Selected Indicators of Child Well-Being), Current Population Reports, Detailed Tables for P70-89, 2003, Internet site http://www.census.gov/population/www/socdemo/00p70-89.html

Most Parents Want Their Children to Graduate from College

Even the poorest families want their children to get a college degree.

Most of today's high school graduates go to college. One reason why college has become the norm is that parents expect their children to get a college degree. Among the nation's 72 million children under age 18, 58 percent have parents who want them to graduate from college and another 28 percent have parents who want them to continue their education beyond college. Only 14 percent of children have parents who want their education to stop at less than a college degree.

Parental desires do not vary much by demographic characteristic, except for education. Among children whose parents have graduate-level degrees, 50 percent have parents who want them to get education and training beyond college. Among children whose parents have a high school education or less, only 21 percent have parents who want them to go beyond college in their educational level.

■ Parents have high expectations and many will be disappointed since only about half the students who enter college eventually graduate.

Most parents want their children to earn a college diploma

(percent distribution of children by educational level parents want for them, 2000)

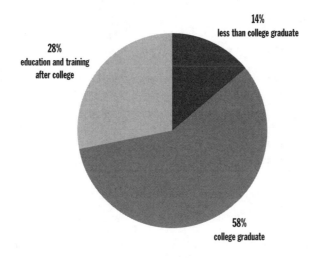

14%
less than college graduate

28%
education and training
after college

58%
college graduate

Table 1.12 Educational Expectations of Parents for Their Children, 2000

(number of children and percent distribution by educational expectation of parents for their children, by charac-teristics of child and parent, 2000; numbers in thousands)

	total	education level parent wants for child				education level parent thinks child will achieve			
		total	less than college graduate	college graduate	education and training after college	total	less than college graduate	college graduate	education and training after college
Total children	**71,663**	**100.0%**	**14.2%**	**57.8%**	**28.0%**	**100.0%**	**20.7%**	**57.1%**	**22.2%**
Sex of child									
Female	34,947	100.0	13.4	58.9	27.8	100.0	19.5	58.1	22.5
Male	36,716	100.0	15.0	56.8	28.2	100.0	21.9	56.2	21.9
Age of child									
Under age 12	47,966	100.0	12.6	58.1	29.3	100.0	18.0	58.9	23.1
Aged 12 to 17	23,697	100.0	17.4	57.2	25.4	100.0	26.2	53.5	20.3
Race and ethnicity of child									
Asian and Pacific Islander	2,509	100.0	9.2	55.5	35.3	100.0	11.8	57.3	30.9
Black	11,377	100.0	16.7	53.0	30.3	100.0	23.6	52.7	23.7
Hispanic	11,636	100.0	19.6	53.6	26.8	100.0	26.2	53.1	20.7
Non-Hispanic white	45,826	100.0	12.4	60.0	27.6	100.0	18.8	59.2	21.9
Marital status of parent									
Married	51,885	100.0	12.1	58.3	29.6	100.0	17.9	58.5	23.6
Separated, divorced, widowed	11,538	100.0	19.3	58.3	22.4	100.0	27.8	55.6	16.6
Never married	8,240	100.0	20.1	53.8	26.1	100.0	28.8	50.4	20.8
Parent's educational level									
High school or less	34,168	100.0	21.0	58.3	20.7	100.0	28.9	55.0	16.1
Some college	12,482	100.0	10.4	60.0	29.6	100.0	18.2	60.3	21.5
Vocational or associate's degree	9,426	100.0	9.4	60.4	30.2	100.0	15.2	61.5	23.3
Bachelor's degree	11,617	100.0	5.8	55.8	38.4	100.0	8.4	59.5	32.1
Advanced degree	3,970	100.0	3.3	46.5	50.2	100.0	6.5	48.3	45.2
Poverty status									
Below poverty level	11,714	100.0	22.9	55.2	21.9	100.0	30.4	52.8	16.8
At or above poverty level	58,526	100.0	12.3	58.3	29.4	100.0	18.5	58.1	23.3
100 to 199 percent of poverty	16,638	100.0	19.1	56.9	24.0	100.0	26.8	54.4	18.8
200 percent of poverty or higher	41,888	100.0	9.6	58.9	31.5	100.0	15.3	59.6	25.1

Source: Bureau of the Census, A Child's Day: 2000 (Selected Indicators of Child Well-Being), *Current Population Reports, Detailed Tables for P70-89, 2003, Internet site http://www.census.gov/population/www/socdemo/00p70-89.html*

Few Parents Are Often Angry at Their Children

But most say their children sometimes bother them.

Raising children can be frustrating, and most parents occasionally feel annoyed at their children's behavior and at how time consuming childrearing can be. The majority of parents (69 percent) say their child is not harder to care for than most children. But the 43 percent minority of parents report that their child never does things that really bother them—leaving the 57 percent majority saying they sometimes are bothered by what their child does. About half admit that caring for children takes more time than they expected. Forty-five percent of parents say they never feel angry with their child, while a perhaps more honest 55 percent say they feel angry at least sometimes. Only 2 percent say they feel angry often or very often.

Those least likely to report problems with their children are the youngest parents, married parents, Asians and Hispanics, and the most highly educated parents.

■ A substantial share of parents admit that raising children is a time-consuming task, with 15 percent saying they often or very often feel it takes more time than they expected.

Asians and Hispanics are least likely to be bothered by their children

(percent of parents who say their child never does things that really bother them, by race and Hispanic origin, 2000)

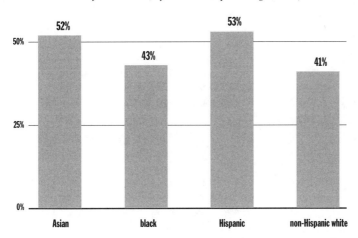

Table 1.13 Parents' Feelings toward Their Children, 2000

(total number of parents and percent with selected feelings towards their children, by characteristics of parent, 2000; numbers in thousands)

		child is much harder to care for than most children		child does things that really bother me		child takes up more time than expected		parent feels angry with child	
	total	never	often or very often	never	often or very often	never	often or very often	never	often or very often
Total parents	**39,836**	**68.7%**	**5.4%**	**43.3%**	**5.1%**	**49.4%**	**15.4%**	**44.5%**	**2.4%**
Age of parent									
Under age 25	3,164	64.5	6.2	49.7	5.0	50.9	17.2	53.2	1.4
Aged 25 to 34	13,083	68.2	5.2	44.9	5.9	50.2	15.0	47.9	2.9
Aged 35 or older	23,590	69.5	5.4	41.5	4.7	48.8	15.4	41.5	2.2
Race and ethnicity of parent									
Asian and Pacific Islander	1,534	65.7	5.6	52.3	3.0	51.9	13.7	49.3	2.0
Black	6,220	68.7	4.7	42.8	6.8	45.8	17.1	49.1	3.1
Hispanic	5,834	67.5	5.0	53.0	3.0	54.6	12.3	49.1	1.7
Non-Hispanic white	26,179	69.5	5.7	41.0	5.3	49.1	15.9	42.7	2.3
Marital status of parent									
Married	27,885	71.2	4.8	44.6	4.0	52.2	13.8	45.2	1.9
Separated, divorced, widowed	6,902	62.8	7.3	38.5	7.8	43.2	19.2	40.9	3.6
Never married	5,049	62.8	6.3	42.4	7.7	42.6	19.2	45.9	3.5
Parent's educational level									
High school or less	18,477	66.8	5.6	43.7	6.1	49.4	16.2	45.4	2.7
Some college	7,143	69.4	4.5	43.2	5.4	47.9	15.2	42.8	2.5
Vocational or associate's degree	5,442	71.1	5.6	41.3	5.0	49.5	15.1	43.2	2.2
Bachelor's degree	6,451	69.5	5.7	42.8	3.1	50.4	14.4	44.1	1.8
Advanced degree	2,322	73.5	4.7	46.3	2.1	51.7	13.7	47.8	1.7
Poverty status									
Below poverty level	5,392	61.6	7.3	40.2	8.1	44.1	20.1	44.3	3.5
At or above poverty level	33,989	70.0	5.1	43.8	4.6	50.4	14.6	44.5	2.2
100 to 199 percent of poverty	8,677	65.9	5.9	43.2	6.2	49.2	14.3	44.2	2.6
200 percent of poverty or higher	25,312	71.4	4.9	43.9	4.0	50.8	14.8	44.6	2.1

Note: Feelings refer to all children living with designated parent.
Source: Bureau of the Census, A Child's Day: 2000 (Selected Indicators of Child Well-Being), *Current Population Reports, Detailed Tables for P70-89, 2003, Internet site http://www.census.gov/population/www/socdemo/00p70-89.html*

Most Teens Are Not Risk Takers

But many engage in risky behavior, including driving after drinking.

When asked whether they have engaged in a variety of risky behaviors, the majority of teens in 9th through 12th grade say no. But a substantial minority of teens are risk takers.

Half of 9th grade boys have been in a physical fight in the past year, as have 30 percent of 9th grade girls. During the past month, 33 percent of 12th graders were passengers in a car with a driver who had been drinking. Twenty-seven to 29 percent of 9th through 12th graders have felt so sad or hopeless almost every day for at least two weeks during the year preceding the survey that they had to stop doing their usual activities. Sixteen to 21 percent seriously considered attempting suicide in the past year.

Some risk taking declines as students mature. The percentage of boys who have been in a physical fight falls from half to 37 percent between 9th and 12th grade. Other risk behavior increases with age. The proportion of students who admit to riding in the past month with a driver who had been drinking rises from 7 percent among 9th graders (most of whom are too young to drive) to 22 percent among 12th graders. Twenty-seven percent of 12th grade boys admit to driving after drinking in the past month.

■ Although most teens do not engage in risky behavior, the substantial portion who do give teens a bad reputation.

Many teen boys drive after drinking

(percent of male students who drove after drinking in the past 30 days, by grade, 2001)

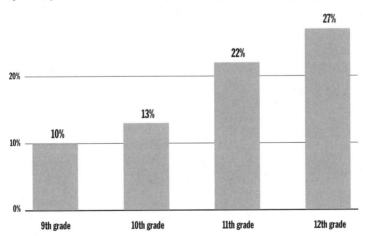

Table 1.14 Risk Behavior of 9th Graders by Sex, 2001

(percent of 9th graders engaging in selected risk behaviors, by sex, 2001)

	9th graders		
	total	female	male
Was in a physical fight in past 12 months	39.5%	30.3%	50.0%
In past 30 days rode with a driver who had been drinking alcohol	30.4	31.3	29.2
Felt so sad/hopeless almost every day for two or more weeks that stopped usual activities	29.4	35.7	22.4
Seriously considered attempting suicide in past 12 months	20.8	26.2	14.7
Rarely or never wore seatbelts when riding in a car driven by someone else	19.9	10.8	19.4
Carried a weapon on at least one day during the past 30 days	19.8	7.4	33.7
Engaged in a physical fight on school property during past 12 months	17.3	10.2	25.1
Was threatened or injured with a weapon on school property during past 12 months	12.7	10.0	15.7
Attempted suicide in past 12 months	11.0	13.2	8.2
Felt too unsafe to go to school in the past 30 days	8.8	9.6	8.0
Was physically hurt by boyfriend/girlfriend on purpose in the past 12 months	8.5	9.2	7.7
Was forced to have sexual intercourse	7.3	8.6	5.9
Carried a gun on at least one day during the past 30 days	6.8	1.0	13.3
Carried a weapon on school property in past 30 days	6.7	2.9	10.7
Drove after drinking alcohol in past 30 days	6.6	3.7	9.9
Suicide attempt required medical attention in past 12 months	3.2	3.8	2.6

Source: Grunbaum, Jo Anne, et al., Youth Risk Behavior Surveillance—United States, 2001, *Mortality and Morbidity Weekly Report, Vol. 51/SS-4, Centers for Disease Control and Prevention, June 28, 2002*

Table 1.15 Risk Behavior of 10th Graders by Sex, 2001

(percent of 10th graders engaging in selected risk behaviors, by sex, 2001)

	10th graders		
	total	female	male
Was in a physical fight in the past 12 months	34.7%	24.9%	45.0%
In past 30 days rode with a driver who had been drinking alcohol	30.6	29.9	31.5
Felt so sad/hopeless almost every day for two or more weeks that stopped usual activities	27.2	34.6	19.7
Seriously considered attempting suicide in past 12 months	19.0	24.1	13.8
Carried a weapon on at least one day during the past 30 days	16.7	5.4	28.4
Engaged in a physical fight on school property during past 12 months	13.5	7.7	19.5
Rarely or never wore seatbelts when riding in a car driven by someone else	13.3	10.3	16.6
Drove after drinking alcohol in past 30 days	10.4	8.4	12.5
Attempted suicide in past 12 months	9.5	12.2	6.7
Was physically hurt by boyfriend/girlfriend on purpose in the past 12 months	9.3	10.6	8.0
Was threatened or injured with a weapon on school property during past 12 months	9.1	6.3	11.9
Was forced to have sexual intercourse	7.5	10.7	4.1
Carried a weapon on school property in past 30 days	6.7	2.9	10.5
Felt too unsafe to go to school in the past 30 days	6.3	7.0	5.6
Carried a gun on at least one day during the past 30 days	4.9	1.0	9.0
Suicide attempt required medical attention in past 12 months	3.0	3.6	2.5

Source: Grunbaum, Jo Anne, et al., Youth Risk Behavior Surveillance—United States, 2001, Mortality and Morbidity Weekly Report, Vol. 51/SS-4, Centers for Disease Control and Prevention, June 28, 2002

Table 1.16   Risk Behavior of 11th Graders by Sex, 2001

(percent of 11th graders engaging in selected risk behaviors, by sex, 2001)

	11th graders		
	total	female	male
In past 30 days rode with a driver who had been drinking alcohol	29.1%	25.4%	32.8%
Was in a physical fight in the past 12 months	29.1	20.3	38.0
Felt so sad/hopeless almost every day for two or more weeks that stopped usual activities	28.7	33.9	23.4
Seriously considered attempting suicide in past 12 months	18.9	23.6	14.1
Carried a weapon on at least one day during the past 30 days	16.8	5.9	28.1
Drove after drinking alcohol in past 30 days	16.7	11.1	22.1
Rarely or never wore seatbelts when riding in a car driven by someone else	13.6	9.7	17.5
Was physically hurt by boyfriend/girlfriend on purpose in the past 12 months	9.5	9.4	9.6
Engaged in a physical fight on school property during past 12 months	9.4	5.1	13.8
Attempted suicide in past 12 months	8.3	11.5	4.9
Was forced to have sexual intercourse	7.1	9.9	4.3
Was threatened or injured with a weapon on school property during past 12 months	6.9	4.7	9.1
Carried a weapon on school property in past 30 days	6.1	2.9	9.5
Felt too unsafe to go to school in the past 30 days	5.9	6.8	5.0
Carried a gun on at least one day during the past 30 days	5.7	1.8	9.6
Suicide attempt required medical attention in past 12 months	2.2	2.8	1.6

Source: Grunbaum, Jo Anne, et al., Youth Risk Behavior Surveillance—United States, 2001, *Mortality and Morbidity Weekly Report, Vol. 51/SS-4, Centers for Disease Control and Prevention, June 28, 2002*

Table 1.17 Risk Behavior of 12th Graders by Sex, 2001

(percent of 12th graders engaging in selected risk behaviors, by sex, 2001)

	12th graders		
	total	female	male
In past 30 days rode with a driver who had been drinking alcohol	32.8%	31.3%	34.5%
Felt so sad/hopeless almost every day for two or more weeks that stopped usual activities	27.0	33.2	20.5
Was in a physical fight in the past 12 months	26.5	16.9	36.5
Drove after drinking alcohol in past 30 days	22.1	17.3	27.2
Seriously considered attempting suicide in past 12 months	16.4	18.9	13.7
Carried a weapon on at least one day during the past 30 days	15.1	5.3	25.6
Rarely or never wore seatbelts when riding in a car driven by someone else	13.9	9.4	18.6
Was physically hurt by boyfriend/girlfriend on purpose in the past 12 months	10.7	9.8	11.7
Was forced to have sexual intercourse	9.0	12.2	5.8
Engaged in a physical fight on school property during past 12 months	7.5	4.4	10.7
Carried a weapon on school property in past 30 days	6.0	2.7	9.6
Attempted suicide in past 12 months	5.5	6.5	4.4
Was threatened or injured with a weapon on school property during past 12 months	5.3	3.0	7.7
Carried a gun on at least one day during the past 30 days	4.7	1.2	8.3
Felt too unsafe to go to school in the past 30 days	4.4	5.0	3.9
Suicide attempt required medical attention in past 12 months	1.6	1.7	1.5

Source: Grunbaum, Jo Anne, et al., Youth Risk Behavior Surveillance—United States, 2001, Mortality and Morbidity Weekly Report, Vol. 51/SS-4, Centers for Disease Control and Prevention, June 28, 2002

Delinquent Behavior Is Not the Norm

Most 12th graders do not engage in delinquent behavior, but a substantial minority cross the line.

Most teenagers follow the rules, but not all of them. When asked which delinquent behaviors they had participated in during the past year, 29 percent of 12th graders admit taking something worth less than $50 that did not belong to them. Twenty-eight percent have taken something from a store without paying for it. Fourteen percent have gotten into a serious fight at school or work.

Boys are more likely than girls to engage in most types of problem behavior. While 18 percent of 12th grade boys have hurt someone badly enough in the past year that they needed bandages or a doctor, only 5 percent of girls have done so. Fourteen percent of boys say they have been arrested and taken to a police station in the past year versus 4 percent of girls. Thirty-seven percent of boys have received a traffic ticket or warning for a moving violation versus 25 percent of girls. The only problem behavior girls are more likely to engage in than boys is arguing with parents—92 percent of girls have done so in the past 12 months versus 85 percent of boys.

■ While delinquent behavior is not the norm among teens, it is widespread enough to raise alarm among parents, teachers, and community leaders.

Many boys engage in delinquent behavior

(percent of 12th grade boys engaging in delinquent behavior in the past 12 months, 2002)

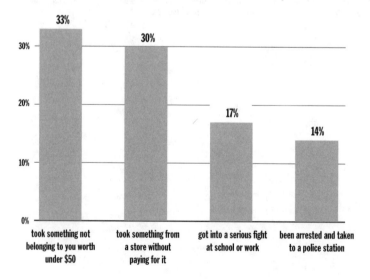

Table 1.18 Delinquent Behavior of 12th Graders, 2002

(percent of 12th graders reporting delinquent behavior in the past 12 months, by type of behavior and sex, 2002)

	total	females	males
Argued or had a fight with either of your parents	87.7%	91.5%	84.9%
Received traffic ticket or warning for a moving violation	30.5	24.5	37.0
Took something not belonging to you worth under $50	28.8	24.8	32.9
Took something from a store without paying for it	27.9	25.8	29.9
Went into a house or building when you weren't supposed to be there	22.6	18.8	26.5
Got into a serious fight at school or work	13.7	9.8	16.6
Hurt someone badly enough to need bandages or a doctor	11.7	5.1	17.5
Damaged school property on purpose	11.5	6.6	15.8
Took something not belonging to you worth over $50	10.1	5.4	14.2
Been arrested and taken to a police station	9.3	4.3	13.5
Took part in a fight with a group of friends	7.1	14.3	19.0
Damaged property at work on purpose	6.5	1.6	11.1
Took a car that didn't belong to someone in your family without permission	4.9	2.7	6.9
Took part of a car without permission	4.7	2.1	7.0
Used a knife, gun, or other weapon to get something from someone	3.2	0.9	5.1
Set fire to someone's property on purpose	3.1	1.2	4.7
Hit an instructor or supervisor	3.0	1.3	4.6

Source: Bureau of Justice Statistics, Sourcebook of Criminal Justice Statistics 2002, Internet site http://www.albany.edu/sourcebook

Most Children Use the Internet

Three out of four teens are online.

Computers and the Internet are used by the majority of children aged 8 or older, according to a study by the National Center for Education Statistics. Fully 81 percent of children aged 5 to 7 use computers, and the proportion rises to 93 percent among 15–to-17-year-olds. Thirty-one percent of 5-to-7-year-olds use the Internet, with the proportion rising to 77 percent among 15-to-17-year-olds. Playing games is the most popular computer activity, and more than half of all children do so. Among those with computers at home, more than 90 percent play games on their computer.

Among children who use the Internet, most are online to complete school assignments. The proportion rises from 37 percent among children aged 5 to 7 to fully 86 percent among those aged 15 to 17. E-mailing, instant messaging, and game playing are done by the majority of children aged 8 or older who are online. Twenty percent of 15-to-17-year-olds have bought something online.

■ Most children are computer literate and Internet savvy, often more so than their parents.

The majority of children aged 8 or older are online

(percent of children aged 5 to 17 who use the Internet, by age, 2001)

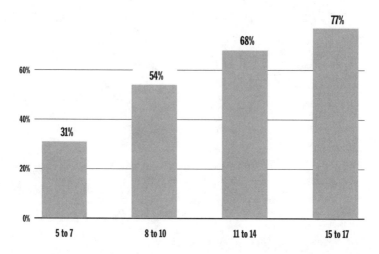

Table 1.19 Computer and Internet Use among Children, 2001

(number and percent of children aged 5 to 17 using computers and the Internet, by age, 2001)

	total children	5–7	8–10	11–14	15–17
Percent using computers at any location	**89.5%**	**80.5%**	**90.5%**	**92.6%**	**93.4%**
Percent using computers at home	65.2	56.4	62.7	68.6	72.0
Percent using computers at school	80.7	68.2	83.1	85.2	84.5
Percent using the Internet	**58.5**	**31.4**	**53.5**	**68.3**	**77.1**
Percent of total children aged 5 to 17 using computers for					
Word processing	32.4	9.4	23.8	42.1	50.9
Connecting to the Internet	45.6	22.6	39.5	54.1	62.9
E-mailing	34.4	9.5	23.9	43.3	57.7
Spreadsheets/databases	–	–	–	–	17.1
Graphics/design	–	–	–	–	23.6
Completion of school assignments	44.2	13.8	37.7	56.6	64.2
Playing games	59.2	54.0	58.8	62.9	59.6
Percent of home computer users aged 5 to 17 using computers for					
Word processing	49.7	16.7	38.0	61.4	70.7
Connecting to the Internet	69.9	40.1	63.0	78.9	87.4
E-mailing	52.7	16.9	38.1	63.1	80.2
Spreadsheets/databases	–	–	–	–	23.8
Graphics/design	–	–	–	–	32.8
Completion of school assignments	67.8	24.4	60.1	82.6	89.2
Playing games	90.8	95.8	93.8	91.8	82.8
Percent of Internet users aged 5 to 17 who use the Internet at					
Own home	77.9	72.0	74.0	79.2	81.6
School	67.7	53.3	63.4	70.8	72.9
Public library	15.4	10.1	12.2	17.3	17.6
Community center	1.1	0.8	0.8	1.3	1.3
Someone else's home	15.1	8.7	11.4	16.6	18.4
Some other place	1.2	1.7	0.9	1.2	1.1
Percent of Internet users aged 5 to 17 using the Internet for					
Completing school assignments	72.0	37.2	59.7	79.5	85.8
E-mail or instant messaging	65.0	35.5	50.1	68.8	82.8
Playing games	62.3	65.3	63.0	63.0	59.8
Learning about news/weather/sports	37.3	14.7	24.4	40.1	52.2
Finding information on products	34.0	12.5	18.6	34.6	53.1
Visiting chat rooms or listservs	20.3	4.1	6.6	20.9	36.1
Watching/listening to TV, movies, radio	18.9	9.4	12.2	19.0	27.4
Making purchases	10.6	2.1	4.2	9.3	20.2
Making phone calls	3.2	1.7	2.0	2.7	5.3
Taking a course online	0.9	0.6	0.8	0.6	1.5
Finding government information	–	–	–	–	9.8
Finding health information	–	–	–	–	9.7
Finding a job	–	–	–	–	4.7
Online banking	–	–	–	–	2.3
Trading stocks	–	–	–	–	0.9

Note: (–) means sample is too small to make a reliable estimate.
Source: National Center for Health Statistics, Computer and Internet Use by Children and Adolescents in 2001, *NCES 2004-014, 2003, Internet site http://nces.ed.gov/pubsearch/pubsinfo.asp?pubid=2004014*

Most Students Go to College Close to Home

The majority have college-educated parents.

The 54 percent majority of college freshmen attend a college that is no more than 100 miles from their home, according to the 2003 American Freshman Survey of UCLA's Higher Education Research Institute. Only 12 percent are attending a college that is more than 500 miles from their home.

Because college costs are high and rising, college students are more likely to come from high-income than low-income families. Only 9 percent of college freshmen are from families with incomes of less than $20,000, while 47 percent are from families with incomes of $75,000 or more. Parental education also plays a role in college attendance. More than half of today's college freshmen have mothers and fathers who are college graduates.

A large share of college freshmen (24 percent) have parents who are divorced or living apart. The 76 percent majority has parents who are white. Nine percent have black parents, and 7 percent have Asian parents. A substantial 13 percent of college freshmen have immigrant parents, although only 3 percent are not U.S. citizens.

■ As college costs continue to soar, the children who can afford to go to college are increasingly from high-income, highly educated families.

Nearly half of college freshmen are from families with incomes of $75,000 or more

(percent distribution of college freshmen by parents' total income, 2003)

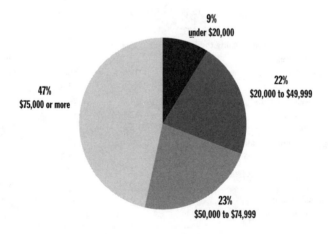

9%
under $20,000

22%
$20,000 to $49,999

47%
$75,000 or more

23%
$50,000 to $74,999

Table 1.20 Family Characteristics of College Freshmen, 2003

(percent distribution of college freshmen in insitutions offering baccalaureate degrees by family characteristics, 2003)

	percent distribution
How many miles from college is your permanent home?	
Ten or less	11.0%
11 to 50	25.6
51 to 100	16.9
101 to 500	34.1
More than 500	12.4
Estimate of parents' total income	
Under $20,000	8.6
$20,000 to $49,999	22.0
$50,000 to $74,999	22.5
$75,000 to $99,999	15.7
$100,000 to $149,999	16.4
$150,000 or more	14.8
Father's educational attainment	
Less than high school graduate	6.6
High school graduate	20.7
Some college or vocational school	19.2
College graduate	28.2
Some graduate school or graduate degree	25.3
Mother's educational attainment	
Less than high school graduate	5.4
High school graduate	21.0
Some college or vocational school	22.4
College graduate	31.2
Some graduate school or graduate degree	20.0
Parents' living arrangements	
Both alive and living with each other	72.7
Both alive, divorced or living apart	23.8
One or both deceased	3.5
Father's ethnic background	
American Indian/Alaska Native	0.9
Asian	6.8
Black	9.3
Hispanic/Mexican	3.1
Hispanic/other	2.6
Native Hawaiian/Pacific Islander	0.7
White	75.8

	percent distribution
Mother's ethnic background	
American Indian/Alaska Native	1.0%
Asian	7.3
Black	9.0
Hispanic/Mexican	3.1
Hispanic/other	2.8
Native Hawaiian/Pacific Islander	0.8
White	75.8
Parents born in the U.S.?	
Both	80.4
Father only	3.0
Mother only	3.2
Neither	13.4
Student's citizenship status	
U.S. citizen	96.6
Permanent resident (green card)	2.3
Neither	1.1

Source: The American Freshman: National Norms for Fall 2003, *Linda J. Sax, Alexander W. Astin, Jennifer A. Lindholm, William S. Korn, Victor B. Saenz, and Kathryn M. Mahoney, Higher Education Research Institute, UCLA, 2003*

Most College Freshmen Are Wired

Computer and Internet use are the norm.

Every year for more than 30 years, the Higher Education Research Institute of UCLA has asked the nation's college freshmen a battery of questions about their attitudes, experiences, college plans, and life objectives. Over the decades, those answers reveal the character of each generation of Americans. Based on the answers supplied by college freshmen in 2003, it's apparent that the Millennial generation is not only wired, but also connected to the community. More than 80 percent frequently use a personal computer. Seventy-eight to 85 percent frequently use the Internet for research or homework. Seventy percent communicate frequently via instant messaging, and 58 to 69 percent communicate frequently via email.

Seventy-eight to 87 percent of male and female college freshmen have performed volunteer work in the past twelve months. About the same proportion have attended religious services. Sixty-seven to 71 percent have socialized with someone from another racial or ethnic group. The majority has visited an art gallery or museum.

Women freshmen are more likely than their male counterparts to frequently feel overwhelmed by all they have to do (35 versus 16 percent). They are more likely to communicate frequently via email, do volunteer work, and use the Internet for research or homework. Men are significantly more likely than women to drink beer and to frequently discuss politics.

■ The familiarity of the younger generation with computers and the Internet will reshape business and government.

College freshmen are more likely to communicate via instant messaging than email

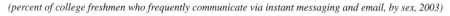

(percent of college freshmen who frequently communicate via instant messaging and email, by sex, 2003)

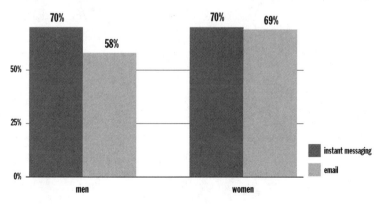

Table 1.21 Experiences of College Freshmen by Sex, 2003

(percent of college freshmen in institutions offering baccalaureate degrees who have participated in selected activities in the past year, by sex, 2003)

	men	women	percentage point difference between men and women
Used a personal computer frequently	85.5%	83.7%	1.8
Performed volunteer work	78.3	87.0	−8.7
Used the Internet for research or homework frequently	78.2	84.5	−6.3
Attended a religious service	77.6	82.6	−5.0
Communicated via instant messaging frequently	70.2	70.2	0.0
Socialized with someone of another racial/ethnic group	67.0	70.5	−3.5
Communicated via email frequently	57.8	69.3	−11.5
Visited an art gallery or museum	53.4	60.2	−6.8
Drank wine or liquor	50.4	51.0	−0.6
Drank beer	49.9	40.7	9.2
Played a musical instrument	44.6	41.0	3.6
Participated in organized demonstrations	44.1	48.5	−4.4
Discussed religion frequently	27.9	30.9	−3.0
Discussed politics frequently	27.0	18.8	8.2
Voted in student elections frequently	20.7	22.1	−1.4
Frequently felt overwhelmed by all I had to do	15.9	35.1	−19.2
Smoked cigarettes frequently	6.2	6.4	−0.2
Frequently felt depressed	5.6	8.9	−3.3

Source: The American Freshman: National Norms for Fall 2003, *Linda J. Sax, Alexander W. Astin, Jennifer A. Lindholm, William S. Korn, Victor B. Saenz, and Kathryn M. Mahoney, Higher Education Research Institute, UCLA, 2003*

College Freshmen Are a Mix of Liberal and Conservative

Their top objectives are to make a lot of money and raise a family.

The great majority of college freshmen believe in gun control, but they also believe the courts are too concerned with the rights of criminals, according to the Higher Education Research Institute's American Freshman Survey. They think colleges should prohibit racist/sexist speech, but many also think affirmative action should be abolished. They support legal abortion, but not the legalization of marijuana.

Women are far more liberal than men on some issues including gun control, affirmative action, women's roles, and homosexuality. The 67 percent majority of freshmen women believe same-sex couples should have the legal right to marry versus only 50 percent of their male counterparts. Just 17 percent of women believe the activities of married women are best confined to the home and family versus 28 percent of men.

Both men and women want to make a lot of money, however. Fully 75 percent of men and 73 percent of women say that being very well off financially is essential or very important to them. Seventy-four percent of men and 76 percent of women say raising a family is essential or very important. Women are more likely than men to want to help others in difficulty, while men are more likely than women to want to be successful in their own business.

■ The differences in the opinions of young men and women—particularly men's more conservative views toward the role of women—may cause problems in their romantic relationships.

Women are more liberal than men

(percent of college freshmen who think same-sex couples should have the right to legal marital status, by sex, 2003)

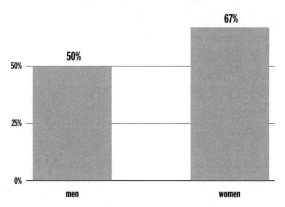

Table 1.22 Attitudes of College Freshmen by Sex, 2003

(percent of college freshmen in institutions offering baccalaureate degrees who somewhat or strongly agree with selected statements, by sex, 2003)

	men	women	percentage point difference between men and women
Federal government should do more to control the sale of handguns	67.6%	83.7%	–16.1
There is too much concern in the courts for the rights of criminals	63.3	59.3	4.0
Affirmative action in college admissions should be abolished	58.4	48.2	10.2
Abortion should be legal	55.0	54.1	0.9
Colleges should prohibit racist/sexist speech on campus	53.5	62.5	–9.0
Wealthy people should pay a larger share of taxes than they do now	52.6	53.5	–0.9
Same-sex couples should have the right to legal marital status	50.2	66.9	–16.7
Marijuana should be legalized	44.3	34.3	10.0
Federal military spending should be increased	43.5	34.3	9.2
People should not obey laws that violate their personal values	39.1	30.9	8.2
It is important to have laws prohibiting homosexual relations	34.6	19.2	15.4
Realistically, an individual can do little to bring about changes in our society	32.3	24.6	7.7
The death penalty should be abolished	28.8	35.8	–7.0
The activities of married women are best confined to the home and family	28.1	16.5	11.6
Racial discrimination is no longer a major problem in America	27.4	18.3	9.1

Source: The American Freshman: National Norms for Fall 2003, *Linda J. Sax, Alexander W. Astin, Jennifer A. Lindholm, William S. Korn, Victor B. Saenz, and Kathryn M. Mahoney, Higher Education Research Institute, UCLA, 2003; calculations by New Strategist*

Table 1.23 Objectives of College Freshmen by Sex, 2003

(percent of college freshmen in institutions offering baccalaureate degrees who say the objective is essential or very important, by sex, 2003)

	men	women	percentage point difference between men and women
Being very well off financially	75.4%	72.5%	2.9
Raising a family	73.7	75.7	–2.0
Becoming an authority in my field	61.5	59.2	2.3
Helping others who are in difficulty	55.1	70.7	–15.6
Obtaining recognition from my colleagues for contributions to my special field	52.8	52.6	0.2
Becoming successful in a business of my own	45.4	36.4	9.0
Developing a meaningful philosophy of life	40.4	38.4	2.0
Improving my understanding of other countries and cultures	40.2	47.8	–7.6
Keeping up to date with political affairs	38.1	30.5	7.6
Integrating spirituality into my life	36.7	43.4	–6.7
Influencing social values	35.3	41.2	–5.9
Becoming a community leader	32.6	31.8	0.8
Helping to promote racial understanding	28.0	32.5	–4.5
Influencing the political structure	23.3	17.6	5.7
Making a theoretical contribution to science	19.9	14.8	5.1
Participating in a community action program	18.7	26.1	–7.4
Becoming involved in programs to clean up the environment	17.0	17.7	–0.7
Writing original works	16.2	14.8	1.4
Creating artistic work	14.8	17.5	–2.7
Becoming accomplished in one of the performing arts	14.7	16.8	–2.1

Source: The American Freshman: National Norms for Fall 2003, *Linda J. Sax, Alexander W. Astin, Jennifer A. Lindholm, William S. Korn, Victor B. Saenz, and Kathryn M. Mahoney, Higher Education Research Institute, UCLA, 2003; calculations by New Strategist*

Most Students Depend on Family to Pay the Bills

Many are worried about college costs.

Eighty percent of college freshmen are paying for tuition, room, and board with money from their parents or other relatives, according UCLA's Higher Education Research Institute's American Freshman Survey. The majority of students say they will receive at least $3,000 from parents or relatives to pay for their first-year expenses, and 29 percent say they will receive $10,000 or more.

Grants, scholarships, and military funding—aid that does not have to be paid back—ranks second as a source of funding for tuition, room, and board. Sixty-four percent of students will receive at least some funding from this type of source, and 16 percent will receive $10,000 or more. A student's personal resources from work or work-study rank third in importance, with 59 percent using money from this source. The amount of funding expected from personal sources is small, however, with most saying it will amount to less than $3,000. Surprisingly, the 52 percent majority of students say they are not using student loans to pay for first-year expenses. Only 8 percent say they are depending on loans of $10,000 or more.

Paying for college is a big worry for many students. When asked how concerned they are about their ability to finance their college education, only 34 percent of college freshmen say they have no concerns. The 53 percent majority has "some" concerns. Thirteen percent have major concerns, not knowing whether they will have enough to pay for school.

■ As college tuitions skyrocket, many colleges are offering grants to lure the best students to their campus.

Many freshmen worry about paying for college

(percent distribution of college freshmen by level of concern about paying for college, 2003)

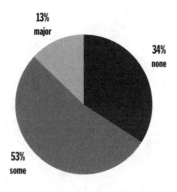

13%
major

34%
none

53%
some

Table 1.24 How Students Will Pay for College, 2003

(percent distribution of college freshmen in institutions offering baccalaureate degrees by amount paid for tuition, fees, room, and board by selected sources, and concern about ability to pay for college, 2003)

How much of your first year's educational expenses do you expect to cover from...

Family resources (parents, relatives, spouses, etc.):

None	19.9%
Less than $1,000	11.2
$1,000 to $2,999	14.0
$3,000 to $5,999	14.1
$6,000 to $9,999	11.8
$10,000 or more	28.9

My own resources (savings from work, work-study, other):

None	40.8
Less than $1,000	27.1
$1,000 to $2,999	22.1
$3,000 to $5,999	6.7
$6,000 to $9,999	1.9
$10,000 or more	1.5

Aid which need not be repaid (grants, scholarships, military funding, etc.):

None	36.4
Less than $1,000	8.0
$1,000 to $2,999	16.1
$3,000 to $5,999	13.5
$6,000 to $9,999	10.0
$10,000 or more	16.1

Aid which must be repaid (loans, etc.):

None	52.0
Less than $1,000	4.2
$1,000 to $2,999	16.0
$3,000 to $5,999	12.3
$6,000 to $9,999	7.7
$10,000 or more	7.8

Do you have any concern about your ability to finance your college education?

None (I am confident that I will have sufficient funds)	34.3
Some (but I probably will have enough funds)	52.6
Major (not sure I will have enough funds to complete college)	13.0

Source: The American Freshman: National Norms for Fall 2003, *Linda J. Sax, Alexander W. Astin, Jennifer A. Lindholm, William S. Korn, Victor B. Saenz, and Kathryn M. Mahoney, Higher Education Research Institute, UCLA, 2003*

Education

■ The oldest members of the Millennial generation have graduated from college and are embarking on a career. The youngest are still in elementary school. Consequently, the educational attainment of Millennials is rising rapidly.

■ Among people aged 15 to 25, Asian women have the highest level of education and Hispanic men the lowest. Fully 56 percent of Asian women aged 15 to 25 have college experience. Only 42 percent of Hispanic men in the age group have graduated from high school.

■ Among householders with children under age 14, fully 78 percent are satisfied with the elementary school in their area. Only 7 percent are not satisfied.

■ SAT scores are rising. The average verbal SAT score rose 5 points between 1990–91 and 2001–02. The average math SAT score rose 16 points during those years.

■ Going to college is no longer an elite privilege, but the norm. Today, 64 percent of young women and 60 percent of young men enroll in college after graduating from high school.

■ Among the nation's 13 million undergraduates in 2002, nearly 10 million were Millennials (students under age 25). Eighty-five percent attend school full-time.

Millennials Are in High School and College

More than half of 20-to-24-year-olds have college experience.

In 2002, Millennials were between 8 and 25 years of age. Thus, the oldest members of the Millennial generation have graduated from college and are embarking on a career, while the youngest are still in elementary school. The educational attainment of Millennials is rising rapidly. Among men aged 18 and 19, 52 percent are high school graduates. The figure is a much higher 83 percent among men aged 20 to 24. Women are further along than men. Sixty percent of 18- and 19-year-old women and 86 percent of those aged 20 to 24 are high school graduates.

Among women aged 20 to 24, 13 percent are college graduates. The figure is a smaller 9 percent for their male counterparts. Since it takes, on average, six years to get a bachelor's degree today, it's little wonder so few in their early twenties have earned a college degree. Among 25-to-29-year-olds, fully 32 percent of women and 27 percent of men have a college degree.

■ Millennial women appear to be more serious about getting an education than their male counterparts. This may narrow the income gap between men and women in the years ahead.

Among 20-to-24-year-olds, women are better educated than men

(percent distribution of people aged 20 to 24 by educational attainment, by sex, 2002)

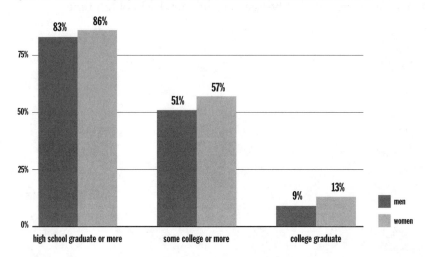

Table 2.1 Educational Attainment of Millennial Men, 2002

(number and percent distribution of men aged 15 or older, aged 15 to 25, and aged 15 to 29 in five-year age groups, by highest level of education, 2002; numbers in thousands)

	total aged 15 or older	aged 15 to 25 exactly	age groups 15 to 17	18 to 19	20 to 24	25 to 29
Total men	**106,910**	**21,756**	**6,209**	**4,026**	**9,679**	**9,150**
Not a high school graduate	23,760	9,983	6,111	1,937	1,618	1,399
High school graduate	31,308	4,947	74	1,117	3,169	2,767
Some college, no degree	19,093	4,816	15	944	3,473	1,843
Associate's degree	7,008	699	3	22	517	684
Bachelor's degree or more	16,805	1,232	4	5	871	2,012
Master's degree	5,620	53	–	2	23	313
Professional degree	1,803	17	–	–	7	93
Doctoral degree	1,514	5	–	–	–	39
High school graduate or more	83,151	11,769	97	2,090	8,060	7,751
Some college or more	51,843	6,822	23	973	4,891	4,984
Bachelor's degree or more	25,742	1,307	5	7	901	2,457
Total men	**100.0%**	**100.0%**	**100.0%**	**100.0%**	**100.0%**	**100.0%**
Not a high school graduate	22.2	45.9	98.4	48.1	16.7	15.3
High school graduate	29.3	22.7	1.2	27.7	32.7	30.2
Some college, no degree	17.9	22.1	0.2	23.4	35.9	20.1
Associate's degree	6.6	3.2	0.1	0.5	5.3	7.5
Bachelor's degree or more	15.7	5.7	0.1	0.1	9.0	22.0
Master's degree	5.3	0.2	–	0.1	0.2	3.4
Professional degree	1.7	0.1	–	–	0.1	1.0
Doctoral degree	1.4	0.0	–	–	–	0.4
High school graduate or more	77.8	54.1	1.6	51.9	83.3	84.7
Some college or more	48.5	31.4	0.4	24.2	50.5	54.5
Bachelor's degree or more	24.1	6.0	0.1	0.2	9.3	26.9

Note: (–) means number is less than 500 or sample is too small to make a reliable estimate.
Source: Bureau of the Census, Educational Attainment in the United States: March 2002, detailed tables (PPL-169); Internet site http://www.census.gov/population/www/socdemo/education/ppl-169.html; calculations by New Strategist

Table 2.2 Educational Attainment of Millennial Women, 2002

(number and percent distribution of women aged 15 or older, aged 15 to 25, and aged 15 to 29 in five-year age groups, by highest level of education, 2002; numbers in thousands)

	total aged 15 or older	aged 15 to 25 exactly	age groups 15 to 17	18 to 19	20 to 24	25 to 29
Total women	**114,681**	**21,361**	**5,928**	**3,883**	**9,724**	**9,159**
Not a high school graduate	23,587	8,958	5,813	1,541	1,377	1,088
High school graduate	35,523	4,490	75	1,159	2,780	2,433
Some college, no degree	21,240	5,318	36	1,154	3,721	1,903
Associate's degree	9,181	738	2	29	565	821
Bachelor's degree	17,567	1,695	–	1	1,210	2,276
Master's degree	5,956	135	2	–	62	486
Professional degree	950	17	–	–	8	114
Doctoral degree	676	1	–	–	–	39
High school graduate or more	91,093	12,394	115	2,343	8,346	8,072
Some college or more	55,570	7,904	40	1,184	5,566	5,639
Bachelor's degree or more	25,149	1,848	2	1	1,280	2,915
Total women	**100.0%**	**100.0%**	**100.0%**	**100.0%**	**100.0%**	**100.0%**
Not a high school graduate	20.6	41.9	98.1	39.7	14.2	11.9
High school graduate	31.0	21.0	1.3	29.8	28.6	26.6
Some college, no degree	18.5	24.9	0.6	29.7	38.3	20.8
Associate's degree	8.0	3.5	0.0	0.7	5.8	9.0
Bachelor's degree	15.3	7.9	–	0.0	12.4	24.8
Master's degree	5.2	0.6	–	–	0.6	5.3
Professional degree	0.8	0.1	–	–	0.1	1.2
Doctoral degree	0.6	0.0	–	–	–	0.4
High school graduate or more	79.4	58.0	1.9	60.3	85.8	88.1
Some college or more	48.5	37.0	0.7	30.5	57.2	61.6
Bachelor's degree or more	21.9	8.7	0.0	0.0	13.2	31.8

Note: (–) means number is less than 500 or sample is too small to make a reliable estimate.
Source: Bureau of the Census, Educational Attainment in the United States: March 2002, detailed tables (PPL-169); Internet site http://www.census.gov/population/www/socdemo/education/ppl-169.html; calculations by New Strategist

Asian Women Are the Best Educated Millennials

Hispanic men are the least educated.

Among people aged 15 to 25, Asian women have the highest level of education. Fifty-six percent have college experience and 16 percent have a bachelor's degree. Asian men rank second in educational attainment, with 49 percent having college experience and 14 percent having a college degree.

Hispanics are the least educated among Millennials. Only 42 percent of men and 48 percent of women aged 15 to 25 are high school graduates. Just 2 to 3 percent have a college degree. Many Hispanics are immigrants from countries that offer little schooling.

■ Although the educational attainment of Millennials will rise as more complete high school and go to college, the gaps by race and Hispanic origin will persist.

Asians are far better educated than others

(percent of people aged 15 to 25 who have college experience, by race and Hispanic origin, 2002)

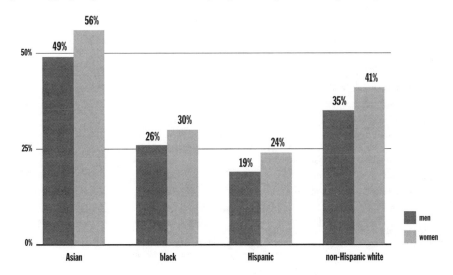

Table 2.3 Educational Attainment of Millennial Men by Race and Hispanic Origin, 2002

(number and percent distribution of men aged 15 to 25 by educational attainment, race, and Hispanic origin, 2002; numbers in thousands)

	non-Hispanic			Hispanic
	Asian	black	white	
Total men	**1,117**	**2,886**	**13,611**	**3,957**
Not a high school graduate	430	1,453	5,697	2,282
High school graduate	135	682	3,154	917
Some college, no degree	346	616	3,276	567
Associate's degree	39	51	508	103
Bachelor's degree	150	83	917	79
Master's degree	6	2	40	4
Professional degree	5	2	10	–
Doctoral degree	–	–	4	–
High school graduate or more	681	1,436	7,909	1,670
Some college or more	546	754	4,755	753
Bachelor's degree or more	161	87	971	83
Total men	**100.0%**	**100.0%**	**100.0%**	**100.0%**
Not a high school graduate	38.5	50.3	41.9	57.7
High school graduate	12.1	23.6	23.2	23.2
Some college, no degree	31.0	21.3	24.1	14.3
Associate's degree	3.5	1.8	3.7	2.6
Bachelor's degree	13.4	2.9	6.7	2.0
Master's degree	0.5	0.1	0.3	0.1
Professional degree	–	0.1	0.1	–
Doctoral degree	–	–	0.0	–
High school graduate or more	61.0	49.8	58.1	42.2
Some college or more	48.9	26.1	34.9	19.0
Bachelor's degree or more	14.4	3.0	7.1	2.1

Note: Numbers will not add to total because not all races are shown and Hispanics may be of any race; (–) means number is less than 500 or sample is too small to make a reliable estimate.
Source: Bureau of the Census, Educational Attainment in the United States: March 2002, detailed tables (PPL-169); Internet site http://www.census.gov/population/www/socdemo/education/ppl-169.html; calculations by New Strategist

Table 2.4 Educational Attainment of Millennial Women by Race and Hispanic Origin, 2000

(number and percent distribution of women aged 15 to 25 by educational attainment, race, and Hispanic origin, 2002; numbers in thousands)

| | non-Hispanic | | | |
	Asian	black	white	Hispanic
Total women	**1,057**	**3,161**	**13,461**	**3,470**
Not a high school graduate	323	1,433	5,301	1,795
High school graduate	139	780	2,682	838
Some college, no degree	382	709	3,538	653
Associate's degree	43	96	493	95
Bachelor's degree or more	156	132	1,325	80
Master's degree	11	14	104	5
Professional degree	1	–	14	2
Doctoral degree	–	–	1	–
High school graduate or more	732	1,731	8,157	1,673
Some college or more	593	951	5,475	835
Bachelor's degree or more	168	146	1,444	87
Total women	**100.0%**	**100.0%**	**100.0%**	**100.0%**
Not a high school graduate	30.6	45.3	39.4	51.7
High school graduate	13.2	24.7	19.9	24.1
Some college, no degree	36.1	22.4	26.3	18.8
Associate's degree	4.1	3.0	3.7	2.7
Bachelor's degree	14.8	4.2	9.8	2.3
Master's degree	1.0	0.4	0.8	0.1
Professional degree	0.1	–	0.1	0.1
Doctoral degree	–	–	0.0	–
High school graduate or more	69.3	54.8	60.6	48.2
Some college or more	56.1	30.1	40.7	24.1
Bachelor's degree or more	15.9	4.6	10.7	2.5

Note: Numbers will not add to total because not all races are shown and Hispanics may be of any race; (–) means number is less than 500 or sample is too small to make a reliable estimate.
Source: Bureau of the Census, Educational Attainment in the United States: March 2002, *detailed tables (PPL-169); Internet site http://www.census.gov/population/www/socdemo/education/ppl-169.html; calculations by New Strategist*

Most Millennials Are Students

More than three out of four people under age 25 are in school.

Among the nation's 74 million students, 67 million—or 91 percent—are under age 25. More than 90 percent of children aged 5 to 17 are in school. The figure falls with age, but remains above 50 percent through age 20. Only 20 percent of 24-year-olds are in school.

The number of students enrolled in kindergarten through 12th grade stood at 53 million in 2002 (33 million in grades K through 8, and 16 million in grades 9 through 12). These lofty numbers have not been seen since the Baby-Boom generation filled classrooms decades ago.

■ School enrollments will continue at a high level thanks to immigration and the beginning of childbearing by the large Millennial generation. Communities will have to invest more in facilities, teachers, and supplies.

School enrollment drops sharply among people in their early twenties

(percent of people aged 18 to 24 enrolled in school, by age, 2002)

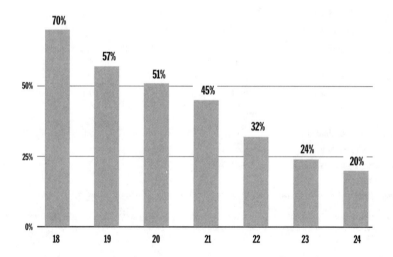

Table 2.5 School Enrollment by Age, 2002

(number of people aged 3 or older, and number and percent enrolled in school, by age, fall 2002; numbers in thousands)

	total	enrolled	
		number	percent
Total people	**270,919**	**74,046**	**27.3%**
Under age 25	88,077	67,462	76.6
Aged 3	3,821	1,619	42.4
Aged 4	3,858	2,568	66.6
Aged 5	3,802	3,540	93.1
Aged 6	3,922	3,813	97.2
Aged 7	4,008	3,938	98.3
Aged 8	4,099	3,998	97.5
Aged 9	3,994	3,922	98.2
Aged 10	4,127	4,064	98.5
Aged 11	4,300	4,219	98.1
Aged 12	4,304	4,243	98.6
Aged 13	4,194	4,140	98.7
Aged 14	4,093	4,026	98.4
Aged 15	4,056	3,995	98.5
Aged 16	4,075	3,932	96.5
Aged 17	4,056	3,737	92.1
Aged 18	4,031	2,807	69.6
Aged 19	3,876	2,201	56.8
Aged 20	3,938	1,998	50.7
Aged 21	3,794	1,699	44.8
Aged 22	4,154	1,318	31.7
Aged 23	3,796	914	24.1
Aged 24	3,779	771	20.4
Aged 25 to 29	18,141	2,196	12.1
Aged 30 or older	164,699	4,388	2.7

Source: Bureau of the Census, School Enrollment—Social and Economic Characteristics of Students: October 2002, *detailed tables; Internet site http://www.census.gov/population/www/socdemo/school/cps2002.html*

Table 2.6 Enrollment in Kindergarten through College, 2002

(number and percent distribution of people attending kindergarten through high school and of those attending college, fall 2002; numbers in thousands)

	number	percent
Total students, K–12	**53,075**	**100.0%**
Kindergarten	**3,571**	**6.7**
Elementary and middle, total	**33,130**	**62.4**
1st grade	4,190	7.9
2nd grade	4,022	7.6
3rd grade	4,028	7.6
4th grade	4,038	7.6
5th grade	4,209	7.9
6th grade	4,243	8.0
7th grade	4,247	8.0
8th grade	4,153	7.8
High school, total	**16,374**	**30.9**
9th grade	4,086	7.7
10th grade	4,180	7.9
11th grade	3,927	7.4
12th grade	4,181	7.9
College, total	**16,497**	**100.0**
1st year	4,416	26.8
2nd year	3,486	21.1
3rd year	3,109	18.8
4th year	2,414	14.6
5th year	1,157	7.0
6th year	1,915	11.6

Source: Bureau of the Census, School Enrollment—Social and Economic Characteristics of Students: October 2002, detailed tables; Internet site http://www.census.gov/population/www/socdemo/school/cps2002.html

Most Parents Are Satisfied with the Local Elementary School

But some are so bothered by their school that they want to move.

Complaints about public schools have become commonplace, but in fact few households with elementary-school-aged children are dissatisfied with the local public elementary school. Among households with children under age 14, 78 percent are satisfied with the public elementary school in their area. Only 7 percent are not satisfied. Three percent of households are so bothered by the local school that they want to move. Renters are slightly more likely than homeowners to be dissatisfied with the local school.

Among households with children aged 5 to 15, 86 percent send at least one child to public school. A substantial 11 percent send a child to private school. Only 1 percent home-school their children. Not surprisingly, homeowners are nearly twice as likely as renters to send a child to private school, 13 versus 7 percent.

■ While the great majority of parents are satisfied with the local elementary school, the more than 2 million dissatisfied parents are one of the pressure points for educational reform.

Homeowners are more likely than renters to be satisfied with the local elementary school

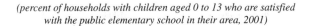

(percent of households with children aged 0 to 13 who are satisfied with the public elementary school in their area, 2001)

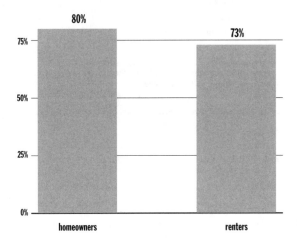

Table 2.7 Satisfaction with Local Elementary School by Homeownership Status, 2001

(number and percent distribution of households with children aged 5 to 15 by school status and opinion of local elementary school, by homeownership status, 2001; numbers in thousands)

	total	owner	renter
Total households with children aged 5 to 15	**27,641**	**19,350**	**8,291**
Attend public school, K–12	23,704	16,265	7,440
Attend private school, K–12	3,112	2,567	545
Attend ungraded school, preschool	287	170	117
Home schooled	366	292	74
Not in school	479	265	213
Households with children aged 0 to 13	**31,381**	**21,003**	**10,379**
Satisfactory public elementary school	24,482	16,889	7,593
Unsatisfactory public elementary school	2,130	1,481	649
So bothered by school they want to move	893	510	384
PERCENT DISTRIBUTION			
Total households with children aged 5 to 15	**100.0%**	**100.0%**	**100.0%**
Attend public school, K–12	85.8	84.1	89.7
Attend private school, K–12	11.3	13.3	6.6
Attend ungraded school, preschool	1.0	0.9	1.4
Home schooled	1.3	1.5	0.9
Not in school	1.7	1.4	2.6
Households with children aged 0 to 13	**100.0**	**100.0**	**100.0**
Satisfactory public elementary school	78.0	80.4	73.2
Unsatisfactory public elementary school	6.8	7.1	6.3
So bothered by school they want to move	2.8	2.4	3.7

Note: Numbers will not add to total because not reported is not shown.
Source: Bureau of the Census, American Housing Survey for the United States in 2001; *Internet site http://www.census.gov/hhes/www/housing/ahs/ahs01/ahs01.html; calculations by New Strategist*

Little Change Forecast in School Enrollment

The number of high school graduates should increase 12 percent, however.

School enrollment is projected to increase in the coming decade as the oldest memers of the Millennial generation (born from 1977 through 1994) begin to send their own children to school. Overall, enrollment in kindergarten through 12th grade is projected to increase 6 percent between 2000 and 2013. The National Center for Education Statistics foresees a bigger increase in private high school enrollment—up 10 percent during those years. Private school students will not change much as a proportion of all students, remaining at about 12 percent.

The number of high school graduates will rise as the Millennial generation finishes high school. The overall figure is projected to climb 12 percent between 2000 and 2013, from 2.8 million to 3.2 million graduates. The projected growth will be much greater for graduates from private high schools—up 19 percent during those years.

■ Colleges are benefiting from the growing numbers of high school graduates as applications increase and competition stiffens among potential students.

More high school graduates are on the way

(number of high school graduates, 2000 to 2013; in millions)

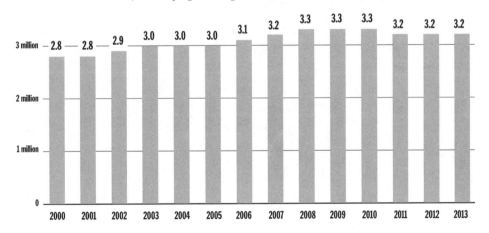

Table 2.8 Projected Enrollment in Kindergarten through 12th Grade, 2000 to 2013

(number of people enrolled in kindergarten through 12th grade by control of institution, fall 2000 to 2013; percent change, 2000–13; numbers in thousands)

	total			public			private		
	total	K–8th	9th–12th	total	K–8th	9th–12th	total	K–8th	9th–12th
2000	53,385	38,584	14,801	47,223	33,709	13,514	6,162	4,875	1,287
2001	53,890	38,832	15,058	47,688	33,952	13,736	6,202	4,880	1,322
2002	54,158	38,827	15,331	47,918	33,942	13,976	6,241	4,885	1,356
2003	54,296	38,719	15,577	48,040	33,843	14,198	6,256	4,876	1,379
2004	54,455	38,541	15,914	48,175	33,669	14,506	6,279	4,871	1,408
2005	54,615	38,412	16,203	48,304	33,534	14,770	6,311	4,878	1,433
2006	54,907	38,522	16,385	48,524	33,589	14,936	6,383	4,933	1,449
2007	55,049	38,605	16,445	48,640	33,654	14,986	6,409	4,950	1,458
2008	55,124	38,766	16,358	48,690	33,791	14,899	6,434	4,975	1,459
2009	55,223	38,995	16,228	48,761	33,994	14,767	6,461	5,001	1,461
2010	55,386	39,283	16,103	48,890	34,243	14,648	6,495	5,040	1,455
2011	55,618	39,688	15,930	49,084	34,597	14,487	6,534	5,091	1,443
2012	55,946	40,154	15,792	49,367	35,006	14,361	6,579	5,148	1,430
2013	56,364	40,638	15,726	49,737	35,430	14,307	6,627	5,208	1,419

Percent change

	total			public			private		
2000 to 2013	5.6%	5.3%	6.2%	5.3%	5.1%	5.9%	7.5%	6.8%	10.3%

Source: National Center for Education Statistics, Projections of Education Statistics to 2013; *Internet site http://nces.ed.gov/ programs/projections/tables/table_01.asp; calculations by New Strategist*

Table 2.9 Projections of High School Graduates, 2000 to 2013

(number of people graduating from high school by control of institution, 2000 to 2013; percent change 2000–13; numbers in thousands)

	total	public	private
2000	2,833	2,554	279
2001	2,852	2,569	283
2002	2,917	2,630	287
2003	2,986	2,685	301
2004	3,002	2,698	305
2005	3,037	2,728	308
2006	3,101	2,785	316
2007	3,172	2,850	322
2008	3,262	2,931	331
2009	3,274	2,942	332
2010	3,262	2,930	331
2011	3,237	2,906	331
2012	3,202	2,870	331
2013	3,176	2,843	333
Percent change			
2000 to 2013	12.1%	11.3%	19.4%

Source: National Center for Education Statistics, Projections of Education Statistics to 2013; Internet site http://nces.ed.gov/ programs/projections/tables/table_23.asp; calculations by New Strategist

SAT Scores Rise

Most demographic segments have made gains.

The number of high school students who take the Scholastic Assessment Test (or SAT) expanded enormously over the past few decades. Once limited to the elite, the SAT has been embraced by the masses—as have the nation's college campuses. Despite the greater numbers of students taking the test, SAT scores have increased for most demographic segments.

The average verbal SAT score rose 5 points between 1990–91 and 2001–02. The biggest gainers by race and Hispanic origin were Puerto Ricans and Asians. Mexican-Americans were the only ones to lose ground on the verbal test (down 8 points). The average math SAT score rose 16 points overall between 1990–91 and 2001–02, including a 21 point rise for Asians. Again, Mexican Americans were the only ones to lose ground (down 2 points).

■ The SAT test is changing in 2005 to include a written essay, which will make it more difficult to compare scores over time.

Verbal and math scores are up

(average verbal and math SAT scores, 1990–91 and 2001–02)

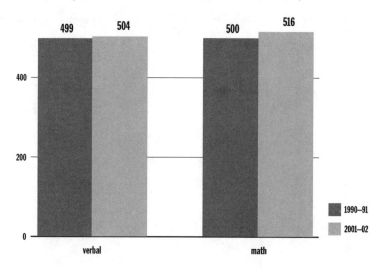

Table 2.10 **Scholastic Assessment Test Scores by Sex, Race, and Hispanic Origin, 1990–91 and 2001–02**

(average SAT scores and change in scores by sex, race, and Hispanic origin of student, 1990–91 and 2001–02)

	2001–02	1990–91	change
VERBAL SAT			
Total students	**504**	**499**	**5**
Male	507	503	4
Female	502	495	7
White	527	518	9
Black	430	427	3
Hispanic or Latino	458	458	0
Mexican American	446	454	–8
Puerto Rican	455	436	19
Asian American	501	485	16
American Indian	479	470	9
Other	502	486	16
MATH SAT			
Total students	**516**	**500**	**16**
Male	534	520	14
Female	500	482	18
White	533	513	20
Black	427	419	8
Hispanic or Latino	464	462	2
Mexican American	457	459	–2
Puerto Rican	451	439	12
Asian American	569	548	21
American Indian	483	468	15
Other	514	492	22

Source: National Center for Education Statistics, Digest of Education Statistics 2002; *http://nces.ed.gov/pubs2003/digest02/index.asp; calculations by New Strategist*

Most Children from Affluent Families Go to College

The majority of families with children aged 18 to 24 and incomes of $50,000 or more have at least one child in college.

It is no surprise that family income is one of the best predictors of whether children have the opportunity to go to college. Among the nation's 11 million families with children aged 18 to 24, 47 percent have at least one child in college full-time. The proportion rises with income to a high of 63 percent for families with incomes of $75,000 or more.

Among families with children aged 18 to 24 whose income is below $20,000, only 27 percent have a child in college full-time.

■ Children of the affluent can devote full attention to their studies because their parents are paying the bills. Many children from less affluent families attend school part-time because they must work to pay the bills.

College attendance rises with family income

(among families with children aged 18 to 24, percentage who have at least one child attending college full-time, by household income, 2002)

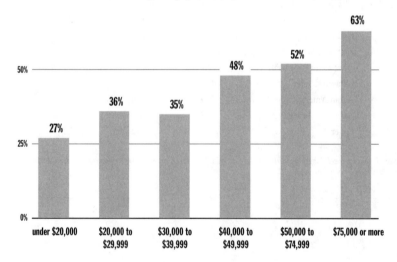

Table 2.11 **Families with Children in College, 2002**

(total number of families, number with children aged 18 to 24, and number and percent with children aged 18 to 24 attending college full-time by household income, 2002; numbers in thousands)

	total	with children aged 18–24	with one or more children attending college full-time		
			number	percent of total families	percent of families with children 18–24
Total families	**75,837**	**11,007**	**5,161**	**6.8%**	**46.9%**
Under $20,000	10,242	1,267	343	3.3	27.1
$20,000 to $29,999	8,598	1,053	383	4.5	36.4
$30,000 to $39,999	8,010	1,065	370	4.6	34.7
$40,000 to $49,999	6,254	889	425	6.8	47.8
$50,000 to $74,999	13,073	2,099	1,092	8.4	52.0
$75,000 or more	17,319	2,948	1,859	10.7	63.1

Note: Numbers will not add to total because not reported is not shown.
Source: Bureau of the Census, School Enrollment—Social and Economic Characteristics of Students: October 2002, *detailed tables; Internet site http://www.census.gov/population/www/socdemo/school/cps2002.html*

The Majority of High School Grads Go to College

Women are more likely to go than men.

Going to college is no longer an elite privilege, but the norm. Most high school graduates continue their education on a college campus. Forty years ago, male high school graduates were much more likely than their female counterparts to go to college—54 versus 38 percent. Today, the opposite is the case, with 66 percent of girls and a smaller 60 percent of boys continuing their education.

White high school graduates are much more likely than black or Hispanic graduates to go to college—64 percent of whites go to college within 12 months of graduating from high school versus only 55 percent of blacks and 49 percent of Hispanics. College enrollment rates have declined for all racial and ethnic groups since the late 1990s, thanks to stock market declines and the recession of 2001.

■ As the cost of private and public colleges rises, the college enrollment rate may fall as families struggle to pay the tuition.

Women have had higher college enrollment rates for decades

(percent of people aged 16 to 24 who graduated from high school in the previous twelve months and had enrolled in college as of October of the respective year, by sex and selected year, 1960 to 2001)

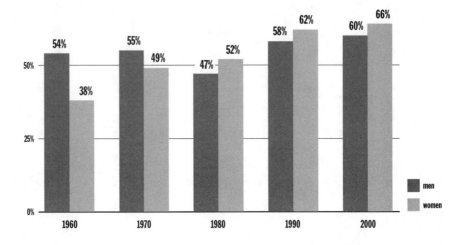

Table 2.12 College Enrollment Rate by Sex, 1960 to 2001

(percent of people aged 16 to 24 graduating from high school in the previous twelve months who were enrolled in college as of October of the respective year, by sex; percentage point difference in enrollment rates of men and women, 1960–2001)

	men	women	percentage point difference
2001	59.7	63.6	–3.9
2000	59.9	66.2	–6.3
1999	61.4	64.4	–3.0
1998	62.4	69.1	–6.7
1997	63.5	70.3	–6.8
1996	60.1	69.7	–9.6
1995	62.6	61.4	1.2
1994	60.6	63.2	–2.6
1993	59.9	65.2	–5.7
1992	60.0	63.8	–4.2
1991	57.9	67.1	–9.5
1990	58.0	62.0	–4.2
1989	57.6	61.6	–4.0
1988	57.0	60.8	–3.8
1987	58.4	55.3	3.1
1986	55.9	51.9	4.0
1985	58.6	56.9	1.7
1980	46.7	51.8	–5.1
1975	52.6	49.0	3.6
1970	55.2	48.5	6.7
1965	57.3	45.3	12.0
1960	54.0	37.9	16.1

Source: National Center for Education Statistics, Digest of Education Statistics 2002; *http://nces.ed.gov/pubs2003/digest02/index.asp; calculations by New Strategist*

Table 2.13 College Enrollment Rate by Race and Hispanic Origin, 1977 to 2001

(percent of people aged 16 to 24 graduating from high school in the previous twelve months who were enrolled in college as of October of the respective year, by race and Hispanic origin, 1977–2001)

	white	black	Hispanic
2001	64.2%	54.6%	–
2000	65.7	54.9	49.0%
1999	66.3	58.9	47.5
1998	68.5	61.9	51.8
1997	68.2	58.5	54.6
1996	67.4	56.0	56.7
1995	64.3	51.2	51.2
1994	64.5	50.8	55.0
1993	62.9	55.6	55.4
1992	64.3	48.2	58.1
1991	65.4	46.4	51.6
1990	63.0	46.8	51.7
1989	60.7	53.4	51.6
1988	61.1	44.4	48.6
1987	58.6	52.2	44.9
1986	56.8	36.9	42.9
1985	60.1	42.2	46.5
1980	49.8	42.7	49.8
1977	50.8	49.5	48.5

Note: Hispanic enrollment rates are a three-year moving average. (–) means data not available.
Source: National Center for Education Statistics, Digest of Education Statistics 2002; *Internet site http://nces.ed.gov/pubs2003/digest02/index.asp*

Millennials Are the Majority of Undergraduates

Most college students under age 25 attend school full-time.

Among the nation's 13 million undergraduates in 2002, nearly 10 million were Millennials (under age 25). Eighty-five percent attend school full-time. The percentage of students attending school full-time falls with age, from 90 percent of those under age 20 to 74 percent of those aged 22 to 24. Even among undergraduates aged 25 to 29, 56 percent attend school full-time. A minority of undergraduates aged 30 or older go to school full-time.

Three million students attend the nation's graduate schools, but only 22 percent are under age 25. Most graduate students under age 30 attend full-time. In contrast, most of those aged 30 or older are part-time students.

■ With Millennials heading to college, many middle-aged parents face enormous tuition bills.

Full-timers outnumber part-timers

(percent distribution of undergraduates under age 25 by attendance status, 2002)

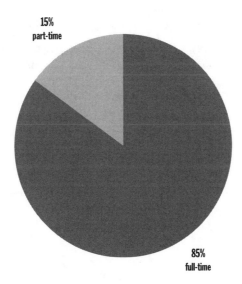

15%
part-time

85%
full-time

Table 2.14 College Students by Sex, Age, and Attendance Status, 2002

(number and percent distribution of people aged 15 or older enrolled in institutions of higher education by sex, age, and attendance status, 2002; numbers in thousands)

| | | undergraduate | | | | graduate | | |
| | | two-year | | four-year | | | | |
	total	full-time	part-time	full-time	part-time	total	full-time	part-time
Total students	**13,425**	**2,464**	**1,914**	**7,271**	**1,776**	**3,072**	**1,406**	**1,666**
Under age 25	9,557	1,891	769	6,262	635	671	523	148
Aged 15 to 17	189	72	17	95	5	6	6	–
Aged 18 to 19	3,554	903	235	2,287	129	27	25	2
Aged 20 to 21	3,459	572	206	2,487	194	67	61	6
Aged 22 to 24	2,355	344	311	1,393	307	571	431	140
Aged 25 to 29	1,346	255	302	503	286	747	411	336
Aged 30 or older	2,521	319	843	505	854	1,655	471	1,184
Female students	**7,496**	**1,362**	**1,132**	**3,910**	**1,092**	**1,760**	**773**	**987**
Under age 25	5,153	993	425	3,349	386	366	272	94
Aged 15 to 17	110	45	11	53	1	5	5	–
Aged 18 to 19	1,938	482	119	1,244	93	8	8	–
Aged 20 to 21	1,854	287	105	1,347	115	32	30	2
Aged 22 to 24	1,251	179	190	705	177	321	229	92
Aged 25 to 29	734	140	190	244	160	441	241	200
Aged 30 or older	1,607	228	516	317	546	956	261	695
Male students	**5,928**	**1,101**	**782**	**3,361**	**684**	**1,310**	**631**	**679**
Under age 25	4,405	898	345	2,914	248	306	251	55
Aged 15 to 17	79	27	6	42	4	1	1	–
Aged 18 to 19	1,616	421	116	1,043	36	19	17	2
Aged 20 to 21	1,605	285	101	1,141	78	35	31	4
Aged 22 to 24	1,105	165	122	688	130	251	202	49
Aged 25 to 29	611	115	111	259	126	307	171	136
Aged 30 or older	915	90	327	189	309	698	209	489

| | undergraduate | | | | graduate | | |
| | two-year | | four-year | | | | |
	total	full-time	part-time	full-time	part-time	total	full-time	part-time
PERCENT DISTRIBUTION BY AGE								
Total students	100.0%	100.0%	100.0%	100.0%	100.0%	100.0%	100.0%	100.0%
Under age 25	71.2	76.7	40.2	86.1	35.8	21.8	37.2	8.9
Aged 15 to 17	1.4	2.9	0.9	1.3	0.3	0.2	0.4	–
Aged 18 to 19	26.5	36.6	12.3	31.5	7.3	0.9	1.8	0.1
Aged 20 to 21	25.8	23.2	10.8	34.2	10.9	2.2	4.3	0.4
Aged 22 to 24	17.5	14.0	16.2	19.2	17.3	18.6	30.7	8.4
Aged 25 to 29	10.0	10.3	15.8	6.9	16.1	24.3	29.2	20.2
Aged 30 or older	18.8	12.9	44.0	6.9	48.1	53.9	33.5	71.1
Female students	100.0%	100.0%	100.0%	100.0%	100.0%	100.0%	100.0%	100.0%
Under age 25	68.7	72.9	37.5	85.7	35.3	20.8	35.2	9.5
Aged 15 to 17	1.5	3.3	1.0	1.4	0.1	0.3	0.6	–
Aged 18 to 19	25.9	35.4	10.5	31.8	8.5	0.5	1.0	–
Aged 20 to 21	24.7	21.1	9.3	34.5	10.5	1.8	3.9	0.2
Aged 22 to 24	16.7	13.1	16.8	18.0	16.2	18.2	29.6	9.3
Aged 25 to 29	9.8	10.3	16.8	6.2	14.7	25.1	31.2	20.3
Aged 30 or older	21.4	16.7	45.6	8.1	50.0	54.3	33.8	70.4
Male students	100.0%	100.0%	100.0%	100.0%	100.0%	100.0%	100.0%	100.0%
Under age 25	74.3	81.6	44.1	86.7	36.3	23.4	39.8	8.1
Aged 15 to 17	1.3	2.5	0.8	1.2	0.6	0.1	0.2	–
Aged 18 to 19	27.3	38.2	14.8	31.0	5.3	1.5	2.7	0.3
Aged 20 to 21	27.1	25.9	12.9	33.9	11.4	2.7	4.9	0.6
Aged 22 to 24	18.6	15.0	15.6	20.5	1.9	19.2	32.0	7.2
Aged 25 to 29	10.3	10.4	14.2	7.7	18.4	23.4	27.1	20.0
Aged 30 or older	15.4	8.2	41.8	5.6	45.2	53.3	33.1	72.0

| | | undergraduate | | | | graduate | | |
| | | two-year | | four-year | | | | |
	total	full-time	part-time	full-time	part-time	total	full-time	part-time
PERCENT DISTRIBUTION BY								
ENROLLMENT STATUS								
Total students	**100.0%**	**18.4%**	**14.3%**	**54.2%**	**13.2%**	**22.9%**	**10.5%**	**12.4%**
Under age 25	100.0	19.8	8.1	65.5	6.6	7.0	5.5	1.5
Aged 15 to 17	100.0	38.1	9.0	50.3	2.6	3.2	3.2	–
Aged 18 to 19	100.0	25.4	6.6	64.4	3.6	0.8	0.7	0.1
Aged 20 to 21	100.0	16.5	6.0	71.9	5.6	1.9	1.8	0.2
Aged 22 to 24	100.0	14.6	13.2	59.2	13.0	24.2	18.3	5.9
Aged 25 to 29	100.0	18.9	22.4	37.4	21.2	55.5	30.5	25.0
Aged 30 or older	100.0	12.7	33.4	20.0	33.9	65.6	18.7	47.0
Female students	**100.0%**	**18.2%**	**15.1%**	**52.2%**	**14.6%**	**23.5%**	**10.3%**	**13.2%**
Under age 25	100.0	19.3	8.2	65.0	7.5	7.1	5.3	1.8
Aged 15 to 17	100.0	40.9	10.0	48.2	0.9	4.5	4.5	–
Aged 18 to 19	100.0	24.9	6.1	64.2	4.8	0.4	0.4	–
Aged 20 to 21	100.0	15.5	5.7	72.7	6.2	1.7	1.6	0.1
Aged 22 to 24	100.0	14.3	15.2	56.4	14.1	25.7	18.3	7.4
Aged 25 to 29	100.0	19.1	25.9	33.2	21.8	60.1	32.8	27.2
Aged 30 or older	100.0	14.2	32.1	19.7	34.0	59.5	16.2	43.2
Male students	**100.0%**	**18.6%**	**13.2%**	**56.7%**	**11.5%**	**22.1%**	**10.6%**	**11.5%**
Under age 25	100.0	20.4	7.8	66.2	5.6	6.9	5.7	1.2
Aged 15 to 17	100.0	34.2	7.6	53.2	5.1	1.3	1.3	–
Aged 18 to 19	100.0	26.1	7.2	64.5	2.2	1.2	1.1	0.1
Aged 20 to 21	100.0	17.8	6.3	71.1	4.9	2.2	1.9	0.2
Aged 22 to 24	100.0	14.9	11.0	62.3	11.8	22.7	18.3	4.4
Aged 25 to 29	100.0	18.8	18.2	42.4	20.6	50.2	28.0	22.3
Aged 30 or older	100.0	9.8	35.7	20.7	33.8	76.3	22.8	53.4

Source: Bureau of the Census, School Enrollment—Social and Economic Characteristics of Students: October 2002, *detailed tables; Internet site http://www.census.gov/population/www/socdemo/school/cps2002.html; calculations by New Strategist*

College Students Are Getting Younger

The growing majority of college students are under age 25.

As the large Millennial generation replaces the much smaller Generation X on college campuses, the student body has been getting younger. This trend has just about peaked as Millennials entirely filled the young-adult age group. In 2000, 61 percent of college students were under age 25. The figure will rise to a slightly larger 62 percent by 2013.

The number of college students under age 25 is projected to grow 22 percent between 2000 and 2013, less than the 29 percent increase projected for students aged 25 to 29 as Millennials move into their late twenties. The number of students aged 30 or older is projected to grow only 7 percent during those years.

Among college students under age 25, the number of females is projected to increase much faster than the number of males—up 25 percent for females and 18 percent for males. By 2013, there will be 1.2 million more female than male college students under age 25.

■ With more women than men on college campuses, the educational attainment of young women will continue to surpass that of young men.

Most college students will continue to be under age 25

(percent distribution of college students, by age, 2013)

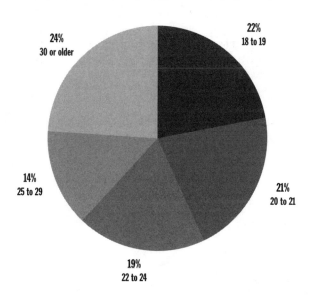

24%
30 or older

22%
18 to 19

14%
25 to 29

21%
20 to 21

19%
22 to 24

Table 2.15 Projections of College Enrollment by Sex and Age, 2000 and 2013

(number and percent distribution of people enrolled in institutions of higher education by sex and age, 2000 and 2013; percent change in number, 2000–13; numbers in thousands)

	2000 number	2000 percent	2013 number	2013 percent	percent change 2000–13
Total people	**15,312**	**100.0%**	**18,151**	**100.0%**	**18.5%**
Under age 25	9,338	61.0	11,344	62.5	21.5
Aged 14 to 17	145	0.9	163	0.9	12.3
Aged 18 to 19	3,531	23.1	3,921	21.6	11.1
Aged 20 to 21	3,045	19.9	3,749	20.7	23.1
Aged 22 to 24	2,617	17.1	3,511	19.3	34.1
Aged 25 to 29	1,961	12.8	2,520	13.9	28.5
Aged 30 or older	4,014	26.2	4,286	23.6	6.8
Total men	**6,722**	**100.0**	**7,734**	**100.0**	**15.1**
Under age 25	4,321	64.3	5,090	65.8	17.8
Aged 14 to 17	63	0.9	65	0.8	3.5
Aged 18 to 19	1,583	23.5	1,733	22.4	9.5
Aged 20 to 21	1,382	20.6	1,691	21.9	22.4
Aged 22 to 24	1,293	19.2	1,601	20.7	23.8
Aged 25 to 29	862	12.8	1,096	14.2	27.2
Aged 30 or older	1,539	22.9	1,549	20.0	0.6
Total women	**8,591**	**100.0**	**10,416**	**100.0**	**21.2**
Under age 25	5,017	58.4	6,255	60.1	24.7
Aged 14 to 17	82	1.0	99	1.0	20.3
Aged 18 to 19	1,948	22.7	2,188	21.0	12.3
Aged 20 to 21	1,663	19.4	2,058	19.8	23.7
Aged 22 to 24	1,324	15.4	1,910	18.3	44.3
Aged 25 to 29	1,099	12.8	1,424	13.7	29.6
Aged 30 or older	2,474	28.8	2,737	26.3	10.6

Source: National Center for Education Statistics, Projections of Education Statistics to 2013; *Internet site http://nces.ed.gov/ programs/projections/tables/table_11.asp; calculations by New Strategist*

Most Teens and Young Adults Participate in Adult Education

The share of 16-to-24-year-olds who take adult education courses is rising.

As Americans gain in education, they become more appreciative of education. Teens and young adults are no exception. Fifty-three percent of people aged 16 to 24 participated in adult education in 2001, up 20 percentage points from 1991. And this lofty figure does not include full-time college students.

Young and middle-aged adults are more likely than their elders to participate in adult education, primarily because they need training to further their careers. As people grow older, their reasons for participating in adult education shift to more personal ones.

■ Young adults who can't afford a college degree are eager customers of adult education courses designed to give them skills to boost their earnings.

Participation in adult education is the norm among teens and young adults

(percent of people aged 16 or older participating in adult education, by age, 2001)

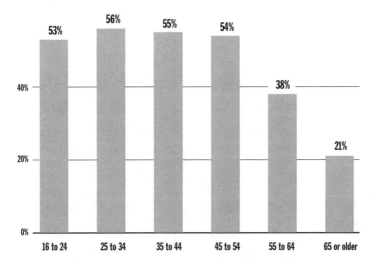

Table 2.16 Participation in Adult Education by Age, 1991 and 2001

(percent of people aged 16 or older participating in adult education activities, by age, 1991 and 2001; percentage point change, 1991–2001)

	2001	1991	percentage point change 1991–01
Total people	**47%**	**32%**	**15**
Aged 16 to 24	53	33	20
Aged 25 to 34	56	37	19
Aged 35 to 44	55	44	11
Aged 45 to 54	54	32	22
Aged 55 to 64	38	23	15
Aged 65 or older	21	10	11

Note: Adult education activities include apprenticeships, courses for basic skills, personal development, English as a second language, work-related courses, and credential programs in organizations other than postsecondary institutions. Excludes full-time participation in postsecondary institutions leading to a college degree, diploma, or certificate.
Source: National Center for Education Statistics, Adult Education and Lifelong Learning Survey of the National Household Education Surveys Program; Internet site http://nces.ed.gov/programs/coe/2003/section1/tables/t08_2.asp; calculations by New Strategist

3

Health

■ The 56 percent majority of children under age 18 are in excellent health, according to their parents. Only 2 percent of parents report their children's health as only fair or poor.

■ Among high school girls, 17 to 20 percent are overweight or at risk for becoming overweight. A larger share of girls (33 to 36 percent) think they are overweight, and even more are trying to lose weight (62 to 63 percent).

■ The 51 percent majority of 12th grade girls are currently sexually active—meaning they had sexual intercourse during the past three months. The figure is a slightly lower 45 percent among 12th grade boys.

■ Twenty-six percent of the population aged 12 or older have smoked cigarettes in the past month. The proportion peaks at 46 percent among 21-year-olds.

■ Young adults are much more likely to be current drug users than is the average person. From 13 to 23 percent of 15-to-24-year-olds have used an illicit drug in the past month.

■ Among 18-to-24-year-olds, fully 30 percent do not have health insurance—a larger share than in any other age group. People under age 25 account for fully 38 percent of the nation's uninsured.

Most Children Are in Excellent Health

The proportion falls among young adults, however.

The 56 percent majority of children under age 18 are in excellent health, according to their parents. Not surprisingly, the figure is much higher than that reported for adults, who are prone to stresses and chronic conditions that lead to health problems. Only about 2 percent of parents report that their children's health is only fair or poor.

The situation is different for 18-to-24-year-olds, who self-reported their health status in a different survey. Only 25 percent said they were in excellent health, but an additional 39 percent reported "very good" health. Seven percent of young adults report being in fair or poor health.

■ Although young adults report being in better health than their elders, the majority of Americans under age 55 say their health is very good to excellent.

Few children are in poor health

(percent distribution of children under age 18 by parent-reported health status, 2001)

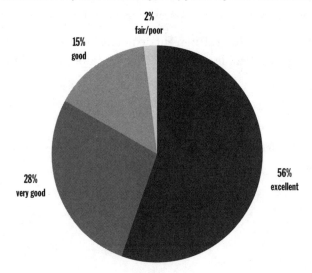

2%
fair/poor

15%
good

28%
very good

56%
excellent

Table 3.1 Health Status of People under Age 25, 2001

(parent- or self-reported health status of people under age 25, by age, 2001)

	excellent	very good	good	fair/poor
Total under age 18	**55.5%**	**28.1%**	**14.6%**	**1.8%**
Under age 5	58.6	26.8	13.2	1.4
Aged 5 to 17	54.3	28.6	15.2	1.9
Aged 5 to 11	55.7	27.9	14.5	1.8
Aged 12 to 17	52.7	29.4	15.9	2.0
Aged 18 to 24	**24.6**	**39.5**	**28.9**	**7.1**

Source: National Center for Health Statistics, Summary Health Statistics for U.S. Children: National Health Interview Survey, 2001, *Series 10, No. 216, 2003; and Centers for Disease Control and Prevention, Behavioral Risk Factor Surveillance System Prevalence Data, 2001; Internet site http://apps.nccd.cdc.gov/brfss/index.asp*

Teens Worry about Being Overweight

Although few are overweight, many are trying to shed pounds.

About 15 percent of children in both the 6-to-11 and 12-to-19 age groups are overweight, according to government studies. Blacks and Hispanics are more likely to be overweight than non-Hispanic whites.

The proportion of female high school students who are overweight or at risk for becoming overweight ranges from 17 to 20 percent. A larger share of girls (33 to 36 percent) think they are overweight, and even more are trying to lose weight (62 to 63 percent).

Boys in 9th to 12th grade are more likely than girls to be overweight or at risk for becoming overweight (13 to 20 percent), but less likely to think they are overweight (22 to 24 percent). Only 27 to 32 percent of boys are trying to lose weight. For both boys and girls, exercise and eating less are the most common ways of trying to lose weight.

■ Although many girls will face weight problems later in life, perhaps a bigger problem for girls in their teen years is the fear of being overweight, which can lead to eating disorders.

Many girls think they are overweight

(percent of girls in 9th to 12th grade who are overweight or at risk for becoming overweight and percent who think they are overweight, 2001

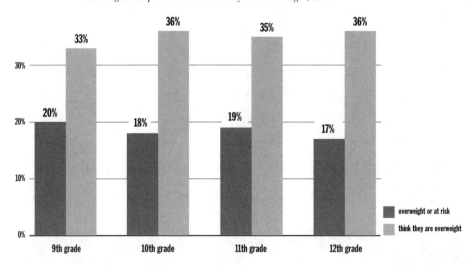

overweight or at risk

think they are overweight

Table 3.2 Overweight Children, 1999–2000

(percent of children aged 6 to 19 who are overweight, by sex, race, Hispanic origin, and age, 1999–2000)

	aged 6 to 11	aged 12 to 19
TOTAL CHILDREN	**15.3%**	**15.5%**
Females	**14.5**	**15.5**
Black, non-Hispanic	22.1	25.7
Mexican	19.6	19.4
White, non-Hispanic	12.0	12.2
Males	**16.0**	**15.5**
Black, non-Hispanic	17.6	20.5
Mexican	27.3	27.5
White, non-Hispanic	11.9	13.0

Note: Being overweight is defined as having a body mass index at or above the sex- and age-specific 95th percentile BMI cutoff points from the 2000 CDC growth charts.
Source: National Center for Health Statistics, Health, United States, 2003, Internet site http://www.cdc.gov/nchs/hus.htm

Table 3.3 Weight Problems and Dieting Behavior of 9th to 12th Graders by Sex, 2001

(percent of 9th to 12th graders by weight status and dieting behavior, by sex, 2001)

	9th grade	10th grade	11th grade	12th grade
Total				
At risk for becoming overweight*	15.7%	13.6%	12.6%	11.8%
Overweight**	10.5	10.8	10.6	9.6
Thought they were overweight	28.8	29.8	29.0	29.1
Were trying to lose weight	47.8	45.7	44.7	45.3
Exercised to lose weight or to avoid gaining weight in past 30 days	64.2	60.4	56.3	57.2
Ate less food, fewer calories, or foods low in fat to lose weight or to avoid gaining weight in past 30 days	44.0	44.5	41.6	45.2
Went without eating for at least 24 hours to lose weight or to avoid gaining weight in past 30 days	15.4	14.5	11.5	11.5
Took diet pills, powders, or liquids without a doctor's advice to lose weight or avoid gaining weight in past 30 days	8.2	9.3	8.9	10.6
Vomited or took a laxative to lose weight or to avoid gaining weight in past 30 days	6.1	6.0	4.4	4.7
Females	**20.0**	**17.9**	**18.9**	**17.3**
At risk for becoming overweight*	12.3	11.3	12.2	11.0
Overweight**	7.7	6.6	6.7	6.3
Thought they were overweight	33.4	35.6	35.2	35.9
Were tring to lose weight	62.1	62.1	62.1	63.1
Exercised to lose weight or to avoid gaining weight in past 30 days	71.5	68.4	65.8	66.9
Ate less food, fewer calories, or foods low in fat to lose weight or to avoid gaining weight in past 30 days	57.0	60.1	56.1	61.5
Went without eating for at least 24 hours to lose weight or to avoid gaining weight in past 30 days	21.1	21.2	16.3	16.4
Took diet pills, powders, or liquids without a doctor's advice to lose weight or avoid gaining weight in past 30 days	10.1	13.1	12.2	15.9
Vomited or took a laxative to lose weight or to avoid gaining weight in past 30 days	8.5	8.5	6.6	7.0

	9th grade	10th grade	11th grade	12th grade
Males	**33.1%**	**31.1%**	**27.6%**	**25.9%**
At risk for becoming overweight*	19.5	15.9	12.9	12.7
Overweight**	13.6	15.2	14.7	13.2
Thought they were overweight	23.7	23.9	22.7	22.2
Were trying to lose weight	31.8	28.6	26.9	26.8
Exercised to lose weight or to avoid gaining weight in past 30 days	56.1	52.1	46.8	47.1
Ate less food, fewer calories, or foods low in fat to lose weight or to avoid gaining weight in past 30 days	29.4	28.2	26.6	28.1
Went without eating for at least 24 hours to lose weight or to avoid gaining weight in past 30 days	9.2	7.6	6.5	6.4
Took diet pills, powders, or liquids without a doctor's advice to lose weight or avoid gaining weight in past 30 days	6.1	5.2	5.5	5.1
Vomited or took a laxative to lose weight or to avoid gaining weight in past 30 days	3.4	3.4	2.2	2.3

Students at risk of becoming overweight were between the 85th and 95th percentile for body mass index, by age and sex, based on reference data.
*** Students who were overweight were at or above the 95th percentile for body mass index, by age and sex, based on reference data.*
Source: Centers for Disease Control and Prevention, "Youth Risk Behavior Surveillance–United States, 2001," Mortality and Morbidity Weekly Report, Vol. 51/SS-4, June 28, 2002

Bicycling Is the Most Popular Recreational Activity among Children

Basketball ranks number-one among teens.

Among selected recreational activities examined by the National Sporting Goods Association, bicycling is most popular among children aged 7 to 11, with more than 9 million (47 percent) taking part at least once in 2002. In-line skating ranks second, slightly ahead of basketball. Among teens aged 12 to 17, basketball is most popular, with nearly 8 million (32 percent) participating at least once in 2002. Bicycling is second, followed by in-line skating.

Many children take part in organized physical activities on a weekly basis, but a much larger share enjoy being physically active during their free time. According to a study by the Centers for Disease Control and Prevention, 40 percent of children participate in organized physical activities during an average week. A much larger 77 percent participate in free-time physical activities on a weekly basis. Expense is the biggest barrier to children's participation in physical activities, cited by 47 percent of parents.

Among 18-to-24-year-olds, only 40 percent take part in regular leisure-time physical activities. Among men, 47 percent participate regularly, while the figure is a much lower 33 percent among women.

■ Cost and transportation problems are bigger barriers for black and Hispanic families than for non-Hispanic white families.

Cost is a barrier to participation in physical activities for many children

(percent of parents reporting barriers to children's participation in physical education, 2002)

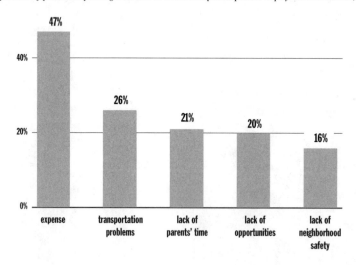

Table 3.4 Sports Participation of Children Aged 7 to 17, 2002

(number and percent of people aged 7 to 17 participating in selected sports at least once during past year, by age, 2002; numbers in thousands)

Children aged 7 to 11	number	percent	Children aged 12 to 17	number	percent
	20,095	100.0%		24,264	100.0%
Bicycle riding	9,378	46.7	Basketball	7,787	32.1
In-line skating	6,734	33.5	Bicycle riding	7,405	30.5
Basketball	6,240	31.1	In-line skating	4,789	19.7
Soccer	5,851	29.1	Fishing	4,446	18.3
Baseball	5,070	25.2	Baseball	3,937	16.2
Fishing	4,783	23.8	Skateboarding	3,834	15.8
Skateboarding	4,023	20.0	Soccer	3,722	15.3
Softball	2,169	10.8	Volleyball	3,091	12.7
Volleyball	1,382	6.9	Softball	3,078	12.7
Tennis	976	4.9	Golf	2,405	9.9
Snowboarding	969	4.8	Tennis	2,048	8.4
Golf	968	4.8	Snowboarding	1,659	6.8
Skiing (alpine)	895	4.5	Skiing (alpine)	1,276	5.3
Ice hockey	132	0.7	Ice hockey	539	2.2

Source: National Sporting Goods Association, Internet site http://www.nsga.org

Table 3.5 Participation of Children Aged 9 to 13 in Physical Activities, 2002

(percent of children aged 9 to 13 participating in physical activities during past seven days and percent of parents reporting barriers to children's participation, by selected demographic characteristics, 2002)

	participated in organized physical activity during past seven days	participated in free-time physical activity during past seven days	barriers to children's participation in physical activities				
			transportation problems	lack of opportunities	expense	lack of parents' time	lack of neighborhood safety
TOTAL CHILDREN	**39.5%**	**77.4%**	**25.6%**	**20.1%**	**46.6%**	**21.0%**	**16.1%**
Sex							
Female	38.6	74.1	26.9	20.8	47.5	22.8	17.6
Male	38.3	80.5	24.4	19.5	45.8	19.2	14.6
Age							
Aged 9	36.1	75.8	25.6	20.5	46.3	20.3	16.9
Aged 10	37.5	77.0	26.2	19.2	46.4	21.6	18.0
Aged 11	43.1	78.0	26.1	21.1	46.0	20.7	16.9
Aged 12	37.7	77.5	24.9	20.0	49.0	20.8	15.9
Aged 13	38.1	78.0	25.2	19.8	45.4	21.5	12.4
Race and Hispanic origin							
Black, non-Hispanic	24.1	74.7	32.6	30.6	54.9	23.3	13.3
Hispanic	25.9	74.6	36.9	30.8	62.3	23.3	41.2
White, non-Hispanic	46.6	79.3	18.9	13.4	39.5	19.1	8.5
Parental education							
Not a high school graduate	19.4	75.3	42.7	36.7	65.9	27.3	42.9
High school graduate	28.3	75.4	32.3	23.8	54.8	20.5	18.2
Some college or more	46.8	78.7	19.3	15.4	39.2	20.0	10.2
Household income							
Less than $25,000	23.5	74.1	44.5	35.6	70.6	25.6	29.4
$25,000 to $50,000	32.8	78.6	28.9	21.9	53.6	20.4	17.8
$50,000 or more	49.1	78.3	14.4	11.5	30.8	19.0	8.6

Source: Centers for Disease Control and Prevention, "Physical Activity Levels among Children Aged 9–13 Years—United States, 2002," Mortality and Morbidity Weekly Report, *Vol. 52, No. 33, August 22, 2003*

Table 3.6 Leisure-Time Physical Activity Level of Young Adults by Sex, 1999–2001

(percent distribution of people aged 18 to 24 by leisure-time physical activity level, percent participating in regular leisure-time physical activity by level, and percent participating in strengthening activities, by sex, 1999–2001)

	total	men	women
Total aged 18 to 24	100.0%	100.0%	100.0%
Physically inactive	29.9	25.3	34.4
At least some physical activity	70.1	74.7	65.6
Regular physical activity			
Any	39.7	46.6	32.8
Light to moderate	17.8	20.6	15.1
Vigorous	31.7	39.1	24.5
Strengthening activities	36.5	45.3	27.8

Note: "Physically inactive" means no light to moderate or vigorous leisure-time physical activity. "At least some" includes light to moderate or vigorous leisure-time physical activities. "Regular physical activity" includes activities done at least three to five times per week. Regular "light to moderate" activity is defined as engaging in light to moderate activity at least five times per week for at least thirty minutes each time. Regular "vigorous" activity is defined as engaging in vigorous activity at least three times per week for at least twenty minutes each time. "Any" regular activity is defined as meeting either criterion or both critera. Light to moderate activity is leisure-time physical activity that causes only light sweating or a light to moderate increase in breathing or heart rate and is done for at least ten minutes per episode. Vigorous activity is leisure-time physical activity that causes heavy sweating or large increases in breathing or heart rate and is done for at least ten minutes per episode. "Strengthening" activities are those designed to strengthen muscles such as weight lifting or calisthenics. Minimum duration and frequency were not asked. Those engaging in strengthening activities may be included in the physically inactive if they did not engage in any other type of physical activity. Numbers will not add to 100 because people may be in more than one category.
Source: National Center for Health Statistics, Health Behaviors of Adults: United States, 1999–2001, *Vital and Health Statistics, Series 10, No. 219, 2004*

Sex Is Common among Teens

Many high school seniors have had four or more sexual partners.

If teenagers are to be believed, then most 12th grade girls and most 11th and 12th grade boys have had sexual intercourse. One in five senior girls has had four or more sexual partners, as has one in four senior boys.

Slightly more than half (51 percent) of 12th grade girls are currently sexually active—meaning they had sexual intercourse during the past three months. The figure is slightly lower among 12th grade boys (45 percent). Fortunately, the majority of high school students, both boys and girls, engage in responsible sexual behavior—that is, they either never had sexual intercourse, or they abstained during the past three months, or they used a condom during their last sexual experience.

■ With sexually active teenagers, preventing pregnancy and sexually transmitted diseases is of prime concern to parents and schools.

The majority of 11th and 12th graders have had sex

(percent of 9th to 12th graders who have had sexual intercourse, 2001)

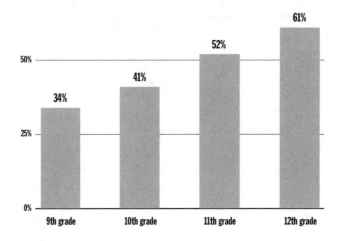

Table 3.7 Sexual Behavior of 9th to 12th Graders by Sex, 2001

(percent of 9th to 12th graders engaging in selected sexual activities, by sex, 2001)

	9th grade	10th grade	11th grade	12th grade
Total				
Ever had sexual intercourse	34.4%	40.8%	51.9%	60.5%
First sexual intercourse before age 13	9.2	7.5	4.6	3.6
Four or more sex partners during lifetime	9.6	12.6	15.2	21.6
Currently sexually active*	22.7	29.7	38.1	47.9
Responsible sexual behavior**	92.8	88.3	84.5	75.8
Females				
Ever had sexual intercourse	29.1	39.3	49.7	60.1
First sexual intercourse before age 13	5.4	4.7	2.9	2.2
Four or more sex partners during lifetime	5.8	10.4	12.6	19.5
Currently sexually active*	19.9	30.7	38.1	51.0
Responsible sexual behavior**	93.5	85.4	82.1	70.1
Males				
Ever had sexual intercourse	40.5	42.2	54.0	61.0
First sexual intercourse before age 13	13.7	10.6	6.4	5.0
Four or more sex partners during lifetime	13.9	15.0	17.8	23.6
Currently sexually active*	25.9	28.6	37.8	44.6
Responsible sexual behavior**	92.2	91.4	87.0	81.9

Had sexual intercourse during the three months preceding the survey.
** Includes those who have never had sexual intercourse, those who have had sexual intercourse but not during the past three months, and those who used a condom the last time they had sex.
Source: Centers for Disease Control and Prevention, "Youth Risk Behavior Surveillance—United States, 2001," Mortality and Morbidity Weekly Report, Vol. 51/SS-4, June 28, 2002

Birth Rate Has Dropped among Teens and Young Adults

Most 20-to-24-year-old women have not yet had children.

The birth rate for women under age 25 has been falling for decades as a growing number of girls have gone to college and embarked on careers. The birth rate among 15-to-19-year-olds fell 28 percent between 1990 and 2002, while the rate for women aged 20 to 24 fell 11 percent. Just 8 percent of 15-to-19-year-old girls have had children. Among women aged 20 to 24, only 33 percent are mothers.

Only 38 percent of women who gave birth in the past year were under age 25. But among those having borne their first child in the past year, nearly half are under age 25. Many teens and young adults who give birth are not married, putting them at an economic disadvantage.

■ Women in their twenties are experiencing one of the most important transitions in life—becoming a parent for the first time.

Most women become mothers during their late twenties

(percent of women who have had children, by age, 2002)

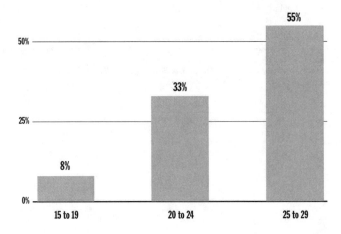

Table 3.8 Birth Rates by Age of Mother, 1990 to 2002

(number of live births per 1,000 women in age group and percent change in rate, 1990–2002)

	15 to 19	20 to 24	25 to 29	30 to 34	35 to 39	40 to 44	45 to 49
2002	43.0	103.6	113.6	91.5	41.4	8.3	0.5
2001	45.3	106.2	113.4	91.9	40.6	8.1	0.5
2000	47.7	109.7	113.5	91.2	39.7	8.0	0.5
1999	48.8	107.9	111.2	87.1	37.8	7.4	0.4
1998	50.3	108.4	110.2	85.2	36.9	7.4	0.4
1997	51.3	107.3	108.3	83.0	35.7	7.1	0.4
1996	53.5	107.8	108.6	82.1	34.9	6.8	0.3
1995	56.0	107.5	108.8	81.1	34.0	6.6	0.3
1994	58.2	109.2	111.0	80.4	33.4	6.4	0.3
1993	59.0	111.3	113.2	79.9	32.7	6.1	0.3
1992	60.3	113.7	115.7	79.6	32.3	5.9	0.3
1991	61.8	115.3	117.2	79.2	31.9	5.5	0.2
1990	59.9	116.5	120.2	80.8	31.7	5.5	0.2

Percent change

1990 to 2002	−28.2%	−11.1%	−5.5%	13.2%	30.6%	50.9%	150.0%

Source: National Center for Health Statistics, Revised Birth and Fertility Rates for the 1990s and New Rates for the Hispanic Populations 2000 and 2001: United States, *National Vital Statistics Report, Vol. 51, No. 12, 2003; calculations by New Strategist*

Table 3.9 Number of Children Born to Women Aged 15 to 44, 2002

(total number of women aged 15 to 44, and percent distribution of women by number of children ever borne, by age, 2002; numbers in thousands)

	total		number of children						
	number	percent	none	one	two	three	four	five	six or more
Aged 15 to 44	**61,361**	**100.0%**	**43.5%**	**17.5%**	**22.2%**	**11.2%**	**3.8%**	**1.5%**	**0.3%**
Aged 15 to 19	9,809	100.0	91.2	5.2	2.4	0.8	0.2	0.1	0.0
Aged 20 to 24	9,683	100.0	67.0	19.6	9.3	3.2	0.6	0.3	0.1
Aged 25 to 29	9,221	100.0	45.2	22.2	19.8	9.1	2.7	0.9	0.1
Aged 30 to 34	10,284	100.0	27.6	21.8	29.6	14.1	4.7	1.9	0.2
Aged 35 to 39	10,803	100.0	20.2	18.6	32.4	18.8	6.9	2.6	0.5
Aged 40 to 44	11,561	100.0	17.9	17.4	35.4	18.9	6.8	2.8	0.8

Source: Bureau of the Census, Fertility of American Women: June 2002, *detailed tables, Internet site http://www.census.gov/population/www/socdemo/fertility/cps2002.html*

Table 3.10 Characteristics of Women Aged 15 to 44 Who Gave Birth in the Past Year, 2002

(total number of women aged 15 to 44, percent childless, number and percent distribution of those who gave birth in the past year and who had a first birth in past year, by selected characteristics, 2002; numbers in thousands)

	total	percent childless	giving birth in past year number	giving birth in past year percent distribution	first birth in past year number	first birth in past year percent distribution
Total aged 15 to 44	**61,361**	**43.5%**	**3,766**	**100.0%**	**1,415**	**100.0%**
Aged 15 to 19	9,809	91.2	549	14.6	272	19.2
Aged 20 to 24	9,683	67.0	872	23.2	438	31.0
Aged 25 to 29	9,221	45.2	897	23.8	306	21.6
Aged 30 to 34	10,284	27.6	859	22.8	272	19.2
Aged 35 to 39	10,803	20.2	452	12.0	85	6.0
Aged 40 to 44	11,561	17.9	137	3.6	42	3.0
Marital Status						
Married, husband present	27,828	18.5	2,382	63.3	825	58.3
Married, husband absent/separated	2,446	21.1	124	3.3	42	3.0
Widowed or divorced	5,303	21.1	143	3.8	35	2.5
Never married	25,782	77.2	1,118	29.7	513	36.3
Race and Hispanic origin						
Asian	3,267	50.8	181	4.8	89	6.3
Black	8,846	39.0	571	15.2	197	13.9
Hispanic	9,141	35.8	750	19.9	278	19.6
Non-Hispanic white	40,017	45.6	2,262	60.1	854	60.4
Educational attainment						
Not a high school graduate	13,096	58.8	812	21.6	264	18.7
High school, four years	16,644	30.7	1,005	26.7	380	26.9
Some college, no degree	12,451	45.9	750	19.9	298	21.1
Associate's degree	5,113	33.0	221	5.9	79	5.6
Bachelor's degree	10,592	46.6	683	18.1	266	18.8
Graduate or professional degree	3,465	44.6	294	7.8	128	9.0
Employment status						
Employed	40,150	43.2	1,867	49.6	741	52.4
Unemployed	3,210	52.8	189	5.0	106	7.5
Not in labor force	18,001	42.4	1,710	45.4	568	40.1
Occupation						
Managerial and professional	13,021	43.8	717	19.0	309	21.8
Technical, sales, admin. support	17,163	44.0	770	20.4	326	23.0
Service occupations	9,102	46.6	436	11.6	165	11.7
Farming, forestry, and fishing	493	47.8	16	0.4	2	0.1
Precision prod., craft and repair	819	33.9	37	1.0	13	0.9
Operators, fabricators, and laborers	2,884	32.9	118	3.1	38	2.7

	total	percent childless	giving birth in past year		first birth in past year	
			number	percent distribution	number	percent distribution
Household income						
Under $10,000	4,203	40.0%	355	9.4%	128	9.0%
$10,000 to $19,999	5,760	39.9	472	12.5	200	14.1
$20,000 to $24,999	3,348	38.2	215	5.7	73	5.2
$25,000 to $29,999	3,464	41.9	194	5.2	55	3.9
$30,000 to $34,999	3,612	43.7	264	7.0	84	5.9
$35,000 to $49,999	8,477	43.0	457	12.1	161	11.4
$50,000 to $74,999	10,613	43.6	554	14.7	247	17.5
$75,000 and over	13,771	47.2	826	21.9	294	20.8
Region						
Northeast	11,616	46.1	694	18.4	247	17.5
Midwest	14,041	43.8	780	20.7	303	21.4
South	21,680	40.9	1,453	38.6	561	39.6
West	14,024	45.1	838	22.3	305	21.6
Metropolitan status						
In central cities	18,804	46.4	1,163	30.9	430	30.4
Outside central cities	31,950	43.8	1,869	49.6	719	50.8
Nonmetropolitan	10,606	37.3	734	19.5	266	18.8
Nativity						
Native born	52,428	44.8	3,129	83.1	1,153	81.5
Foreign born	8,933	35.6	637	16.9	262	18.5

Source: Bureau of the Census, Fertility of American Women: June 2002, *detailed tables, Internet site http://www.census.gov/ population/www/socdemo/fertility/cps2002.html*

The Millennial Generation Accounts for More than One-Third of Births

More than 1.4 million babies were born to women under age 25 in 2002.

Although the birth rate for women under age 25 has been falling, the under-25 age group still accounts for a substantial share of births. In 2002, 36 percent of babies were born to women under age 25. More than 1 million babies were born to women aged 20 to 24. The 56 percent majority of women under age 25 giving birth in 2002 were having their first child.

Non-Hispanic whites accounted for fewer than half the babies born to women under age 25 in 2002. Twenty-seven percent of the newborns were Hispanic and 21 percent were black. The younger the mothers are, the smaller is the percentage of babies borne who are non-Hispanic white. Only 20 percent of babies born to girls under age 15 are non-Hispanic white.

Thirty-four percent of babies born in 2002 had single mothers. The proportion is a much higher 60 percent among babies born to women under age 25, with the figure ranging from fully 97 percent of those born to girls under age 15 to a still substantial 52 percent of those born to women aged 20 to 24. Only 19 percent of babies born to women aged 25 or older are out-of-wedlock.

■ In another five years, the majority of the nation's newborns will have mothers belonging to the Millennial generation.

Non-Hispanic whites account for fewer than half of births to women under age 25

(percent distribution of births to women under age 25 by race and Hispanic origin of mother, 2002)

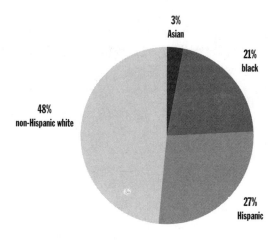

3% Asian
21% black
48% non-Hispanic white
27% Hispanic

Table 3.11 Births to Women by Age and Birth Order, 2002

(number and percent distribution of births by age of mother and birth order, 2002)

	total births	first child	second child	third child	fourth or later child
Total births	**4,021,726**	**1,594,921**	**1,306,786**	**675,270**	**434,527**
Total under age 25	1,454,914	816,186	424,389	154,360	56,357
Under age 15	7,315	7,149	145	2	1
Aged 15 to 17	138,731	123,777	13,428	1,105	84
Aged 18 to 19	286,762	212,284	61,124	11,013	1,600
Aged 20 to 24	1,022,106	472,976	349,692	142,240	54,672
Aged 25 or older	2,566,812	778,735	882,397	520,910	378,170
PERCENT DISTRIBUTION BY AGE					
Total births	**100.0%**	**100.0%**	**100.0%**	**100.0%**	**100.0%**
Total under age 25	36.2	51.2	32.5	22.9	13.0
Under age 15	0.2	0.4	0.0	0.0	0.0
Aged 15 to 17	3.4	7.8	1.0	0.2	0.0
Aged 18 to 19	7.1	13.3	4.7	1.6	0.4
Aged 20 to 24	25.4	29.7	26.8	21.1	12.6
Aged 25 or older	63.8	48.8	67.5	77.1	87.0
PERCENT DISTRIBUTION BY BIRTH ORDER					
Total births	**100.0%**	**39.7%**	**32.5%**	**16.8%**	**10.8%**
Total under age 25	100.0	56.1	29.2	10.6	3.9
Under age 15	100.0	97.7	2.0	0.0	0.0
Aged 15 to 17	100.0	89.2	9.7	0.8	0.1
Aged 18 to 19	100.0	74.0	21.3	3.8	0.6
Aged 20 to 24	100.0	46.3	34.2	13.9	5.3
Aged 25 or older	100.0	30.3	34.4	20.3	14.7

Note: Numbers will not add to total because not stated is not included.
Source: National Center for Health Statistics, Births: Final Data for 2002, *National Vital Statistics Report, Vol. 52, No. 10, 2002, calculations by New Strategist*

Table 3.12 Births to Women by Age, Race, and Hispanic Origin, 2002

(number and percent distribution of births by age, race, and Hispanic origin of mother, 2002)

		race				Hispanic origin	
	total	American Indian	Asian	black	white	Hispanic	non-Hispanic white
Total births	**4,021,726**	**42,368**	**210,907**	**593,691**	**3,174,760**	**876,642**	**2,298,156**
Total under age 25	1,454,914	22,183	38,172	301,687	1,092,872	395,556	700,157
Under age 15	7,315	133	110	3,188	3,884	2,421	1,493
Aged 15 to 17	138,731	2,663	2,315	37,889	95,864	46,740	49,756
Aged 18 to 19	286,762	5,044	5,688	65,906	210,124	81,160	129,755
Aged 20 to 24	1,022,106	14,343	30,059	194,704	783,000	265,235	519,153
Aged 25 or older	2,566,812	20,185	172,735	292,004	2,081,888	481,086	1,597,999

PERCENT DISTRIBUTION BY AGE

Total births	**100.0%**	**100.0%**	**100.0%**	**100.0%**	**100.0%**	**100.0%**	**100.0%**
Total under age 25	36.2	52.4	18.1	50.8	34.4	45.1	30.5
Under age 15	0.2	0.3	0.1	0.5	0.1	0.3	0.1
Aged 15 to 17	3.4	6.3	1.1	6.4	3.0	5.3	2.2
Aged 18 to 19	7.1	11.9	2.7	11.1	6.6	9.3	5.6
Aged 20 to 24	25.4	33.9	14.3	32.8	24.7	30.3	22.6
Aged 25 or older	63.8	47.6	81.9	49.2	65.6	54.9	69.5

PERCENT DISTRIBUTION BY RACE AND HISPANIC ORIGIN

Total births	**100.0%**	**1.1%**	**5.2%**	**14.8%**	**78.9%**	**21.8%**	**57.1%**
Total under age 25	100.0	1.5	2.6	20.7	75.1	27.2	48.1
Under age 15	100.0	1.8	1.5	43.6	53.1	33.1	20.4
Aged 15 to 17	100.0	1.9	1.7	27.3	69.1	33.7	35.9
Aged 18 to 19	100.0	1.8	2.0	23.0	73.3	28.3	45.2
Aged 20 to 24	100.0	1.4	2.9	19.1	76.6	25.9	50.8
Aged 25 or older	100.0	0.8	6.7	11.4	81.1	18.7	62.3

Note: Numbers will not add to total because Hispanics may be of any race and not stated is not included.
Source: National Center for Health Statistics, Births: Final Data for 2002, *National Vital Statistics Report, Vol. 52, No. 10, 2002, calculations by New Strategist*

Table 3.13 Births to Women by Age and Marital Status, 2002

(total number of births and number and percent to unmarried women by age, race, and Hispanic origin of mother, 2002)

		race				Hispanic origin	
	total	American Indian	Asian	black	white	Hispanic	non-Hispanic white
Total births	**4,021,726**	**42,368**	**210,907**	**593,691**	**3,174,760**	**876,642**	**2,298,156**
Total under age 25	1,454,914	22,183	38,172	301,687	1,092,872	395,556	700,157
Under age 15	7,315	133	110	3,188	3,884	2,421	1,493
Aged 15 to 17	138,731	2,663	2,315	37,889	95,864	46,740	49,756
Aged 18 to 19	286,762	5,044	5,688	65,906	210,124	81,160	129,755
Aged 20 to 24	1,022,106	14,343	30,059	194,704	783,000	265,235	519,153
Aged 25 or older	2,566,812	20,185	172,735	292,004	2,081,888	481,086	1,597,999
BIRTHS TO UNMARRIED WOMEN							
Total births	**1,365,966**	**25,297**	**31,344**	**404,864**	**904,461**	**381,466**	**528,535**
Total under age 25	874,936	16,355	16,505	260,825	581,251	233,118	351,288
Under age 15	7,093	129	107	3,174	3,683	2,266	1,446
Aged 15 to 17	122,791	2,502	1,896	37,361	81,032	38,698	42,971
Aged 18 to 19	217,395	4,176	3,830	62,014	147,375	55,785	92,342
Aged 20 to 24	527,657	9,548	10,672	158,276	349,161	136,369	214,529
Aged 25 or older	491,030	8,942	14,839	144,039	323,210	148,348	177,247
PERCENT OF BIRTHS TO UNMARRIED WOMEN							
Total births	**34.0%**	**59.7%**	**14.9%**	**68.2%**	**28.5%**	**43.5%**	**23.0%**
Total under age 25	60.1	73.7	43.2	86.5	53.2	58.9	50.2
Under age 15	97.0	97.0	97.3	99.6	94.8	93.6	96.9
Aged 15 to 17	88.5	94.0	81.9	98.6	84.5	82.8	86.4
Aged 18 to 19	75.8	82.8	67.3	94.1	70.1	68.7	71.2
Aged 20 to 24	51.6	66.6	35.5	81.3	44.6	51.4	41.3
Aged 25 or older	19.1	44.3	8.6	49.3	15.5	30.8	11.1

Note: Births by race and Hispanic origin will not add to total because Hispanics may be of any race, not all races are shown, and not stated is not included.
Source: National Center for Health Statistics, Births: Final Data for 2002, *National Vital Statistics Report, Vol. 52, No. 10, 2002, calculations by New Strategist*

Table 3.14 Birth Delivery Method by Age, 2002

(number and percent distribution of births by age and method of delivery, 2002)

| | total | vaginal | | Caesarean | | |
		total	after previous Caesarean	total	first	repeat
Total births	**4,021,726**	**2,958,423**	**59,248**	**1,043,846**	**634,426**	**409,420**
Total under age 25	1,454,914	1,153,190	12,416	295,802	212,688	83,114
Under age 20	432,808	353,653	1,506	77,563	67,741	9,822
Aged 20 to 24	1,022,106	799,537	10,910	218,239	144,947	73,292
Aged 25 or older	2,566,812	1,805,233	46,832	748,044	421,738	326,306
PERCENT DISTRIBUTION BY AGE						
Total births	**100.0%**	**100.0%**	**100.0%**	**100.0%**	**100.0%**	**100.0%**
Total under age 25	36.2	39.0	21.0	28.3	33.5	20.3
Under age 20	10.8	12.0	2.5	7.4	10.7	2.4
Aged 20 to 24	25.4	27.0	18.4	20.9	22.8	17.9
Aged 25 or older	63.8	61.0	79.0	71.7	66.5	79.7
PERCENT DISTRIBUTION BY DELIVERY METHOD						
Total births	**100.0%**	**73.6%**	**1.5%**	**26.0%**	**15.8%**	**10.2%**
Total under age 25	100.0	79.3	0.9	20.3	14.6	5.7
Under age 20	100.0	81.7	0.3	17.9	15.7	2.3
Aged 20 to 24	100.0	78.2	1.1	21.4	14.2	7.2
Aged 25 or older	100.0	70.3	1.8	29.1	16.4	12.7

Note: Numbers will not add to total because not stated is not included.
Source: National Center for Health Statistics, Births: Final Data for 2002, *National Vital Statistics Report, Vol. 52, No. 10, 2002, calculations by New Strategist*

Cigarette Smoking Is above Average among Millennials

More than 40 percent of 20-to-23-year-olds have smoked cigarettes in the past month.

Cigarette smoking has been declining in the population as a whole, but among young adults it remains stubbornly high. Either antismoking campaigns are backfiring, or Hollywood's cigarette-smoking role models are overcoming the warnings about the dangers of cigarettes.

Overall, 26 percent of people aged 12 or older smoked cigarettes in the past month, according to a 2002 survey. The proportion surpasses the national average among 17-year-olds and peaks at 46 percent among 21-year-olds.

Cigarette smoking remains popular among teens and young adults although their peers are increasingly likely to disapprove of smoking. Surveys of 8th, 10th, and 12th graders show a larger percentage disapproving or strongly disapproving of cigarettes in 2002 than in 1992. The percentage of teenagers who believe cigarette smoking presents a "great" physical risk is also up, ranging from 58 percent among 8th graders to 74 percent among 12th graders.

■ Until smoking stops being "cool," many teens will experiment with cigarettes and many will become hooked on smoking.

Many teens and young adults smoke cigarettes

(percent of people who have smoked cigarettes in the past month, by age, 2002)

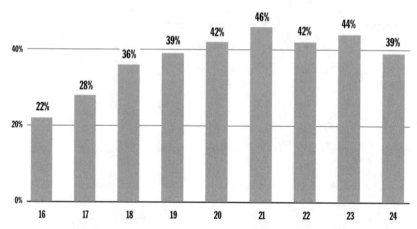

Table 3.15 Cigarette Smoking among People Aged 12 to 25, 2002

(percent of people aged 12 or older and aged 12 to 25 reporting any, past year, and past month use of cigarettes, 2002)

	ever used	used in past year	used in past month
Total people	**69.1%**	**30.3%**	**26.0%**
Aged 12	9.2	4.4	1.7
Aged 13	18.7	10.0	4.7
Aged 14	28.5	16.2	8.5
Aged 15	39.7	23.4	14.1
Aged 16	48.4	31.2	21.9
Aged 17	56.9	38.2	28.1
Aged 18	65.4	46.2	35.8
Aged 19	66.6	47.1	38.7
Aged 20	71.2	50.7	41.8
Aged 21	74.4	54.0	46.2
Aged 22	74.1	51.1	42.2
Aged 23	74.7	50.8	44.1
Aged 24	72.2	46.9	39.4
Aged 25	72.4	45.0	38.1

Source: SAMHSA, Office of Applied Studies, National Survey on Drug Use and Health, 2002; Internet site http://www.samhsa.gov/

Table 3.16 Attitudes toward Cigarette Smoking by 8th, 10th, and 12th Graders, 1992 and 2002

(percent of 8th, 10th, and 12th graders who think cigarettes present a "great" physical risk, and percent who "disapprove" or "strongly disapprove" of cigarette smoking, 1992 and 2002; percentage point change, 1992–2002)

	2002	1992	percentage point change 1992–02
Great risk			
8th graders	57.5%	50.8%	6.7
10th graders	64.3	59.3	5.0
12th graders	74.2	69.2	5.0
Disapprove			
8th graders	84.6	82.3	2.3
10th graders	80.6	77.8	2.8
12th graders	73.6	73.5	0.1

Source: Institute for Social Research, University of Michigan, Monitoring the Future Survey, 2002; Internet site http://monitoringthefuture.org/data/02data.html

Most Teens Don't Wait for Legal Drinking Age

The majority of 19- and 20-year-olds have had an alcoholic beverage in the past month.

More than half of Americans aged 12 or older have had an alcoholic beverage in the past month. The share of those who imbibed climbs above 50 percent among 19-year-olds although the legal drinking age is 21.

Many teens and young adults take part in binge drinking, meaning they had five or more drinks on one occasion in the past month. At least one in ten 18-to-24-year-olds is a heavy drinker, that is, has participated in binge drinking at least five times in the past month.

Full-time college students aged 18 to 22 are more likely to drink alcohol than other 18-to-22-year olds. Sixty-four percent of college students have drunk alcohol in the past month, and 44 percent have been on a binge. College students are less likely than other 18-to-22-year-olds to use tobacco, however. Thirty-three percent of college students have smoked cigarettes in the past month versus 46 percent of other 18-to-22-year-olds. College students are also slightly less likely to use illicit drugs than their noncollege counterparts (21 versus 22 percent).

■ Heavy drinking is a problem on many college campuses. With 44 percent of college students aged 18 to 22 taking part in binge drinking during the past month, campus authorities have a problem to address.

Many teens drink alcohol

(percent of people aged 16 to 20 who have consumed alcoholic beverages in the past month, by age, 2002)

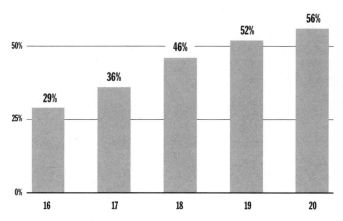

Table 3.17 Alcohol Use by People Aged 12 to 25, 2002

(percent of people aged 12 or older and aged 12 to 25 who drank alcoholic beverages during the past month, by level of alcohol use, 2002)

	any time	binge	heavy
Total people	**51.0%**	**22.9%**	**6.7%**
Aged 12	2.0	0.8	0.0
Aged 13	6.5	2.8	0.5
Aged 14	13.4	7.0	1.4
Aged 15	19.9	11.6	2.4
Aged 16	29.0	17.9	4.0
Aged 17	36.2	25.0	7.2
Aged 18	46.3	32.6	11.2
Aged 19	51.6	38.3	14.1
Aged 20	55.5	38.7	15.1
Aged 21	70.9	50.2	20.1
Aged 22	67.0	46.1	17.0
Aged 23	66.2	43.5	16.6
Aged 24	64.9	39.4	13.2
Aged 25	64.4	39.3	11.6

Note: Binge drinking is defined as having five or more drinks on the same occasion on at least one day in the 30 days prior to the survey. Heavy drinking is having five or more drinks on the same occasion on each of five or more days in 30 days prior to the survey.
Source: SAMHSA, Office of Applied Studies, National Survey on Drug Use and Health, 2002; Internet site http://www.samhsa.gov/

Table 3.18 **Cigarette, Alcohol, and Drug Use of 18-to-22-Year-Olds by College Enrollment Status, 2002**

(percent of people aged 18 to 22 who have smoked cigarettes, consumed alcohol, or used illicit drugs in the past month, by college enrollment status, 2002)

	full-time undergraduates	others
Cigarettes	32.6%	45.8%
Alcohol	64.1	54.3
Binge drinking	44.4	38.9
Heavy drinking	18.8	13.4
Illicit drugs	20.7	22.4

Note: Binge drinking is defined as having five or more drinks on the same occasion on at least one day in the 30 days prior to the survey. Heavy drinking is having five or more drinks on the same occasion on each of five or more days in 30 days prior to the survey. Illicit drugs include marijuana, cocaine, heroin, hallucinogens, inhalants, and nonmedical use of prescription-type pain relievers, tranquilizers, stimulants, and sedatives.
Source: Substance Abuse and Mental Health Services Administration, National Household Survey on Drug Use and Health, 2002; Internet site http://www.samhsa.gov/oas/nhsda/2k2nsduh/Results/2k2results.htm#chap2

Drug Use Is Prevalent among Teens and Young Adults

More than one in five 17-to-21-year-olds has used an illicit drug in the past month.

Only 8 percent of Americans aged 12 or older have used an illicit drug in the past month. Young adults are much more likely to be current drug users than the average person. From 13 to 23 percent of 15-to-24-year-olds have used an illicit drug in the past month.

A survey of teenagers shows widespread and growing drug use. Ten percent of 8th graders have used an illicit drug in the past month, up from 7 percent in 1992. The figure rises to 21 percent in 10th grade and to 25 percent in 12th grade. The most commonly used drug is marijuana. Nearly half of 12th graders have used marijuana at some time in their lives, as have 39 percent of 10th graders and 19 percent of 8th graders.

Behind these shockingly high rates of drug use are changing attitudes among teens. A shrinking share of 12th graders believe illicit drug use presents a "great" physical risk or disapprove of it.

■ The greater acceptance of drug use among teens may stem from the ambivalence of their Baby-Boom parents, most of whom experimented with marijuana during their young-adult years.

Many teens and young adults use illicit drugs

(percent of people who have used illicit drugs in the past month, by age, 2002)

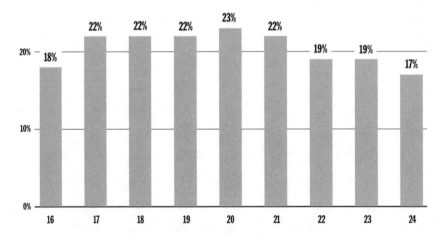

Table 3.19 Drug Use by People Aged 12 to 25, 2002

(percent of people aged 12 or older and aged 12 to 25 who ever used any illicit drug, who used an illicit drug in the past year, and who used an illicit drug in the past month, 2002)

	ever used	used in past year	used in past month
Total people	**46.0%**	**14.9%**	**8.3%**
Aged 12	12.4	7.1	3.3
Aged 13	18.0	11.2	5.1
Aged 14	26.7	18.9	9.1
Aged 15	35.3	26.1	13.3
Aged 16	43.7	32.6	17.5
Aged 17	50.6	38.5	22.1
Aged 18	54.5	40.3	22.3
Aged 19	57.5	39.6	22.3
Aged 20	59.7	38.4	22.8
Aged 21	66.8	39.4	21.7
Aged 22	60.4	33.7	19.4
Aged 23	61.9	33.5	19.4
Aged 24	59.7	29.2	17.0
Aged 25	58.4	26.7	15.0

Note: Illicit drugs include marijuana/hashish, cocaine (including crack), heroin, hallucinogens, inhalants, and any prescription-type psychotherapeutic used nonmedically.
Source: SAMHSA, Office of Applied Studies, National Survey on Drug Use and Health, 2002; Internet site http://www.samhsa.gov/

Table 3.20 Lifetime Marijuana Use by People Aged 12 to 25, 1965 to 2002

(percent of people aged 12 to 25 who have ever used marijuana, 1965 to 2002)

	12 to 17	18 to 25
2002	20.6%	53.8%
2001	21.9	53.0
2000	20.4	51.8
1999	19.7	50.3
1998	19.9	47.0
1997	18.6	45.7
1996	17.9	44.3
1995	16.4	44.1
1994	13.9	43.5
1993	12.4	43.4
1992	11.8	44.5
1991	11.5	45.1
1990	11.9	46.6
1989	12.5	47.3
1988	13.2	48.8
1987	14.9	49.7
1986	15.2	50.4
1985	15.4	51.5
1984	15.6	53.2
1983	16.0	53.8
1982	16.9	54.4
1981	17.6	54.3
1980	19.4	53.0
1979	19.6	52.1
1978	18.0	51.0
1977	18.7	48.6
1976	17.9	44.9
1975	15.8	41.6
1974	14.8	39.3
1973	13.2	34.5
1972	11.0	30.8
1971	9.4	27.1
1970	7.4	22.0
1969	5.9	16.0
1968	4.9	10.6
1967	2.8	7.7
1966	1.8	6.1
1965	1.8	5.1

Source: SAMHSA, Office of Applied Studies, National Survey on Drug Use and Health, 2002; Internet site http://www.samhsa.gov/

Table 3.21 Marijuana Use by 9th to 12th Graders, 2001

(percent of 9th to 12th graders who have ever used marijuana or who have used marijuana in the past 30 days, by sex, 2001)

	lifetime	past month
Total 9th graders	**32.7%**	**19.4%**
Female	28.6	16.5
Male	37.3	22.6
Total 10th graders	**41.7**	**24.8**
Female	37.5	21.5
Male	46.1	28.3
Total 11th graders	**47.2**	**25.8**
Female	42.6	21.4
Male	51.7	30.2
Total 12th graders	**51.5**	**26.9**
Female	48.9	21.8
Male	54.2	32.3

Source: Centers for Disease Control and Prevention, "Youth Risk Behavior Surveillance—United States, 2001," Mortality and Morbidity Weekly Report, *Vol. 51/SS-4, June 28, 2002*

Table 3.22 Lifetime Drug Use by 8th, 10th, and 12th Graders, 1992 and 2002

(percent of 8th, 10th, and 12th graders who have ever used illicit drugs by type of drug, 1992 and 2002; percentage point change, 1992–2002)

	2002	1992	percentage point change 1992–02
8TH GRADERS			
Any illicit drug	**24.5%**	**20.6%**	**3.9**
Marijuana	19.2	11.2	8.0
Inhalants	15.2	17.4	–2.2
Hallucinogens	4.1	3.8	0.3
Cocaine	3.6	2.9	0.7
Heroin	1.6	1.4	0.2
Amphetamines	8.7	10.8	–2.1
Steroids	2.5	1.7	0.8
10TH GRADERS			
Any illicit drug	**44.6**	**29.8**	**14.8**
Marijuana	38.7	21.4	17.3
Inhalants	13.5	16.6	–3.1
Hallucinogens	7.8	6.4	1.4
Cocaine	6.1	3.3	2.8
Heroin	1.8	1.2	0.6
Amphetamines	14.9	13.1	1.8
Steroids	3.5	1.7	1.8
12TH GRADERS			
Any illicit drug	**53.0**	**40.7**	**12.3**
Marijuana	47.8	32.6	15.2
Inhalants	11.7	16.6	–4.9
Hallucinogens	12.0	9.2	2.8
Cocaine	7.8	6.1	1.7
Heroin	1.7	1.2	0.5
Amphetamines	16.8	13.9	2.9
Steroids	4.0	2.1	1.9

Source: Institute for Social Research, University of Michigan, Monitoring the Future Survey, 2002; Internet site http://monitoringthefuture.org/data/02data.html

Table 3.23 Past Month Drug Use by 8th, 10th, and 12th Graders, 1992 and 2002

(percent of 8th, 10th, and 12th graders who have used illicit drugs in the past 30 days, by type of drug, 1992 and 2002; percentage point change, 1992–2002)

	2002	1992	percentage point change 1992–02
8TH GRADERS			
Any illicit drug	**10.4%**	**6.8%**	**3.6**
Marijuana	8.3	3.7	4.6
Inhalants	3.8	4.7	–0.9
Hallucinogens	1.2	1.1	0.1
Cocaine	1.1	0.7	0.4
Heroin	0.5	0.4	0.1
Amphetamines	2.8	3.3	–0.5
Steroids	0.8	0.5	0.3
10TH GRADERS			
Any illicit drug	**20.8**	**11.0**	**9.8**
Marijuana	17.8	8.1	9.7
Inhalants	2.4	2.7	–0.3
Hallucinogens	1.6	1.8	–0.2
Cocaine	1.6	0.7	0.9
Heroin	0.5	0.2	0.3
Amphetamines	5.2	3.6	1.6
Steroids	1.0	0.6	0.4
12TH GRADERS			
Any illicit drug	**25.4**	**14.4**	**11.0**
Marijuana	21.5	11.9	9.6
Inhalants	1.5	2.3	–0.8
Hallucinogens	2.3	2.1	0.2
Cocaine	2.3	1.3	1.0
Heroin	0.5	0.3	0.2
Amphetamines	5.5	2.8	2.7
Steroids	1.4	0.6	0.8

Source: Institute for Social Research, University of Michigan, Monitoring the Future Survey, 2002; Internet site http:// monitoringthefuture.org/data/02data.html

Table 3.24 Attitudes toward Drug Use among 12th Graders, 1992 and 2002

(percentage of high school seniors who think the use of illicit drugs is a "great" physical risk and percent who "disapprove" or "strongly disapprove" of drug use by people aged 18 or older, by type of use, 1992 and 2002; percentage point change, 1992–2002)

	2002	1992	percentage point change 1992–02
Great risk			
Try marijuana once or twice	16.1%	24.5%	–8.4
Smoke marijuana occasionally	23.2	39.6	–16.4
Smoke marijuana regularly	53.0	76.5	–23.5
Try cocaine once or twice	51.2	56.8	–5.6
Take cocaine occasionally	68.3	75.1	–6.8
Take cocaine regularly	84.5	90.2	–5.7
Try one or two drinks of an alcoholic beverage	7.6	8.6	–1.0
Take one or two drinks nearly every day	21.0	30.6	–9.6
Smoke one or more packs of cigarettes per day	74.2	69.2	–5.0
Disapprove			
Try marijuana once or twice	51.6	69.9	–18.3
Smoke marijuana occasionally	63.4	79.7	–16.3
Smoke marijuana regularly	78.3	90.1	–11.8
Try cocaine once or twice	89.0	93.0	–4.0
Take cocaine regularly	95.0	96.9	–1.9
Try one or two drinks of an alcoholic beverage	26.3	33.0	–6.7
Take one or two drinks nearly every day	69.1	75.9	–6.8
Smoke one or more packs of cigarettes per day	73.6	73.5	0.1

Source: Institute for Social Research, University of Michigan, Monitoring the Future Survey, 2002; Internet site http:// monitoringthefuture.org/data/02data.html; calculations by New Strategist

Children under Age 18 Account for One-Fifth of the Uninsured

More than 8 million children do not have health insurance.

Among all Americans, 44 million lacked health insurance in 2002—or 15 percent of the population. The figure is 12 percent among children under age 18, many of whom are covered under the government's Medicaid program. Among 18-to-24-year-olds, fully 30 percent do not have health insurance—a larger share than in any other age group. People under age 25 account for fully 38 percent of the uninsured.

The children most likely to be without health insurance are Hispanic (25 percent have no health insurance), poor (22 percent), and foreign born (38 percent). Among children without health insurance, 36 percent are Hispanic and 73 percent live in the South or West.

For 61 percent of the population, health insurance is provided by an employer. Among 18-to-24-year-olds, however, only 49 percent have employment-based health insurance.

■ Young adults without health insurance are vulnerable to financial catastrophe in the event of major illness or injury.

Many young adults are without health insurance

(percent of people who do not have health insurance, by age, 2002)

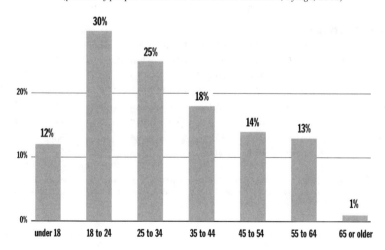

Table 3.25 Health Insurance Coverage of People by Age, 2002

(number and percent distribution of people by age and health insurance coverage status, 2002; numbers in thousands)

| | | covered by private or government health insurance | | | | | | | not covered |
| | | private health insurance | | | government health insurance | | | | |
	total	total	total	employment based	total	Medicaid	Medicare	military	
Total people	**285,933**	**242,360**	**198,973**	**175,296**	**73,624**	**33,246**	**38,448**	**10,063**	**43,574**
Under age 18	73,312	64,781	49,473	46,182	19,662	17,526	524	2,148	8,531
Aged 18 to 24	27,438	19,310	16,562	13,429	3,738	2,909	183	779	8,128
Aged 25 to 34	39,243	29,474	26,492	24,800	3,944	2,801	455	922	9,769
Aged 35 to 44	44,074	36,292	33,240	31,180	4,240	2,728	881	1,121	7,781
Aged 45 to 54	40,234	34,648	31,724	29,617	4,345	2,227	1,382	1,351	5,586
Aged 55 to 64	27,399	23,879	20,797	18,505	4,882	1,773	2,392	1,482	3,521
Aged 65 or older	34,234	33,976	20,685	11,583	32,813	3,283	32,631	2,259	258
PERCENT DISTRIBUTION BY AGE									
Total people	**100.0%**	**100.0%**	**100.0%**	**100.0%**	**100.0%**	**100.0%**	**100.0%**	**100.0%**	**100.0%**
Under age 18	25.6	26.7	24.9	26.3	26.7	52.7	1.4	21.3	19.6
Aged 18 to 24	9.6	8.0	8.3	7.7	5.1	8.7	0.5	7.7	18.7
Aged 25 to 34	13.7	12.2	13.3	14.1	5.4	8.4	1.2	9.2	22.4
Aged 35 to 44	15.4	15.0	16.7	17.8	5.8	8.2	2.3	11.1	17.9
Aged 45 to 54	14.1	14.3	15.9	16.9	5.9	6.7	3.6	13.4	12.8
Aged 55 to 64	9.6	9.9	10.5	10.6	6.6	5.3	6.2	14.7	8.1
Aged 65 or older	12.0	14.0	10.4	6.6	44.6	9.9	84.9	22.4	0.6
PERCENT DISTRIBUTION BY TYPE OF COVERAGE									
Total people	**100.0%**	**84.8%**	**69.6%**	**61.3%**	**25.7%**	**11.6%**	**13.4%**	**3.5%**	**15.2%**
Under age 18	100.0	88.4	67.5	63.0	26.8	23.9	0.7	2.9	11.6
Aged 18 to 24	100.0	70.4	60.4	48.9	13.6	10.6	0.7	2.8	29.6
Aged 25 to 34	100.0	75.1	67.5	63.2	10.1	7.1	1.2	2.3	24.9
Aged 35 to 44	100.0	82.3	75.4	70.7	9.6	6.2	2.0	2.5	17.7
Aged 45 to 54	100.0	86.1	78.8	73.6	10.8	5.5	3.4	3.4	13.9
Aged 55 to 64	100.0	87.2	75.9	67.5	17.8	6.5	8.7	5.4	12.9
Aged 65 or older	100.0	99.2	60.4	33.8	95.8	9.6	95.3	6.6	0.8

Note: Numbers may not add to total because some people have more than one type of health insurance coverage.
Source: Bureau of the Census, unpublished tables from the 2003 Current Population Survey, Internet site http://www.census.gov/hhes/hlthins/historic/hihistt2.html; calculations by New Strategist

Table 3.26 Health Insurance Coverage of Children under Age 19, 2001

(number and percent distribution of children under age 19 by selected characteristics and health insurance coverage status, 2001; numbers in thousands)

| | | covered by private or government health insurance | | | | | | | |
| | | private health insurance | | | government health insurance | | | | |
	total	total	total	employment based	total	Medicaid/ state based/ SCHIP	Medicare	military	not covered
Total children under 19	76,559	67,322	52,352	48,699	19,522	17,089	451	2,488	9,237
Age									
Under age 5	23,373	20,870	15,062	14,264	7,322	6,546	156	810	2,503
Aged 6 to 15	41,133	36,254	28,640	26,997	10,057	8,734	214	1,351	4,879
Aged 16 to 18	12,054	10,199	8,650	7,438	2,144	1,810	81	327	1,855
Under age 18	72,628	64,119	49,647	46,439	18,822	16,502	423	2,381	8,509
Race and Hispanic origin									
American Indian and Alaskan Native	1,246	968	530	488	520	490	11	35	278
Asian and Pacific Islander	3,408	2,997	2,400	2,188	764	609	17	146	411
Black	12,307	10,543	6428	6102	5,041	4,651	160	396	1,764
Hispanic	13,529	10,166	5,870	5,480	4,934	4,648	94	278	3,363
White	59,599	52,814	42,994	39,920	13,197	11,339	262	1,911	6,785
Non-Hispanic	46,870	43,303	37,455	34,745	8,627	7,036	175	1,656	3,567
Family income-to-poverty ratio									
Less than 100 percent	12,352	9,638	2,754	2,262	7,669	7,456	220	198	2,714
100 to less than 133 percent	5,493	4,359	2,155	1,885	2,645	2,481	59	178	1,134
133 to less than 200 percent	11,004	9,134	6,220	5,647	3,831	3,381	57	481	1,870
200 to less than 250 percent	7,539	6,559	5,547	5,144	1,584	1,344	28	252	980
250 percent or higher	39,564	37,249	35,521	33,617	3,551	2,201	78	1,361	2,315
Nativity									
Native	73,171	65,221	50,859	47,352	18,813	16,423	430	2,449	7,950
Foreign born	3,388	2,100	1,493	1,347	709	666	22	39	1,288
Naturalized citizen	478	402	299	280	120	101	3	19	76
Not a citizen	2,910	1,698	1,194	1,067	589	565	19	20	1,212
Region									
Northeast	12,964	11,841	9,386	8,940	3,180	2,954	54	237	1,123
Midwest	16,442	15,132	12,691	11,844	3,401	3,096	98	295	1,310
South	28,150	24,148	18,095	16,814	7,889	6,669	200	1,258	4,002
West	19,003	16,201	12,179	11,101	5,052	4,370	99	698	2,802
Metropolitan status									
Inside metropolitan area	62,604	55,019	43255	40,383	15,180	13,233	320	2,007	7,585
Inside central cities	22,215	18,915	12,646	11,788	7,527	6,870	175	683	3,300
Outside central cities	40,389	36,104	30,609	28,595	7,652	6,363	145	1,323	4,285
Outside metropolitan area	13,955	12,303	9,097	8,316	4,343	3,856	131	481	1,652

		covered by private or government health insurance							
		private health insurance			government health insurance				
	total	total	total	employment based	total	Medicaid/ state based/ SCHIP	Medicare	military	not covered
Total children under 19	**100.0%**	**87.9%**	**68.4%**	**63.6%**	**25.5%**	**22.3%**	**0.6%**	**3.2%**	**12.1%**
Age									
Under age 5	100.0	89.3	64.4	61.0	31.3	28.0	0.7	3.5	10.7
Aged 6 to 15	100.0	88.1	69.6	65.6	24.4	21.2	0.5	3.3	11.9
Aged 16 to 18	100.0	84.6	71.8	61.7	17.8	15.0	0.7	2.7	15.4
Under age 18	100.0	88.3	68.4	63.9	25.9	22.7	0.6	3.3	11.7
Race and Hispanic origin									
American Indian and									
Alaskan Native	100.0	77.7	42.5	39.2	41.7	39.3	0.9	2.8	22.3
Asian and Pacific Islander	100.0	87.9	70.4	64.2	22.4	17.9	0.5	4.3	12.1
Black	100.0	85.7	52.2	49.6	41.0	37.8	1.3	3.2	14.3
Hispanic	100.0	75.1	43.4	40.5	36.5	34.4	0.7	2.1	24.9
White	100.0	88.6	72.1	67.0	22.1	19.0	0.4	3.2	11.4
Non-Hispanic	100.0	92.4	79.9	74.1	18.4	15.0	0.4	3.5	7.6
Family income-to-poverty ratio									
Less than 100 percent	100.0	78.0	22.3	18.3	62.1	60.4	1.8	1.6	22.0
100 to less than 133 percent	100.0	79.4	39.2	34.3	48.2	45.2	1.1	3.2	20.6
133 to less than 200 percent	100.0	83.0	56.5	51.3	34.8	30.7	0.5	4.4	17.0
200 to less than 250 percent	100.0	87.0	73.6	68.2	21.0	17.8	0.4	3.3	13.0
250 percent or higher	100.0	94.1	89.8	85.0	9.0	5.6	0.2	3.4	5.9
Nativity									
Native	100.0	89.1	69.5	64.7	25.7	22.4	0.6	3.3	10.9
Foreign born	100.0	62.0	44.1	39.8	20.9	19.7	0.6	1.2	38.0
Naturalized citizen	100.0	84.1	62.6	58.6	25.1	21.1	0.6	4.0	15.9
Not a citizen	100.0	58.4	41.0	36.7	20.2	19.4	0.7	0.7	41.6
Region									
Northeast	100.0	91.3	72.4	69.0	24.5	22.8	0.4	1.8	8.7
Midwest	100.0	92.0	77.2	72.0	20.7	18.8	0.6	1.8	8.0
South	100.0	85.8	64.3	59.7	28.0	23.7	0.7	4.5	14.2
West	100.0	85.3	64.1	58.4	26.6	23.0	0.5	3.7	14.7
Metropolitan status									
Inside metropolitan area	100.0	87.9	69.1	64.5	24.2	21.1	0.5	3.2	12.1
Inside central cities	100.0	85.1	56.9	53.1	33.9	30.9	0.8	3.1	14.9
Outside central cities	100.0	89.4	75.8	70.8	18.9	15.8	0.4	3.3	10.6
Outside metropolitan area	100.0	88.2	65.2	59.6	31.1	27.6	0.9	3.4	11.8

Source: Bureau of the Census, Children with Health Insurance: 2001, *Current Population Reports, P20-224, 2003; calculations by New Strategist*

Table 3.27 Children under Age 19 without Health Insurance, 2001

(number and percent distribution of children under age 19 without health insurance by selected characteristics, 2001; numbers in thousands)

	children without health insurance		
	number	percent	percent distribution
Total children under age 19	**9,237**	**12.1%**	**100.0%**
Age			
Under age 5	2,503	10.7	27.1
Aged 6 to 15	4,879	11.9	52.8
Aged 16 to 18	1,855	15.4	20.1
Under age 18	8,509	11.7	92.1
Race and Hispanic origin			
American Indian, Alaskan Native	278	22.3	3.0
Asian and Pacific Islander	411	12.1	4.4
Black	1,764	14.3	19.1
Hispanic	3,363	24.9	36.4
White	6,785	11.4	73.5
Non-Hispanic	3,567	7.6	38.6
Family income-to-poverty ratio			
Less than 100 percent	2,714	22.0	29.4
100 to less than 133 percent	1,134	20.6	12.3
133 to less than 200 percent	1,870	17.0	20.2
200 to less than 250 percent	980	13.0	10.6
250 percent or higher	2,315	5.9	25.1
Nativity			
Native	7,950	10.9	86.1
Foreign born	1,288	38.0	13.9
Naturalized citizen	76	15.9	8.0
Not a citizen	1,212	41.6	13.1
Region			
Northeast	1,123	8.7	12.2
Midwest	1,310	8.0	14.2
South	4,002	14.2	43.3
West	2,802	14.7	30.3
Metropolitan status			
Inside metropolitan area	7,585	12.1	82.1
Inside central cities	3,300	14.9	35.7
Outside central cities	4,285	10.6	46.4
Outside metropolitan area	1,652	11.8	17.9

Source: Bureau of the Census, Children with Health Insurance: 2001, *Current Population Reports, P20-224, 2003*

Asthma and Allergies Affect Many Children

Boys are more likely than girls to have learning disabilities.

Asthma is a growing problem among children. Fully 13 percent of the nation's 73 million children under age 18 have been diagnosed with asthma. Six percent have had an asthma attack in the past year. Boys are more likely to have asthma than girls (15 versus 11 percent). The percentage of black children with asthma is double the Mexican-American figure (16 versus 8 percent). Children in single-parent families headed by women are far more likely to have asthma than those from two-parent families (17 versus 11 percent).

More than 4 million children (8 percent) have been diagnosed with a learning disability, and nearly 4 million (6 percent) have attention deficit disorder. Boys are far more likely than girls to suffer from these conditions, accounting for two-thirds of those with learning disabilities and three-fourths of those with attention deficit disorder.

Many children use prescription medications. More than 8 million children have taken prescription medications regularly for at least three months during the past year. That's 12 percent of the nation's children—or one in eight.

■ The number of children with asthma is likely to increase unless researchers determine its underlying cause and halt the rise in the incidence of the disease.

Asthma is a big problem for the nation's children

(percent of people under age 18 diagnosed with asthma, by age, 2001)

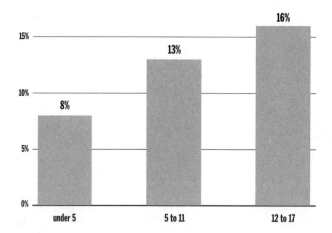

Table 3.28 Health Conditions among Children by Selected Characteristics, 2001

(number of people under age 18 with selected health conditions, by type of condition and selected characteristics, 2001; numbers in thousands)

| | total children | diagnosed with asthma | experienced in last 12 months | | | | ever told they had* | | take prescription medication regularly, at least 3 months |
			asthma attack	hay fever	respiratory allergies	other allergies	learning disability	attention deficit hyper-activity disorder	
Total children	**72,649**	**9,185**	**4,156**	**7,365**	**9,151**	**7,755**	**4,667**	**3,862**	**8,668**
Sex									
Female	35,499	3,786	1,768	3,297	4,215	3,862	1,634	1,024	3,629
Male	37,151	5,398	2,388	4,068	4,936	3,893	3,033	2,838	5,039
Age									
Aged 0 to 4	19,740	1,553	926	936	1,736	2,420	119	63	1,350
Aged 5 to 17	52,910	7,632	3,231	6,429	7,415	5,336	4,548	3,799	7,318
Aged 5 to 11	28,673	3,802	1,807	2,999	3,782	2,808	2,122	1,798	3,364
Aged 12 to 17	24,237	3,830	1,424	3,430	3,634	2,527	2,426	2,002	3,954
Race									
One race	70,764	8,861	4,015	7,163	8,839	7,454	4,525	3,799	8,448
Asian	2,338	263	112	143	189	271	54	49	159
Black	10,691	1,712	826	875	1,236	1,304	825	545	1,141
White	54,069	6,426	2,902	5,854	7,054	5,583	3,391	3,084	6,892
Two or more races	1,886	324	142	201	312	302	141	64	221
Hispanic origin and race									
Hispanic	12,185	1,359	482	747	911	896	637	340	775
Mexican American	8,255	694	226	453	555	497	328	170	457
Not Hispanic	60,464	7,826	3,674	6,617	8,240	6,859	4,029	3,523	7,893
White, single race	45,480	5,539	2,588	5,343	6,487	5,002	2,999	2,878	6,338
Black, single race	10,452	1,643	801	866	1,207	1,283	781	501	1,118
Family structure									
Mother and father	53,118	5,935	2,577	5,383	6,614	5,574	2,764	2,413	6,070
Mother, no father	15,644	2,653	1,264	1,659	2,159	1,919	1,554	1,097	2,153
Father, no mother	2,193	285	160	183	184	120	191	188	253
Neither mother nor father	1,685	309	155	140	194	142	157	164	192
Parent's education									
Less than high school diploma	9,578	1,139	495	667	818	684	757	328	726
High school diploma or GED	16,493	2,174	950	1,211	1,790	1,528	1,178	933	1,959
More than high school	44,537	5,520	2,554	5,314	6,340	5,382	2,570	2,411	5,766
Family income									
Less than $20,000	12,351	1,971	876	1,080	1,513	1,193	1,175	682	1,468
$20,000 or more	56,793	6,812	3,134	6,042	7,347	6,292	3,355	3,075	6,884
$20,000 to $34,999	10,222	1,305	569	943	1,185	1,060	638	457	1,201
$35,000 to $54,999	12,000	1,417	655	1,302	1,587	1,348	925	814	1,406
$55,000 to $74,999	9,524	1,102	494	918	1,035	1,050	476	468	1,156
$75,000 or more	15,960	2,025	1,024	2,105	2,588	2,077	887	837	2,295

| | | | experienced in last 12 months | | | | | ever told they had[*] | take prescription medication regularly, |
Metropolitan status	total children	diagnosed with asthma	asthma attack	hay fever	respiratory allergies	other allergies	learning disability	attention deficit hyper-activity disorder	at least 3 months
Metropolitan areas, populations 1+ million	34,526	4,358	1,925	3,466	4,072	3,669	2,072	1,687	3,684
Metropolitan areas, populations < 1 million	23,603	2,950	1,385	2,520	3,362	2,631	1,719	1,338	3,098
Nonmetropolitan area	14,520	1,876	846	1,379	1,717	1,455	875	837	1,886
Region									
Northeast	13,438	1,982	881	1,498	1,625	1,608	1,101	674	1,679
Midwest	16,933	1,864	953	1,640	1,879	1,875	1,116	1,022	2,250
South	26,070	3,416	1,540	2,553	3,935	2,627	1,685	1,564	3,432
West	16,208	1,923	783	1,673	1,712	1,645	765	602	1,307

* "Ever told" by a school representative or health professional. Data exclude children under age 3.
Note: "Other, non-Hispanic" includes American Indian, Alaska Native, Asian, and Pacific Islander children. "Mother and father" can include biological, adoptive, step, in-law, or foster relationships. Legal guardians are classified as "neither mother nor father." Parent's education is the education level of the parent with the higher level of education. Other allergies include food or digestive allergies, eczema, and other skin allergies.
Source: National Center for Health Statistics, Summary Health Statistics for U.S. Children: National Health Interview Survey, 2001, Series 10, No. 216, 2003

Table 3.29 Percent of Children with Health Conditions by Selected Characteristics, 2001

(percent of people under age 18 with selected health conditions, by type of condition and selected characteristics, 2001)

	total children	diagnosed with asthma	asthma attack	hay fever	respiratory allergies	other allergies	learning disability	attention deficit hyper-activity disorder	take prescription medication regularly, at least 3 months
Total children	100.0%	12.7%	5.7%	10.2%	12.6%	10.7%	7.7%	6.3%	11.9%
Sex									
Female	100.0	10.7	5.0	9.3	11.9	10.9	5.5	3.5	10.2
Male	100.0	14.5	6.4	11.0	13.3	10.5	9.7	9.1	13.6
Age									
Aged 0 to 4	100.0	7.9	4.7	4.8	8.8	12.3	1.5	0.8	6.8
Aged 5 to 17	100.0	14.4	6.1	12.2	14.1	10.1	8.6	7.2	13.8
Aged 5 to 11	100.0	13.3	6.3	10.5	13.2	9.8	7.4	6.3	11.7
Aged 12 to 17	100.0	15.8	5.9	14.2	15.0	10.4	10.0	8.3	16.3
Race									
One race	100.0	12.5	6.7	10.1	12.5	10.5	6.4	7.6	11.9
Asian	100.0	11.3	4.8	6.1	8.1	11.6	2.8	2.6	6.8
Black	100.0	16.0	7.7	8.2	11.6	12.2	9.2	6.1	10.7
White	100.0	11.9	5.4	10.9	13.1	10.3	7.5	6.8	12.8
Two or more races	100.0	17.2	7.6	10.8	16.8	16.0	9.5	4.3	11.7
Hispanic origin and race									
Hispanic	100.0	11.2	4.0	6.1	7.5	7.4	6.5	3.5	6.4
Mexican American	100.0	8.4	2.7	5.5	6.7	6.0	5.0	2.6	5.5
Not Hispanic	100.0	13.0	6.1	11.0	13.7	11.4	7.9	6.9	13.1
White, single race	100.0	12.2	5.7	11.8	14.3	11.0	7.8	7.5	13.9
Black, single race	100.0	15.7	7.7	8.3	11.6	12.3	8.9	5.7	10.7
Family structure									
Mother and father	100.0	11.2	4.9	10.2	12.5	10.5	6.3	5.5	11.4
Mother, no father	100.0	17.0	8.1	10.7	13.9	12.3	11.5	8.1	13.8
Father, no mother	100.0	13.0	7.3	8.3	8.4	5.5	9.3	9.2	11.5
Neither mother nor father	100.0	18.3	9.2	8.3	11.5	8.5	10.0	10.5	11.4
Parent's education									
Less than high school diploma	100.0	11.9	5.2	7.0	8.6	7.1	9.6	4.2	7.6
High school diploma or GED	100.0	13.2	5.8	7.4	10.9	9.3	8.6	6.8	11.9
More than high school	100.0	12.4	5.7	12.0	14.3	12.1	6.9	6.4	12.9
Family income									
Less than $20,000	100.0	16.0	7.1	8.8	12.3	9.7	11.8	6.8	11.9
$20,000 or more	100.0	12.0	5.5	10.7	13.0	11.1	7.0	6.4	12.1
$20,000 to $34,999	100.0	12.8	5.6	9.3	11.6	10.4	7.6	5.4	11.7
$35,000 to $54,999	100.0	11.8	5.5	10.9	13.3	11.2	9.3	8.2	11.7
$55,000 to $74,999	100.0	11.6	5.2	9.7	10.9	11.0	5.9	5.8	12.1
$75,000 or more	100.0	12.7	6.4	13.2	16.3	13.0	6.4	6.0	14.4

	total children	diagnosed with asthma	experienced in last 12 months				learning disability	ever told they had[*]	take prescription medication regularly, at least 3 months
			asthma attack	hay fever	respiratory allergies	other allergies		attention deficit hyper-activity disorder	
Metropolitan status									
Metropolitan areas, populations 1+ million	100.0%	12.6%	5.6%	10.1%	11.8%	10.6%	7.2%	5.9%	10.7%
Metropolitan areas, populations < 1 million	100.0	12.5	5.9	10.7	14.3	11.2	8.7	6.8	13.1
Nonmetropolitan area	100.0	12.9	5.8	9.5	11.9	10.0	7.0	6.7	13.0
Region									
Northeast	100.0	14.8	6.6	11.2	12.2	12.0	9.5	5.8	12.5
Midwest	100.0	11.0	5.6	9.7	11.1	11.1	7.8	7.2	13.3
South	100.0	13.1	5.9	9.8	15.1	10.1	7.8	7.3	13.2
West	100.0	11.9	4.8	10.3	10.6	10.2	5.6	4.4	8.1

* *"Ever told" by a school representative or health professional. Data exclude children under age 3.*
Note: "Other, non-Hispanic" includes American Indian, Alaska Native, Asian, and Pacific Islander children. "Mother and father" can include biological, adoptive, step, in-law, or foster relationships. Legal guardians are classified as "neither mother nor father." Parent's education is the education level of the parent with the higher level of education. Other allergies include food or digestive allergies, eczema, and other skin allergies.
Source: National Center for Health Statistics, Summary Health Statistics for U.S. Children: National Health Interview Survey, 2001, *Series 10, No. 216, 2003*

Table 3.30 Distribution of Health Conditions by Selected Characteristics of Children, 2001

(percent distribution of people under age 18 with health condition by selected characteristics, 2001)

	total children	diagnosed with asthma	experienced in last 12 months — asthma attack	hay fever	respiratory allergies	other allergies	ever told they had* — learning disability	attention deficit hyper-activity disorder	take prescription medication regularly, at least 3 months
Total children	100.0%	100.0%	100.0%	100.0%	100.0%	100.0%	100.0%	100.0%	100.0%
Sex									
Female	48.9	41.2	42.5	44.8	46.1	49.8	35.0	26.5	41.9
Male	51.1	58.8	57.5	55.2	53.9	50.2	65.0	73.5	58.1
Age									
Aged 0 to 4	27.2	16.9	22.3	12.7	19.0	31.2	2.5	1.6	15.6
Aged 5 to 17	72.8	83.1	77.7	87.3	81.0	68.8	97.5	98.4	84.4
Aged 5 to 11	39.5	41.4	43.5	40.7	41.3	36.2	45.5	46.6	38.8
Aged 12 to 17	33.4	41.7	34.3	46.6	39.7	32.6	52.0	51.8	45.6
Race									
One race	97.4	96.5	96.6	97.3	96.6	96.1	97.0	98.4	97.5
Asian	3.2	2.9	2.7	1.9	2.1	3.5	1.2	1.3	1.8
Black	14.7	18.6	19.9	11.9	13.5	16.8	17.7	14.1	13.2
White	74.4	70.0	69.8	79.5	77.1	72.0	72.7	79.9	79.5
Two or more races	2.6	3.5	3.4	2.7	3.4	3.9	3.0	1.7	2.5
Hispanic origin and race									
Hispanic	16.8	14.8	11.6	10.1	10.0	11.6	13.6	8.8	8.9
Mexican American	11.4	7.6	5.4	6.2	6.1	6.4	7.0	4.4	5.3
Not Hispanic	83.2	85.2	88.4	89.8	90.0	88.4	86.3	91.2	91.1
White, single race	62.6	60.3	62.3	72.5	70.9	64.5	64.3	74.5	73.1
Black, single race	14.4	17.9	19.3	11.8	13.2	16.5	16.7	13.0	12.9
Family structure									
Mother and father	73.1	64.6	6.2	73.1	72.3	71.9	59.2	62.5	70.0
Mother, no father	21.5	28.9	30.4	22.5	23.6	24.7	33.3	28.4	24.8
Father, no mother	3.0	3.1	3.8	2.5	2.0	1.5	4.1	4.9	2.9
Neither mother nor father	2.3	3.4	3.7	1.9	2.1	1.8	3.4	4.2	2.2
Parent's education									
Less than high school diploma	13.2	12.4	11.9	9.1	8.9	8.8	16.2	8.5	8.4
High school diploma or GED	22.7	23.7	22.9	16.4	19.6	19.7	25.2	24.2	22.6
More than high school	61.3	60.1	61.5	72.2	69.3	69.4	55.1	62.4	66.5
Family income									
Less than $20,000	17.0	21.5	21.1	14.7	16.5	15.4	25.2	17.7	16.9
$20,000 or more	78.2	74.2	75.4	82.0	80.3	81.1	71.9	79.6	79.4
$20,000 to $34,999	14.1	14.2	13.7	12.8	12.9	13.7	13.7	11.8	13.9
$35,000 to $54,999	16.5	15.4	15.8	17.7	17.3	17.4	19.8	21.1	16.2
$55,000 to $74,999	13.1	12.0	11.9	12.5	11.3	13.5	10.2	12.1	13.3
$75,000 or more	22.0	22.1	24.6	28.6	28.3	26.8	19.0	21.7	26.5

	total children	diagnosed with asthma	experienced in last 12 months				ever told they had*		take prescription medication regularly, at least 3 months
			asthma attack	hay fever	respiratory allergies	other allergies	learning disability	attention deficit hyperactivity disorder	
Metropolitan status									
Metropolitan areas, populations 1+ million	47.5%	47.4%	46.3%	47.1%	44.5%	47.3%	44.4%	43.7%	42.5%
Metropolitan areas, populations < 1 million	32.5	32.1	33.3	34.2	36.7	33.9	36.8	34.6	35.7
Nonmetropolitan area	20.0	20.4	20.4	18.7	18.8	18.8	18.7	21.7	21.8
Region									
Northeast	18.5	21.6	21.2	20.3	17.8	20.7	23.6	17.5	19.4
Midwest	23.3	20.3	22.9	22.3	20.5	24.2	23.9	26.5	26.0
South	35.9	37.2	37.1	34.7	43.0	33.9	36.1	40.5	39.6
West	22.3	20.9	18.8	22.7	18.7	21.2	16.4	15.6	15.1

* "Ever told" by a school representative or health professional. Data exclude children under age 3.
Note: "Other, non-Hispanic" includes American Indian, Alaska Native, Asian, and Pacific Islander children. "Mother and father" can include biological, adoptive, step, in-law, or foster relationships. Legal guardians are classified as "neither mother nor father." Parent's education is the education level of the parent with the higher level of education. Other allergies include food or digestive allergies, eczema, and other skin allergies.
Source: National Center for Health Statistics, Summary Health Statistics for U.S. Children: National Health Interview Survey, 2001, Series 10, No. 216, 2003; calculations by New Strategist

Table 3.31 AIDS Cases by Sex and Age, through June 2002

(cumulative number and percent distribution of AIDS cases by age at diagnosis and sex for those aged 13 or older, through June 2002)

	number	percent of total cases
Total cases	**831,112**	**100.0%**
Under age 1	3,249	0.4
Aged 1 to 12	5,558	0.7
Aged 13 to 19	4,627	0.6
Aged 20 to 29	134,170	16.1
Aged 30 to 39	365,924	44.0
Aged 40 to 49	223,467	26.9
Aged 50 to 59	68,988	8.3
Aged 60 or older	25,129	3.0
Females		
Aged 13 or older	**145,696**	**17.5**
Aged 13 to 19	1,995	0.2
Aged 20 to 29	29,996	3.6
Aged 30 to 39	63,504	7.6
Aged 40 to 49	35,168	4.2
Aged 50 to 59	10,243	1.2
Aged 60 or older	4,790	0.6
Males		
Aged 13 or older	**676,609**	**81.4**
Aged 13 to 19	2,632	0.3
Aged 20 to 29	104,174	12.5
Aged 30 to 39	302,420	36.4
Aged 40 to 49	188,299	22.7
Aged 50 to 59	58,745	7.1
Aged 60 or older	20,339	2.4

Source: National Center for Health Statistics, Health, United States, 2003*; calculations by New Strategist*

Millions of Children Are Disabled

The numbers vary widely, however, depending on who's counting.

Population surveys and censuses measure disability in many different ways. A 1997 Census Bureau survey counted 4.0 million disabled children aged 6 to 14, whereas the 2000 census counted 2.6 million disabled children aged 5 to 15.

No matter who's doing the counting, boys are more likely than girls to be classified as disabled. In the 1997 survey, 14 percent of boys and 8 percent of girls aged were classified as disabled. In the 2000 census, 7 percent of boys and 4 percent of girls had a disability. Behind the sex difference is the greater difficulty boys have in doing school work, which is the most common disability experienced by the age group. Nine percent of boys aged 6 to 14 have difficulty doing their regular school work—double the 4.5 percent rate among girls, according to the 1997 survey. The 2000 census found 6 percent of boys with a mental disability versus only 3 percent of girls.

According to the Census Bureau's Current Population Survey, 4 percent of young adults aged 16 to 24 have a work disability—meaning they have a health problem that prevents them from working or limits the kind or amount of work they can do. This is less than half the 10 percent work disability rate for the entire working-age population, aged 16 to 64.

■ Problems with school work can be the result of children being placed in school at a level beyond their abilities. As children mature, many will outgrow their learning difficulties.

Most disabled children have mental problems, often learning disabilities

(number of children aged 5 to 15 with disabilities, by type, 2000)

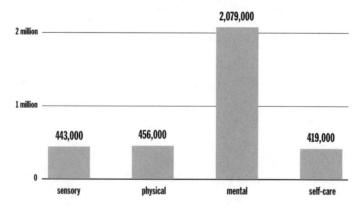

Table 3.32 Children under Age 15 with Disabilities, 1997

(number and percent distribution of children under age 15 by disability status, age and sex, 1997; numbers in thousands)

	total		male		female	
	number	percent distribution	number	percent distribution	number	percent distribution
Under age 3	**11,619**	**100.0%**	**5,947**	**100.0%**	**5,671**	**100.0%**
With no disability	11,386	98.0	5,809	97.7	5,576	98.3
With a disability	233	2.0	138	2.3	95	1.7
With a developmental delay	206	1.8	121	2.0	85	1.5
Has difficulty moving arms or legs	58	0.5	38	0.6	19	0.3
Age 3 to 5 years	**12,192**	**100.0**	**6,229**	**100.0**	**5,963**	**100.0**
With no disability	11,782	96.6	5,990	96.2	5,792	97.1
With a disability	410	3.4	239	3.8	171	2.9
With a developmental delay	335	2.7	194	3.1	141	2.4
Has difficulty running or playing	218	1.8	125	2.0	94	1.6
Age 6 to 14 years	**35,795**	**100.0**	**18,317**	**100.0**	**17,478**	**100.0**
With no disability	31,777	88.8	15,679	85.6	16,097	92.1
With a disability	4,018	11.2	2,638	14.4	1,381	7.9
Severe	1,715	4.8	1,187	6.5	528	3.0
Not severe	2,303	6.4	1,450	7.9	853	4.9
Has difficulty doing regular school work	2,446	6.8	1,655	9.0	791	4.5
Has difficulty getting along with others	647	1.8	451	2.5	196	1.1
With one or more selected conditions	2,818	7.9	1,882	10.3	935	5.4
A learning disability	1,867	5.2	1,209	6.6	658	3.8
Mental retardation	307	0.9	185	1.0	122	0.7
Other developmental disability	240	0.7	167	0.9	73	0.4
Other developmental condition	1,314	3.7	900	4.9	414	2.4
With a developmental disability or condition	1,611	4.5	1,109	6.1	503	2.9
Uses a wheelchair	70	0.2	30	0.2	40	0.2
Uses cane/crutches/walker	20	0.1	8	0.0	12	0.1
Has used for six months or more	12	0.0	6	0.0	6	0.0
Has difficulty seeing words/letters	264	0.7	160	0.9	104	0.6
Severe	45	0.1	23	0.1	22	0.1
Not severe	219	0.6	136	0.7	83	0.5
Has difficulty hearing conversation	234	0.7	141	0.8	93	0.5
Severe	57	0.2	37	0.2	20	0.1
Not severe	177	0.5	104	0.6	73	0.4
Has difficulty with speech	752	2.1	546	3.0	205	1.2
Severe	154	0.4	115	0.6	38	0.2
Not severe	598	1.7	431	2.4	167	1.0
Has difficulty walking or running	758	2.1	431	2.4	327	1.9

Note: For the definition of disability, see the glossary.
Source: Bureau of the Census, Americans with Disabilities: 1997, *detailed tables from Current Population Reports P70–73, 2001; Internet site http://www.census.gov/hhes/www/disable/sipp/disab97/ds97t5.html*

Table 3.33 Disability Status of People by Age, 2000 Census

(total number of people aged 5 or older and number and percent with disabilities, by age and type of disability, 2000)

	total		female		male	
	number	percent	number	percent	number	percent
TOTAL PEOPLE	**257,167,527**	**100.0%**	**132,530,702**	**100.0%**	**124,636,825**	**100.0%**
With any disability	49,746,248	19.3	25,306,717	19.1	24,439,531	19.6
PEOPLE AGED 5 TO 15	**45,133,667**	**100.0**	**22,008,343**	**100.0**	**23,125,324**	**100.0**
With any disability	**2,614,919**	**5.8**	**948,689**	**4.3**	**166,230**	**7.2**
Sensory	442,894	1.0	200,188	0.9	242,706	1.0
Physical	455,461	1.0	203,609	0.9	251,852	1.1
Mental	2,078,502	4.6	691,109	3.1	1,387,393	6.0
Self-care	419,018	0.9	174,194	0.8	244,824	1.1
PEOPLE AGED 16 TO 64	**178,687,234**	**100.0**	**91,116,651**	**100.0**	**87,570,583**	**100.0**
With any disability	**33,153,211**	**18.6**	**16,014,192**	**17.6**	**17,139,019**	**19.6**
Sensory	4,123,902	2.3	1,735,781	1.9	2,388,121	2.7
Physical	11,150,365	6.2	5,870,634	6.4	5,279,731	6.0
Mental	6,764,439	3.8	3,329,808	3.7	3,434,631	3.9
Self-care	3,149,875	1.8	1,686,691	1.9	1,463,184	1.7
Difficulty going outside the home	11,414,508	6.4	5,845,146	6.4	5,569,362	6.4
Employment disability	21,287,570	11.9	9,913,784	10.9	11,373,786	13.0
PEOPLE AGED 65+	**33,346,626**	**100.0**	**19,405,708**	**100.0**	**13,940,918**	**100.0**
With any disability	13,978,118	41.9	8,343,836	43.0	5,634,282	40.4
Sensory	4,738,479	14.2	2,561,263	13.2	2,177,216	15.6
Physical	9,545,680	28.6	5,955,541	30.7	3,590,139	25.8
Mental	3,592,912	10.8	2,212,852	11.4	1,380,060	9.9
Self-care	3,183,840	9.5	2,138,930	11.0	1,044,910	7.5
Difficulty going outside the home	6,795,517	20.4	4,456,389	23.0	2,339,128	16.8

Note: Sensory disabilities are long-lasting impairments of vision and hearing; physical disabilities are limitations such as difficulty walking or climbing stairs; mental disabilities are difficulty with cognitive tasks such as learning, remembering, and concentrating; self-care disabilities are difficulty taking care of personal needs like dressing and bathing; employment disabilities are physical, mental, or emotional conditions making it difficult for people to work at a job; difficulty going outside the home is difficulty shopping or visiting the doctor.
Source: Bureau of the Census, Disability Status: 2000, *Census 2000 Brief, 2003*

Table 3.34 People Aged 16 to 24 with a Work Disability, 2002

(number and percent of people aged 16 to 64 and 16 to 24 with a work disability, by education and severity of disability, 2002; numbers in thousands)

		with a work disability					
		total		not severe		severe	
	total	number	percent	number	percent	number	percent
Total aged 16 to 64	**183,018**	**18,120**	**9.9%**	**5,487**	**3.0%**	**12,632**	**6.9%**
Not a high school graduate	33,185	5,041	15.2	801	2.4	4,240	12.8
High school graduate	54,676	6,579	12.0	1,878	3.4	4,701	8.6
Associate's degree or some college	50,118	4,442	8.9	1,776	3.5	2,666	5.3
Bachelor's degree or more	45,038	2,058	4.6	1,032	2.3	1,026	2.3
Total aged 16 to 24	**35,261**	**1,264**	**3.6**	**421**	**1.2**	**843**	**2.4**
Not a high school graduate	14,409	599	4.2	162	1.1	438	3.0
High school graduate	8,273	410	5.0	114	1.4	296	3.6
Associate's degree or some college	10,405	227	2.2	128	1.2	99	1.0
Bachelor's degree or more	2,174	28	1.3	17	0.8	11	0.5

Note: A person is considered to have a work disability if one or more of the following conditions are met: 1) identified by the March supplement question "Does anyone in this household have a health problem or disability which prevents them from working or which limits the kind or amount of work they can do?"; 2) identified by the March supplement question "Is there anyone in this household who ever retired or left a job for health reasons?"; 3) identified by the core questionnaire as currently not in the labor force because of a disability; 4) identified by the March supplement as a person who did not work at all in the previous year because of illness or disability; 5) under 65 years old and covered by Medicare in previous year; 6) under 65 years old and received Supplemental Security Income in previous year; 7) received Veterans Administration disability income in previous year. If one or more of conditions 3, 4, 5, and 6 are met, the person is considered to have a severe work disability.
Source: Bureau of the Census, 2002 Current Population Survey Annual Demographic Supplement, Internet site http://www .census.gov/hhes/www/disable/cps/cps102.html

Young Adults Are Least Likely to See a Doctor

People aged 15 to 24 visit doctors less than twice a year, on average.

In 2001, Americans visited physicians a total of 880 million times. People under age 25 made 24 percent of the visits. Children under age 15 visited a doctor 146 million times in 2001 as parents brought them into the office an average of 2.4 times a year for immunizations or treatment for ear infections, colds, and other childhood ailments. Young adults aged 15 to 24 visited a doctor only 1.7 times a year, for a total of 66 million visits, in part because the age group is least likely to be covered by health insurance.

People under age 25 account for 34 percent of hospital outpatients and represent the largest share of people visiting the outpatient department because of an acute health problem. The under-25 age group accounts for an even bigger 37 percent share of visits to hospital emergency departments. This is the age group whose emergency visits are least likely to be deemed "emergent"—or a true emergency. Many head to the emergency room because they lack health insurance and have no other source of health care.

■ Among children under age 15, boys visit doctors slightly more often than girls. This is the only age group in which males go to the doctor more frequently than females.

People aged 15 to 24 see doctors less frequently than any other age group

(average number of physician visits per person per year, by age, 2001)

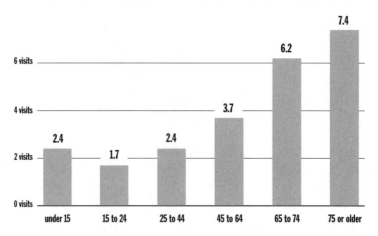

Table 3.35 Physician Office Visits by Sex and Age, 2001

(total number, percent distribution, and number of physician office visits per person per year, by sex and age, 2001; numbers in thousands)

	total	percent distribution	average visits per year
Total visits	**880,487**	**100.0%**	**3.1**
Under age 15	146,683	16.7	2.4
Aged 15 to 24	65,632	7.5	1.7
Aged 25 to 44	200,636	22.8	2.4
Aged 45 to 64	239,106	27.2	3.7
Aged 65 to 74	112,978	12.8	6.2
Aged 75 or older	115,452	13.1	7.4
Visits by females	**520,110**	**59.1**	**3.6**
Under age 15	69,614	7.9	2.4
Aged 15 to 24	42,071	4.8	2.2
Aged 25 to 44	131,664	15.0	3.1
Aged 45 to 64	142,657	16.2	4.3
Aged 65 to 74	64,029	7.3	6.5
Aged 75 or older	70,075	8.0	7.3
Visits by males	**360,377**	**40.9**	**2.6**
Under age 15	77,069	8.8	2.5
Aged 15 to 24	23,562	2.7	1.2
Aged 25 to 44	68,971	7.8	1.7
Aged 45 to 64	96,449	11.0	3.1
Aged 65 to 74	48,950	5.6	6.0
Aged 75 or older	45,376	5.2	7.6

Source: National Center for Health Statistics, National Ambulatory Medical Care Survey: 2001 Summary, *Advance Data No. 337, 2003*

Table 3.36 Hospital Outpatient Department Visits by Age and Reason, 2001

(number and percent distribution of visits to hospital outpatient departments by age and major reason for visit, 2001; numbers in thousands)

	total	acute problem	chronic problem, routine	chronic problem, flare-up	pre- or post-surgery	preventive care	unknown
				major reason for visit			
Total visits	**83,715**	**31,738**	**26,017**	**6,619**	**3,230**	**12,969**	**3,142**
Under age 15	18,319	7,970	4,258	1,106	588	3,936	460
Aged 15 to 24	9,834	3,881	1,977	663	272	2,737	304
Aged 25 to 44	20,576	8,790	5,243	1,643	795	3,267	838
Aged 45 to 64	21,590	7,128	8,750	2,033	911	1,831	938
Aged 65 to 74	7,299	2,190	3,044	665	376	661	363
Aged 75 or older	6,097	1,779	2,745	510	288	536	238
PERCENT DISTRIBUTION BY AGE							
Total visits	**100.0%**	**100.0%**	**100.0%**	**100.0%**	**100.0%**	**100.0%**	**100.0%**
Under age 15	21.9	25.1	16.4	16.7	18.2	30.3	14.6
Aged 15 to 24	11.7	12.2	7.6	10.0	8.4	21.1	9.7
Aged 25 to 44	24.6	27.7	20.2	24.8	24.6	25.2	26.7
Aged 45 to 64	25.8	22.5	33.6	30.7	28.2	14.1	29.9
Aged 65 to 74	8.7	6.9	11.7	10.1	11.6	5.1	11.6
Aged 75 or older	7.3	5.6	10.6	7.7	8.9	4.1	7.6
PERCENT DISTRIBUTION BY MAJOR REASON							
Total visits	**100.0%**	**37.9%**	**31.1%**	**7.9%**	**3.9%**	**15.5%**	**3.8%**
Under age 15	100.0	43.5	23.2	6.0	3.2	21.5	2.5
Aged 15 to 24	100.0	39.5	20.1	6.7	2.8	27.8	3.1
Aged 25 to 44	100.0	42.7	25.5	8.0	3.9	15.9	4.1
Aged 45 to 64	100.0	33.0	40.5	9.4	4.2	8.5	4.3
Aged 65 to 74	100.0	30.0	41.7	9.1	5.2	9.1	5.0
Aged 75 or older	100.0	29.2	45.0	8.4	4.7	8.8	3.9

Source: National Center for Health Statistics, National Hospital Ambulatory Medical Care Survey: 2001 Outpatient Department Summary, *Advance Data No. 338, 2003*

Table 3.37 Emergency Department Visits by Age and Urgency of Problem, 2001

(number of visits to emergency rooms and percent distribution by age and urgency of problem, 2001; numbers in thousands)

| | number | percent distribution | percent distribution by urgency of problem | | | | | |
			total	emergent	urgent	semiurgent	nonurgent	unknown
Total visits	**107,490**	**100.0%**	**100.0%**	**19.2%**	**31.7%**	**16.3%**	**9.1%**	**23.6%**
Under age 15	22,245	20.7	100.0	14.9	31.2	17.6	8.7	27.6
Aged 15 to 24	17,371	16.2	100.0	15.7	31.4	18.5	11.4	22.9
Aged 25 to 44	32,732	30.5	100.0	17.9	32.2	17.1	10.2	22.6
Aged 45 to 64	19,260	17.9	100.0	22.6	31.5	14.8	8.6	22.5
Aged 65 to 74	6,551	6.1	100.0	26.7	31.3	13.4	6.4	22.1
Aged 75 or older	9,332	8.7	100.0	29.0	32.0	11.4	5.0	22.6

Note: Emergent is a visit in which the patient should be seen in less than 15 minutes; urgent is a visit in which the patient should be seen within 15 to 60 minutes; semiurgent is a visit in which the patient should be seen within 61 to 120 minutes; nonurgent is a visit in which the patient should be seen within 121 minutes to 24 hours; unknown is a visit with no mention of immediacy or triage, or the patient was dead on arrival.
Source: National Center for Health Statistics, National Hospital Ambulatory Medical Care Survey: 2001 Emergency Department Summary, *Advance Data No. 335, 2003*

Accidents Are Leading Cause of Death among Children and Young Adults

Homicide and suicide are important causes of death as well.

Once past infancy, most people under age 25 who die do so in accidents—which means a large portion of deaths in the age group are preventable. Among infants, congenital anomalies and other birth problems are the leading causes of death.

In the 1-to-4 age group, accidents account for more than one-third of deaths, while congenital anomalies rank second. Disturbingly, homicide is the fourth leading cause of death in the age group. Among 5-to-9-year-olds, accidents are the leading cause of death followed by cancer, congenital anomalies, and homicide. Among 10-to-14-year-olds, accidents and cancer rank first and second, but suicide is third. For both the 15-to-19 and 20-to-24 age groups, accidents, homicide, and suicide are the top three causes.

Life expectancy has been rising for decades thanks to the success of medical science at combating the ailments of childhood. In 2001, life expectancy at birth stood at 74 years for males and nearly 80 years for females. At age 25, males and females have more than 50 years of life remaining.

■ As medical science tamed the ailments that once killed many infants and children, accidents became a more important cause of death.

Newborns today can expect to live more than 70 years

(years of life remaining at birth and at age 25, by sex, 2001)

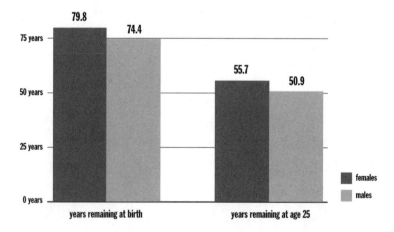

Table 3.38 Leading Causes of Death for Infants, 2001

(number and percent distribution of deaths accounted for by the ten leading causes of death for children under age 1, 2001)

		number	percent distribution
All causes		**27,568**	**100.0%**
1.	Congenital anomalies	5,513	20.0
2.	Disorders relating to short gestation and low birthweight	4,410	16.0
3.	Sudden infant death syndrome	2,234	8.1
4.	Newborn affected by maternal complications of pregnancy	1,499	5.4
5.	Newborn affected by complications of placenta, cord, and membranes	1,018	3.7
6.	Respiratory distress syndrome	1,011	3.7
7.	Accidents (5)	976	3.5
8.	Bacterial sepsis of newborn	696	2.5
9.	Diseases of the circulatory system	622	2.3
10.	Intrauterine hypoxia and birth asphyxia	534	1.9
All other causes		9,055	32.8

Note: Number in parentheses shows rank for all age groups if the cause of death is among top fifteen.
Source: National Center for Health Statistics, Deaths: Leading Causes for 2001, *National Vital Statistics Report, Vol. 52, No. 9, 2003; calculations by New Strategist*

Table 3.39 Leading Causes of Death for Children Aged 1 to 4, 2001

(number and percent distribution of deaths accounted for by the ten leading causes of death for children aged 1 to 4, 2001)

		number	percent distribution
All causes		**5,107**	**100.0%**
1.	Accidents (5)	1,714	33.6
2.	Congenital anomalies	557	10.9
3.	Malignant neoplasms (2)	420	8.2
4.	Homicide (13)	415	8.1
5.	Diseases of heart (1)	225	4.4
6.	Influenza and pneumonia (7)	112	2.2
7.	Septicemia (10)	108	2.1
8.	Certain conditions originating in the perinatal period	72	1.4
9.	Benign neoplasms	58	1.1
10.	Cerebrovascular diseases (3)	54	1.1
All other causes		1,372	26.9

Note: Number in parentheses shows rank for all age groups if the cause of death is among top fifteen.
Source: National Center for Health Statistics, Deaths: Leading Causes for 2001, *National Vital Statistics Report, Vol. 52, No. 9, 2003; calculations by New Strategist*

Table 3.40 Leading Causes of Death for Children Aged 5 to 9, 2001

(number and percent distribution of deaths accounted for by the ten leading causes of death for children aged 5 to 9, 2001)

		number	percent distribution
All causes		**3,093**	**100.0%**
1.	Accidents (5)	1,283	41.5
2.	Malignant neoplasms (2)	493	15.9
3.	Congenital anomalies	182	5.9
4.	Homicide (13)	137	4.4
5.	Diseases of heart (1)	98	3.2
6.	Benign neoplasms	52	1.7
7.	Influenza and pneumonia (7)	46	1.5
8.	Chronic lower respiratory disease (4)	42	1.4
9.	Cerebrovascular diseases (3)	38	1.2
10.	Septicemia	29	0.9
	All other causes	693	22.4

Note: Number in parentheses shows rank for all age groups if the cause of death is among top fifteen.
Source: National Center for Health Statistics, Deaths: Leading Causes for 2001, *National Vital Statistics Report, Vol. 52, No. 9, 2003; calculations by New Strategist*

Table 3.41 Leading Causes of Death for Children Aged 10 to 14, 2001

(number and percent distribution of deaths accounted for by the ten leading causes of death for children aged 10 to 14, 2001)

		number	percent distribution
All causes		**4,002**	**100.0%**
1.	Accidents (5)	1,553	38.8
2.	Malignant neoplasms (2)	515	12.9
3.	Suicide (11)	272	6.8
4.	Congenital anomalies	194	4.8
5.	Homicide (13)	189	4.7
6.	Diseases of heart (1)	174	4.3
7.	Chronic lower respiratory disease (4)	62	1.5
8.	Benign neoplasms	53	1.3
9.	Influenza and pneumonia (7)	46	1.1
10.	Cerebrovascular diseases (3)	42	1.1
All other causes		902	22.5

Note: Number in parentheses shows rank for all age groups if the cause of death is among top fifteen.
Source: National Center for Health Statistics, Deaths: Leading Causes for 2001, *National Vital Statistics Report, Vol. 52, No. 9, 2003; calculations by New Strategist*

Table 3.42 Leading Causes of Death for People Aged 15 to 19, 2001

(number and percent distribution of deaths for the 10 leading causes of death for people aged 15 to 19, 2001)

		number	percent distribution
All causes		**13,555**	**100.0%**
1.	Accidents (5)	6,646	49.0
2.	Homicide (13)	1,899	14.0
3.	Suicide (11)	1,611	11.9
4.	Malignant neoplasms (2)	732	5.4
5.	Diseases of heart (1)	347	2.6
6.	Congenital anomalies	255	1.9
7.	Chronic lower respiratory disease (4)	74	0.5
8.	Cerebrovascular diseases (3)	68	0.5
9.	Influenza and pneumonia (7)	66	0.5
10.	Septicemia	57	0.4
All other causes		1,800	13.3

Note: Number in parentheses shows rank for all age groups if the cause of death is among top fifteen.
Source: National Center for Health Statistics, Deaths: Leading Causes for 2001, *National Vital Statistics Report, Vol. 52, No. 9, 2003; calculations by New Strategist*

Table 3.43 Leading Causes of Death for People Aged 20 to 24, 2001

(number and percent distribution of deaths for the 10 leading causes of death for people aged 20 to 24, 2001)

		number	percent distribution
All causes		**18,697**	**100.0%**
1.	Accidents (5)	7,765	41.5
2.	Homicide (13)	3,398	18.2
3.	Suicide (11)	2,360	12.6
4.	Malignant neoplasms (2)	972	5.2
5.	Diseases of heart (1)	652	3.5
6.	Congenital anomalies	250	1.3
7.	Human immunodeficiency virus infection	183	1.0
8.	Cerebrovascular diseases (3)	128	0.7
9.	Influenza and pneumonia (7)	115	0.6
10.	Diabetes mellitus (6)	103	0.6
All other causes		2,771	14.8

Note: Number in parentheses shows rank for all age groups if the cause of death is among top fifteen.
Source: National Center for Health Statistics, Deaths: Leading Causes for 2001, *National Vital Statistics Report, Vol. 52, No. 9, 2003; calculations by New Strategist*

Table 3.44 Life Expectancy by Age and Sex, 2002

(years of life remaining at selected ages, by sex, 2002)

	total	females	males
At birth	77.4	79.9	74.7
Aged 1	76.9	79.4	74.3
Aged 5	73.0	75.5	70.4
Aged 10	68.1	70.6	65.4
Aged 15	63.1	65.6	60.5
Aged 20	58.3	60.7	55.8
Aged 25	53.6	55.9	51.1
Aged 30	48.8	51.0	46.5
Aged 35	44.1	46.2	41.8
Aged 40	39.4	41.5	37.2
Aged 45	34.9	36.8	32.7
Aged 50	30.4	32.2	28.4
Aged 55	26.2	27.8	24.2
Aged 60	22.0	23.5	20.3
Aged 65	18.2	19.5	16.6
Aged 70	14.7	15.8	13.3
Aged 75	11.6	12.5	10.4
Aged 80	8.9	9.5	8.0
Aged 85	6.7	7.0	5.9
Aged 90	4.9	5.1	4.4
Aged 95	3.7	3.8	3.3
Aged 100	2.8	2.8	2.6

Source: National Center for Health Statistics, Deaths: Preliminary Data for 2002, *National Vital Statistics Report, Vol. 52, No. 13, 2004*

4

Housing

■ The nation's homeownership rate climbed by more than 4 percentage points between 1990 and 2003, to a record high of 68.3 percent. The homeownership rate of householders under age 25 rose much faster than average, by 7 percentage points.

■ Although the homeownership rate has been rising among young adults, the great majority are renters. Fully 77 percent of householders under age 25 rent their home, while only 23 percent are homeowners.

■ According to the 2000 census, 21 percent of non-Hispanic white householders under age 25 owned their home. Hispanics ranked second, with a homeownership rate of 15 percent.

■ Sixty-three percent of American households live in detached single-family homes. But among householders under age 25, the 57 percent majority live in multi-unit apartment buildings.

■ Only 10 percent of people aged 30 or older move in a typical year, but among people aged 20 to 29, the percentage of movers in a year is about three times as great. One of the big reasons for moving among 20-to-24-year-olds is to attend or leave college.

More Young Adults Are Homeowners

Growth in homeownership has been much faster than average for householders under age 25.

The nation's homeownership rate has climbed considerably since 1990, rising more than 4 percentage points to a record high of 68.3 percent in 2003. The homeownership rate of house-holders under age 25 (Millennials were aged 26 and younger in 2003) rose much faster than average, up 7 percentage points. Twenty-three percent of householders under age 25 were homeowners in 2003, up from 16 percent in 1990.

Behind the rise in the homeownership rate of young adults are low interest rates and, perhaps, the financial help of their Boomer parents. Figuring that now is the time to get into the housing market, Boomers may be urging their children to invest in a starter home.

■ As housing prices rise, young adult homeowners will reap the rewards of their housing investment throughout their lives.

Homeownership increased the most for the youngest adults

(percentage point change in homeownership rate, by age of householder, 1990 to 2003)

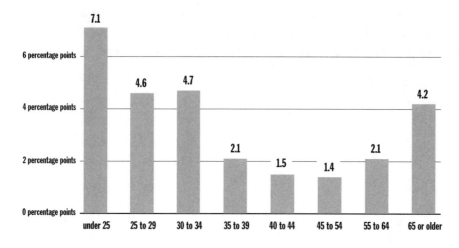

Table 4.1 Homeownership by Age of Householder, 1990 to 2003

(percentage of householders who own their home by age of householder, 1990 to 2003; percentage point change for selected years)

	2003	2000	1990	percentage point change 2000–03	percentage point change 1990–03
Total households	**68.3%**	**67.4%**	**63.9%**	**0.9**	**4.4**
Under age 25	22.8	21.7	15.7	1.1	7.1
Aged 25 to 29	39.8	38.1	35.2	1.7	4.6
Aged 30 to 34	56.5	54.6	51.8	1.9	4.7
Aged 35 to 44	68.3	67.9	66.3	0.4	2.0
Aged 45 to 54	76.6	76.5	75.2	0.1	1.4
Aged 55 to 64	81.4	80.3	79.3	1.1	2.1
Aged 65 or older	80.5	80.4	76.3	0.1	4.2

Source: Bureau of the Census, Housing Vacancy Surveys, Internet site http://www.census.gov/hhes/www/housing/hvs/annual03/ann03ind.html; calculations by New Strategist

Homeownership Rises with Age

Most young adults are renters.

Although the homeownership rate has been rising among young adults, the great majority are renters. Fully 77 percent of householders under age 25 rent their home, while only 23 percent are homeowners.

The homeownership rate climbs steeply as people enter their thirties and forties. During the past two decades, Boomers have filled those age groups, fueling the real estate, construction, and home improvement industries. When the large Millennial generation enters its thirties and forties beginning in another few years, it will add more fuel to the fire under the housing market.

■ Millennials today are giving the rental market a boost as they inflate the young-adult age group.

Few young adults own a home

(percent distribution of householders under age 25 by homeownership status, 2003)

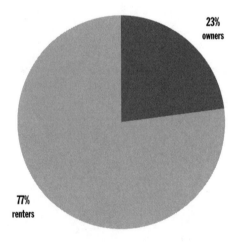

23%
owners

77%
renters

Table 4.2 Owners and Renters by Age of Householder, 2003

(number and percent distribution of householders by age and homeownership status, 2003; numbers in thousands)

		owners			renters		
	total	number	percent distribution	share of total	number	percent distribution	share of total
Total households	**105,560**	**72,054**	**100.0%**	**68.3%**	**33,506**	**100.0%**	**31.7%**
Under age 25	6,441	1,469	2.0	22.8	4,972	14.8	77.2
Aged 25 to 29	8,213	3,272	4.5	39.8	4,941	14.7	60.2
Aged 30 to 34	10,084	5,698	7.9	56.5	4,386	13.1	43.5
Aged 35 to 44	22,525	15,394	21.4	68.3	7,131	21.3	31.7
Aged 45 to 54	21,535	16,499	22.9	76.6	5,036	15.0	23.4
Aged 55 to 64	15,326	12,468	17.3	81.4	2,858	8.5	18.6
Aged 65 or older	21,436	17,253	23.9	80.5	4,183	12.5	19.5

Source: Bureau of the Census, Housing Vacancy Survey, Internet site http://www.census.gov/hhes/www/housing/hvs/historic/ histt12.html; calculations by New Strategist

Few Millennial Couples Are Homeowners

Male-headed families are more likely to own a home.

Although married couples are much more likely to own a home than other household types, this is not true among the youngest adults. Among householders under age 25, only 33 percent of couples are homeowners. The figure is a higher 40 percent among male-headed families in the age group. Twenty-three percent of female-headed families under age 25 are homeowners, as are 13 to 16 percent of men and women who live alone.

The homeownership rate rises with age for every household type. The majority of couples are homeowners beginning in the 25-to-29 age group. Homeownership does not reach majority status until ages 40 or older for most other household types.

■ The homeownership of married couples quickly surpasses that of other household types because married-couple households are most likely to have two incomes.

Among young adults, homeownership is highest for male-headed families

(percent of householders under age 25 who own their home, by household type, 2003)

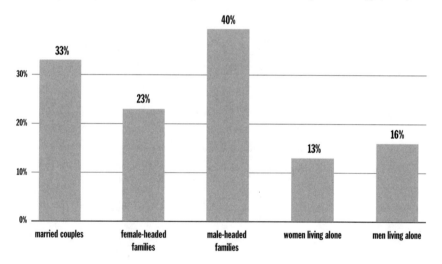

Table 4.3 Homeownership Rate by Age of Householder and Type of Household, 2003

(percent of households owning their home, by age of householder and type of household, 2003)

		family households			people living alone	
	total	married couples	female householder, no spouse present	male householder, no spouse present	females	males
Total households	**68.3%**	**83.3%**	**49.6%**	**57.9%**	**59.1%**	**50.0%**
Under age 25	22.8	32.8	23.1	40.4	12.7	16.0
Aged 25 to 29	39.8	57.9	23.0	39.0	23.8	28.2
Aged 30 to 34	56.5	71.6	33.3	49.2	37.3	38.1
Aged 35 to 39	65.1	78.9	43.2	53.5	45.2	44.6
Aged 40 to 44	71.3	84.9	51.6	63.7	49.8	49.6
Aged 45 to 49	75.4	88.3	60.0	69.6	54.2	50.4
Aged 50 to 54	77.9	90.2	61.1	71.5	60.9	55.4
Aged 55 to 59	80.9	91.6	65.8	75.2	65.4	58.7
Aged 60 to 64	81.9	92.2	71.3	75.0	68.6	61.4
Aged 65 or older	80.5	92.1	81.6	81.9	70.0	67.8

Source: Bureau of the Census, Housing Vacancy Survey, Internet site http://www.census.gov/hhes/www/housing/hvs/annual03/ann03t15.html

Non-Hispanic Whites Have the Highest Homeownership Rate

Hispanics rank a distant second in homeownership.

Nationally, the homeownership rate of non-Hispanic whites stood at 72 percent, according to the 2000 census. The rate was a much lower 53 percent among Asians, and below the 50 percent majority among blacks and Hispanics. Regardless of race and Hispanic origin, however, homeownership rises with age as people acquire the savings and income needed to become homeowners.

Among householders under age 25 in 2000 (Millennials were aged 23 or younger in that year), 21 percent of non-Hispanic whites owned a home. Hispanics ranked second, with a homeownership rate of 15 percent. Asians and blacks in the age group are least likely to own a home, with rates of 11 and 10 percent, respectively.

■ One reason for the higher homeownership rate of young non-Hispanic whites is the greater wealth of their parents, who may be helping them buy their first home.

Among young adults, blacks are least likely to be homeowners

(homeownership rate of householders under age 25, by race and Hispanic origin, 2000)

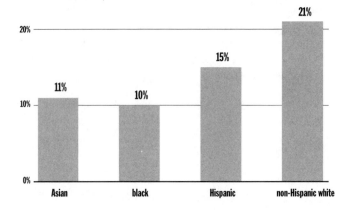

Table 4.4 Homeowners by Age, Race, and Hispanic Origin of Householder, 2000 Census

(percent of households owning their home by age, race, and Hispanic origin of householder, 2000)

	total	Asian	black	Hispanic	non-Hispanic white
Total households	**66.2%**	**52.8%**	**46.0%**	**45.7%**	**72.4%**
Under age 25	17.9	11.3	10.4	15.3	20.5
Aged 25 to 34	45.6	32.1	27.2	32.9	53.0
Aged 35 to 44	66.2	57.8	44.4	48.8	73.2
Aged 45 to 54	74.9	67.9	55.2	56.8	80.3
Aged 55 to 64	79.8	71.2	61.6	61.9	84.1
Aged 65 or older	78.1	62.0	64.3	62.8	80.6

Note: Each racial category includes those who identified themselves as being of the race alone and those who identified themselves as being of the race in combination with one or more other races. Hispanics may be of any race. Non-Hispanic whites include only those who identified themselves as white alone and non-Hispanic.
Source: Bureau of the Census, Census 2000, American Factfinder, Internet site http://factfinder.census.gov/home/saff/main.html?_lang=en

Few Young Adults Live in Single-Family Homes

The majority of the youngest adults live in apartment buildings.

Most American households (63 percent) live in detached single-family homes. But there is great variation by age. While the majority of householders aged 30 or older live in this type of home, the figure is a minority among those under age 30. The under-30 age group accounts for only 7 percent of householders in detached single-family homes.

Fifty-seven percent of householders under age 25 live in multi-unit buildings, as do 42 percent of householders aged 25 to 29. The share drops to just 19 percent among those aged 30 or older. Householders under age 30 account for 28 percent of apartment dwellers.

Seven percent of householders live in mobile homes, a proportion that does not vary much by age. Householders under age 30 account for 15 percent of mobile home householders.

■ As the number of young adults grows with the aging of the Millennial generation, the demand for apartments is likely to be strong.

Young adults are most likely to live in multi-unit buildings

(percent of households living in multi-unit buildings, by age of householder, 2001)

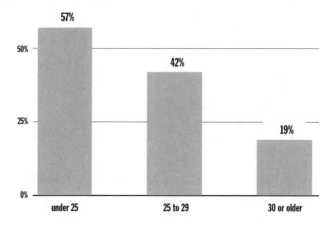

Table 4.5 Number of Units in Structure by Age of Householder, 2001

(number and percent distribution of households by age of householder and number of units in structure of home, 2001; numbers in thousands)

	total	one, detached	one, attached	multi-unit dwellings total	2 to 4	5 to 9	10 to 19	20 to 49	50 or more	mobile homes
Total households	**106,261**	**67,129**	**7,305**	**24,609**	**8,200**	**4,994**	**4,620**	**3,253**	**3,543**	**7,219**
Under age 25	6,206	1,613	632	3,545	1,022	887	838	468	330	416
Aged 25 to 29	8,143	3,260	803	3,435	1,188	760	739	428	321	646
Aged 30 or older	91,911	62,255	5,871	17,628	5,990	3,347	3,043	2,358	2,892	6,156
Median age	47	49	43	39	39	37	36	41	52	46

PERCENT DISTRIBUTION BY AGE OF HOUSEHOLDER

	total	one, detached	one, attached	total	2 to 4	5 to 9	10 to 19	20 to 49	50 or more	mobile homes
Total households	**100.0%**	**100.0%**	**100.0%**	**100.0%**	**100.0%**	**100.0%**	**100.0%**	**100.0%**	**100.0%**	**100.0%**
Under age 25	5.8	2.4	8.7	14.4	12.5	17.8	18.1	14.4	9.3	5.8
Aged 25 to 29	7.7	4.9	11.0	14.0	14.5	15.2	16.0	13.2	9.1	8.9
Aged 30 or older	86.5	92.7	80.4	71.6	73.1	67.0	65.9	72.5	81.6	85.3

PERCENT DISTRIBUTION BY UNITS IN STRUCTURE

	total	one, detached	one, attached	total	2 to 4	5 to 9	10 to 19	20 to 49	50 or more	mobile homes
Total households	**100.0%**	**63.2%**	**6.9%**	**23.2%**	**7.7%**	**4.7%**	**4.3%**	**3.1%**	**3.3%**	**6.8%**
Under age 25	100.0	26.0	10.2	57.1	16.5	14.3	13.5	7.5	5.3	6.7
Aged 25 to 29	100.0	40.0	9.9	42.2	14.6	9.3	9.1	5.3	3.9	7.9
Aged 30 or older	100.0	67.7	6.4	19.2	6.5	3.6	3.3	2.6	3.1	6.7

Source: Bureau of the Census, American Housing Survey for the United States in 2001, *Internet site http://www.census.gov/hhes/www/housing/ahs/ahs01/ahs01.html*

Many Younger Homeowners Live in New Homes

Few older homeowners are in recently built homes.

New homes are the province of the young. Overall, only 6 percent of homeowners live in a new home—meaning one built in the past four years. The share is much greater among young homeowners, however. Fourteen percent of homeowners under age 25 live in a new home, as do 15 percent of those aged 25 to 29. In contrast, only 6 percent of homeowners aged 30 or older are in a new home. Older homeowners usually are in homes they have owned for many years. Even if new at the time they bought it, the home has aged along with its owner.

Overall, 3 percent of renters are in housing units built in the past four years. The proportion is a significantly higher 7 percent among renters under age 25, but falls to 4 percent among those aged 25 to 29 and to 3 percent among those aged 30 or older.

■ The large Millennial generation is likely to boost sales of new homes as they reach adulthood.

Few homeowners aged 30 or older are in new homes

(percent of homeowners living in homes built in the past four years, by age of householder, 2001)

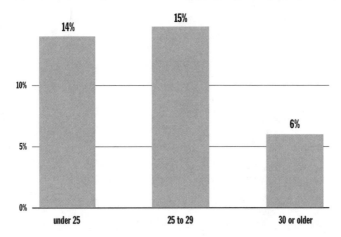

Table 4.6 **Owners and Renters of New Homes by Age of Householder, 2001**

(number of total occupied housing units, number and percent built in the past four years, and percent distribution of new units by housing tenure and age of householder, 2001; numbers in thousands)

	total	in new homes		
		number	percent of total	percent distribution
Total households	**106,261**	**5,853**	**5.5%**	**100.0%**
Under age 25	6,206	502	8.1	8.6
Aged 25 to 29	8,143	683	8.4	11.7
Aged 30 or older	91,911	4,667	5.1	79.7
Owners	**72,265**	**4,690**	**6.5**	**100.0**
Under age 25	1,320	182	13.8	3.9
Aged 25 to 29	3,256	494	15.2	10.5
Aged 30 or older	67,689	4,014	5.9	85.6
Renters	**33,996**	**1,163**	**3.4**	**100.0**
Under age 25	4,886	321	6.6	27.6
Aged 25 to 29	4,887	189	3.9	16.3
Aged 30 or older	24,223	652	2.7	56.1

Source: Bureau of the Census, American Housing Survey for the United States in 2001, *Internet site http://www.census.gov/hhes/www/housing/ahs/ahs01/ahs01.html*

Housing Costs Are Rising for Millennials

Costs are lowest for homeowners aged 65 or older.

Monthly housing costs for the average household in 2001 stood at a median of $658, including mortgage interest and utilities. For homeowners, median monthly housing cost was $685, and for renters the figure was a slightly smaller $632.

Among married-couple homeowners, housing costs are relatively low for those under age 25, a median of just $690 per month. But costs rise sharply as couples age into their late twenties, in part because they buy bigger homes to make room for their growing families. Home owning couples in the 25-to-29 age group have median monthly housing costs of $914. Costs peak for couples aged 30 to 44, at more than $1,000 per month.

Housing costs are lowest for married-couple homeowners aged 65 or older. For older renters, however, housing costs do not decline with age. Among married householders aged 65 or older, homeowners paid a median of $383 for housing while renters paid a median of $651.

■ The financial advantages of homeownership grow as householders pay off their mortgages in middle and old age.

Housing costs rise steeply for couples in the 25-to-29 age group

(median monthly housing costs for married couples, by age of householder, 2001)

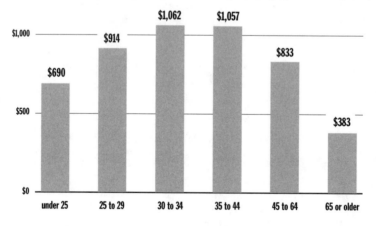

Table 4.7 Median Monthly Housing Costs of Married Couples by Age of Householder, 2001

(median monthly housing costs and indexed costs of married couples by age of householder and housing tenure, 2001)

	median monthly cost				indexed cost		
	total	owners	renters		total	owners	renters
TOTAL HOUSEHOLDS	**$658**	**$685**	**$632**		**100**	**104**	**96**
Married couples	**783**	**811**	**721**		**119**	**123**	**110**
Under age 25	638	690	622		97	105	95
Aged 25 to 29	796	914	691		121	139	105
Aged 30 to 34	928	1,062	737		141	161	112
Aged 35 to 44	979	1,057	775		149	161	118
Aged 45 to 64	815	833	740		124	127	113
Aged 65 or older	395	383	651		60	58	99

Source: Bureau of the Census, American Housing Survey for the United States in 2001, *Internet site http://www.census.gov/hhes/ www/housing/ahs/ahs01/ahs01.html; calculations by New Strategist*

The Homes of the Youngest Adults Are below Average in Value

Home values rise as young couples trade in their starter homes for more expensive models.

The median value of America's owned homes stood at $124,624 in 2001. Median home value is an even higher $139,364 among the nation's married couples. Home values peak among couples aged 35 to 44, with a median value of $147,327.

The value of the homes owned by married couples under age 25 is well below average ($94,774) because many have small starter homes. Among couples aged 25 to 29, median home value stood at $109,988 in 2001. After age 30, home values surge as families move into bigger homes with more room for children. The median value of the homes owned by couples aged 30 to 34 is close to the married-couple average, at $135,904 in 2001. More than one in four own a home worth at least $200,000.

■ Home values have been rising steadily and are now significantly higher than the 2001 figures shown in this table.

Home values peak in the 35-to-44 age group

(median value of homes owned by married couples, by age of householder, 2001)

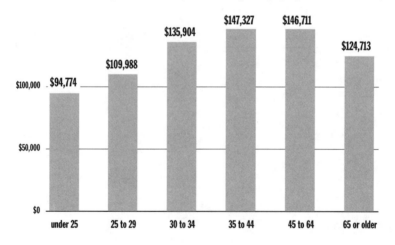

Table 4.8 Value of Homes Owned by Married Couples by Age of Householder, 2001

(total number of married-couple homeowners and percent distribution by value of home, median value of housing unit, and indexed median value, by age of householder, 2001)

	total		under $100,000	$100,000 to $149,999	$150,000 to $199,999	$200,000 to $249,999	$250,000 to $299,999	$300,000 or more	median value of home	indexed median value
	number (in 000s)	percent								
TOTAL HOMEOWNERS	**72,265**	**100.0%**	**39.3%**	**21.6%**	**14.1%**	**7.9%**	**5.2%**	**11.8%**	**$124,624**	**100**
Married couples	**44,618**	**100.0**	**32.8**	**21.9**	**15.5**	**9.4**	**6.3**	**14.1**	**139,364**	**112**
Under age 25	490	100.0	53.7	19.2	11.2	6.5	3.1	5.9	94,774	76
Aged 25 to 29	2,039	100.0	44.9	25.7	14.4	6.0	3.4	5.6	109,988	88
Aged 30 to 34	3,744	100.0	31.8	25.3	15.7	9.6	7.0	10.6	135,904	109
Aged 35 to 44	11,182	100.0	29.1	22.0	16.5	10.2	7.1	15.1	147,327	118
Aged 45 to 64	18,681	100.0	30.0	21.4	15.8	10.0	6.4	16.5	146,711	118
Aged 65 or older	8,482	100.0	39.8	20.6	14.1	8.3	5.4	11.8	124,713	100

Source: Bureau of the Census, American Housing Survey for the United States in 2001, *Internet site http://www.census.gov/hhes/www/housing/ahs/ahs01/ahs01.html*

People in Their Twenties Are Most Likely to Move

More than one in four move each year.

Young adults are far more likely than their elders to move from one home to another. Only 10 percent of people aged 30 or older move in a typical year, but among people aged 20 to 29, the percentage who move in a year is about three times as great. Among children under age 18, a much smaller percentage move as parents try to stay put while their children are in school. Households with school-aged children are less likely to move (12 percent) than those with preschoolers (24 percent) and those without children (14 percent).

Among twentysomething movers, most stay within the same county. Only 18 percent cross state lines, a slightly smaller share than the 19 percent of all movers who head to a different state.

One of the bigger reasons for moving among 20-to-24-year-olds is to attend or leave college, cited as the primary reason by 8 percent of movers. A slightly smaller 7 percent of 25-to-29-year-olds moved because of a new job or job transfer. Twelve percent moved to establish their own household (i.e., moved out of their parents' home), and 17 percent moved because they wanted a better home or apartment.

■ Americans are moving less than they once did. Several factors are behind the lower mobility rate, including the aging of the population, the rise in homeownership, and the proliferation of dual-income couples.

Mobility rate is high among people aged 20 to 29

(percent of people who moved between March 2002 and March 2003, by age)

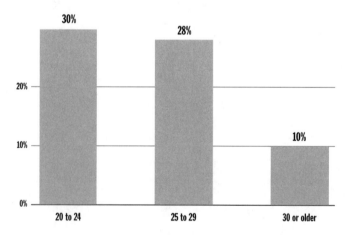

Table 4.9 Geographical Mobility by Age, 2002 to 2003

(total number and percent distribution of people aged 1 or older by mobility status between March 2002 and March 2003, by selected age groups; numbers in thousands)

	total	nonmovers	total movers	same county	different county, same state	different state, same division	different division, same region	different region	abroad
Total, aged 1 or older	**282,556**	**242,463**	**40,093**	**23,468**	**7,728**	**3,752**	**1,181**	**2,695**	**1,269**
Total under age 30	116,093	92,570	23,520	14,153	4,475	1,987	672	1,481	752
Aged 1 to 4	16,408	12,896	3,512	2,237	637	248	95	201	94
Aged 5 to 9	19,708	16,584	3,123	1,935	579	238	98	188	85
Aged 10 to 14	21,190	18,388	2,800	1,729	500	223	89	172	87
Aged 15 to 17	12,628	11,126	1,501	892	289	131	38	111	40
Aged 18 to 19	7,554	6,200	1,353	803	294	112	24	85	35
Aged 20 to 24	19,884	13,906	5,979	3,547	1,156	552	173	385	166
Aged 25 to 29	18,721	13,470	5,252	3,010	1,020	483	155	339	245
Aged 30 or older	166,462	149,893	16,568	9,314	3,252	1,765	507	1,214	516

PERCENT DISTRIBUTION BY AGE

	total	nonmovers	total movers	same county	different county, same state	different state, same division	different division, same region	different region	abroad
Total, aged 1 or older	**100.0%**	**100.0%**	**100.0%**	**100.0%**	**100.0%**	**100.0%**	**100.0%**	**100.0%**	**100.0%**
Total under age 30	41.1	38.2	58.7	60.3	57.9	53.0	56.9	55.0	59.3
Aged 1 to 4	5.8	5.3	8.8	9.5	8.2	6.6	8.0	7.5	7.4
Aged 5 to 9	7.0	6.8	7.8	8.2	7.5	6.3	8.3	7.0	6.7
Aged 10 to 14	7.5	7.6	7.0	7.4	6.5	5.9	7.5	6.4	6.9
Aged 15 to 17	4.5	4.6	3.7	3.8	3.7	3.5	3.2	4.1	3.2
Aged 18 to 19	2.7	2.6	3.4	3.4	3.8	3.0	2.0	3.2	2.8
Aged 20 to 24	7.0	5.7	14.9	15.1	15.0	14.7	14.6	14.3	13.1
Aged 25 to 29	6.6	5.6	13.1	12.8	13.2	12.9	13.1	12.6	19.3
Aged 30 or older	58.9	61.8	41.3	39.7	42.1	47.0	42.9	45.1	40.7

PERCENT DISTRIBUTION BY MOBILITY STATUS

	total	nonmovers	total movers	same county	different county, same state	different state, same division	different division, same region	different region	abroad
Total, aged 1 or older	**100.0%**	**85.8%**	**14.2%**	**8.3%**	**2.7%**	**1.3%**	**0.4%**	**1.0%**	**0.4%**
Total under age 30	100.0	79.7	20.3	12.2	3.9	1.7	0.6	1.3	0.6
Aged 1 to 4	100.0	78.6	21.4	13.6	3.9	1.5	0.6	1.2	0.6
Aged 5 to 9	100.0	84.1	15.8	9.8	2.9	1.2	0.5	1.0	0.4
Aged 10 to 14	100.0	86.8	13.2	8.2	2.4	1.1	0.4	0.8	0.4
Aged 15 to 17	100.0	88.1	11.9	7.1	2.3	1.0	0.3	0.9	0.3
Aged 18 to 19	100.0	82.1	17.9	10.6	3.9	1.5	0.3	1.1	0.5
Aged 20 to 24	100.0	69.9	30.1	17.8	5.8	2.8	0.9	1.9	0.8
Aged 25 to 29	100.0	72.0	28.1	16.1	5.4	2.6	0.8	1.8	1.3
Aged 30 or older	100.0	90.1	10.0	5.6	2.0	1.1	0.3	0.7	0.3

	total	nonmovers	total movers	same county	different county, same state	different state, same division	different division, same region	different region	abroad
PERCENT DISTRIBUTION OF									
MOVERS BY TYPE OF MOVE									
Total, aged 1 or older	–	–	**100.0%**	**58.5%**	**19.3%**	**9.4%**	**2.9%**	**6.7%**	**3.2%**
Total under age 30	–	–	100.0	60.2	19.0	8.4	2.9	6.3	3.2
Aged 1 to 4	–	–	100.0	63.7	18.1	7.1	2.7	5.7	2.7
Aged 5 to 9	–	–	100.0	62.0	18.5	7.6	3.1	6.0	2.7
Aged 10 to 14	–	–	100.0	61.8	17.9	8.0	3.2	6.1	3.1
Aged 15 to 17	–	–	100.0	59.4	19.3	8.7	2.5	7.4	2.7
Aged 18 to 19	–	–	100.0	59.3	21.7	8.3	1.8	6.3	2.6
Aged 20 to 24	–	–	100.0	59.3	19.3	9.2	2.9	6.4	2.8
Aged 25 to 29	–	–	100.0	57.3	19.4	9.2	3.0	6.5	4.7
Aged 30 or older	–	–	100.0	56.2	19.6	10.7	3.1	7.3	3.1

Note: (–) means not applicable.
Source: Bureau of the Census, Geographical Mobility: March 2002 to March 2003, Detailed Tables for P20-549, 2003 Current Population Survey, Internet site http://www.census.gov/population/www/socdemo/migrate/p20-549.html; calculations by New Strategist

Table 4.10 Mobility of Families with Children, 2002 to 2003

(total number and percent distribution of householders aged 15 to 54 by presence of own children under age 18 at home and mobility status between March 2002 and March 2003; numbers in thousands)

	total	nonmovers	total movers	same county	different county, same state	different state, same division	different division, same region	different region	abroad
Total householders	**52,593**	**44,635**	**7,958**	**4,828**	**1,489**	**693**	**221**	**533**	**194**
No children under 18	17,841	15,415	2,426	1,327	483	267	71	191	87
With children under 18	34,753	29,220	5,533	3,501	1,007	426	150	342	107
Under age 6 only	8,355	6,337	2,019	1,282	374	137	51	135	40
Under age 6 and 6 to 17	7,097	5,851	1,245	788	200	104	44	72	37
Aged 6 to 17 only	19,301	17,032	2,269	1,431	433	185	55	135	30

PERCENT DISTRIBUTION BY MOBILITY STATUS

	total	nonmovers	total movers	same county	different county, same state	different state, same division	different division, same region	different region	abroad
Total householders	**100.0%**	**84.9%**	**15.1%**	**9.2%**	**2.8%**	**1.3%**	**0.4%**	**1.0%**	**0.4%**
No children under 18	100.0	86.4	13.6	7.4	2.7	1.5	0.4	1.1	0.5
With children under 18	100.0	84.1	15.9	10.1	2.9	1.2	0.4	1.0	0.3
Under age 6 only	100.0	75.8	24.2	15.3	4.5	1.6	0.6	1.6	0.5
Under age 6 and 6 to 17	100.0	82.4	17.5	11.1	2.8	1.5	0.6	1.0	0.5
Aged 6 to 17 only	100.0	88.2	11.8	7.4	2.2	1.0	0.3	0.7	0.2

PERCENT DISTRIBUTION OF MOVERS BY TYPE OF MOVE

	total	nonmovers	total movers	same county	different county, same state	different state, same division	different division, same region	different region	abroad
Total householders	–	–	**100.0%**	**60.7%**	**18.7%**	**8.7%**	**2.8%**	**6.7%**	**2.4%**
No children under 18	–	–	100.0	54.7	19.9	11.0	2.9	7.9	3.6
With children under 18	–	–	100.0	63.3	18.2	7.7	2.7	6.2	1.9
Under age 6 only	–	–	100.0	63.5	18.5	6.8	2.5	6.7	2.0
Under age 6 and 6 to 17	–	–	100.0	63.3	16.1	8.4	3.5	5.8	3.0
Aged 6 to 17 only	–	–	100.0	63.1	19.1	8.2	2.4	5.9	1.3

Note: (–) means not applicable.
Source: Bureau of the Census, Geographical Mobility: March 2002 to March 2003, *Detailed Tables for P20-549, 2003 Current Population Survey, Internet site http://www.census.gov/population/www/socdemo/migrate/p20-549.html; calculations by New Strategist*

Table 4.11 **Reason for Moving by Age, 2002 to 2003**

(number and percent distribution of movers between March 2002 and March 2003 by primary reason for move and age; numbers in thousands)

	total	under 16	16 to 19	20 to 24	25 to 29	30 to 64	65 or older
TOTAL MOVERS	**40,093**	**9,912**	**2,381**	**5,979**	**5,252**	**15,199**	**1,371**
Family reasons	**10,548**	**2,716**	**800**	**1,758**	**1,401**	**3,473**	**401**
Change in marital status	2,679	564	147	397	396	1,110	65
To establish own household	2,814	579	261	718	460	764	33
Other family reason	5,055	1,573	392	643	545	1,599	303
Job reasons	**6,247**	**1,374**	**281**	**903**	**992**	**2,628**	**69**
New job or job transfer	3,546	868	152	429	566	1,508	23
To look for work or lost job	749	121	40	165	126	298	–
To be closer to work/easier commute	1,275	272	64	227	213	492	5
Retired	101	2	–	3	1	64	32
Other job-related reason	576	111	25	79	86	266	9
Housing reasons	**20,578**	**5,473**	**1,071**	**2,651**	**2,518**	**8,224**	**636**
Wanted own home, not rent	4,078	1,110	166	411	636	1,704	50
Wanted new or better home/apartment	7,942	2,246	475	1,016	916	3,108	181
Wanted better neighborhood/less crime	1,530	439	85	178	179	609	39
Wanted cheaper housing	2,622	616	104	457	286	1,042	116
Other housing reason	4,406	1,062	241	589	501	1,761	250
Other reasons	**2,722**	**350**	**229**	**667**	**341**	**873**	**261**
To attend or leave college	1,010	61	128	499	176	142	3
Change of climate	160	12	–	14	15	92	26
Health reasons	565	83	16	14	35	220	197
Other reasons	987	194	85	140	115	419	35

PERCENT DISTRIBUTION BY REASON	total	under 16	16 to 19	20 to 24	25 to 29	30 to 64	65 or older
TOTAL MOVERS	100.0%	100.0%	100.0%	100.0%	100.0%	100.0%	100.0%
Family reasons	**26.3**	**27.4**	**33.6**	**29.4**	**26.7**	**22.9**	**29.2**
Change in marital status	6.7	5.7	6.2	6.6	7.5	7.3	4.7
To establish own household	7.0	5.8	11.0	12.0	8.8	5.0	2.4
Other family reason	12.6	15.9	16.5	10.8	10.4	10.5	22.1
Job reasons	**15.6**	**13.9**	**11.8**	**15.1**	**18.9**	**17.3**	**5.0**
New job or job transfer	8.8	8.8	6.4	7.2	10.8	9.9	1.7
To look for work or lost job	1.9	1.2	1.7	2.8	2.4	2.0	–
To be closer to work/easier commute	3.2	2.7	2.7	3.8	4.1	3.2	0.4
Retired	0.3	0.0	–	0.1	0.0	0.4	2.3
Other job-related reason	1.4	1.1	1.1	1.3	1.6	1.8	0.7
Housing reasons	**51.3**	**55.2**	**45.0**	**44.3**	**47.9**	**54.1**	**46.4**
Wanted own home, not rent	10.2	11.2	7.0	6.9	12.1	11.2	3.6
Wanted new or better home/apartment	19.8	22.7	19.9	17.0	17.4	20.4	13.2
Wanted better neighborhood/less crime	3.8	4.4	3.6	3.0	3.4	4.0	2.8
Wanted cheaper housing	6.5	6.2	4.4	7.6	5.4	6.9	8.5
Other housing reason	11.0	10.7	10.1	9.9	9.5	11.6	18.2
Other reasons	**6.8**	**3.5**	**9.6**	**11.2**	**6.5**	**5.7**	**19.0**
To attend or leave college	2.5	0.6	5.4	8.3	3.4	0.9	0.2
Change of climate	0.4	0.1	–	0.2	0.3	0.6	1.9
Health reasons	1.4	0.8	0.7	0.2	0.7	1.4	14.4
Other reasons	2.5	2.0	3.6	2.3	2.2	2.8	2.6

PERCENT DISTRIBUTION BY AGE	total	under 16	16 to 19	20 to 24	25 to 29	30 to 64	65 or older
TOTAL MOVERS	**100.0%**	**24.7%**	**5.9%**	**14.9%**	**13.1%**	**37.9%**	**3.4%**
Family reasons	**100.0**	**25.7**	**7.6**	**16.7**	**13.3**	**32.9**	**3.8**
Change in marital status	100.0	21.1	5.5	14.8	14.8	41.4	2.4
To establish own household	100.0	20.6	9.3	25.5	16.3	27.1	1.2
Other family reason	100.0	31.1	7.8	12.7	10.8	31.6	6.0
Job reasons	**100.0**	**22.0**	**4.5**	**14.5**	**15.9**	**42.1**	**1.1**
New job or job transfer	100.0	24.5	4.3	12.1	16.0	42.5	0.6
To look for work or lost job	100.0	16.2	5.3	22.0	16.8	39.8	–
To be closer to work/easier commute	100.0	21.3	5.0	17.8	16.7	38.6	0.4
Retired	100.0	2.0	–	3.0	1.0	63.4	31.7
Other job-related reason	100.0	19.3	4.3	13.7	14.9	46.2	1.6
Housing reasons	**100.0**	**26.6**	**5.2**	**12.9**	**12.2**	**40.0**	**3.1**
Wanted own home, not rent	100.0	27.2	4.1	10.1	15.6	41.8	1.2
Wanted new or better home/apartment	100.0	28.3	6.0	12.8	11.5	39.1	2.3
Wanted better neighborhood/less crime	100.0	28.7	5.6	11.6	11.7	39.8	2.5
Wanted cheaper housing	100.0	23.5	4.0	17.4	10.9	39.7	4.4
Other housing reason	100.0	24.1	5.5	13.4	11.4	40.0	5.7
Other reasons	**100.0**	**12.9**	**8.4**	**24.5**	**12.5**	**32.1**	**9.6**
To attend or leave college	100.0	6.0	12.7	49.4	17.4	14.1	0.3
Change of climate	100.0	7.5	–	8.8	9.4	57.5	16.2
Health reasons	100.0	14.7	2.8	2.5	6.2	38.9	34.9
Other reasons	100.0	19.7	8.6	14.2	11.7	42.5	3.5

Note: (–) means number is less than 500 or sample is too small to make a reliable estimate.
Source: Bureau of the Census, Geographical Mobility: March 2002 to March 2003, Detailed Tables for P20-549, 2003 Current Population Survey, Internet site http://www.census.gov/population/www/socdemo/migrate/p20-549.html; calculations by New Strategist

5

Income

■ The median income of households fell 3 percent between 2000 and 2002, after adjusting for inflation. Among householders under age 25 (Millennials were aged 25 or younger in 2002), the decline was an even larger 4 percent.

■ Householders under age 25 had a median income of $27,828 in 2002, well below the $42,409 national median. Within the age group, black householders have the lowest incomes, while non-Hispanic whites and Asians have the highest incomes.

■ In most age groups, married couples are the most affluent household type. Among households headed by people under age 25, however, the median income of male-headed families is higher than that of married couples.

■ Among families with children under age 18 at home, the median income of married couples stood at $65,399 in 2002 compared with a median of $32,154 for male-headed families and just $22,537 for female-headed families.

■ The median incomes of men and women under age 25 are low—less than $10,000 in 2002—because many in the age group are in college and few work full-time.

■ Children and young adults are much more likely to be poor than middle-aged or older adults. While 12.1 percent of all Americans were poor in 2002, the poverty rate among the Millennial generation was a much larger 16.6 percent.

Incomes of Millennial Householders Have Slipped from Their Peak

Young adults have gained ground over the past two decades, however.

The median income of households fell 3 percent between 2000 and 2002, after adjusting for inflation. Among householders under age 25 (Millennials were aged 25 or younger in 2002), the decline was an even larger 4 percent. The recession of 2001 and the loss of millions of jobs limited the earnings of young adults.

The economic fortunes of young adults have had their ups and downs over the past two decades. On the down side is the fact that the minimum wage has not kept pace with inflation, leaving some young adults behind since many have minimum-wage jobs. In addition, a growing proportion of young adults are going to college and, thus, more have part-time rather than full-time jobs, limiting their incomes. On the up side, the tight labor market of the 1990s boosted the incomes of householders under age 25. Despite the decline since 2000, the median household income of young adults was greater in 2002 than in 1990 or 1980.

■ Because the Millennial generation is large, competition for jobs will be tough, limiting the income growth of young adults even when the labor market recovers.

Young adults have seen their incomes rise and fall

(median income of households headed by people under age 25 in selected years; in 2002 dollars)

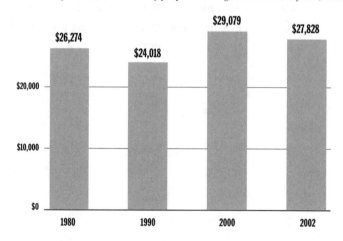

Table 5.1 **Median Income of Households Headed by People under Age 25, 1980 to 2002**

(median income of total households and households headed by people under age 25, 1980 to 2002; percent change for selected years; in 2002 dollars)

	total households	15 to 24
2002	$42,409	$27,828
2001	42,899	28,644
2000	43,848	29,079
1999	44,044	27,162
1998	42,844	25,963
1997	41,346	25,232
1996	40,503	24,465
1995	39,931	24,584
1994	38,725	23,213
1993	38,287	23,694
1992	38,482	22,186
1991	38,790	23,580
1990	39,949	24,018
1989	40,484	26,138
1988	39,766	24,890
1987	39,453	24,899
1986	38,975	23,967
1985	37,648	23,988
1984	36,921	23,107
1983	35,774	22,956
1982	35,986	24,649
1981	36,042	25,023
1980	36,608	26,274
Percent change		
2000–2002	–3.3%	–4.3%
1990–2002	6.2	15.9
1980–2002	15.8	5.9

Source: Bureau of the Census, data from the Current Population Survey Annual Demographic Supplements, Internet site http://www.census.gov/hhes/income/histinc/h10.html; calculations by New Strategist

Household Incomes Differ Sharply by Race and Hispanic Origin

Among householders under age 25, blacks have the lowest incomes.

Householders under age 25 had a median income of $27,828 in 2002, well below the $42,409 national median. Within the age group, black householders have the lowest incomes by far—a median of just $20,342. Non-Hispanic whites and Asians have the highest median household income, at $30,841 and $30,666, respectively. Hispanics are in the middle, with a median household income of $26,662.

Household income rises substantially in the 25-to-29 age group as young men and women marry and more households have two incomes. The median income of householders aged 25 to 29 is close to the national average at $41,388. Within the age group, Asians have the highest median income, at $49,304 in 2002.

■ Differences in household income among young adults by race and Hispanic origin stem from differences in household composition and educational attainment.

Asians and non-Hispanic whites have the highest incomes

(median income of householders under age 25, by race and Hispanic origin, 2002)

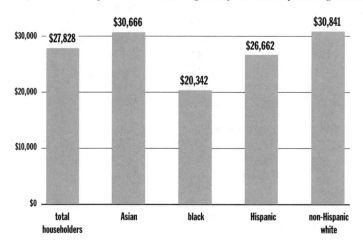

Table 5.2 Income of Households Headed by People under Age 30, 2002: Total Households

(number and percent distribution of total households and households headed by people under age 30, by household income, 2002; households in thousands as of 2003)

	total	15 to 24	25 to 29
Total households	**111,278**	**6,611**	**8,535**
Under $10,000	10,090	1,056	673
$10,000 to $19,999	15,063	1,241	968
$20,000 to $29,999	14,362	1,206	1,213
$30,000 to $39,999	12,795	978	1,223
$40,000 to $49,999	10,743	715	1,029
$50,000 to $59,999	9,226	476	857
$60,000 to $69,999	7,633	256	716
$70,000 to $79,999	6,695	230	549
$80,000 to $89,999	5,039	134	369
$90,000 to $99,999	3,952	106	226
$100,000 or more	15,676	214	713
Median income	$42,409	$27,828	$41,388
Total households	**100.0%**	**100.0%**	**100.0%**
Under $10,000	9.1	16.0	7.9
$10,000 to $19,999	13.5	18.8	11.3
$20,000 to $29,999	12.9	18.2	14.2
$30,000 to $39,999	11.5	14.8	14.3
$40,000 to $49,999	9.7	10.8	12.1
$50,000 to $59,999	8.3	7.2	10.0
$60,000 to $69,999	6.9	3.9	8.4
$70,000 to $79,999	6.0	3.5	6.4
$80,000 to $89,999	4.5	2.0	4.3
$90,000 to $99,999	3.6	1.6	2.6
$100,000 or more	14.1	3.2	8.4

Source: Bureau of the Census, data from the 2003 Current Population Survey Annual Social and Economic Supplement, Internet site http://ferret.bls.census.gov/macro/032003/hhinc/new02_000.htm; calculations by New Strategist

Table 5.3 Income of Households Headed by People under Age 30, 2002: Asian Households

(number and percent distribution of total Asian households and Asian households headed by people under age 30, by household income, 2002; households in thousands as of 2003)

	total	15 to 24	25 to 29
Total Asian households	**4,079**	**313**	**420**
Under $10,000	329	64	40
$10,000 to $19,999	379	43	34
$20,000 to $29,999	407	45	44
$30,000 to $39,999	436	47	50
$40,000 to $49,999	359	38	45
$50,000 to $59,999	355	24	48
$60,000 to $69,999	270	8	31
$70,000 to $79,999	261	12	19
$80,000 to $89,999	228	9	16
$90,000 to $99,999	166	8	15
$100,000 or more	889	15	77
Median income	$52,285	$30,666	$49,304
Total Asian households	**100.0%**	**100.0%**	**100.0%**
Under $10,000	8.1	20.4	9.5
$10,000 to $19,999	9.3	13.7	8.1
$20,000 to $29,999	10.0	14.4	10.5
$30,000 to $39,999	10.7	15.0	11.9
$40,000 to $49,999	8.8	12.1	10.7
$50,000 to $59,999	8.7	7.7	11.4
$60,000 to $69,999	6.6	2.6	7.4
$70,000 to $79,999	6.4	3.8	4.5
$80,000 to $89,999	5.6	2.9	3.8
$90,000 to $99,999	4.1	2.6	3.6
$100,000 or more	21.8	4.8	18.3

Note: Asian householders include those who identified themselves as Asian alone and those who identified themselves as Asian in combination with one or more other races.
Source: Bureau of the Census, data from the 2003 Current Population Survey Annual Social and Economic Supplement, Internet site http://ferret.bls.census.gov/macro/032003/hhinc/new02_000.htm; calculations by New Strategist

Table 5.4   Income of Households Headed by People under Age 30, 2002: Black Households

(number and percent distribution of total black households and black households headed by people under age 30, by household income, 2002; households in thousands as of 2003)

	total	15 to 24	25 to 29
Total black households	**13,778**	**1,193**	**1,214**
Under $10,000	2,432	330	201
$10,000 to $19,999	2,486	257	246
$20,000 to $29,999	2,111	201	215
$30,000 to $39,999	1,809	161	194
$40,000 to $49,999	1,190	91	95
$50,000 to $59,999	918	58	67
$60,000 to $69,999	698	22	67
$70,000 to $79,999	566	15	52
$80,000 to $89,999	384	11	22
$90,000 to $99,999	280	17	13
$100,000 or more	904	32	44
Median income	$29,177	$20,342	$27,658
Total black households	**100.0%**	**100.0%**	**100.0%**
Under $10,000	17.7	27.7	16.6
$10,000 to $19,999	18.0	21.5	20.3
$20,000 to $29,999	15.3	16.8	17.7
$30,000 to $39,999	13.1	13.5	16.0
$40,000 to $49,999	8.6	7.6	7.8
$50,000 to $59,999	6.7	4.9	5.5
$60,000 to $69,999	5.1	1.8	5.5
$70,000 to $79,999	4.1	1.3	4.3
$80,000 to $89,999	2.8	0.9	1.8
$90,000 to $99,999	2.0	1.4	1.1
$100,000 or more	6.6	2.7	3.6

Note: Black householders include those who identified themselves as black alone and those who identified themselves as black in combination with one or more other races.
Source: Bureau of the Census, data from the 2003 Current Population Survey Annual Social and Economic Supplement, Internet site http://ferret.bls.census.gov/macro/032003/hhinc/new02_000.htm; calculations by New Strategist

Table 5.5 Income of Households Headed by People under Age 30, 2002: Hispanic Households

(number and percent distribution of total Hispanic households and Hispanic households headed by people under age 30, by household income, 2002; households in thousands as of 2003)

	total	15 to 24	25 to 29
Total Hispanic households	**11,339**	**1,073**	**1,368**
Under $10,000	1,247	147	125
$10,000 to $19,999	1,879	218	215
$20,000 to $29,999	1,949	242	265
$30,000 to $39,999	1,574	147	202
$40,000 to $49,999	1,109	99	163
$50,000 to $59,999	945	71	115
$60,000 to $69,999	693	27	90
$70,000 to $79,999	505	36	55
$80,000 to $89,999	372	15	41
$90,000 to $99,999	249	18	29
$100,000 or more	815	48	69
Median income	$33,103	$26,662	$33,485
Total Hispanic households	**100.0%**	**100.0%**	**100.0%**
Under $10,000	11.0	13.7	9.1
$10,000 to $19,999	16.6	20.3	15.7
$20,000 to $29,999	17.2	22.6	19.4
$30,000 to $39,999	13.9	13.7	14.8
$40,000 to $49,999	9.8	9.2	11.9
$50,000 to $59,999	8.3	6.6	8.4
$60,000 to $69,999	6.1	2.5	6.6
$70,000 to $79,999	4.5	3.4	4.0
$80,000 to $89,999	3.3	1.4	3.0
$90,000 to $99,999	2.2	1.7	2.1
$100,000 or more	7.2	4.5	5.0

Note: Hispanics may be of any race.
Source: Bureau of the Census, data from the 2003 Current Population Survey Annual Social and Economic Supplement, Internet site http://ferret.bls.census.gov/macro/032003/hhinc/new02_000.htm; calculations by New Strategist

Table 5.6   **Income of Households Headed by People under Age 30, 2002:**
Non-Hispanic White Households

(number and percent distribution of total non-Hispanic white households and non-Hispanic white households headed by people under age 30, by household income, 2002; households in thousands as of 2003)

	total	15 to 24	25 to 39
Total non-Hispanic white households	**81,166**	**3,979**	**5,465**
Under $10,000	5,977	508	297
$10,000 to $19,999	10,170	709	466
$20,000 to $29,999	9,797	709	674
$30,000 to $39,999	8,829	612	755
$40,000 to $49,999	7,982	479	722
$50,000 to $59,999	6,958	322	625
$60,000 to $69,999	5,926	199	529
$70,000 to $79,999	5,301	161	415
$80,000 to $89,999	4,034	98	290
$90,000 to $99,999	3,235	64	170
$100,000 or more	12,958	119	523
Median income	$46,900	$30,841	$46,816
Total non-Hispanic white households	**100.0%**	**100.0%**	**100.0%**
Under $10,000	7.4	12.8	5.4
$10,000 to $19,999	12.5	17.8	8.5
$20,000 to $29,999	12.1	17.8	12.3
$30,000 to $39,999	10.9	15.4	13.8
$40,000 to $49,999	9.8	12.0	13.2
$50,000 to $59,999	8.6	8.1	11.4
$60,000 to $69,999	7.3	5.0	9.7
$70,000 to $79,999	6.5	4.1	7.6
$80,000 to $89,999	5.0	2.5	5.3
$90,000 to $99,999	4.0	1.6	3.1
$100,000 or more	16.0	3.0	9.6

Note: Non-Hispanic white householders include only those who identified themselves as white alone and non-Hispanic.
Source: Bureau of the Census, data from the 2003 Current Population Survey Annual Social and Economic Supplement, Internet site http://ferret.bls.census.gov/macro/032003/hhinc/new02_000.htm; calculations by New Strategist

Male-Headed Families Have the Highest Incomes

Among householders under age 25, the median income of male-headed families is slightly higher than that of married couples.

For most age groups, married couples are the most affluent household type. Among households headed by people under age 25, however, the $37,386 median income of male-headed families is higher than the $34,630 median of married couples. Female-headed family households had a median income of just $19,754, while women who live alone had the lowest incomes, a median of just $14,544.

Behind the higher incomes of male-headed families are the number of earners in the household. In fully 34 percent of married couples under age 25, only the husband is in the labor force—a larger proportion than in any other age group. Many of these couples have young children, and the wife is taking care of the kids rather than working outside the home. Male-headed families often have more than one working adult in the household, boosting their incomes.

In the 25-to-29 age group, the incomes of married couples soar as dual-earners become more common. The median income of married couples aged 25 to 29 is $52,728, well above that of any other household type.

■ Young adult households are diverse, many having only one or even no earners, limiting their incomes.

Women who live alone have the lowest incomes

(median income of householders under age 25 by household type, 2002)

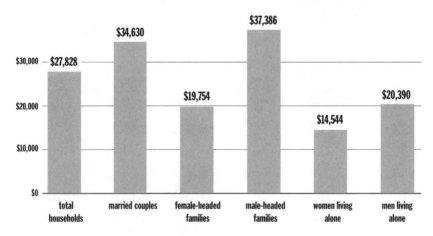

Table 5.7 Income of Households by Household Type, 2002: Aged 15 to 24

(number and percent distribution of households headed by people aged 15 to 24, by household income and household type, 2002; households in thousands as of 2003)

	total	family households			nonfamily households			
					female householder		male householder	
		married couples	female hh, no spouse present	male hh, no spouse present	total	living alone	total	living alone
Total householders aged 15 to 24	**6,611**	**1,379**	**1,383**	**789**	**1,552**	**817**	**1,507**	**722**
Under $10,000	1,056	78	397	62	310	247	211	169
$10,000 to $19,999	1,241	201	301	89	374	301	276	183
$20,000 to $29,999	1,206	309	234	137	254	126	274	167
$30,000 to $39,999	978	210	153	136	229	74	252	102
$40,000 to $49,999	715	217	81	87	159	46	169	44
$50,000 to $59,999	476	131	62	62	95	17	128	24
$60,000 to $69,999	256	80	32	53	33	2	58	6
$70,000 to $79,999	230	51	42	55	40	4	41	12
$80,000 to $89,999	134	33	21	23	24	–	32	3
$90,000 to $99,999	106	28	16	29	12	–	20	7
$100,000 or more	214	40	46	57	22	–	49	6
Median income	$27,828	$34,630	$19,754	$37,386	$22,324	$14,544	$29,607	$20,390
Total householders aged 15 to 24	**100.0%**	**100.0%**	**100.0%**	**100.0%**	**100.0%**	**100.0%**	**100.0%**	**100.0%**
Under $10,000	16.0	5.7	28.7	7.9	20.0	30.2	14.0	23.4
$10,000 to $19,999	18.8	14.6	21.8	11.3	24.1	36.8	18.3	25.3
$20,000 to $29,999	18.2	22.4	16.9	17.4	16.4	15.4	18.2	23.1
$30,000 to $39,999	14.8	15.2	11.1	17.2	14.8	9.1	16.7	14.1
$40,000 to $49,999	10.8	15.7	5.9	11.0	10.2	5.6	11.2	6.1
$50,000 to $59,999	7.2	9.5	4.5	7.9	6.1	2.1	8.5	3.3
$60,000 to $69,999	3.9	5.8	2.3	6.7	2.1	0.2	3.8	0.8
$70,000 to $79,999	3.5	3.7	3.0	7.0	2.6	0.5	2.7	1.7
$80,000 to $89,999	2.0	2.4	1.5	2.9	1.5	–	2.1	0.4
$90,000 to $99,999	1.6	2.0	1.2	3.7	0.8	–	1.3	1.0
$100,000 or more	3.2	2.9	3.3	7.2	1.4	–	3.3	0.8

Note: (–) means number is less than 500 or sample is too small to make a reliable estimate.
Source: Bureau of the Census, data from the 2003 Current Population Survey Annual Social and Economic Supplement, Internet site http://ferret.bls.census.gov/macro/032003/hhinc/new02_000.htm; calculations by New Strategist

Table 5.8 Income of Households by Household Type, 2002: Aged 25 to 29

(number and percent distribution of households headed by people aged 25 to 29, by income and household type, 2002; households in thousands as of 2003)

| | | family households | | | nonfamily households | | | |
| | | | | | female householder | | male householder | |
	total	married couples	female hh, no spouse present	male hh, no spouse present	total	living alone	total	living alone
Total householders								
aged 25 to 29	**8,535**	**3,760**	**1,391**	**508**	**1,223**	**783**	**1,653**	**1,021**
Under $10,000	673	99	303	26	103	86	141	120
$10,000 to $19,999	968	250	356	54	121	101	188	163
$20,000 to $29,999	1,213	429	245	80	195	154	265	201
$30,000 to $39,999	1,223	459	192	90	235	191	246	182
$40,000 to $49,999	1,029	489	100	55	171	117	214	131
$50,000 to $59,999	857	485	53	57	106	45	158	65
$60,000 to $69,999	716	409	46	49	85	40	124	61
$70,000 to $79,999	549	358	35	24	59	20	73	25
$80,000 to $89,999	369	212	18	19	52	3	66	27
$90,000 to $99,999	226	141	6	16	22	8	42	6
$100,000 or more	713	428	36	38	76	16	134	39
Median income	$41,388	$52,728	$21,270	$40,408	$37,815	$31,833	$39,082	$31,016
Total householders								
aged 25 to 29	**100.0%**	**100.0%**	**100.0%**	**100.0%**	**100.0%**	**100.0%**	**100.0%**	**100.0%**
Under $10,000	7.9	2.6	21.8	5.1	8.4	11.0	8.5	11.8
$10,000 to $19,999	11.3	6.6	25.6	10.6	9.9	12.9	11.4	16.0
$20,000 to $29,999	14.2	11.4	17.6	15.7	15.9	19.7	16.0	19.7
$30,000 to $39,999	14.3	12.2	13.8	17.7	19.2	24.4	14.9	17.8
$40,000 to $49,999	12.1	13.0	7.2	10.8	14.0	14.9	12.9	12.8
$50,000 to $59,999	10.0	12.9	3.8	11.2	8.7	5.7	9.6	6.4
$60,000 to $69,999	8.4	10.9	3.3	9.6	7.0	5.1	7.5	6.0
$70,000 to $79,999	6.4	9.5	2.5	4.7	4.8	2.6	4.4	2.4
$80,000 to $89,999	4.3	5.6	1.3	3.7	4.3	0.4	4.0	2.6
$90,000 to $99,999	2.6	3.8	0.4	3.1	1.8	1.0	2.5	0.6
$100,000 or more	8.4	11.4	2.6	7.5	6.2	2.0	8.1	3.8

Source: Bureau of the Census, data from the 2003 Current Population Survey Annual Social and Economic Supplement, Internet site http://ferret.bls.census.gov/macro/032003/hhinc/new02_000.htm; calculations by New Strategist

Children in Married-Couple Families Are Better Off

Among families with children, married couples are far more affluent than single parents.

Many members of the Millennial generation (aged 8 to 25 in 2002) are children, and their financial well-being depends greatly on the type of household in which they live. Those living with married parents are better off than those living in other household types.

Among all families with children under age 18 at home, the median income of married couples stood at $65,399 in 2002 compared with a median of $32,154 for male-headed families and just $22,637 for female-headed families with children.

Married couples with school-aged children, aged 6 to 17, have the highest incomes, a median of $71,151 in 2002. Fully 27 percent have incomes of $100,000 or more. The incomes of male- and female-headed families with school-aged children also surpass the incomes of those with preschoolers. Most householders with school-aged children are in their peak earning years, which accounts for their above-average incomes. Female-headed families with a combination of preschoolers and school-aged children have the lowest incomes—a median of just $17,764 in 2002.

■ Black children have higher poverty rates than non-Hispanic white children because they are much less likely to live in married-couple families.

Single-parent families have the lowest incomes

(median income of families with children under age 18 at home, by family type, 2002)

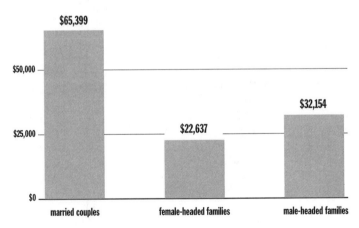

Table 5.9 Household Income of Children under Age 18 by Family Type, 2002

(number and percent distribution of families with related children under age 18 at home, by household income and family type, 2002; families in thousands as of 2003)

	total families	married couples	female-headed families	male-headed families
Total families with children	**38,846**	**27,052**	**9,414**	**2,380**
Under $10,000	2,711	542	1,957	211
$10,000 to $19,999	3,918	1,329	2,199	391
$20,000 to $29,999	4,493	2,248	1,774	470
$30,000 to $39,999	4,118	2,474	1,245	402
$40,000 to $49,999	3,806	2,696	819	292
$50,000 to $59,999	3,374	2,707	491	174
$60,000 to $69,999	2,995	2,565	304	127
$70,000 to $79,999	2,783	2,493	192	98
$80,000 to $89,999	2,135	1,938	135	61
$90,000 to $99,999	1,691	1,588	70	34
$100,000 or more	6,823	6,475	226	122
Median income	$50,851	$65,399	$22,637	$32,154

DISTRIBUTION OF FAMILIES BY INCOME

	total families	married couples	female-headed families	male-headed families
Total families with children	**100.0%**	**100.0%**	**100.0%**	**100.0%**
Under $10,000	7.0	0.2	20.8	8.9
$10,000 to $19,999	10.1	4.9	23.4	16.4
$20,000 to $29,999	11.6	8.3	18.8	19.7
$30,000 to $39,999	10.6	9.1	13.2	16.9
$40,000 to $49,999	9.8	10.0	8.7	12.3
$50,000 to $59,999	8.7	1.0	5.2	7.3
$60,000 to $69,999	7.7	9.5	3.2	5.3
$70,000 to $79,999	7.2	9.2	2.0	4.1
$80,000 to $89,999	5.5	7.2	1.4	2.6
$90,000 to $99,999	4.4	5.9	0.7	1.4
$100,000 or more	17.6	23.9	2.4	5.1

DISTRIBUTION OF FAMILIES BY FAMILY TYPE

	total families	married couples	female-headed families	male-headed families
Total families	**100.0%**	**69.6%**	**24.2%**	**6.1%**
Under $10,000	100.0	20.0	72.2	7.8
$10,000 to $19,999	100.0	33.9	56.1	10.0
$20,000 to $29,999	100.0	50.0	39.5	10.5
$30,000 to $39,999	100.0	60.1	30.2	9.8
$40,000 to $49,999	100.0	70.8	21.5	7.7
$50,000 to $59,999	100.0	80.2	14.6	5.2
$60,000 to $69,999	100.0	85.6	10.2	4.2
$70,000 to $79,999	100.0	89.6	6.9	3.5
$80,000 to $89,999	100.0	90.8	6.3	2.9
$90,000 to $99,999	100.0	93.9	4.1	2.0
$100,000 or more	100.0	94.9	3.3	1.8

Source: Bureau of the Census, data from the 2003 Current Population Survey Annual Social and Economic Supplement, http:// ferret.bls.census.gov/macro/032003/faminc/new03_000.htm; calculations by New Strategist

Table 5.10 Household Income of Children under Age 18 Living in Married-Couple Families, 2002

(number and percent distribution of total married-couple households and those with related children under age 18 at home, by household income and age of children, 2002; households in thousands as of 2003)

	total	with one or more children			
		total	all under 6	some under 6, some 6 to 17	all 6 to 17
Total married-couple families	**57,327**	**27,052**	**6,546**	**5,955**	**14,551**
Under $10,000	1,436	542	169	138	235
$10,000 to $19,999	3,819	1,329	419	345	565
$20,000 to $29,999	5,693	2,248	646	659	943
$30,000 to $39,999	5,811	2,474	624	671	1,178
$40,000 to $49,999	5,640	2,696	670	662	1,363
$50,000 to $59,999	5,540	2,707	652	655	1,400
$60,000 to $69,999	5,083	2,565	611	550	1,404
$70,000 to $79,999	4,770	2,493	585	507	1,401
$80,000 to $89,999	3,795	1,938	428	383	1,128
$90,000 to $99,999	3,082	1,588	360	285	943
$100,000 or more	12,659	6,475	1,383	1,101	3,991
Median income	$61,130	$65,399	$61,026	$56,947	$71,151
Total married-couple families	**100.0%**	**100.0%**	**100.0%**	**100.0%**	**100.0%**
Under $10,000	2.5	0.2	2.6	2.3	1.6
$10,000 to $19,999	6.7	4.9	6.4	5.8	3.9
$20,000 to $29,999	9.9	8.3	9.9	11.1	6.5
$30,000 to $39,999	10.1	9.1	9.5	11.3	8.1
$40,000 to $49,999	9.8	10.0	10.2	11.1	9.4
$50,000 to $59,999	9.7	10.0	10.0	11.0	9.6
$60,000 to $69,999	8.9	9.5	9.3	9.2	9.6
$70,000 to $79,999	8.3	9.2	8.9	8.5	9.6
$80,000 to $89,999	6.6	7.2	6.5	6.4	7.8
$90,000 to $99,999	5.4	5.9	5.5	4.8	6.5
$100,000 or more	22.1	23.9	21.1	18.5	27.4

Source: Bureau of the Census, data from the 2003 Current Population Survey Annual Social and Economic Supplement, http:// ferret.bls.census.gov/macro/032003/faminc/new03_000.htm; calculations by New Strategist

Table 5.11 Household Income of Children under Age 18 Living in Female-Headed Families, 2002

(number and percent distribution of total female-headed households and those with related children under age 18 at home, by household income and age of children, 2002; households in thousands as of 2003)

		with one or more children			
	total	total	all under 6	some under 6, some 6 to 17	all 6 to 17
Total female-headed families	**13,626**	**9,414**	**2,002**	**1,763**	**5,649**
Under $10,000	2,281	1,957	608	499	850
$10,000 to $19,999	2,896	2,199	461	464	1,275
$20,000 to $29,999	2,437	1,774	355	316	1,105
$30,000 to $39,999	1,915	1,245	226	202	815
$40,000 to $49,999	1,365	819	110	105	604
$50,000 to $59,999	877	491	76	59	354
$60,000 to $69,999	578	304	61	39	204
$70,000 to $79,999	375	192	37	19	136
$80,000 to $89,999	252	135	28	13	94
$90,000 to $99,999	157	70	14	9	48
$100,000 or more	494	226	26	38	161
Median income	$26,423	$22,637	$17,986	$17,764	$26,001
Total female-headed families	**100.0%**	**100.0%**	**100.0%**	**100.0%**	**100.0%**
Under $10,000	16.7	20.8	30.4	28.3	15.1
$10,000 to $19,999	21.3	23.4	23.0	26.3	22.6
$20,000 to $29,999	17.9	18.8	17.7	17.9	19.6
$30,000 to $39,999	14.1	13.2	11.3	11.5	14.4
$40,000 to $49,999	10.0	8.7	5.5	6.0	10.7
$50,000 to $59,999	6.4	5.2	3.8	3.3	6.3
$60,000 to $69,999	4.2	3.2	3.1	2.2	3.6
$70,000 to $79,999	2.8	2.0	1.8	1.1	2.4
$80,000 to $89,999	1.8	1.4	1.4	0.7	1.7
$90,000 to $99,999	1.2	0.7	0.7	0.5	0.8
$100,000 or more	3.6	2.4	1.3	2.2	2.9

Source: Bureau of the Census, data from the 2003 Current Population Survey Annual Social and Economic Supplement, http://ferret.bls.census.gov/macro/032003/faminc/new03_000.htm; calculations by New Strategist

Table 5.12 Household Income of Children under Age 18 Living in Male-Headed Families, 2002

(number and percent distribution of total male-headed households and those with related children under age 18 at home, by household income and age of children, 2002; households in thousands as of 2003)

	total	with one or more children			
		total	all under 6	some under 6, some 6 to 17	all 6 to 17
Total male-headed families	**4,663**	**2,380**	**607**	**286**	**1,487**
Under $10,000	330	211	66	27	118
$10,000 to $19,999	606	391	124	69	198
$20,000 to $29,999	792	470	159	54	257
$30,000 to $39,999	721	402	107	44	252
$40,000 to $49,999	610	292	63	31	198
$50,000 to $59,999	406	174	29	26	119
$60,000 to $69,999	344	127	17	12	98
$70,000 to $79,999	261	98	12	7	79
$80,000 to $89,999	146	61	13	6	42
$90,000 to $99,999	102	34	1	2	30
$100,000 or more	344	122	16	10	96
Median income	$37,739	$32,154	$26,246	$28,451	$36,403
Total male-headed families	**100.0%**	**100.0%**	**100.0%**	**100.0%**	**100.0%**
Under $10,000	7.1	8.9	10.9	9.4	7.9
$10,000 to $19,999	13.0	16.4	20.4	24.1	13.3
$20,000 to $29,999	17.0	19.7	26.2	18.9	17.3
$30,000 to $39,999	15.5	16.9	17.6	15.4	16.9
$40,000 to $49,999	13.1	12.3	10.4	10.8	13.3
$50,000 to $59,999	8.7	7.3	4.8	9.1	8.0
$60,000 to $69,999	7.4	5.3	2.8	4.2	6.6
$70,000 to $79,999	5.6	4.1	2.0	2.4	5.3
$80,000 to $89,999	3.1	2.6	2.1	2.1	2.8
$90,000 to $99,999	2.2	1.4	0.2	0.7	2.0
$100,000 or more	7.4	5.1	2.6	3.5	6.5

Source: Bureau of the Census, data from the 2003 Current Population Survey Annual Social and Economic Supplement, http://ferret.bls.census.gov/macro/032003/faminc/new03_000.htm; calculations by New Strategist

Young Adults Have Seen Incomes Decline Since 2000

But their incomes are higher than in 1980 or 1990.

Between 2000 and 2002, men under age 25 saw their median income fall 3.3 percent, after adjusting for inflation. Women under age 25 experienced a 1.3 percent decline in median income during those years. Behind the decline was the recession of 2001 and the prolonged jobless recovery.

Despite the decline since 2000, the median income of young men and women was greater in 2002 than in 1980 or 1990. For men, income growth was a slight 1.5 percent between 1980 and 2002, after adjusting for inflation. For their female counterparts, median income grew a substantial 17 percent as more women went to work. In 2002, men under age 25 had a median income of $9,642, while women in the age group had a median income of $7,582.

■ The median income of men and women under age 25 is low because many are going to school and working part-time or not at all. As these young adults earn their degree, their incomes will rise.

Among young adults, women's incomes have grown faster than men's

(median income of people under age 25, by sex, 1980 and 2002; in 2002 dollars)

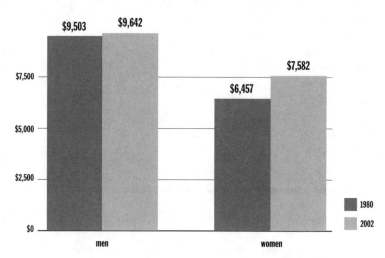

Table 5.13 Median Income of Men under Age 25, 1980 to 2002

(median income of men aged 15 or older and under age 25, 1980 to 2002; percent change for selected years; in 2002 dollars)

	total men	15 to 24
2002	$29,238	$9,642
2001	29,564	9,449
2000	29,597	9,968
1999	29,433	8,959
1998	29,189	9,024
1997	28,170	8,345
1996	27,199	7,942
1995	26,439	8,101
1994	26,070	8,459
1993	25,862	7,879
1992	25,694	7,910
1991	26,357	8,088
1990	27,075	8,431
1989	27,861	8,841
1988	27,618	8,535
1987	26,925	8,261
1986	26,791	8,270
1985	26,000	7,963
1984	25,696	7,756
1983	25,061	7,338
1982	24,888	7,898
1981	25,459	5,805
1980	25,900	9,503
Percent change		
2000–2002	–1.2%	–3.3%
1990–2002	8.0	14.4
1980–2002	12.9	1.5

Source: Bureau of the Census, data from the Current Population Survey Annual Demographic Supplements, Internet site http://www.census.gov/hhes/income/histinc/p08.html; calculations by New Strategist

Table 5.14 Median Income of Women under Age 25, 1980 to 2002

(median income of women aged 15 or older and under age 25, 1980 to 2002; percent change for selected years; in 2002 dollars)

	total women	15 to 24
2002	$16,812	$7,582
2001	16,878	7,586
2000	16,774	7,685
1999	16,523	7,218
1998	15,899	7,200
1997	15,311	7,086
1996	14,624	6,711
1995	14,215	6,222
1994	13,762	6,612
1993	13,537	6,558
1992	13,458	6,494
1991	13,489	6,692
1990	13,435	6,540
1989	13,479	6,637
1988	12,977	6,552
1987	12,558	6,673
1986	11,914	6,331
1985	11,504	6,043
1984	11,313	5,945
1983	10,823	5,922
1982	10,502	5,981
1981	10,313	3,772
1980	10,170	6,457

Percent change

2000–2002	0.2%	–1.3%
1990–2002	25.1	15.9
1980–2002	65.3	17.4

Source: Bureau of the Census, data from the Current Population Survey Annual Demographic Supplements, Internet site http://www.census.gov/hhes/income/histinc/p08.html; calculations by New Strategist

The Incomes of Millennial Men Are Low

Their incomes are low because few work full-time.

The median income of men under age 25 stood at just $9,642 in 2002 (Millennials were aged 25 or younger in 2002). Behind the low figure is the fact that few men in the age group work full-time—only 23 percent are full-time workers versus 54 percent of all men aged 16 or older. A much larger 69 percent of men aged 25 to 29 work full-time, and their incomes are a higher $27,256.

Among men under age 25, Hispanics have the highest median income ($12,454) because they are most likely to work full-time. Among the 32 percent with full-time jobs, their median income was $18,547 in 2002. Only 18 percent of Asian men under age 25 work full-time because most are in college, which explains their modest median income of $9,783. The median income of non-Hispanic white men under age 25 is a slightly smaller $8,857 because they, too, are likely to be in college—only 22 percent work full-time. As with Asians and non-Hispanic whites, few black men under age 25 work full-time—only 18 percent in 2002. Unlike the situation with Asians and non-Hispanic whites, however, the low labor force participation rate of young black men primarily stems from their difficulty in finding full-time employment.

■ Men's incomes rise steeply as they enter their late twenties and the majority get full-time jobs.

Among young men, Hispanics have the highest incomes

(median income of men under age 25, by race and Hispanic origin, 2002)

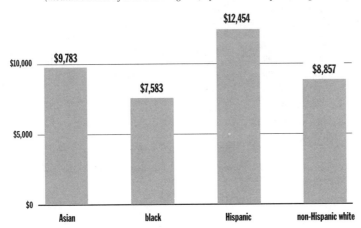

Table 5.15 Income of Men under Age 30, 2002: Total Men

(number and percent distribution of men aged 16 or older and under age 30 by income, 2002; median income by work status, and percent working year-round, full-time; men in thousands as of 2003)

	total	15 to 24	25 to 29
TOTAL MEN	**108,814**	**20,216**	**9,382**
Without income	**9,026**	**6,096**	**527**
With income	**99,788**	**14,120**	**8,855**
Under $10,000	16,061	7,202	1,013
$10,000 to $19,999	18,536	3,434	1,828
$20,000 to $29,999	16,206	1,951	1,991
$30,000 to $39,999	13,528	854	1,657
$40,000 to $49,999	9,485	385	989
$50,000 to $59,999	7,048	134	527
$60,000 to $69,999	4,735	34	330
$70,000 to $79,999	3,769	42	194
$80,000 to $89,999	2,355	26	104
$90,000 to $99,999	1,512	19	57
$100,000 or more	6,556	42	164
Median income of men with income	$29,238	$9,642	$27,256
Median income of full-time workers	40,507	21,342	31,356
Percent working full-time	54.0%	23.1%	68.6%
TOTAL MEN	**100.0%**	**100.0%**	**100.0%**
Without income	**8.3**	**30.2**	**5.6**
With income	**91.7**	**69.8**	**94.4**
Under $10,000	14.8	35.6	10.8
$10,000 to $19,999	17.0	17.0	19.5
$20,000 to $29,999	14.9	9.7	21.2
$30,000 to $39,999	12.4	4.2	17.7
$40,000 to $49,999	8.7	1.9	10.5
$50,000 to $59,999	6.5	0.7	5.6
$60,000 to $69,999	4.4	0.2	3.5
$70,000 to $79,999	3.5	0.2	2.1
$80,000 to $89,999	2.2	0.1	1.1
$90,000 to $99,999	1.4	0.1	0.6
$100,000 or more	6.0	0.2	1.7

Source: Bureau of the Census, data from the 2003 Current Population Survey Annual Social and Economic Supplement, Internet site http://ferret.bls.census.gov/macro/032003/perinc/toc.htm; calculations by New Strategist

Table 5.16 Income of Men under Age 30, 2002: Asian Men

(number and percent distribution of Asian men aged 16 or older and under age 30 by income, 2002; median income by work status, and percent working year-round, full-time; men in thousands as of 2003)

	total	15 to 24	25 to 29
TOTAL ASIAN MEN	**4,688**	**915**	**543**
Without income	**549**	**335**	**56**
With income	**4,139**	**580**	**487**
Under $10,000	708	295	69
$10,000 to $19,999	701	144	67
$20,000 to $29,999	589	63	76
$30,000 to $39,999	536	44	90
$40,000 to $49,999	371	22	50
$50,000 to $59,999	235	1	41
$60,000 to $69,999	206	1	35
$70,000 to $79,999	199	3	16
$80,000 to $89,999	141	4	8
$90,000 to $99,999	95	2	9
$100,000 or more	360	2	25
Median income of men with income	$30,839	$9,783	$31,665
Median income of full-time workers	42,448	24,823	40,250
Percent working full-time	56.2%	18.1%	61.0%
TOTAL ASIAN MEN	**100.0%**	**100.0%**	**100.0%**
Without income	**11.7**	**36.6**	**10.3**
With income	**88.3**	**63.4**	**89.7**
Under $10,000	15.1	32.2	12.7
$10,000 to $19,999	15.0	15.7	12.3
$20,000 to $29,999	12.6	6.9	14.0
$30,000 to $39,999	11.4	4.8	16.6
$40,000 to $49,999	7.9	2.4	9.2
$50,000 to $59,999	5.0	0.1	7.6
$60,000 to $69,999	4.4	0.1	6.4
$70,000 to $79,999	4.2	0.3	2.9
$80,000 to $89,999	3.0	0.4	1.5
$90,000 to $99,999	2.0	0.2	1.7
$100,000 or more	7.7	0.2	4.6

Note: Asians include those who identified themselves as Asian alone and those who identified themselves as Asian in combination with one or more other races.
Source: Bureau of the Census, data from the 2003 Current Population Survey Annual Social and Economic Supplement, Internet site http://ferret.bls.census.gov/macro/032003/perinc/toc.htm; calculations by New Strategist

Table 5.17 Income of Men under Age 30, 2002: Black Men

(number and percent distribution of black men aged 16 or older and under age 30 by income, 2002; median income by work status, and percent working year-round, full-time; men in thousands as of 2003)

	total	15 to 24	25 to 29
TOTAL BLACK MEN	**12,188**	**2,935**	**1,111**
Without income	**2,092**	**1,322**	**138**
With income	**10,096**	**1,613**	**973**
Under $10,000	2,416	928	214
$10,000 to $19,999	2,254	354	233
$20,000 to $29,999	1,813	203	199
$30,000 to $39,999	1,373	64	164
$40,000 to $49,999	829	36	75
$50,000 to $59,999	527	17	36
$60,000 to $69,999	264	3	20
$70,000 to $79,999	214	3	13
$80,000 to $89,999	115	0	7
$90,000 to $99,999	70	0	4
$100,000 or more	221	5	10
Median income of men with income	$21,509	$7,583	$21,738
Median income of full-time workers	31,966	20,229	27,560
Percent working full-time	45.2%	17.6%	55.4%
TOTAL BLACK MEN	**100.0%**	**100.0%**	**100.0%**
Without income	**17.2**	**45.0**	**12.4**
With income	**82.8**	**55.0**	**87.6**
Under $10,000	19.8	31.6	19.3
$10,000 to $19,999	18.5	12.1	21.0
$20,000 to $29,999	14.9	6.9	17.9
$30,000 to $39,999	11.3	2.2	14.8
$40,000 to $49,999	6.8	1.2	6.8
$50,000 to $59,999	4.3	0.6	3.2
$60,000 to $69,999	2.2	0.1	1.8
$70,000 to $79,999	1.8	0.1	1.2
$80,000 to $89,999	0.9	0.0	0.6
$90,000 to $99,999	0.6	0.0	0.4
$100,000 or more	1.8	0.2	0.9

Note: Blacks include those who identified themselves as black alone and those who identified themselves as black in combination with one or more other races.
Source: Bureau of the Census, data from the 2003 Current Population Survey Annual Social and Economic Supplement, Internet site http://ferret.bls.census.gov/macro/032003/perinc/toc.htm; calculations by New Strategist

Table 5.18 Income of Men under Age 30, 2002: Hispanic Men

(number and percent distribution of Hispanic men aged 16 or older and under age 30 by income, 2002; median income by work status, and percent working year-round, full-time; men in thousands as of 2003)

	total	15 to 24	25 to 29
TOTAL HISPANIC MEN	**14,353**	**3,602**	**2,114**
Without income	**1,729**	**1,218**	**117**
With income	**12,624**	**2,384**	**1,997**
Under $10,000	2,395	866	265
$10,000 to $19,999	3,629	888	640
$20,000 to $29,999	2,715	379	512
$30,000 to $39,999	1,526	135	295
$40,000 to $49,999	869	64	129
$50,000 to $59,999	566	18	63
$60,000 to $69,999	304	4	42
$70,000 to $79,999	201	6	18
$80,000 to $89,999	104	6	14
$90,000 to $99,999	63	4	2
$100,000 or more	251	14	14
Median income of men with income	$20,702	$12,454	$21,179
Median income of full-time workers	26,137	18,547	24,591
Percent working full-time	57.0%	32.2%	70.8%
TOTAL HISPANIC MEN	**100.0%**	**100.0%**	**100.0%**
Without income	**12.1**	**33.8**	**5.5**
With income	**88.0**	**66.2**	**94.5**
Under $10,000	16.7	24.0	12.5
$10,000 to $19,999	25.3	24.7	30.3
$20,000 to $29,999	18.9	10.5	24.2
$30,000 to $39,999	10.6	3.7	14.0
$40,000 to $49,999	6.1	1.8	6.1
$50,000 to $59,999	3.9	0.5	3.0
$60,000 to $69,999	2.1	0.1	2.0
$70,000 to $79,999	1.4	0.2	0.9
$80,000 to $89,999	0.7	0.2	0.7
$90,000 to $99,999	0.4	0.1	0.1
$100,000 or more	1.7	0.4	0.7

Note: Hispanics may be of any race.
Source: Bureau of the Census, data from the 2003 Current Population Survey Annual Social and Economic Supplement, Internet site http://ferret.bls.census.gov/macro/032003/perinc/toc.htm; calculations by New Strategist

Table 5.19 Income of Men under Age 30, 2002: Non-Hispanic White Men

(number and percent distribution of non-Hispanic white men aged 16 or older and under age 30 by income, 2002; median income by work status, and percent working year-round, full-time; men in thousands as of 2003)

	total	15 to 24	25 to 29
TOTAL NON-HISPANIC			
WHITE MEN	**76,722**	**12,632**	**5,565**
Without income	**4,576**	**3,181**	**205**
With income	**72,146**	**9,451**	**5,360**
Under $10,000	10,338	5,030	451
$10,000 to $19,999	11,849	2,063	881
$20,000 to $29,999	10,984	1,297	1,198
$30,000 to $39,999	8,664	2,249	1,139
$40,000 to $49,999	6,633	1,664	936
$50,000 to $59,999	5,164	1,023	643
$60,000 to $69,999	3,841	330	311
$70,000 to $79,999	3,139	30	149
$80,000 to $89,999	1,973	17	75
$90,000 to $99,999	1,270	12	39
$100,000 or more	5,703	21	112
Median income of men with income	$32,034	$8,857	$30,797
Median income of full-time workers	45,153	22,403	34,447
Percent working full-time	54.8%	22.3%	71.3%
TOTAL NON-HISPANIC			
WHITE MEN	**100.0%**	**100.0%**	**100.0%**
Without income	**6.0**	**25.2**	**3.7**
With income	**94.0**	**74.8**	**96.3**
Under $10,000	13.5	39.8	8.1
$10,000 to $19,999	15.4	16.3	15.8
$20,000 to $29,999	14.3	10.3	21.5
$30,000 to $39,999	11.3	17.8	20.5
$40,000 to $49,999	8.6	13.2	16.8
$50,000 to $59,999	6.7	8.1	11.6
$60,000 to $69,999	5.0	2.6	5.6
$70,000 to $79,999	4.1	0.2	2.7
$80,000 to $89,999	2.6	0.1	1.3
$90,000 to $99,999	1.7	0.1	0.7
$100,000 or more	7.4	0.2	2.0

Note: Non-Hispanic whites include only those who identified themselves as white alone and non-Hispanic.
Source: Bureau of the Census, data from the 2003 Current Population Survey Annual Social and Economic Supplement, Internet site http://ferret.bls.census.gov/macro/032003/perinc/toc.htm; calculations by New Strategist

The Incomes of Young Women Are Low

Fewer than 20 percent of women under age 25 work full-time.

The median income of women under age 25 is even lower than that of their male counter-parts, standing at just $7,582 in 2002. Behind the low figures for both men and women is the fact that few in the age group work full-time. Only 17 percent of women under age 25 work full-time compared with 36 percent of all women aged 16 or older. Among those who work full-time, median income was $19,570, well below the $30,970 median of all women who work full-time.

Among women under age 25, Asians are least likely to work full-time (12 percent) because they are most likely to attend college. The median income of Asian women under age 25 was just $7,761 in 2002. The median income of non-Hispanic white women in the age group is about the same ($7,589), although a larger share (18 percent) have full-time jobs. The figures are similar for black women, who have a median income of $7,115. Just 16 percent of black women under age 25 work full-time. The median income of Hispanic women under age 25 is higher than that of Asians, blacks, or non-Hispanic whites, at $8,851 in 2002. By the 25-to-29 age group, however, Hispanic women have the lowest incomes.

■ Young women are even more likely to be in school than young men, with many working part-time or not at all. Their incomes will rise as they gain the credentials to advance in the job market.

Among young women, Hispanics have the highest incomes

(median income of women under age 25, by race and Hispanic origin, 2002)

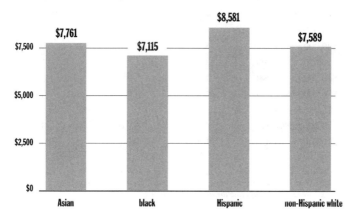

Table 5.20 Income of Women under Age 30, 2002: Total Women

(number and percent distribution of women aged 16 or older and under age 30 by income, 2002; median income by work status, and percent working year-round, full-time; women in thousands as of 2003)

	total	15 to 24	25 to 29
TOTAL WOMEN	**116,436**	**19,850**	**9,339**
Without income	**13,949**	**6,266**	**1,168**
With income	**102,487**	**13,584**	**8,171**
Under $10,000	33,026	7,820	1,996
$10,000 to $19,999	24,289	3,461	1,772
$20,000 to $29,999	16,626	1,432	1,824
$30,000 to $39,999	11,180	530	1,287
$40,000 to $49,999	6,784	216	621
$50,000 to $59,999	3,886	53	291
$60,000 to $69,999	2,264	31	157
$70,000 to $79,999	1,428	13	92
$80,000 to $89,999	787	–	41
$90,000 to $99,999	558	4	32
$100,000 or more	1,658	27	58
Median income of women with income	$16,812	$7,582	$21,376
Median income of full-time workers	30,970	19,570	29,051
Percent working full-time	36.0%	17.1%	48.2%
TOTAL WOMEN	**100.0%**	**100.0%**	**100.0%**
Without income	**12.0**	**31.6**	**12.5**
With income	**88.0**	**68.4**	**87.5**
Under $10,000	28.4	39.4	21.4
$10,000 to $19,999	20.9	17.4	19.0
$20,000 to $29,999	14.3	7.2	19.5
$30,000 to $39,999	9.6	2.7	13.8
$40,000 to $49,999	5.8	1.1	6.6
$50,000 to $59,999	3.3	0.3	3.1
$60,000 to $69,999	1.9	0.2	1.7
$70,000 to $79,999	1.2	0.1	1.0
$80,000 to $89,999	0.7	–	0.4
$90,000 to $99,999	0.5	0.0	0.3
$100,000 or more	1.4	0.1	0.6

Note: (–) means number is less than 500 or sample is too small to make a reliable estimate.
Source: Bureau of the Census, data from the 2003 Current Population Survey Annual Social and Economic Supplement, Internet site http://ferret.bls.census.gov/macro/032003/perinc/toc.htm; calculations by New Strategist

Table 5.21 Income of Women under Age 30, 2002: Asian Women

(number and percent distribution of Asian women aged 16 or older and under age 30 by income, 2002; median income by work status, and percent working year-round, full-time; women in thousands as of 2003)

	total	15 to 24	25 to 29
TOTAL ASIAN WOMEN	**5,131**	**909**	**563**
Without income	**994**	**371**	**105**
With income	**4,137**	**538**	**458**
Under $10,000	1,373	303	134
$10,000 to $19,999	804	140	75
$20,000 to $29,999	642	54	98
$30,000 to $39,999	396	19	49
$40,000 to $49,999	291	13	27
$50,000 to $59,999	214	4	40
$60,000 to $69,999	118	1	9
$70,000 to $79,999	92	2	7
$80,000 to $89,999	45	–	4
$90,000 to $99,999	40	–	8
$100,000 or more	125	2	6
Median income of women with income	$17,898	$7,761	$21,211
Median income of full-time workers	32,031	19,490	31,223
Percent working full-time	37.0%	12.3%	40.5%
TOTAL ASIAN WOMEN	**100.0%**	**100.0%**	**100.0%**
Without income	**19.4**	**40.8**	**18.7**
With income	**80.6**	**59.2**	**81.3**
Under $10,000	26.8	33.3	23.8
$10,000 to $19,999	15.7	15.4	13.3
$20,000 to $29,999	12.5	5.9	17.4
$30,000 to $39,999	7.7	2.1	8.7
$40,000 to $49,999	5.7	1.4	4.8
$50,000 to $59,999	4.2	0.4	7.1
$60,000 to $69,999	2.3	0.1	1.6
$70,000 to $79,999	1.8	0.2	1.2
$80,000 to $89,999	0.9	–	0.7
$90,000 to $99,999	0.8	–	1.4
$100,000 or more	2.4	0.2	1.1

Note: Asians include those who identified themselves as Asian alone and those who identified themselves as Asian in combination with one or more other races. (–) means less than 500 or sample is too small to make a reliable estimate.
Source: Bureau of the Census, data from the 2003 Current Population Survey Annual Social and Economic Supplement, Internet site http://ferret.bls.census.gov/macro/032003/perinc/toc.htm; calculations by New Strategist

Table 5.22 Income of Women under Age 30, 2002: Black Women

(number and percent distribution of black women aged 16 or older and under age 30 by income, 2002; median income by work status, and percent working year-round, full-time; women in thousands as of 2003)

	total	15 to 24	25 to 29
TOTAL BLACK WOMEN	**14,887**	**3,113**	**1,372**
Without income	**2,222**	**1,245**	**138**
With income	**12,665**	**1,868**	**1,234**
Under $10,000	4,069	1,137	296
$10,000 to $19,999	3,156	420	356
$20,000 to $29,999	2,196	209	253
$30,000 to $39,999	1,434	63	201
$40,000 to $49,999	774	21	71
$50,000 to $59,999	411	11	22
$60,000 to $69,999	260	6	18
$70,000 to $79,999	143	–	7
$80,000 to $89,999	71	–	7
$90,000 to $99,999	50	–	–
$100,000 or more	100	3	2
Median income of women with income	$16,671	$7,115	$18,893
Median income of full-time workers	27,703	19,610	26,554
Percent working full-time	40.7%	16.0%	50.7%
TOTAL BLACK WOMEN	**100.0%**	**100.0%**	**100.0%**
Without income	**14.9**	**40.0**	**10.1**
With income	**85.1**	**60.0**	**89.9**
Under $10,000	27.3	36.5	21.6
$10,000 to $19,999	21.2	13.5	25.9
$20,000 to $29,999	14.8	6.7	18.4
$30,000 to $39,999	9.6	2.0	14.7
$40,000 to $49,999	5.2	0.7	5.2
$50,000 to $59,999	2.8	0.4	1.6
$60,000 to $69,999	1.7	0.2	1.3
$70,000 to $79,999	1.0	–	0.5
$80,000 to $89,999	0.5	–	0.5
$90,000 to $99,999	0.3	–	–
$100,000 or more	0.7	0.1	0.1

Note: Blacks include those who identified themselves as black alone and those who identified themselves as black in combination with one or more other races. (–) means number is less than 500 or sample is too small to make a reliable estimate.
Source: Bureau of the Census, data from the 2003 Current Population Survey Annual Social and Economic Supplement, Internet site http://ferret.bls.census.gov/macro/032003/perinc/toc.htm; calculations by New Strategist

Table 5.23　Income of Women under Age 30, 2002: Hispanic Women

(number and percent distribution of Hispanic women aged 16 or older and under age 30 by income, 2002; median income by work status, and percent working year-round, full-time; women in thousands as of 2003)

	total	15 to 24	25 to 29
TOTAL HISPANIC			
WOMEN	**13,607**	**3,169**	**1,724**
Without income	**3,589**	**1,456**	**454**
With income	**10,018**	**1,713**	**1,270**
Under $10,000	3,822	940	404
$10,000 to $19,999	2,821	505	349
$20,000 to $29,999	1,602	166	280
$30,000 to $39,999	839	69	130
$40,000 to $49,999	444	21	61
$50,000 to $59,999	215	3	27
$60,000 to $69,999	110	7	7
$70,000 to $79,999	64	–	5
$80,000 to $89,999	30	–	–
$90,000 to $99,999	10	–	1
$100,000 or more	63	3	6
Median income of women with income	$13,364	$8,581	$15,983
Median income of full-time workers	22,355	16,190	23,565
Percent working full-time	33.7%	17.9%	39.1%
TOTAL HISPANIC			
WOMEN	**100.0%**	**100.0%**	**100.0%**
Without income	**26.4**	**45.9**	**26.3**
With income	**73.6**	**54.1**	**73.7**
Under $10,000	28.1	29.7	23.4
$10,000 to $19,999	20.7	15.9	20.2
$20,000 to $29,999	11.8	5.2	16.2
$30,000 to $39,999	6.2	2.2	7.5
$40,000 to $49,999	3.3	0.7	3.5
$50,000 to $59,999	1.6	0.1	1.6
$60,000 to $69,999	0.8	0.2	0.4
$70,000 to $79,999	0.5	–	0.3
$80,000 to $89,999	0.2	–	–
$90,000 to $99,999	0.1	–	0.1
$100,000 or more	0.5	0.1	0.3

Note: Hispanics may be of any race. (–) means number is less than 500 or sample is too small to make a reliable estimate.
Source: Bureau of the Census, data from the 2003 Current Population Survey Annual Social and Economic Supplement, Internet site http://ferret.bls.census.gov/macro/032003/perinc/toc.htm; calculations by New Strategist

Table 5.24 Income of Women under Age 30, 2002: Non-Hispanic White Women

(number and percent distribution of non-Hispanic white women aged 16 or older and under age 30 by income, 2002; median income by work status, and percent working year-round, full-time; women in thousands as of 2003)

	total	15 to 24	25 to 29
TOTAL NON-HISPANIC			
WHITE WOMEN	**81,851**	**12,454**	**5,606**
Without income	**7,037**	**3,166**	**470**
With income	**74,814**	**9,288**	**5,136**
Under $10,000	23,423	5,318	1,114
$10,000 to $19,999	17,326	2,351	988
$20,000 to $29,999	12,052	1,000	1,190
$30,000 to $39,999	8,440	377	899
$40,000 to $49,999	5,230	161	455
$50,000 to $59,999	3,018	33	199
$60,000 to $69,999	1,760	17	124
$70,000 to $79,999	1,120	11	71
$80,000 to $89,999	631	–	29
$90,000 to $99,999	452	4	24
$100,000 or more	1,360	19	45
Median income of women with income	$17,389	$7,589	$23,445
Median income of full-time workers	32,347	20,408	30,701
Percent working full-time	35.6%	17.5%	51.6%
TOTAL NON-HISPANIC			
WHITE WOMEN	**100.0%**	**100.0%**	**100.0%**
Without income	**8.6**	**25.4**	**8.4**
With income	**91.4**	**74.6**	**91.6**
Under $10,000	28.6	42.7	19.9
$10,000 to $19,999	21.2	18.9	17.6
$20,000 to $29,999	14.7	8.0	21.2
$30,000 to $39,999	10.3	3.0	16.0
$40,000 to $49,999	6.4	1.3	8.1
$50,000 to $59,999	3.7	0.3	3.5
$60,000 to $69,999	2.2	0.1	2.2
$70,000 to $79,999	1.4	0.1	1.3
$80,000 to $89,999	0.8	–	0.5
$90,000 to $99,999	0.6	0.0	0.4
$100,000 or more	1.7	0.2	0.8

Note: Non-Hispanic whites include only those who identified themselves as white alone and non-Hispanic. (–) means number is less than 500 or sample is too small to make a reliable estimate.
Source: Bureau of the Census, data from the 2003 Current Population Survey Annual Social and Economic Supplement, Internet site http://ferret.bls.census.gov/macro/032003/perinc/toc.htm; calculations by New Strategist

Jobs Are the Most Important Source of Income for Young Adults

A substantial proportion receive educational grants and loans.

Earnings are the most common source of income for young adults. Eighty-three to 86 percent of women and men aged 15 to 24 received wage and salary income from an employer in 2002.

The second most common source of income for young adults is interest. Twenty-eight to 31 percent of people under age 25 receive interest income, although those with interest income received very little—less than $300 in 2002.

A substantial 13 percent of men and 18 percent of women under age 25 receive educational assistance. On average, they received $4,800 to $5,100 in educational grants and scholarships in 2002, accounting for a substantial portion of the income of many young adults.

■ Earnings from employment will always be young adults' primary source of income. For many, however, educational support is significant.

Educational assistance counts among young adults

(percent of people under age 25 who receive educational assistance, by sex, 2002)

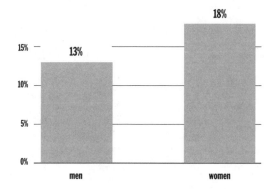

Table 5.25 Sources of Income for Men Aged 15 to 24, 2002

(number and percent distribution of men aged 15 to 24 with income and average income for those with income, by selected sources of income, 2002; people in thousands as of 2003)

	number	percent distribution	average
Men aged 15 to 24 with income	**14,120**	**100.0%**	**$13,504**
Earnings	12,347	87.4	13,740
Wages and salary	12,120	85.8	13,658
Nonfarm self-employment	435	3.1	8,860
Farm self-employment	148	1.1	1,628
Unemployment compensation	397	2.8	3,693
Workers' compensation	61	0.4	–
Social Security	456	3.2	5,679
SSI (Supplemental Security Income)	214	1.5	5,161
Public assistance	93	0.7	2,789
Veterans' benefits	24	0.2	–
Survivors' benefits	27	0.2	–
Disability benefits	21	0.1	–
Retirement income	52	0.4	–
Property income	4,217	29.9	561
Interest	3,960	28.1	298
Dividends	759	5.4	680
Rents, royalties, estates or trusts	91	0.6	7,310
Educational assistance	1,880	13.3	4,891
Pell grant only	326	2.3	2,465
Other government only	272	1.9	5,057
Scholarships only	737	5.2	4,867
Other only	162	1.1	4,187
Combinations	382	2.7	7,191
Child support	94	0.7	3,473
Alimony	3	0.0	–
Financial assistance from other household	432	3.1	6,484
Other income	51	0.4	–

Note: (–) means sample too small to make a reliable estimate.
Source: Bureau of the Census, data from the 2003 Current Population Survey Annual Social and Economic Supplement, http:// ferret.bls.census.gov/macro/032003/perinc/new09_000.htm; calculations by New Strategist

Table 5.26 Sources of Income for Women Aged 15 to 24, 2002

(number and percent distribution of women aged 15 to 24 with income and average income for those with income, by selected sources of income, 2002; people in thousands as of 2003)

	number	percent distribution	average
Women aged 15 to 24 with income	**13,584**	**100.0%**	**$11,071**
Earnings	11,409	84.0	10,955
Wages and salary	11,277	83.0	10,956
Nonfarm self-employment	288	2.1	4,507
Farm self-employment	79	0.6	1,699
Unemployment compensation	264	1.9	2,814
Workers' compensation	30	0.2	–
Social Security	458	3.4	5,543
SSI (Supplemental Security Income)	185	1.4	4,915
Public assistance	474	3.5	2,386
Veterans' benefits	20	0.1	–
Survivors' benefits	45	0.3	–
Disability benefits	20	0.1	–
Retirement income	60	0.4	–
Property income	4,362	32.1	535
Interest	4,204	30.9	254
Dividends	701	5.2	1,089
Rents, royalties, estates or trusts	106	0.8	4,737
Educational assistance	2,509	18.5	5,111
Pell grant only	520	3.8	2,216
Other government only	276	2.0	4,514
Scholarships only	920	6.8	5,386
Other only	178	1.3	5,378
Combinations	615	4.5	7,340
Child support	479	3.5	2,338
Alimony	–	–	–
Financial assistance from other household	565	4.2	5,468
Other income	43	0.3	–

Note: (–) means sample too small to make a reliable estimate.
Source: Bureau of the Census, data from the 2003 Current Population Survey Annual Social and Economic Supplement, http://ferret.bls.census.gov/macro/032003/perinc/new09_000.htm; calculations by New Strategist

Children Have the Highest Poverty Rate

The Millennial generation accounts for nearly half the nation's poor.

Children and young adults are much more likely to be poor than middle-aged or older adults. While 12.1 percent of all Americans were poor in 2002, the poverty rate among the Millennial generation (people under age 26 in 2002) was a much larger 16.6 percent. Millennials account for nearly 50 percent of the nation's poor. Thirty percent of black and 26 percent of Hispanic Millennials are poor, while the poverty rate is just 10 percent among non-Hispanic whites and 13 percent among Asians in the age group. Non-Hispanic whites account for a 38 percent minority of the Millennial poor.

Children under age 18 living in families headed by married couples are much less likely to be poor than those in single-parent families. Only 9 percent of children in married-couple families are poor versus 40 percent of those in female-headed families. The poverty rate is even higher among black and Hispanic children living in single-parent families, 47 to 48 percent being poor.

■ Poverty rates for children are well above average because many live in female-headed families—the poorest household type. Until single parenthood becomes less common, poverty among the young will remain stubbornly high.

The nation's young are most likely to be poor

(percent of people living below poverty level, by age, 2002)

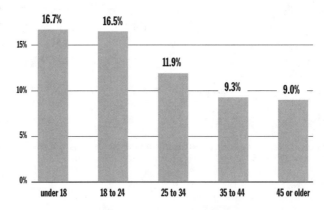

Table 5.27 People below Poverty Level by Age, Race and Hispanic Origin, 2002

(number, percent, and percent distribution of people below poverty level, by age, race and Hispanic origin, 2002; people in thousands as of 2003)

	total	Asian	black	Hispanic	non-Hispanic white
NUMBER IN POVERTY					
TOTAL PEOPLE	**34,570**	**1,243**	**8,884**	**8,555**	**15,567**
Millennials (under 26)	**17,190**	**593**	**5,061**	**4,940**	**6,470**
Under age 18	12,133	353	3,817	3,782	4,090
Under age 5	3,727	83	1,191	1,166	1,261
Aged 5 to 17	8,405	270	2,626	2,616	2,829
Aged 18 to 24	4,536	211	1,119	1,014	2,165
Aged 25 to 34	4,674	207	1,018	1,410	1,980
Aged 35 to 44	4,087	212	968	1,016	1,854
Aged 45 or older	9,140	259	1,963	1,332	5,479
PERCENT IN POVERTY					
TOTAL PEOPLE	**12.1%**	**10.0%**	**23.9%**	**21.8%**	**8.0%**
Millennials (under 26)	**16.6**	**12.7**	**30.4**	**26.3**	**10.3**
Under age 18	16.7	11.0	31.5	28.6	9.4
Under age 5	19.0	8.9	36.5	29.3	11.2
Aged 5 to 17	15.8	11.9	29.7	28.3	8.8
Aged 18 to 24	16.5	16.3	27.5	21.1	12.7
Aged 25 to 34	11.9	9.0	19.7	19.0	8.2
Aged 35 to 44	9.3	10.2	17.4	17.2	6.1
Aged 45 or older	9.0	7.2	19.1	17.0	6.9
PERCENT DISTRIBUTION OF POOR BY AGE					
TOTAL PEOPLE	**100.0%**	**100.0%**	**100.0%**	**100.0%**	**100.0%**
Millennials (under 26)	**49.7**	**47.7**	**57.0**	**57.7**	**41.6**
Under age 18	35.1	28.4	43.0	44.2	26.3
Under age 5	10.8	6.7	13.4	13.6	8.1
Aged 5 to 17	24.3	21.7	29.6	30.6	18.2
Aged 18 to 24	13.1	17.0	12.6	11.9	13.9
Aged 25 to 34	13.5	16.7	11.5	16.5	12.7
Aged 35 to 44	11.8	17.1	10.9	11.9	11.9
Aged 45 or older	26.4	20.8	22.1	15.6	35.2
PERCENT DISTRIBUTION OF POOR BY RACE AND HISPANIC ORIGIN					
TOTAL PEOPLE	**100.0%**	**3.6%**	**25.7%**	**24.7%**	**45.0%**
Millennials (under 26)	**100.0**	**3.4**	**29.4**	**28.7**	**37.6**
Under age 18	100.0	2.9	31.5	31.2	33.7
Under age 5	100.0	2.2	32.0	31.3	33.8
Aged 5 to 17	100.0	3.2	31.2	31.1	33.7
Aged 18 to 24	100.0	4.7	24.7	22.4	47.7
Aged 25 to 34	100.0	4.4	21.8	30.2	42.4
Aged 35 to 44	100.0	5.2	23.7	24.9	45.4
Aged 45 or older	100.0	2.8	21.5	14.6	59.9

Note: Numbers will not add to total because each racial category includes those who identified themselves as being of the race alone and those who identified themselves as being of the race in combination with one or more other races, because Hispanics may be of any race, and because not all races are shown. Non-Hispanic whites include only those who identified themselves as white alone and non-Hispanic.
Source: Bureau of the Census, data from the 2003 Current Population Survey Annual Social and Economic Supplement, Internet sites http://ferret.bls.census.gov/macro/032003/pov/new34_100.htm and http://ferret.bls.census.gov/macro/032003/pov/new01_000.htm; calculations by New Strategist

Table 5.28 Children under Age 18 in Poverty by Family Type, Race, and Hispanic Origin, 2002

(number, percent, and percent distribution of children under age 18 in families with incomes below poverty level by family type, race, and Hispanic origin, 2002; children in thousands as of 2003)

	total	Asian	black	Hispanic	non-Hispanic white
NUMBER OF CHILDREN IN POVERTY					
All family types	**11,704**	**340**	**3,748**	**3,677**	**3,864**
Married couple families	4,358	195	541	1,903	1,682
Female householder, no spouse present	6,593	97	3,001	1,511	1,957
Male householder, no spouse present	752	49	206	262	225
PERCENT OF CHILDREN IN POVERTY					
All family types	**16.3**	**10.7**	**31.3**	**28.2**	**9.0**
Married couple families	8.5	7.3	11.0	21.3	4.9
Female householder, no spouse present	39.6	27.1	46.9	47.8	29.1
Male householder, no spouse present	20.3	31.4	30.4	28.8	12.0
PERCENT DISTRIBUTION OF POOR CHILDREN BY TYPE OF FAMILY					
All family types	**100.0%**	**100.0%**	**100.0%**	**100.0%**	**100.0%**
Married couple families	37.2	57.4	14.4	51.8	43.5
Female householder, no spouse present	56.3	28.5	80.1	41.1	50.6
Male householder, no spouse present	6.4	14.4	5.5	7.1	5.8
PERCENT DISTRIBUTION OF POOR CHILDREN BY RACE AND HISPANIC ORIGIN					
All family types	**100.0%**	**2.9%**	**32.0%**	**31.4%**	**33.0%**
Married couple families	100.0	4.5	12.4	43.7	38.6
Female householder, no spouse present	100.0	1.5	45.5	22.9	29.7
Male householder, no spouse present	100.0	6.5	27.4	34.8	29.9

Note: Numbers will not add to total because each racial group includes those identifying themselves as being of the race alone and those identifying themselves as being of the race in combination with other races. Hispanics may be of any race. Non-Hispanic whites include only those identifying themselves as white alone and non-Hispanic.
Source: Bureau of the Census, 2003 Current Population Survey, Annual Social and Economic Supplement, http://ferret.bls.census.gov/macro/032003/pov/new02_100.htm; calculations by New Strategist

6

Labor Force

■ The percentage of men and women under age 30 who are in the labor force fell sharply between 2000 and 2003. The decline was particularly steep among teenagers.

■ Fifteen percent of the nation's workers are under age 25 and one in four is under age 30. Fully 31 percent of the nation's unemployed are under age 25, and 43 percent are under age 30.

■ A substantial 36 percent of black men aged 16 to 19 are unemployed. In contrast, only 17 percent of white men in the age group are unemployed.

■ Workers under age 25 account for 53 percent of waiters and waitresses, 49 percent of cashiers, 34 percent of cooks, 33 percent of stock clerks, and 32 percent of laborers.

■ Among 16- and 17-year-old workers, 87 percent of men and 92 percent of women hold part-time jobs. Among 18- and 19-year-olds, part-time work is still the norm.

■ Between 2003 and 2012, the Millennial generation will fill the young adult age group. The number of workers aged 20 to 34 will expand by 10 percent during those years.

■ For the Millennial generation, working parents are the norm. Sixty-one percent of married couples with children under age 18 are dual earners.

Fewer Young Adults Are at Work

Labor force participation rates have fallen sharply among young men and women.

The percentage of men and women under age 30 who are in the labor force fell sharply between 2000 and 2003. The decline was particularly steep among teenagers. In 2003, only 44 percent of men aged 16 to 19 were in the labor force, down from the 53 percent majority in 2000 and an even larger 56 percent in 1990. Among their female counterparts, labor force participation fell from 51 to 45 percent between 2000 and 2003. Labor force participation rates are also down among people in their twenties.

The recession of 2001 and massive job losses are factors behind young adults' declining labor force participation rate. Another factor is the increasing proportion of high school graduates who go to college. In a tight labor market, many college students may not even bother looking for a job.

■ When the U.S. labor market begins to grow again, the labor force participation rate of teenagers is likely to rise.

A shrinking share of teens are in the labor force

(percent of people aged 16 to 19 in the labor force, by sex, 2000 and 2003)

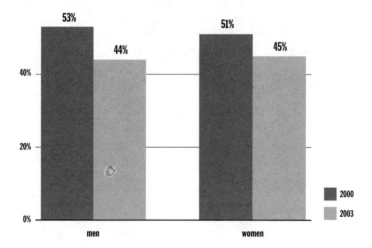

Table 6.1 Labor Force Participation Rate of People under Age 30 by Sex, 1990 to 2003

(civilian labor force participation rate of people aged 16 or older and under age 30, by sex, 1990 to 2003; percentage point change, 2000–2003 and 1990–2003)

				percentage point change	
	2003	2000	1990	2000–03	1990–03
Men aged 16 or older	**73.5%**	**74.8%**	**76.4%**	**−1.3**	**−2.9**
Aged 16 to 19	44.3	52.8	55.7	−8.5	−11.4
Aged 16 to 17	32.2	40.9	43.5	−8.7	−11.3
Aged 18 to 19	58.2	65.0	67.1	−6.8	−8.9
Aged 20 to 24	80.0	82.6	84.4	−2.6	−4.4
Aged 25 to 29	90.6	92.5	93.7	−1.9	−3.1
Women aged 16 or older	**59.5**	**59.9**	**57.9**	**−0.4**	**1.6**
Aged 16 to 19	44.8	51.2	51.6	−6.4	−6.8
Aged 16 to 17	34.6	40.8	41.7	−6.2	−7.1
Aged 18 to 19	56.3	61.3	60.3	−5.0	−4.0
Aged 20 to 24	70.8	73.1	71.3	−2.3	−0.5
Aged 25 to 29	74.4	76.7	73.6	−2.3	0.8

Source: Bureau of Labor Statistics, Public Query Data Tool, Internet site http://www.bls.gov/data; calculations by New Strategist

Labor Force Rates Are Low among Teens

More than half of 18-to-19-year-olds are in the labor force, however.

Fifteen percent of the nation's workers are under age 25 and one in four is under age 30. As the large Millennial generation fills the young-adult age group, the number of young workers is rising. Restraining this growth, however, is higher education. Only 57 percent of 18-to-19-year-olds are in the labor force, in large part because most in the age group are attending college, which limits their work options. Among 20-to-24-year-olds, labor force participation rises to 75 percent. Until age 20 to 24, there is little difference in labor force participation rates by sex.

Fully 31 percent of the nation's unemployed are under age 25, and 43 percent are under age 30. While the unemployment rate stood at 6 percent among all workers, it was a much higher 17 percent among 16-to-19-year-olds and 10 percent among 20-to-24-year-olds.

■ Young adults are much more likely to be unemployed than older workers because they are more often between jobs as they look for the right position and because entry-level workers are more likely to be let go during layoffs.

Teen labor force participation is relatively low

(labor force participation rate of people under age 25, by age, 2003)

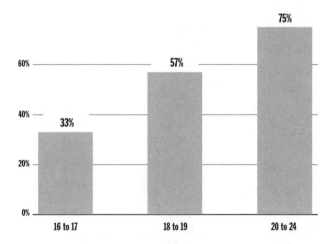

Table 6.2 Employment Status by Sex and Age, 2003

(number and percent of people aged 16 or older in the civilian labor force by sex, age, and employment status, 2003; numbers in thousands)

	civilian noninstitutional population	civilian labor force			unemployed	
		total	percent of population	employed	number	percent of labor force
Total, aged 16 or older	**221,168**	**146,510**	**66.2%**	**137,736**	**8,774**	**6.0%**
Aged 16 to 19	16,096	7,170	44.5	5,919	1,251	17.4
Aged 16 to 17	8,561	2,857	33.4	2,312	545	19.1
Aged 18 to 19	7,535	4,313	57.2	3,607	706	16.4
Aged 20 to 24	19,801	14,928	75.4	13,433	1,495	10.0
Aged 25 to 29	18,625	15,357	82.5	14,339	1,018	6.6
Aged 30 to 64	132,392	104,264	78.8	99,437	4,827	4.6
Aged 65 or older	34,253	4,792	14.0	4,608	183	3.8
Men, aged 16 or older	**106,435**	**78,238**	**73.5**	**73,332**	**4,906**	**6.3**
Aged 16 to 19	8,163	3,614	44.3	2,917	697	19.3
Aged 16 to 17	4,365	1,405	32.2	1,115	291	20.7
Aged 18 to 19	3,797	2,209	58.2	1,802	407	18.4
Aged 20 to 24	9,878	7,906	80.0	7,065	841	10.6
Aged 25 to 29	9,262	8,395	90.6	7,817	578	6.9
Aged 30 to 64	64,637	55,628	86.1	52,948	2,683	4.8
Aged 65 or older	14,496	2,692	18.6	2,585	107	4.0
Women, aged 16 or older	**114,733**	**68,272**	**59.5**	**64,404**	**3,868**	**5.7**
Aged 16 to 19	7,934	3,556	44.8	3,002	554	15.6
Aged 16 to 17	4,195	1,452	34.6	1,197	255	17.6
Aged 18 to 19	3,738	2,104	56.3	1,805	299	14.2
Aged 20 to 24	9,924	7,021	70.7	6,367	654	9.3
Aged 25 to 29	9,363	6,962	74.4	6,522	440	6.3
Aged 30 to 64	67,756	48,635	71.8	46,489	2,144	4.4
Aged 65 or older	19,758	2,099	10.6	2,023	76	3.6

Source: Bureau of Labor Statistics, 2003 Current Population Survey, Internet site http://www.bls.gov/cps/home.htm; calculations by New Strategist

Asian and Black Teens Are Least Likely to Work

Young black men are most likely to be unemployed.

Among teenagers, the labor force participation rate is higher for whites than for Asians, blacks, or Hispanics. While 48 percent of white men aged 16 to 19 are in the labor force, the figure is just 31 percent among blacks, 32 percent among Asians, and 41 percent among Hispanics. The pattern is the same for women. The differences are pronounced in the 20-to-24 age group as well. Among Asian men aged 20 to 24, only 66 percent are in the labor force compared to 83 percent of white men and 86 percent of Hispanic men. One reason for the low labor force participation rate of Asian men is their high college attendance rate.

Unemployment is much higher for black teens than it is for Asians, Hispanics, or whites. Fully 36 percent of black men aged 16 to 19 are unemployed—meaning they want a job but cannot find one. In contrast, only 17 percent of white men in the age group are unemployed. Among women age 16 to 19, the comparable unemployment figures are 30 percent for blacks and 13 percent for whites.

■ The jobless recovery is hurting many, especially young black men.

More than one-third of black teens are unemployed

(percent of men aged 16 to 19 who are unemployed, by race and Hispanic origin, 2003)

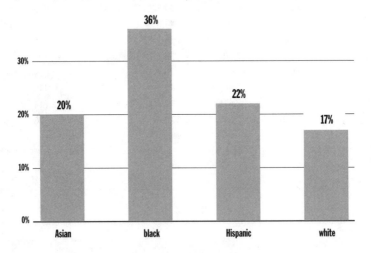

Table 6.3 Employment Status of Men by Race, Hispanic Origin, and Age, 2003

(number and percent of men aged 16 or older in the civilian labor force by race, Hispanic origin, age, and employment status, 2003; numbers in thousands)

	civilian noninstitutional population	civilian labor force			unemployed	
		total	percent of population	employed	number	percent of labor force
ASIAN MEN						
Total aged 16 or older	**4,338**	**3,277**	**75.5%**	**3,073**	**204**	**6.2%**
Aged 16 to 19	313	101	32.2	80	21	20.3
Aged 16 to 17	165	33	19.9	24	8	25.7
Aged 18 to 19	148	68	45.9	56	12	17.8
Aged 20 to 24	410	272	66.4	245	27	9.9
Aged 25 to 29	491	409	83.3	386	23	5.6
Aged 30 to 64	2,716	2,413	88.8	2,282	130	5.4
Aged 65 or older	409	83	20.3	79	4	4.5
BLACK MEN						
Total aged 16 or older	**11,454**	**7,711**	**67.3**	**6,820**	**891**	**11.6**
Aged 16 to 19	1,176	365	31.1	234	132	36.0
Aged 16 to 17	661	138	20.9	89	49	35.6
Aged 18 to 19	515	228	44.2	145	83	36.3
Aged 20 to 24	1,291	918	71.1	726	192	20.9
Aged 25 to 29	1,075	878	81.7	755	123	14.0
Aged 30 to 64	6,819	5,364	78.7	4,930	435	8.1
Aged 65 or older	1,093	186	17.0	176	10	5.6
HISPANIC MEN						
Total aged 16 or older	**14,098**	**11,288**	**80.1**	**10,479**	**809**	**7.2**
Aged 16 to 19	1,301	532	40.9	415	116	21.9
Aged 16 to 17	674	164	24.3	121	42	25.9
Aged 18 to 19	627	368	58.7	294	74	20.1
Aged 20 to 24	1,905	1,642	86.2	1,485	157	9.6
Aged 25 to 29	2,073	1,927	93.0	1,807	120	6.2
Aged 30 to 64	7,958	7,036	88.4	6,627	480	6.8
Aged 65 or older	862	150	17.4	144	5	3.6
WHITE MEN						
Total aged 16 or older	**88,249**	**65,509**	**74.2**	**61,866**	**3,643**	**5.6**
Aged 16 to 19	6,390	3,036	47.5	2,518	518	17.1
Aged 16 to 17	3,378	1,193	35.3	972	221	18.5
Aged 18 to 19	3,012	1,843	61.2	1,546	298	16.1
Aged 20 to 24	7,856	6,479	82.5	5,890	589	9.1
Aged 25 to 29	7,442	6,883	92.5	6,470	413	6.0
Aged 30 to 64	53,744	46,725	86.9	44,694	2,032	4.3
Aged 65 or older	12,818	2,386	18.6	2,295	91	3.8

Note: Race is shown only for those selecting that race group only. People who selected more than one race are not included. Hispanics may be of any race.
Source: Bureau of Labor Statistics, 2003 Current Population Survey, Internet site http://www.bls.gov/cps/home.htm; calculations by New Strategist

Table 6.4 Employment Status of Women by Race, Hispanic Origin, and Age, 2003

(number and percent of women aged 16 or older in the civilian labor force by race, Hispanic origin, age, and employment status, 2003; numbers in thousands)

	civilian noninstitutional population	civilian labor force			unemployed	
		total	percent of population	employed	number	percent of labor force
ASIAN WOMEN						
Total aged 16 or older	4,882	2,845	58.3%	2,683	162	5.7%
Aged 16 to 19	288	77	26.7	66	11	13.8
Aged 16 to 17	148	31	21.2	27	4	12.4
Aged 18 to 19	140	46	32.6	39	7	14.8
Aged 20 to 24	444	252	56.9	232	20	8.1
Aged 25 to 29	531	347	65.3	330	17	4.8
Aged 30 to 64	3,065	2,121	69.2	2,007	113	5.3
Aged 65 or older	555	48	8.7	47	1	3.1
BLACK WOMEN						
Total aged 16 or older	14,232	8,815	61.9	7,919	895	10.2
Aged 16 to 19	1,206	406	33.7	283	123	30.3
Aged 16 to 17	648	151	23.3	107	44	29.1
Aged 18 to 19	558	255	45.6	175	79	31.1
Aged 20 to 24	1,482	973	65.7	790	183	18.8
Aged 25 to 29	1,342	1,045	77.9	919	126	12.1
Aged 30 to 64	8,448	6,209	73.5	5,756	455	7.3
Aged 65 or older	1,753	180	10.3	171	10	5.3
HISPANIC WOMEN						
Total aged 16 or older	13,452	7,525	55.9	6,894	631	8.4
Aged 16 to 19	1,242	428	34.5	353	76	17.7
Aged 16 to 17	672	158	23.5	121	37	23.2
Aged 18 to 19	570	271	47.7	231	39	14.4
Aged 20 to 24	1,628	1,030	63.3	914	116	11.3
Aged 25 to 29	1,736	1,071	61.7	970	102	9.5
Aged 30 to 64	7,683	4,886	63.6	4,552	334	6.8
Aged 65 or older	1,166	109	9.4	105	5	4.4
WHITE WOMEN						
Total aged 16 or older	93,043	55,037	59.2	52,369	2,668	4.8
Aged 16 to 19	6,137	2,937	47.9	2,546	391	13.3
Aged 16 to 17	3,251	1,221	37.6	1,027	194	15.9
Aged 18 to 19	2,886	1,716	59.5	1,519	197	11.5
Aged 20 to 24	7,680	5,584	72.7	5,161	423	7.6
Aged 25 to 29	7,214	5,358	74.3	5,080	278	5.2
Aged 30 to 64	54,796	39,303	71.7	37,793	1,510	3.8
Aged 65 or older	17,216	1,852	10.8	1,788	64	3.5

Note: Race is shown only for those selecting that race group only. People who selected more than one race are not included. Hispanics may be of any race.
Source: Bureau of Labor Statistics, 2003 Current Population Survey, Internet site http://www.bls.gov/cps/home.htm; calculations by New Strategist

Most College Students Are Not in the Labor Force

Among college students, women are more likely to work than men.

Most of today's high school graduates go to college. Among high school graduates in 2002, 65 percent were enrolled in college in October of that year—62 percent of men and 68 percent of women.

College students are far less likely to be in the labor force than those who are not in college. Among 2002 high school graduates, only 45 percent of those who enrolled in college were in the labor force compared to a much larger 80 percent of those who did not go to college. Interestingly, female college students are more likely to work than their male counterparts. Among 2002 high school graduates, 47 percent of college women were in the labor force versus a smaller 44 percent of college men. In contrast, among 2002 high school graduates who did not go to college, men were more likely than women to be in the labor force (83 versus 76 percent).

■ The labor force participation rate of college students may rise as jobs become more plentiful.

A minority of college students are in the labor force

(labor force participation rate of 2002 high school graduates by college enrollment status, 2002)

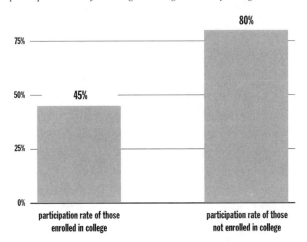

Table 6.5 College Enrollment and Labor Force Participation of 2002 High School Graduates

(number and percent distribution of 2002 high school graduates, by sex, college enrollment, and labor force status, October 2002; numbers in thousands)

	total		in labor force		
	number	percent distribution	number	percent distribution	percent in labor force
Total 2002 high school graduates	**2,796**	**100.0%**	**1,604**	**100.0%**	**57.4%**
Enrolled in college	1,824	65.2	829	51.7	45.4
Not enrolled in college	972	34.8	775	48.3	79.7
Male 2002 high school graduates	**1,412**	**100.0**	**829**	**100.0**	**58.7**
Enrolled in college	877	62.1	385	46.4	43.9
Not enrolled in college	535	37.9	444	53.6	83.0
Female 2002 high school graduates	**1,384**	**100.0**	**774**	**100.0**	**55.9**
Enrolled in college	947	68.4	444	57.4	46.9
Not enrolled in college	437	31.6	330	42.6	75.5

Source: Bureau of Labor Statistics, College Enrollment and Work Activity of 2002 High School Graduates, *USDL 03-330, 2003; calculations by New Strategist*

Most Couples under Age 30 Are Dual Earners

The husband is the sole support of only 30 percent of young couples.

Dual incomes are by far the norm among married couples. Both husband and wife are in the labor force in 56 percent of the nation's couples. In another 22 percent, the husband is the only worker. Not far behind are the 17 percent of couples in which neither spouse is in the labor force. The wife is the sole worker among 6 percent of couples.

Sixty-six percent of couples under age 30 are dual earners. The proportion is just 45 percent among the few married couples under age 20, but leaps to 61 percent among those aged 20 to 24, and rises to 69 percent among those aged 25 to 29. The proportion peaks among couples aged 40 to 54. The dual-earner share falls to just 46 percent among couples aged 55 to 64, in part because of early retirement.

■ The proportion of couples in which the husband is the sole earner is highest among the youngest adults because many wives are at home with newborns.

The youngest couples are most likely to be supported solely by the husband

(percent of married couples in which only the husband is in the labor force, by age, 2002)

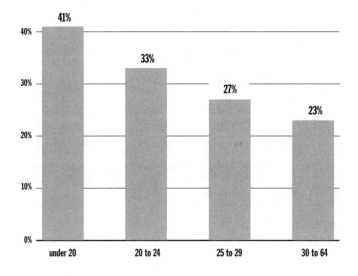

Table 6.6 Labor Force Status of Married-Couple Family Groups by Age of Reference Person, 2002

(number and percent distribution of married-couple family groups by age of reference person and labor force status of husband and wife, 2002; numbers in thousands)

	total	husband and/or wife in labor force husband and wife	husband only	wife only	neither husband nor wife in labor force
Total married-couple family groups	**57,919**	**32,194**	**12,672**	**3,470**	**9,583**
Under age 30	5,474	3,604	1,615	156	98
Under age 20	137	62	56	8	10
Aged 20 to 24	1,574	956	526	61	31
Aged 25 to 29	3,763	2,586	1,033	87	57
Aged 30 to 34	5,889	3,964	1,693	131	102
Aged 35 to 39	6,919	4,739	1,857	207	115
Aged 40 to 44	7,499	5,424	1,686	261	128
Aged 45 to 54	13,375	9,457	2,774	683	460
Aged 55 to 64	9,062	4,206	2,003	1,127	1,726
Aged 65 or older	9,702	797	1,045	905	6,953
PERCENT DISTRIBUTION					
Total married-couple family groups	**100.0%**	**55.6%**	**21.9%**	**6.0%**	**16.5%**
Under age 30	100.0	65.8	29.5	2.8	1.8
Under age 20	100.0	45.3	40.9	5.8	7.3
Aged 20 to 24	100.0	60.7	33.4	3.9	2.0
Aged 25 to 29	100.0	68.7	27.5	2.3	1.5
Aged 30 to 34	100.0	67.3	28.7	2.2	1.7
Aged 35 to 39	100.0	68.5	26.8	3.0	1.7
Aged 40 to 44	100.0	72.3	22.5	3.5	1.7
Aged 45 to 54	100.0	70.7	20.7	5.1	3.4
Aged 55 to 64	100.0	46.4	22.1	12.4	19.1
Aged 65 or older	100.0	8.2	10.8	9.3	71.7

Note: Number of married-couple family groups exceeds number of married-couple householders because some households contain more than one married couple.
Source: Bureau of the Census, 2002 Current Population Survey Annual Demographic Supplement, Internet site http://www.census.gov/population/www/socdemo/hh-fam/cps2002.html; calculations by New Strategist

The Youngest Workers Dominate Many Entry-Level Positions

They account for the majority of child care workers.

Among the 138 million employed Americans in 2003, only 19 million were under age 25—or 14 percent. In some occupations, however, workers under age 25 account for a disproportionately large share. While people aged 16 to 24 are only 6 percent of the nation's managers and professionals, they are 42 percent of food preparation workers.

Workers under age 25 account for 53 percent of waiters and waitresses, 49 percent of cashiers, 34 percent of cooks, 33 percent of stock clerks, and 32 percent of laborers. Most young adults will move out of these entry-level positions as they earn educational credentials and gain job experience. Not surprisingly, young adults account for 35 percent of the nation's athletes. They are also disproportionately well-represented among retail salespersons (30 percent), child care workers (28 percent), security guards (21 percent), customer service representatives (21 percent), and actors (20 percent).

■ Young adults account for a large share of workers in occupations with considerable public contact. Employers should train young adults to relate well to middle-aged and older people if they want customers to return.

Young adult workers often come in contact with the public

(percent of workers under age 25 by occupation, 2003)

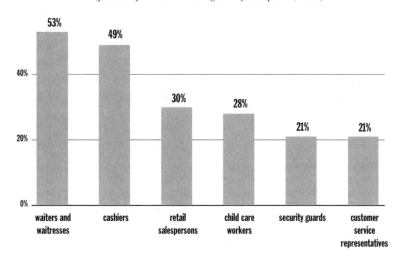

Table 6.7 Occupations of Workers under Age 35, 2003

(number of employed workers aged 16 or older, median age of workers, and number of workers under age 35, by occupation, 2003; numbers in thousands)

	total	median age	under age 25 total	16 to 19	20 to 24	25 to 34
TOTAL WORKERS	**137,736**	**40.4**	**19,352**	**5,919**	**13,433**	**30,383**
Management and professional occupations	**47,929**	**42.6**	**2,978**	**354**	**2,624**	**10,822**
Management, business and financial operations	19,934	44.0	822	53	769	3,839
Management	14,468	44.7	475	37	438	2,526
Business and financial operations	5,465	42.1	347	16	331	1,313
Professional and related occupations	27,995	41.5	2,156	301	1,855	6,984
Computer and mathematical	3,122	38.6	225	18	207	1,050
Architecture and engineering	2,727	41.5	168	12	156	650
Life, physical, and social sciences	1,375	41.2	108	11	97	383
Community and social services	2,184	43.1	166	14	152	497
Legal	1,508	43.1	74	6	68	360
Education, training, and library	7,768	42.6	686	123	563	1,782
Arts, design, entertainment, sports, and media	2,663	40.0	330	83	247	677
Health care practitioner and technician	6,648	41.9	397	33	364	1,584
Service occupations	**22,086**	**36.3**	**5,607**	**2,284**	**3,323**	**4,847**
Health care support	2,926	38.1	511	113	398	720
Protective service	2,727	39.9	359	103	256	663
Food preparation and serving	7,254	28.6	3,081	1,435	1,646	1,533
Building and grounds cleaning and maintenance	4,947	40.8	735	269	466	993
Personal care and service	4,232	37.9	921	365	556	938
Sales and office occupations	**35,496**	**39.7**	**6,418**	**2,176**	**4,242**	**7,293**
Sales and related occupations	15,960	38.8	3,346	1,362	1,984	3,258
Office and administrative support	19,536	40.5	3,072	814	2,258	4,035
Natural resources, construction, and maintenance occupations	**14,205**	**38.9**	**2,012**	**476**	**1,536**	**3,562**
Farming, fishing, and forestry	1,050	36.7	233	105	128	260
Construction and extraction	8,114	38.2	1,217	264	953	2,151
Installation, maintenance, and repair	5,041	40.4	562	107	455	1,152
Production, transportation, and material moving occupations	**18,020**	**40.7**	**2,337**	**629**	**1,708**	**3,858**
Production	9,700	41.1	1,052	196	856	2,088
Transportation and material moving	8,320	40.1	1,285	433	852	1,770

Source: Bureau of Labor Statistics, unpublished data from the 2003 Current Population Survey; calculations by New Strategist

Table 6.8 Distribution of Workers under Age 35 by Occupation, 2003

(percent distribution of employed people aged 16 or older and under age 35 by occupation, 2003)

	total	under age 25 total	16 to 19	20 to 24	25 to 34
TOTAL WORKERS	**100.0%**	**100.0%**	**100.0%**	**100.0%**	**100.0%**
Management and professional occupations	**34.8**	**15.4**	**6.0**	**19.5**	**35.6**
Management, business and financial operations	14.5	4.2	0.9	5.7	12.6
Management	10.5	2.5	0.6	3.3	8.3
Business and financial operations	4.0	1.8	0.3	2.5	4.3
Professional and related occupations	20.3	11.1	5.1	13.8	23.0
Computer and mathematical	2.3	1.2	0.3	1.5	3.5
Architecture and engineering	2.0	0.9	0.2	1.2	2.1
Life, physical, and social sciences	1.0	0.6	0.2	0.7	1.3
Community and social services	1.6	0.9	0.2	1.1	1.6
Legal	1.1	0.4	0.1	0.5	1.2
Education, training, and library	5.6	3.5	2.1	4.2	5.9
Arts, design, entertainment, sports, and media	1.9	1.7	1.4	1.8	2.2
Health care practitioner and technician	4.8	2.1	0.6	2.7	5.2
Service occupations	**16.0**	**29.0**	**38.6**	**24.7**	**16.0**
Health care support	2.1	2.6	1.9	3.0	2.4
Protective service	2.0	1.9	1.7	1.9	2.2
Food preparation and serving	5.3	15.9	24.2	12.3	5.1
Building and grounds cleaning and maintenance	3.6	3.8	4.5	3.5	3.3
Personal care and service	3.1	4.8	6.2	4.1	3.1
Sales and office occupations	**25.8**	**33.2**	**36.8**	**31.6**	**2.4**
Sales and related occupations	11.6	17.3	23.0	14.8	10.7
Office and administrative support	14.2	15.9	13.8	16.8	13.3
Natural resources, construction, and maintenance occupations	**10.3**	**10.4**	**8.0**	**11.4**	**11.7**
Farming, fishing, and forestry	0.8	1.2	1.8	1.0	0.9
Construction and extraction	5.9	6.3	4.5	7.1	7.1
Installation, maintenance, and repair	3.7	2.9	1.8	3.4	3.8
Production, transportation, and material moving occupations	**13.1**	**12.1**	**10.6**	**12.7**	**12.7**
Production	7.0	5.4	3.3	6.4	6.9
Transportation and material moving	6.0	6.6	7.3	6.3	5.8

Source: Calculations by New Strategist based on Bureau of Labor Statistics' unpublished 2003 Current Population Survey data

Table 6.9 Share of Workers under Age 35 by Occupation, 2003

(employed people under age 35 as a percent of total employed people aged 16 or older by occupation, 2003)

	total	under age 25 total	16 to 19	20 to 24	25 to 34
TOTAL WORKERS	100.0%	14.1%	4.3%	9.8%	22.1%
Management and professional occupations	**100.0**	**6.2**	**0.7**	**5.5**	**22.6**
Management, business and financial operations	100.0	4.1	0.3	3.9	19.3
Management	100.0	3.3	0.3	3.0	17.5
Business and financial operations	100.0	6.3	0.3	6.1	24.0
Professional and related occupations	100.0	7.7	1.1	6.6	24.9
Computer and mathematical	100.0	7.2	0.6	6.6	33.6
Architecture and engineering	100.0	6.2	0.4	5.7	23.8
Life, physical, and social sciences	100.0	7.9	0.8	7.1	27.9
Community and social services	100.0	7.6	0.6	7.0	22.8
Legal	100.0	4.9	0.4	4.5	23.9
Education, training, and library	100.0	8.8	1.6	7.2	22.9
Arts, design, entertainment, sports, and media	100.0	12.4	3.1	9.3	25.4
Health care practitioner and technician	100.0	6.0	0.5	5.5	23.8
Service occupations	**100.0**	**25.4**	**10.3**	**15.1**	**21.9**
Health care support	100.0	17.5	3.9	13.6	24.6
Protective service	100.0	13.2	3.8	9.4	24.3
Food preparation and serving	100.0	42.5	19.8	22.7	21.1
Building and grounds cleaning and maintenance	100.0	14.9	5.4	9.4	20.1
Personal care and service	100.0	21.8	8.6	13.1	22.2
Sales and office occupations	**100.0**	**18.1**	**6.1**	**12.0**	**20.5**
Sales and related occupations	100.0	21.0	8.5	12.4	20.4
Office and administrative support	100.0	15.7	4.2	11.6	20.7
Natural resources, construction, and maintenance occupations	**100.0**	**14.2**	**3.4**	**10.8**	**25.1**
Farming, fishing, and forestry	100.0	22.2	10.0	12.2	24.8
Construction and extraction	100.0	15.0	3.3	11.7	26.5
Installation, maintenance, and repair	100.0	11.1	2.1	9.0	22.9
Production, transportation, and material moving occupations	**100.0**	**13.0**	**3.5**	**9.5**	**21.4**
Production	100.0	10.8	2.0	8.8	21.5
Transportation and material moving	100.0	15.4	5.2	10.2	21.3

Source: Calculations by New Strategist based on Bureau of Labor Statistics' unpublished 2003 Current Population Survey data

Table 6.10 Workers under Age 35 by Detailed Occupation, 2003

(number of employed workers aged 16 or older, median age, and number and percent under age 35, by selected detailed occupation, 2003; numbers in thousands)

| | | | under age 25 | | | | | | | |
| | | | total | | aged 16 to 19 | | aged 20 to 24 | | aged 25 to 34 | |
	total workers	median age	number	percent of total	number	percent of total	number	percent of total	number	percent of total
Total workers	137,736	40.4	19,352	14.1%	5,919	4.3%	13,433	9.8%	30,383	22.1%
Chief executives	1,617	48.2	6	0.4	1	0.1	5	0.3	153	9.5
Legislators	14	53.2	1	7.1	–	–	1	7.1	–	–
Marketing and sales managers	888	41.6	35	3.9	1	0.1	34	3.8	227	25.6
Computer and information systems managers	347	41.7	7	2.0	1	0.3	6	1.7	83	23.9
Financial managers	1,041	42.1	38	3.7	3	0.3	35	3.4	233	22.4
Human resources managers	263	45.1	6	2.3	–	–	6	2.3	45	17.1
Farmers and ranchers	825	54.0	17	2.1	4	0.5	13	1.6	82	9.9
Education administrators	748	48.9	24	3.2	2	0.3	22	2.9	94	12.6
Food service managers	875	39.5	110	12.6	10	1.1	100	11.4	220	25.1
Medical and health services managers	480	46.1	6	1.2	–	–	6	1.2	76	15.8
Accountants and auditors	1,639	41.1	103	6.3	4	0.2	99	6.0	436	26.6
Computer scientists and systems analysts	722	40.4	52	7.2	5	0.7	47	6.5	194	26.9
Computer programmers	563	38.7	37	6.6	2	0.4	35	6.2	182	32.3
Computer software engineers	758	38.3	31	4.1	1	0.1	30	4.0	287	37.9
Architects	180	42.0	5	2.8	–	–	5	2.8	51	28.3
Civil engineers	278	42.9	8	2.9	–	–	8	2.9	67	24.1
Electrical engineers	363	42.7	15	4.1	–	–	15	4.1	72	19.8
Mechanical engineers	285	41.0	11	3.9	–	–	11	3.9	77	27.0
Medical scientists	101	39.9	4	4.0	–	–	4	4.0	32	31.7
Psychologists	185	50.2	2	1.1	–	–	2	1.1	31	16.8
Social workers	673	41.4	45	6.7	1	0.1	44	6.5	182	27.0
Clergy	410	49.9	11	2.7	–	–	11	2.7	52	12.7
Lawyers	952	44.4	14	1.5	1	0.1	13	1.4	224	23.5
Postsecondary teachers	1,121	43.8	93	8.3	7	0.6	86	7.7	252	22.5
Preschool, kindergarten teachers	665	38.9	89	13.4	15	2.3	74	11.1	192	28.9
Elementary and middle school teachers	2,557	42.7	152	5.9	3	0.1	149	5.8	651	25.5
Secondary school teachers	1,124	43.7	49	4.4	4	0.4	45	4.0	280	24.9
Librarians	194	49.6	12	6.2	2	1.0	10	5.2	25	12.9
Teacher assistants	932	41.8	131	14.1	35	3.8	96	10.3	153	16.4
Artists	212	43.8	15	7.1	4	1.9	11	5.2	42	19.8
Actors	30	36.6	6	20.0	1	3.3	5	16.7	9	30.0
Athletes	215	30.1	76	35.3	36	16.7	40	18.6	57	26.5
Editors	163	40.8	17	10.4	1	0.6	16	9.8	47	28.8
Writers and authors	190	44.8	9	4.7	–	–	9	4.7	38	20.0
Dentists	188	46.0	2	1.1	–	–	2	1.1	29	15.4
Pharmacists	232	42.1	11	4.7	2	0.9	9	3.9	66	28.4
Physicians and surgeons	819	44.2	6	0.7	–	–	6	0.7	171	20.9
Registered nurses	2,449	43.1	78	3.2	3	0.1	75	3.1	533	21.8

| | | | under age 25 | | | | | | | |
| | | total | | aged 16 to 19 | | aged 20 to 24 | | aged 25 to 34 | |
	total workers	median age	number	percent of total	number	percent of total	number	percent of total	number	percent of total
Physical therapists	182	37.6	8	4.4%	–	–	8	4.4%	77	42.3%
Licensed practical nurses	531	43.3	34	6.4	1	0.2%	33	6.2	98	18.5
Nursing, psychiatric, and home health aides	1,811	39.2	300	16.6	65	3.6	235	13.0	415	22.9
Firefighters	258	38.3	18	7.0	1	0.4	17	6.6	93	36.1
Police, sheriff's patrol officers	612	38.7	35	5.7	1	0.2	34	5.6	216	35.3
Security guards and gaming surveillance officers	781	40.7	161	20.6	23	2.9	138	17.7	153	19.6
Chefs and head cooks	281	37.8	41	14.6	5	1.8	36	12.8	79	28.1
Cooks	1,814	32.1	609	33.6	276	15.2	333	18.4	423	23.3
Food preparation workers	612	29.4	253	41.3	146	23.9	107	17.5	118	19.3
Waiters and waitresses	1,842	24.6	979	53.1	360	19.5	619	33.6	390	21.2
Janitors and building cleaners	1,973	43.2	268	13.6	119	6.0	149	7.6	310	15.7
Maids, housekeeping cleaners	1,370	42.2	134	9.8	35	2.6	99	7.2	274	20.0
Grounds maintenance workers	1,135	34.1	302	26.6	111	9.8	191	16.8	285	25.1
Hairdressers, hair stylists, and cosmetologists	718	39.0	94	13.1	19	2.6	75	10.4	192	26.7
Child care workers	1,284	35.4	358	27.9	161	12.5	197	15.3	289	22.5
Cashiers	2,903	26.1	1,425	49.1	792	27.3	633	21.8	490	16.9
Retail salespersons	3,113	35.9	948	30.5	365	11.7	583	18.7	560	18.0
Insurance sales agents	552	44.1	35	6.3	3	0.5	32	5.8	113	20.5
Securities, commodities, and financial services sale	389	39.8	24	6.2	1	0.3	23	5.9	126	32.4
Sales representatives, wholesale and manufacturing	1,399	41.7	95	6.8	22	1.6	73	5.2	317	22.7
Real estate brokers, sales agents	850	48.6	26	3.1	3	0.4	23	2.7	144	16.9
Bookkeeping, accounting, and auditing clerks	1,545	44.5	117	7.6	13	0.8	104	6.7	263	17.0
Customer service reps.	1,747	36.0	359	20.5	88	5.0	271	15.5	486	27.8
Receptionists, information clerks	1,376	36.9	380	27.6	136	9.9	244	17.7	266	19.3
Stock clerks and order fillers	1,360	33.6	444	32.6	193	14.2	251	18.5	271	19.9
Secretaries and administrative assistants	3,632	43.7	316	8.7	59	1.6	257	7.1	626	17.2
Misc. agricultural workers	741	33.8	202	27.3	96	13.0	106	14.3	201	27.1
Carpenters	1,595	37.4	250	15.7	45	2.8	205	12.9	448	28.1
Construction laborers	1,151	34.8	273	23.7	87	7.6	186	16.2	315	27.4
Automotive service technicians and mechanics	884	37.6	164	18.6	33	3.7	131	14.8	220	24.9
Misc. assemblers, fabricators	1,080	39.9	138	12.8	29	2.7	109	10.1	266	24.6
Machinists	454	42.3	37	8.1	3	0.7	34	7.5	86	18.9
Aircraft pilots, flight engineers	116	44.2	3	2.6	–	–	3	2.6	19	16.4
Driver/sales workers and truck drivers	3,214	42.1	279	8.7	66	2.1	213	6.6	713	22.2
Freight, stock and material movers, hand laborers	1,748	33.4	557	31.9	239	13.7	318	18.2	386	22.1

Note: (–) means number is less than 500 or sample is too small to make a reliable estimate.
Source: Bureau of Labor Statistics, unpublished tables from the 2003 Current Population Survey; calculations by New Strategist

The Youngest Workers Are Part-timers

Among 20-to-24-year-olds, however, most work full-time.

Among people aged 16 or older in the civilian labor force, 11 percent of men and 26 percent of women work part-time. Among 16- and 17-year-old workers, however, 87 percent of men and 92 percent of women hold part-time jobs. Most are high school students with after-school jobs in fast-food restaurants and other entry-level positions.

Among 18- and 19-year-olds in the labor force, part-time is still the norm. Among working men in the age group, 52 percent work part-time, as do 65 percent of their female counterparts. Young women are more likely than young men to work part-time because women are more likely to attend college.

Among 20-to-24-year-olds in the labor force, the majority of both men and women work full-time. Nevertheless, a substantial 23 percent of men and 35 percent of women work part-time.

■ With more high school students going to college, part-time work is becoming increasingly important in the educational plans of young adults.

Part-time work is common among teens

(percent of people aged 16 to 24 in the civilian labor force who work part-time, by, sex, 2003)

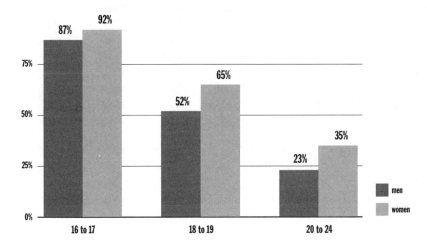

Table 6.11 Full- and Part-time Workers by Age and Sex, 2003

(number and percent distribution of employd people aged 16 or older in the civilian labor force by full- and part-time employment status, by age and sex, 2003; numbers in thousands)

	men			women		
	total	full-time	part-time	total	full-time	part-time
Total employed	**73,332**	**65,379**	**7,953**	**64,405**	**47,946**	**16,459**
Under age 25	9,983	6,477	3,506	9,369	4,882	4,487
Aged 16 to 19	2,917	1,015	1,902	3,002	731	2,271
Aged 16 to 17	1,115	147	968	1,197	95	1,102
Aged 18 to 19	1,802	868	934	1,805	636	1,169
Aged 20 to 24	7,066	5,462	1,604	6,367	4,151	2,216
Aged 25 to 34	16,670	15,666	1,004	13,713	11,034	2,679
Aged 35 or older	46,680	43,236	3,444	41,321	32,028	9,293

PERCENT DISTRIBUTION BY AGE

Total employed	**100.0%**	**100.0%**	**100.0%**	**100.0%**	**100.0%**	**100.0%**
Under age 25	13.6	9.9	44.1	14.5	10.2	27.3
Aged 16 to 19	4.0	1.6	23.9	4.7	1.5	13.8
Aged 16 to 17	1.5	0.2	12.2	1.9	0.2	6.7
Aged 18 to 19	2.5	1.3	11.7	2.8	1.3	7.1
Aged 20 to 24	9.6	8.4	20.2	9.9	8.7	13.5
Aged 25 to 34	22.7	24.0	12.6	21.3	23.0	16.3
Aged 35 or older	63.7	66.1	43.3	64.2	66.8	56.5

PERCENT DISTRIBUTION BY EMPLOYMENT STATUS

Total employed	**100.0%**	**89.2%**	**10.8%**	**100.0%**	**74.4%**	**25.6%**
Under age 25	100.0	64.9	35.1	100.0	52.1	47.9
Aged 16 to 19	100.0	34.8	65.2	100.0	24.4	75.6
Aged 16 to 17	100.0	13.2	86.8	100.0	7.9	92.1
Aged 18 to 19	100.0	48.2	51.8	100.0	35.2	64.8
Aged 20 to 24	100.0	77.3	22.7	100.0	65.2	34.8
Aged 25 to 34	100.0	94.0	6.0	100.0	80.5	19.5
Aged 35 or older	100.0	92.6	7.4	100.0	77.5	22.5

Source: Unpublished data from the Bureau of Labor Statistics; calculations by New Strategist

Few Millennials Are Self-Employed

Self-employment rises with age and experience.

Although many teens and young adults may dream of being their own boss, few are able to do so. Among the nation's 138 million employed workers, only 7.5 percent are self-employed. Among workers under age 25, the figure is a much smaller 1.9 percent. It rises to 5.3 percent among those aged 25 to 34.

As people age, the percentage who are self-employed rises. Nearly one in ten workers aged 35 or older is self-employed. Self-employment increases with age because it takes years of experience to gain marketable skills.

■ Self-employment is becoming a more difficult proposition for Americans because the cost of buying private health insurance can be prohibitive, especially for those starting businesses.

Self-employment rises with age

(percent of workers who are self-employed, by age, 2003)

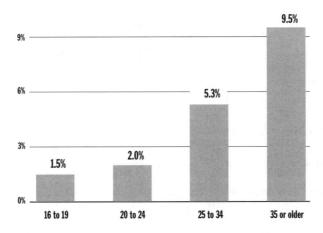

Table 6.12 Self-Employed Workers by Sex and Age, 2003

(number of employed workers aged 16 or older, number and percent who are self-employed, and percent distribution of self-employed, by sex and age, 2003; numbers in thousands)

	total	self-employed number	self-employed percent	percent distribution of self-employed by age
Total workers	**137,736**	**10,295**	**7.5%**	**100.0%**
Under age 25	19,351	359	1.9	3.5
Aged 16 to 19	5,919	91	1.5	0.9
Aged 16 to 17	2,312	46	2.0	0.4
Aged 18 to 19	3,607	44	1.2	0.4
Aged 20 to 24	13,432	269	2.0	2.6
Aged 25 to 34	30,383	1,609	5.3	15.6
Aged 35 or older	88,001	8,326	9.5	80.9
Total men	**73,331**	**6,430**	**8.8**	**100.0**
Under age 25	9,982	244	2.4	3.8
Aged 16 to 19	2,917	64	2.2	1.0
Aged 16 to 17	1,115	32	2.9	0.5
Aged 18 to 19	1,802	32	1.8	0.5
Aged 20 to 24	7,065	180	2.5	2.8
Aged 25 to 34	16,670	982	5.9	15.3
Aged 35 or older	46,680	5,203	11.1	80.9
Total women	**64,404**	**3,866**	**6.0**	**100.0**
Under age 25	9,368	117	1.2	3.0
Aged 16 to 19	3,002	32	1.1	0.8
Aged 16 to 17	1,197	18	1.5	0.5
Aged 18 to 19	1,804	14	0.8	0.4
Aged 20 to 24	6,367	85	1.3	2.2
Aged 25 to 34	13,714	628	4.6	16.2
Aged 35 or older	41,320	3,123	7.6	80.8

Source: Bureau of Labor Statistics, 2003 Current Population Survey, Internet site http://www.bls.gov/cps/home.htm; calculations by New Strategist

Few Young Adults Have Alternative Work Arrangements

But the young are more likely than average to be on-call and temp workers.

Among the nation's 12 million alternative workers, only about 1 million (10 percent) are under age 25. The Bureau of Labor Statistics defines alternative workers as independent contractors, on-call workers (such as substitute teachers), temporary-help agency workers, and people who work for contract firms (such as lawn or janitorial service companies).

Among all age groups, the most popular alternative work arrangement is independent contracting—which includes most of the self-employed. Among the nation's alternative workers, 69 percent are independent contractors. But this group accounts for only 29 percent of alternative workers among those under age 25. A larger 43 percent are on-call workers—such as substitute teachers and construction workers supplied by union hiring halls. People under age 25 are more likely than average to be on-call or temp workers.

The percentage of workers with alternative work arrangements rises with age as independent contracting becomes more popular. Eleven percent of workers aged 35 or older are alternative workers, and one in twelve is an independent contractor.

■ Older workers have more skills and experience, making it easier for them to earn a living by self-employment.

Few young workers are independent contractors

(percent of employed workers who are independent contractors, by age, 2001)

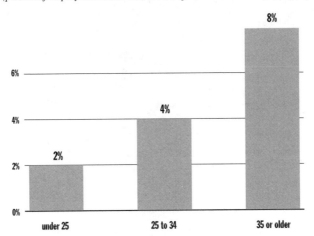

Table 6.13 Alternative Work Arrangements by Age, 2001

(number and percent distribution of employed people aged 16 or older with alternative work arrangements by age and type of alternative work, 2001; numbers in thousands)

	employed	with traditional work arrangements	with alternative work arrangements				
			total	independent contractors	on-call workers	temporary help agency workers	workers provided by contract firms
Total people	**134,605**	**121,917**	**12,476**	**8,585**	**2,089**	**1,169**	**633**
Under age 25	19,856	18,573	1,187	339	511	261	76
Aged 25 to 34	30,079	27,905	2,127	1,314	355	310	148
Aged 35 or older	84,670	75,438	9,162	6,932	1,222	598	410
PERCENT DISTRIBUTION BY ALTERNATIVE WORK STATUS							
Total people	**100.0%**	**90.6%**	**9.3%**	**6.4%**	**1.6%**	**0.9%**	**0.5%**
Under age 25	100.0	93.5	6.0	1.7	2.6	1.3	0.4
Aged 25 to 34	100.0	92.8	7.1	4.4	1.2	1.0	0.5
Aged 35 or older	100.0	89.1	10.8	8.2	1.4	0.7	0.5
PERCENT DISTRIBUTION BY AGE							
Total people	**100.0%**	**100.0%**	**100.0%**	**100.0%**	**100.0%**	**100.0%**	**100.0%**
Under age 25	14.8	15.2	9.5	3.9	24.5	22.3	12.0
Aged 25 to 34	22.3	22.9	17.1	15.3	17.0	26.5	23.4
Aged 35 or older	62.9	61.9	73.4	80.7	58.5	51.2	64.8

Note: Numbers may not add to total because the total employed includes day laborers, an alternative arrangement not shown separately, and a small number of workers who were both on call and provided by contract firms. Independent contractors are self-employed (except incorporated) or wage and salary workers who obtain customers on their own to provide a product or service. On-call workers are in a pool of workers who are called to work only as needed, such as substitute teachers and construction workers supplied by a union hiring hall. Temporary help agency workers are those who said they are paid by a temporary help agency. Workers provided by contract firms are those employed by a company that provides employees or their services to others under contract, such as security, landscaping, and computer programming.
Source: Bureau of Labor Statistics, Contingent and Alternative Employment Arrangements, February 2001, USDL 01-153, Internet site http://www.bls.gov/news.release/conemp.toc.htm; calculations by New Strategist

Many Workers Have Flexible Schedules

Men are more likely than women to have flexible schedules.

Twenty-nine percent of the nation's wage and salary workers have flexible schedules—meaning they may vary the time they begin or end work, according to the Bureau of Labor Statistics. Men are more likely than women to have flexible schedules—30 versus 27 percent in 2001.

Teenage workers are less likely to have flexible schedules than older workers. Among men aged 16 to 19 working full-time, only 17 percent have flexible schedules versus 30 percent of all working men. Among their female counterparts, only 22 percent have flexible schedules versus 27 percent of all women who work full-time.

Fifteen percent of wage and salary workers do not work a regular daytime schedule. The youngest workers are most likely to be shift workers—29 percent of those aged 16 to 19 work the evening, night, or other shift, with evening being most common. Among workers aged 20 to 24, 21 percent are shift workers. The figure falls to 14 percent among those aged 25 to 34.

■ Younger workers are less likely to work a regular daytime shift because many are in school during the day.

Teen workers are less likely than average to have flexible schedules

(percent of full-time wage and salary workers who have flexible work schedules, by sex and age, 2001)

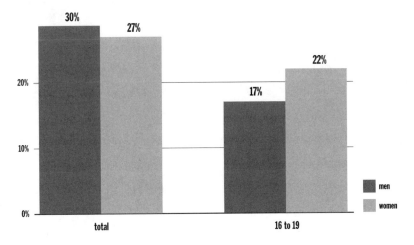

Table 6.14 Workers with Flexible Work Schedules by Age, 2001

(number and percent distribution of full-time wage and salary workers aged 16 or older with flexible work schedules, by sex and age, 2001; numbers in thousands)

| | total | with flexible schedules | |
		number	percent
Full-time wage and salary workers	**99,631**	**28,724**	**28.8%**
Under age 25	11,104	2,666	24.0
Aged 16 to 19	1,761	339	19.3
Aged 20 to 24	9,343	2,327	24.9
Aged 25 or older	88,528	26,058	29.4
Men	**56,066**	**16,792**	**30.0**
Under age 25	6,207	1,370	22.1
Aged 16 to 19	988	167	16.9
Aged 20 to 24	5,219	1,203	23.1
Aged 25 or older	49,860	15,423	30.9
Women	**43,566**	**11,931**	**27.4**
Under age 25	4,897	1,295	26.4
Aged 16 to 19	773	171	22.1
Aged 20 to 24	4,124	1,124	27.3
Aged 25 or older	38,668	10,635	27.5

Note: Flexible schedules are those that allow workers to vary the time they begin or end work.
Source: Bureau of Labor Statistics, Workers on Flexible and Shift Schedules in 2001, *USDL 02-225, 2002, Internet site http:// www.bls.gov/news.release/flex.toc.htm; calculations by New Strategist*

Table 6.15 Workers by Shift Usually Worked and Age, 2001

(number of full-time wage and salary workers aged 16 or older and percent distribution by age and shift ususally worked, 2001; numbers in thousands)

	total	16 to 24	25 to 34	35 to 44	45 to 54	55 to 64	65 or older
Total full-time wage and salary workers, number	**99,631**	**11,104**	**24,552**	**28,702**	**23,946**	**9,971**	**1,357**
Total full-time wage and salary workers, percent	**100.0%**	**100.0%**	**100.0%**	**100.0%**	**100.0%**	**100.0%**	**100.0%**
Regular daytime schedule	84.8	76.6	84.9	86.2	86.3	86.3	84.9
Shift workers	14.5	22.5	14.4	13.2	13.1	13.2	15.0
Evening shift	4.8	9.4	4.9	3.7	4.1	4.5	3.9
Night shift	3.3	4.8	3.3	3.3	2.9	3.1	2.1
Rotating shift	2.3	3.3	2.3	2.3	2.3	1.7	1.7
Split shift	0.4	0.3	0.6	0.4	0.3	0.4	1.3
Employer-arranged irregular schedule	2.8	3.8	2.4	2.8	2.6	2.8	5.5
Other	0.7	0.8	0.8	0.6	0.8	0.6	0.5

Source: Bureau of Labor Statistics, Workers on Flexible and Shift Schedules in 2001, *USDL 02-225, 2002, Internet site http:// www.bls.gov/news.release/flex.toc.htm*

Most Minimum-Wage Workers Are Teens and Young Adults

More than 1 million are under age 25.

Among the nation's 73 million workers who are paid hourly rates, only 2 million (3 percent) make minimum wage or less, according to the Bureau of Labor Statistics. Of those 2 million workers, more than half (53 percent) are under age 25.

The largest share of minimum-wage workers (28 percent) are aged 16 to 19, followed by the 26 percent who are aged 20 to 24. Among workers paid hourly rates in the 16-to-19 age group, 10 percent earn minimum wage or less. Among those in the 20-to-24 age group, 5 percent earn minimum wage or less.

■ Younger workers are most likely to earn minimum wage or less because many are entry-level and/or part-time workers.

Teens and young adults account for the majority of minimum wage workers

(percent distribution of workers earning minimum wage or less, by age, 2002)

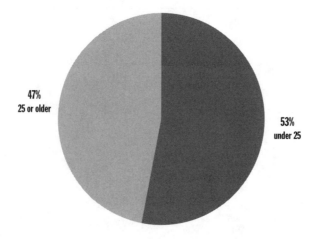

47%
25 or older

53%
under 25

Table 6.16 Workers Earning Minimum Wage by Age, 2002

(number and percent distribution of workers paid hourly rates and workers paid at or below minimum wage, by age, 2002; numbers in thousands)

	total paid hourly rates	at or below minimum wage		
		total	at $5.15/hour	below $5.15/hour
Total aged 16 or older	**72,720**	**2,168**	**570**	**1,598**
Under age 25	16,191	1,158	340	818
Aged 16 to 19	5,808	605	226	379
Aged 20 to 24	10,383	553	114	439
Aged 25 to 29	8,120	208	48	160
Aged 30 or older	48,411	802	182	620
PERCENT DISTRIBUTION BY AGE				
Total aged 16 or older	**100.0%**	**100.0%**	**100.0%**	**100.0%**
Under age 25	22.3	53.4	59.6	51.2
Aged 16 to 19	8.0	27.9	39.6	23.7
Aged 20 to 24	14.3	25.5	20.0	27.5
Aged 25 to 29	11.2	9.6	8.4	10.0
Aged 30 or older	66.6	37.0	31.9	38.8
PERCENT DISTRIBUTION BY WAGE STATUS				
Total aged 16 or older	**100.0%**	**3.0%**	**0.8%**	**2.2%**
Under age 25	100.0	7.2	2.1	5.1
Aged 16 to 19	100.0	10.4	3.9	6.5
Aged 20 to 24	100.0	5.3	1.1	4.2
Aged 25 to 29	100.0	2.6	0.6	2.0
Aged 30 or older	100.0	1.7	0.4	1.3

Source: Bureau of Labor Statistics, Characteristics of Minimum Wage Workers, 2002, *Internet site http://www.bls.gov/cps/minwage2002.htm; calculations by New Strategist*

Few Millennials Belong to Unions

Men are more likely than women to be union members.

Union membership has fallen sharply over the past few decades. In 1970, 30 percent of nonagricultural workers were members of labor unions. In 2003, only 13 percent were union members. A slightly larger 14 percent of workers are represented by unions.

The percentage of workers who belong to a union peaks in the 45-to-54 age group at 20 percent of men and 16 percent of women. A larger percentage of men are union members because they are more likely to work in jobs that are traditional strongholds of labor unions. In fact, the decline of labor unions is partly the result of the shift in jobs from manufacturing to services. Among workers under age 25, only 6 percent of men and 4 percent of women are union members.

■ Union membership will continue to decline because the increasingly cut-throat economy rewards companies with more flexible workforces.

Few workers are union members

(percent of employed wage and salary workers who are members of unions, by age, 2003)

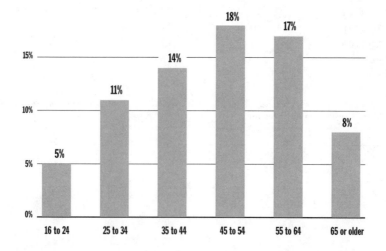

Table 6.17 Union Membership by Sex and Age, 2003

(number and percent of employed wage and salary workers aged 16 or older by union affiliation, sex, and age, 2003; numbers in thousands)

	total employed	represented by unions		members of unions	
		number	percent	number	percent
Total aged 16+	**122,358**	**17,448**	**14.3%**	**15,776**	**12.9%**
Aged 16 to 24	18,904	1,124	5.9	966	5.1
Aged 25 to 34	28,179	3,455	12.3	3,097	11.0
Aged 35 to 44	30,714	4,717	15.4	4,308	14.0
Aged 45 to 54	27,567	5,307	19.3	4,848	17.6
Aged 55 to 64	13,633	2,547	18.7	2,300	16.9
Aged 65 or older	3,361	297	8.8	258	7.7
Men aged 16+	**63,236**	**9,848**	**15.6**	**9,044**	**14.3**
Aged 16 to 24	9,683	685	7.1	595	6.1
Aged 25 to 34	15,263	2,005	13.1	1,826	12.0
Aged 35 to 44	16,080	2,735	17.0	2,535	15.8
Aged 45 to 54	13,723	2,891	21.1	2,684	19.6
Aged 55 to 64	6,776	1,377	20.3	1,271	18.8
Aged 65 or older	1,710	155	9.0	133	7.8
Women aged 16+	**59,122**	**7,601**	**12.9**	**6,732**	**11.4**
Aged 16 to 24	9,221	439	4.8	371	4.0
Aged 25 to 34	12,916	1,451	11.2	1,270	9.8
Aged 35 to 44	14,634	1,982	13.5	1,773	12.1
Aged 45 to 54	13,844	2,416	17.5	2,163	15.6
Aged 55 to 64	6,857	1,170	17.1	1,029	15.0
Aged 65 or older	1,651	142	8.6	125	7.6

Source: Bureau of Labor Statistics, 2003 Current Population Survey, Internet site http://www.bls.gov/cps/home.htm

Millennial Generation Will Expand Young Adult Labor Force

The number of young workers will increase during the coming decade.

Between 2003 and 2012, the Millennial generation will fill the 18-to-34 age group. The number of young-adult workers will increase, reversing the decline of recent years. The number of workers aged 20 to 34 will expand by 10 percent between 2003 and 2012, according to the Bureau of Labor Statistics. At the same time, the number of workers aged 35 to 44 will fall by 6 percent as the small Generation X fills the age group. The labor force participation rates of Millennial men and women are projected to remain stable through the decade, except for an anticipated decline in participation among 16- and 17-year-olds.

The number of older workers is projected to soar during the coming decade. The Bureau of Labor Statistics projects a 42 percent increase in the number of workers aged 55 or older between 2003 and 2012. In contrast, the number of workers under age 55 is projected to grow by just 5 percent during those years.

■ The decline in the labor force participation rate of teenagers may result from competition with their grandparents, as the older age group vies for part-time jobs to supplement its meager retirement income.

The number of workers aged 20 to 34 will increase

(percent change in number of workers by sex and selected age, 2003–12)

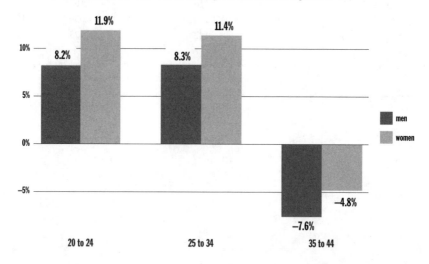

men
women

20 to 24: 8.2% (men), 11.9% (women)
25 to 34: 8.3% (men), 11.4% (women)
35 to 44: −7.6% (men), −4.8% (women)

Table 6.18 Projections of the Labor Force by Sex and Age, 2003 to 2012

(number and percent of people aged 16 or older in the civilian labor force by sex and age, 2003 and 2012; percent change in number and percentage point change in participation rate, 2003–12; numbers in thousands)

	number			participation rate		
	2003	2012	percent change 2003–12	2003	2012	percentage point change 2003–12
Total labor force	**147,003**	**162,269**	**10.4%**	**67.1%**	**67.2%**	**0.1**
Total men in labor force	**78,560**	**85,252**	**8.5**	**74.4**	**73.1**	**–1.3**
Under age 25	11,884	12,461	4.9	66.6	65.7	–0.9
Aged 16 to 19	3,871	3,791	–2.1	47.4	45.6	–1.8
Aged 16 to 17	1,411	1,235	–12.5	34.0	29.9	–4.1
Aged 18 to 19	2,460	2,556	3.9	61.1	61.1	0.0
Aged 20 to 24	8,014	8,670	8.2	81.6	81.4	–0.2
Aged 20 to 21	2,947	3,155	7.1	74.2	73.8	–0.4
Aged 22 to 24	5,067	5,515	8.8	86.7	86.5	–0.2
Aged 25 to 34	17,602	19,069	8.3	93.2	92.5	–0.7
Aged 25 to 29	8,326	9,436	13.3	92.2	91.1	–1.1
Aged 30 to 34	9,276	9,633	3.8	94.0	93.9	–0.1
Aged 35 to 44	19,734	18,244	–7.6	92.3	92.3	0.0
Aged 45 to 54	17,511	19,122	9.2	88.3	88.6	0.3
Aged 55 to 64	9,232	12,714	37.7	69.3	69.9	0.6
Aged 65 or older	2,598	3,641	40.1	18.3	20.8	2.5
Total women in labor force	**68,443**	**77,017**	**12.5**	**60.4**	**61.6**	**1.2**
Under age 25	10,980	11,916	8.5	61.3	63.2	1.9
Aged 16 to 19	3,765	3,845	2.1	47.4	47.4	0.0
Aged 16 to 17	1,445	1,397	–3.3	36.3	35.1	–1.2
Aged 18 to 19	2,319	2,448	5.6	58.4	59.2	0.8
Aged 20 to 24	7,215	8,070	11.9	72.4	75.1	2.7
Aged 20 to 21	2,738	3,066	12.0	68.4	70.9	2.5
Aged 22 to 24	4,477	5,004	11.8	75.0	77.9	2.9
Aged 25 to 34	14,660	16,337	11.4	75.5	78.2	2.7
Aged 25 to 29	7,038	8,164	16.0	75.9	78.0	2.1
Aged 30 to 34	7,623	8,174	7.2	75.2	78.4	3.2
Aged 35 to 44	17,002	16,189	–4.8	76.8	79.9	3.1
Aged 45 to 54	15,824	17,905	13.2	76.3	79.8	3.5
Aged 55 to 64	8,043	11,902	48.0	55.8	60.6	4.8
Aged 65 or older	1,934	2,769	43.2	10.3	12.1	1.8

Source: Bureau of Labor Statistics, Internet site http://www.bls.gov/emp/emplab1.htm; calculations by New Strategist

Most Children Have Working Parents

For the Millennial generation, working mothers are the norm.

Among women with children under age 18, fully 72 percent are in the labor force. Fifty percent of women with children under age 18 work full-time. Even among women with infants, 56 percent are in the labor force—most with full-time jobs.

In 61 percent of married couples with children under age 18, both husband and wife are employed. Seventy-three percent of women heading single-parent families have jobs, as do 84 percent of men who head single-parent families.

Because most parents work, the 61 percent majority of children aged 0 to 6 and not yet in kindergarten are in nonparental care, including 85 percent of children whose mothers work 35 or more hours per week. The largest share of preschoolers (34 percent) are in center-based programs, while 23 percent are cared for by a relative and 16 percent by a nonrelative.

■ Day care is the norm for the Millennial generation while mom and dad are at work. Since this is the only lifestyle most Millennials have ever known, they are likely to do the same as adults.

For most children, parents are at work

(percent of families with children under age 18 by family type and parents' labor force status, 2002)

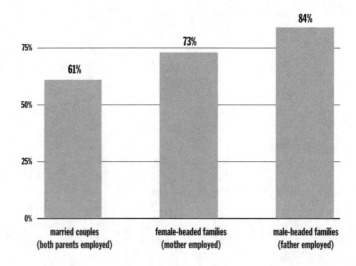

Table 6.19 Labor Force Status of Parents with Children under Age 18, 2002

(number and percent distribution of people aged 16 or older with own children under age 18 by family type, labor force status, and age of children, 2002; numbers in thousands)

		with children under age 18	
	total	aged 6 to 17, none younger	under age 6
NUMBER			
Married couples	**25,191**	**13,891**	**11,300**
One or both parents employed	24,372	13,459	10,913
Mother employed	16,773	10,230	6,543
Both parents employed	15,439	9,386	6,053
Mother employed, not father	1,334	844	490
Father employed, not mother	7,599	3,229	4,370
Neither parent employed	819	432	388
Female-headed families	**8,053**	**4,959**	**3,094**
Mother employed	5,910	3,856	2,054
Mother not employed	2,143	1,102	1,040
Male-headed families	**1,995**	**1,193**	**803**
Father employed	1,673	998	674
Father not employed	323	194	129
PERCENT DISTRIBUTION			
Married couples	**100.0%**	**100.0%**	**100.0%**
One or both parents employed	96.7	96.9	96.6
Mother employed	66.6	73.6	57.9
Both parents employed	61.3	67.6	53.6
Mother employed, not father	5.3	6.1	4.3
Father employed, not mother	30.2	23.2	38.7
Neither parent employed	3.3	3.1	3.4
Female-headed families	**100.0**	**100.0**	**100.0**
Mother employed	73.4	77.8	66.4
Mother not employed	26.6	22.2	33.6
Male-headed families	**100.0**	**100.0**	**100.0**
Father employed	83.9	83.7	83.9
Father not employed	16.2	16.3	16.1

Source: Bureau of Labor Statistics, Employment Characteristics of Families, 2002; *Internet site http://www.bls.gov/cps/home.htm*

Table 6.20 Labor Force Status of Women by Presence of Children, 2002

(labor force status of women by presence and age of own children under age 18, 2002; numbers in thousands)

	total civilian population	total civilian labor force	total employed	employed full-time	employed part-time	not in labor force
NUMBER						
Total women	**112,985**	**67,363**	**63,583**	**47,494**	**16,087**	**45,622**
No children under age 18	76,722	41,327	39,034	29,254	9,779	35,395
With children under age 18	36,263	26,036	24,549	18,240	6,308	10,227
Children 6 to 17, none younger	20,250	15,830	15,099	11,638	3,461	4,420
Children under age 6	16,013	10,206	9,450	6,602	2,848	5,807
Children under age 3	9,350	5,632	5,181	3,513	1,667	3,718
Children under age 1	3,091	1,734	1,571	1,038	533	1,357
PERCENT DISTRIBUTION						
Total women	**100.0%**	**59.6%**	**56.3%**	**42.0%**	**14.2%**	**40.4%**
No children under age 18	100.0	53.9	50.9	38.1	12.7	46.1
With children under age 18	100.0	71.8	67.7	50.3	17.4	28.2
Children 6 to 17, none younger	100.0	78.2	74.6	57.5	17.1	21.8
Children under age 6	100.0	63.7	59.0	41.2	17.8	36.3
Children under age 3	100.0	60.2	55.4	37.6	17.8	39.8
Children under age 1	100.0	56.1	50.8	33.6	17.2	43.9

Source: Bureau of Labor Statistics, Employment Characteristics of Families, *2002; Internet site http://www.bls.gov/cps/home.htm; calculations by New Strategist*

Table 6.21 Child Care Experiences of Children through Age Six, 2001

(percent of children under age 6 and not yet in kindergarten by type of care arrangement and child and family characteristics, 2001)

| | parental care only | nonparental care | | | |
| | | total | care in home | | center-based program |
			by a relative	by a nonrelative	
Total children aged 0 to 6, not in kindergarten	**39%**	**61%**	**23%**	**16%**	**34%**
Age					
Aged 0 to 2	48	52	23	18	17
Aged 3 to 6	26	74	22	14	56
Race and Hispanic origin					
Black, non-Hispanic	26	75	34	14	41
Hispanic	53	47	23	12	20
White, non-Hispanic	38	62	20	19	35
Other, non-Hispanic	35	65	23	15	37
Poverty status					
Below poverty level	46	54	26	10	27
At or above poverty level	37	63	22	18	35
Mother's educational attainment					
Less than high school	56	44	21	9	21
High school graduate	43	58	26	14	28
Vocational/technical or some college	37	64	25	16	36
College graduate	32	69	17	23	42
Mother's employment status					
Works 35 or more hours per week	15	85	33	26	42
Works fewer than 35 hours per week	29	71	32	20	36
Looking for work	57	43	16	9	25
Not in the labor force	68	32	6	5	24

Source: America's Children: Key National Indicators of Well-Being, *2003, Federal Interagency Forum on Child and Family Statistics, Internet site http://www.childstats.gov/americaschildren/*

7

Living Arrangements

■ Of the nation's 111 million households in 2003, people under age 30 headed 15 million, or a little less than 14 percent.

■ The living arrangements of young adults depend greatly on their race and Hispanic origin. Married couples account for fully 44 percent of households headed by Hispanics under age 30 but for only 16 percent of black households in the age group.

■ The 56 percent majority of black and Hispanic householders under age 30 have children under age 18 at home. This compares with only 18 percent of Asian householders in the age group.

■ The proportion of children living with two parents ranges from a low of 38 percent among black children to a high of 82 percent among Asian children.

■ Among the nation's children under age 18, the 80 percent majority has siblings at home. Sixty-one percent have parents in the 30-to-44 age group, and 60 percent have a parent with college experience.

■ Adopted children live in households with higher incomes than biological or stepchildren. Similarly, the educational level of the parents of adopted children is significantly higher than those of other children.

■ The majority of men and women under age 25 have never married. Among men aged 20 to 24, fully 85 percent are single. The figure is 74 percent among their female counterparts.

The Millennial Generation Heads Few Households

Only 14 percent of households are headed by people under age 30.

Only 15 million households were headed by people under age 30 in 2003 (Millennials were aged 9 to 26 in that year). Young adults today are slow to establish their own households because many are in college and still financially dependent on their parents. In addition, entry-level pay has fallen sharply over the past few decades as the minimum wage has been eroded by inflation. Consequently, few young adults can afford to strike out on their own.

Households headed by young adults are extremely diverse. Married couples account for the 34 percent plurality of households headed by people under age 30. Fully 22 percent are men and women who live alone, while another 18 percent are female-headed families. Seventeen percent of householders under age 30 live with nonrelatives, many of them co-habiting with romantic partners. Nine percent of householders under age 30 are male-headed families, including 12 percent of households headed by people under age 25—the largest share held by this household type among all age groups.

■ The diversity of young adults' living arrangement makes it difficult for marketers, politicians, or community organizations to reach them.

Households headed by young adults are diverse

(percent distribution of households headed by people under age 30, by type of household, 2003)

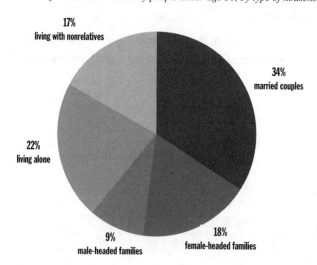

17%
living with nonrelatives

34%
married couples

22%
living alone

9%
male-headed families

18%
female-headed families

Table 7.1 Households Headed by People under Age 30 by Household Type, 2003: Total Households

(number and percent distribution of total households and households headed by people under age 30, by household type, 2003; numbers in thousands)

	total	aged 15 to 29		
		total	15 to 24	25 to 29
Total households	**111,278**	**15,146**	**6,611**	**8,535**
Family households	75,596	9,210	3,551	5,659
Married couples	57,320	5,139	1,379	3,760
Female householder, no spouse present	13,620	2,774	1,383	1,391
Male householder, no spouse present	4,656	1,297	789	508
Nonfamily households	35,682	5,935	3,059	2,876
Female householder	19,662	2,775	1,552	1,223
Living alone	16,919	1,600	817	783
Male householder	16,020	3,160	1,507	1,653
Living alone	12,511	1,743	722	1,021
PERCENT DISTRIBUTION BY TYPE				
Total households	**100.0%**	**100.0%**	**100.0%**	**100.0%**
Family households	67.9	60.8	53.7	66.3
Married couples	51.5	33.9	20.9	44.1
Female householder, no spouse present	12.2	18.3	20.9	16.3
Male householder, no spouse present	4.2	8.6	11.9	6.0
Nonfamily households	32.1	39.2	46.3	33.7
Female householder	17.7	18.3	23.5	14.3
Living alone	15.2	10.6	12.4	9.2
Male householder	14.4	20.9	22.8	19.4
Living alone	11.2	11.5	10.9	12.0
PERCENT DISTRIBUTION BY AGE				
Total households	**100.0%**	**13.6%**	**5.9%**	**7.7%**
Family households	100.0	12.2	4.7	7.5
Married couples	100.0	9.0	2.4	6.6
Female householder, no spouse present	100.0	20.4	10.2	10.2
Male householder, no spouse present	100.0	27.9	16.9	10.9
Nonfamily households	100.0	16.6	8.6	8.1
Female householder	100.0	14.1	7.9	6.2
Living alone	100.0	9.5	4.8	4.6
Male householder	100.0	19.7	9.4	10.3
Living alone	100.0	13.9	5.8	8.2

Source: Bureau of the Census, 2003 Current Population Survey, Annual Social and Economic Supplement, Internet site http://ferret.bls.census.gov/macro/032003/hhinc/new02_000.htm; calculations by New Strategist

Young Adult Households Differ by Race and Hispanic Origin

Hispanics account for a large share of the nation's young married couples.

Among householders under age 30, non-Hispanic whites head the 62 percent majority. But the figure varies greatly by type of household. Non-Hispanic whites account for 72 percent of nonfamily householders under age 30, but for only 42 percent of female-headed families in the age group. Among married couples under age 30, Hispanics head 21 percent and blacks just 8 percent.

Female-headed families account for the 42 percent plurality of black households headed by young adults. In contrast only 9 percent of Asian and 12 percent of non-Hispanic white households under age 30 are female-headed families. Married couples account for 44 percent of households headed by Hispanic young adults, but for only 16 percent of black households in the age group.

Among young adults, nonfamilies (people who live alone or with nonrelatives) account for 45 percent of households headed by non-Hispanic whites and for an even larger 53 percent of households headed by Asians. In contrast, they account for only 21 percent of households headed by Hispanics and 30 percent of those headed by blacks.

■ Young adults have different wants and needs depending on their living arrangements.

Asians are most likely to live alone

(percent of householders under age 30 who live alone, by race and Hispanic origin, 2003)

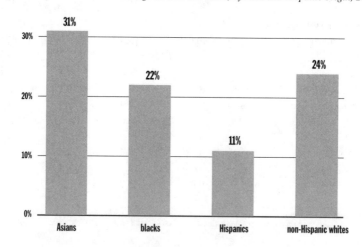

Table 7.2 Households Headed by People under Age 30 by Household Type, Race, and Hispanic Origin, 2003

(number and percent distribution of households headed by people under age 30, by household type, race, and Hispanic origin, 2003; numbers in thousands)

	total	Asian	black	Hispanic	non-Hispanic white
Total householders under age 30	**15,146**	**733**	**2,407**	**2,441**	**9,444**
Family households	9,210	347	1,680	1,923	5,200
Married couples	5,139	183	395	1,076	3,459
Female householder, no spouse present	2,774	67	1,014	520	1,154
Male householder, no spouse present	1,297	97	270	327	586
Nonfamily households	5,935	386	727	518	4,244
Female householder	2,775	175	366	207	2,002
Living alone	1,600	101	282	113	1,097
Male householder	3,160	211	361	309	2,242
Living alone	1,743	125	250	144	1,199

PERCENT DISTRIBUTION BY RACE AND HISPANIC ORIGIN

	total	Asian	black	Hispanic	non-Hispanic white
Total householders under age 30	**100.0%**	**4.8%**	**15.9%**	**16.1%**	**62.4%**
Family households	100.0	3.8	18.2	20.9	56.5
Married couples	100.0	3.6	7.7	20.9	67.3
Female householder, no spouse present	100.0	2.4	36.6	18.7	41.6
Male householder, no spouse present	100.0	7.5	20.8	25.2	45.2
Nonfamily households	100.0	6.5	12.2	8.7	71.5
Female householder	100.0	6.3	13.2	7.5	72.1
Living alone	100.0	6.3	17.6	7.1	68.6
Male householder	100.0	6.7	11.4	9.8	70.9
Living alone	100.0	7.2	14.3	8.3	68.8

Note: Numbers will not add to total because each racial group includes householders identifying themselves as the race alone and householders identifying themselves as the race in combination with other races. Hispanics may be of any race. Non-Hispanic white households include only householders identifying themselves as white alone and non-Hispanic.
Source: Bureau of the Census, 2003 Current Population Survey, Annual Social and Economic Supplement, Internet site http://ferret.bls.census.gov/macro/032003/hhinc/new02_000.htm; calculations by New Strategist

Table 7.3 Households Headed by People under Age 30 by Household Type, 2003: Asian Households

(number and percent distribution of total households headed by Asians and households headed by Asians under age 30, by household type, 2003; numbers in thousands)

	total	aged 15 to 29 total	aged 15 to 29 15 to 24	aged 15 to 29 25 to 29
Total Asian households	**4,079**	**733**	**313**	**420**
Family households	2,939	347	136	211
Married couples	2,344	183	36	147
Female householder, no spouse present	354	67	38	29
Male householder, no spouse present	241	97	62	35
Nonfamily households	1,140	386	177	209
Female householder	567	175	83	92
Living alone	435	101	47	54
Male householder	573	211	94	117
Living alone	411	125	53	72
PERCENT DISTRIBUTION BY TYPE				
Total Asian households	**100.0%**	**100.0%**	**100.0%**	**100.0%**
Family households	72.1	47.3	43.5	50.2
Married couples	57.5	25.0	11.5	35.0
Female householder, no spouse present	8.7	9.1	12.1	6.9
Male householder, no spouse present	5.9	13.2	19.8	8.3
Nonfamily households	27.9	52.7	56.5	49.8
Female householder	13.9	23.9	26.5	21.9
Living alone	10.7	13.8	15.0	12.9
Male householder	14.1	28.8	30.0	27.9
Living alone	10.1	17.1	16.9	17.1
PERCENT DISTRIBUTION BY AGE				
Total Asian households	**100.0%**	**18.0%**	**7.7%**	**10.3%**
Family households	100.0	11.8	4.6	7.2
Married couples	100.0	7.8	1.5	6.3
Female householder, no spouse present	100.0	18.9	10.7	8.2
Male householder, no spouse present	100.0	40.2	25.7	14.5
Nonfamily households	100.0	33.9	15.5	18.3
Female householder	100.0	30.9	14.6	16.2
Living alone	100.0	23.2	10.8	12.4
Male householder	100.0	36.8	16.4	20.4
Living alone	100.0	30.4	12.9	17.5

Note: Number of Asian households includes both those identifying themselves as Asian alone and those identifying themselves as Asian in combination with other races.
Source: Bureau of the Census, 2003 Current Population Survey, Annual Social and Economic Supplement, Internet site http:// ferret.bls.census.gov/macro/032003/hhinc/new02_000.htm; calculations by New Strategist

Table 7.4 Households Headed by People under Age 30 by Household Type, 2003: Black Households

(number and percent distribution of total households headed by blacks and households headed by blacks under age 30, by household type, 2003; numbers in thousands)

	total	aged 15 to 29 total	15 to 24	25 to 29
Total black households	**13,778**	**2,407**	**1,193**	**1,214**
Family households	9,128	1,680	800	880
Married couples	4,268	395	120	275
Female householder, no spouse present	4,069	1,014	486	528
Male householder, no spouse present	791	270	193	77
Nonfamily households	4,650	727	393	334
Female householder	2,550	366	215	151
Living alone	2,318	282	156	126
Male householder	2,100	361	178	183
Living alone	1,753	250	114	136
PERCENT DISTRIBUTION BY TYPE				
Total black households	**100.0%**	**100.0%**	**100.0%**	**100.0%**
Family households	66.3	69.8	67.1	72.5
Married couples	31.0	16.4	10.1	22.7
Female householder, no spouse present	29.5	42.1	40.7	43.5
Male householder, no spouse present	5.7	11.2	16.2	6.3
Nonfamily households	33.7	30.2	32.9	27.5
Female householder	18.5	15.2	18.0	12.4
Living alone	16.8	11.7	13.1	10.4
Male householder	15.2	15.0	14.9	15.1
Living alone	12.7	10.4	9.6	11.2
PERCENT DISTRIBUTION BY AGE				
Total black households	**100.0%**	**17.5%**	**8.7%**	**8.8%**
Family households	100.0	18.4	8.8	9.6
Married couples	100.0	9.3	2.8	6.4
Female householder, no spouse present	100.0	24.9	11.9	13.0
Male householder, no spouse present	100.0	34.1	24.4	9.7
Nonfamily households	100.0	15.6	8.5	7.2
Female householder	100.0	14.4	8.4	5.9
Living alone	100.0	12.2	6.7	5.4
Male householder	100.0	17.2	8.5	8.7
Living alone	100.0	14.3	6.5	7.8

Note: Number of black households includes both those identifying themselves as black alone and those identifying themselves as black in combination with other races.
Source: Bureau of the Census, 2003 Current Population Survey, Annual Social and Economic Supplement, Internet site http://ferret.bls.census.gov/macro/032003/hhinc/new02_000.htm; calculations by New Strategist

Table 7.5 Households Headed by People under Age 30 by Household Type, 2003: Hispanic Households

(number and percent distribution of total households headed by Hispanics and households headed by Hispanics under age 30, by household type, 2003; numbers in thousands)

	total	aged 15 to 29 total	15 to 24	25 to 29
Total Hispanic households	**11,339**	**2,441**	**1,073**	**1,368**
Family households	9,090	1,923	822	1,101
Married couples	6,189	1,076	361	715
Female householder, no spouse present	2,029	520	272	248
Male householder, no spouse present	872	327	188	139
Nonfamily households	2,249	518	251	267
Female householder	1,021	207	115	92
Living alone	791	113	57	56
Male householder	1,228	309	135	174
Living alone	809	144	53	91
PERCENT DISTRIBUTION BY TYPE				
Total Hispanic households	**100.0%**	**100.0%**	**100.0%**	**100.0%**
Family households	80.2	78.8	76.6	80.5
Married couples	54.6	44.1	33.6	52.3
Female householder, no spouse present	17.9	21.3	25.3	18.1
Male householder, no spouse present	7.7	13.4	17.5	10.2
Nonfamily households	19.8	21.2	23.4	19.5
Female householder	9.0	8.5	10.7	6.7
Living alone	7.0	4.6	5.3	4.1
Male householder	10.8	12.7	12.6	12.7
Living alone	7.1	5.9	4.9	6.7
PERCENT DISTRIBUTION BY AGE				
Total Hispanic households	**100.0%**	**21.5%**	**9.5%**	**12.1%**
Family households	100.0	21.2	9.0	12.1
Married couples	100.0	17.4	5.8	11.6
Female householder, no spouse present	100.0	25.6	13.4	12.2
Male householder, no spouse present	100.0	37.5	21.6	15.9
Nonfamily households	100.0	23.0	11.2	11.9
Female householder	100.0	20.3	11.3	9.0
Living alone	100.0	14.3	7.2	7.1
Male householder	100.0	25.2	11.0	14.2
Living alone	100.0	17.8	6.6	11.2

Source: Bureau of the Census, 2003 Current Population Survey, Annual Social and Economic Supplement, Internet site http:// ferret.bls.census.gov/macro/032003/hhinc/new02_000.htm; calculations by New Strategist

Table 7.6 Households Headed by People under Age 30 by Household Type, 2003: Non-Hispanic White Households

(number and percent distribution of total households headed by non-Hispanic whites and households headed by non-Hispanic whites under age 30, by household type, 2003; numbers in thousands)

	total	aged 15 to 29		
		total	15 to 24	25 to 29
Total non-Hispanic white households	**81,166**	**9,444**	**3,979**	**5,465**
Family households	53,845	5,200	1,773	3,427
Married couples	44,101	3,459	870	2,589
Female householder, no spouse present	7,070	1,154	570	584
Male householder, no spouse present	2,674	586	333	253
Nonfamily households	27,321	4,244	2,206	2,038
Female householder	15,353	2,002	1,127	875
Living alone	13,233	1,097	556	541
Male householder	11,968	2,242	1,079	1,163
Living alone	9,421	1,199	490	709
PERCENT DISTRIBUTION BY TYPE				
Total non-Hispanic white households	**100.0%**	**100.0%**	**100.0%**	**100.0%**
Family households	66.3	55.1	44.6	62.7
Married couples	54.3	36.6	21.9	47.4
Female householder, no spouse present	8.7	12.2	14.3	10.7
Male householder, no spouse present	3.3	6.2	8.4	4.6
Nonfamily households	33.7	44.9	55.4	37.3
Female householder	18.9	21.2	28.3	16.0
Living alone	16.3	11.6	14.0	9.9
Male householder	14.7	23.7	27.1	21.3
Living alone	11.6	12.7	12.3	13.0
PERCENT DISTRIBUTION BY AGE				
Total non-Hispanic white households	**100.0%**	**11.6%**	**4.9%**	**6.7%**
Family households	100.0	9.7	3.3	6.4
Married couples	100.0	7.8	2.0	5.9
Female householder, no spouse present	100.0	16.3	8.1	8.3
Male householder, no spouse present	100.0	21.9	12.5	9.5
Nonfamily households	100.0	15.5	8.1	7.5
Female householder	100.0	13.0	7.3	5.7
Living alone	100.0	8.3	4.2	4.1
Male householder	100.0	18.7	9.0	9.7
Living alone	100.0	12.7	5.2	7.5

Note: Number of non-Hispanic white households includes only those identifying themselves as white alone and non-Hispanic.
Source: Bureau of the Census, 2003 Current Population Survey, Annual Social and Economic Supplement, Internet site http://ferret.bls.census.gov/macro/032003/hhinc/new02_000.htm; calculations by New Strategist

The Households of Young Adults Are of Average Size

Between two and three people live in the average household headed by someone under age 30.

Households headed by people under age 30 are home to an average of 2.53 to 2.83 people—close to the national average of 2.58 people. Because so many young adults live alone or with nonrelatives, they average fewer than one child per household.

Household size grows as householders age through their thirties. It peaks among householders aged 35 to 39—at 3.29 people—because this age group is most likely to have at least one child at home. As householders age into their forties, the nest empties and household size shrinks.

■ As young adults marry and have children, the nest will become increasingly crowded, fueling the real estate and home furnishings industries.

Average household size rises above three people among householders in their thirties

(average household size by age of householder, 2002)

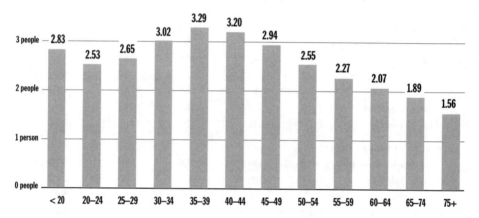

Table 7.7 Average Size of Household by Age of Householder, 2002

(number of households, average number of people per household, and average number of people under age 18 per household, by age of householder, 2002; numbers in thousands)

	number	average number of people	average number of people under age 18
Total households	**109,297**	**2.58**	**0.66**
Under age 20	907	2.83	0.80
Aged 20 to 24	5,484	2.53	0.58
Aged 25 to 29	8,412	2.65	0.86
Aged 30 to 34	10,576	3.02	1.22
Aged 35 to 39	11,599	3.29	1.42
Aged 40 to 44	12,432	3.20	1.20
Aged 45 to 49	11,754	2.94	0.78
Aged 50 to 54	10,455	2.55	0.39
Aged 55 to 59	8,611	2.27	0.20
Aged 60 to 64	6,592	2.07	0.14
Aged 65 to 74	11,472	1.89	0.09
Aged 75 or older	11,004	1.56	0.03

Source: Bureau of the Census, 2002 Current Population Survey Annual Demographic Supplement, http://www.census.gov/population/www/socdemo/hh-fam/cps2002.html

A Minority of Young Adult Households include Children

Most black and Hispanic householders under age 30 have children at home, however.

Among all households headed by people under age 30, only 39 percent include children under age 18. The figure is a higher 63 percent for married-couple householders in the age group, and an even higher 80 percent for female-headed families.

The percentage of households that include children under age 18 varies greatly by race and Hispanic origin. The 56 percent majority of black and Hispanic householders under age 30 have children under age 18 at home. This compares with a smaller 33 percent of non-Hispanic whites and only 18 percent of Asians in the age group. Regardless of race or Hispanic origin, the majority of young married couples have children under age 18 at home.

■ The lifestyles of young adults are diverse, ranging from students with class schedules to parents with family and work schedules.

Few households headed by Asians under age 30 include children

(percent of householders under age 30 with children under age 18 at home, by race and Hispanic origin, 2002)

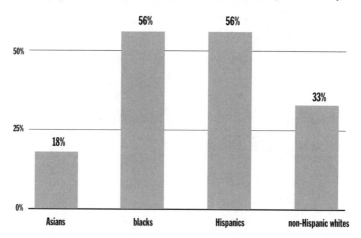

Table 7.8 **Households by Type, Age of Householder, and Presence of Children, 2002: Total Households**

(total number of households and number and percent with own children under age 18 at home, by household type and age of householder, 2002; numbers in thousands)

	total	with own children under age 18	
		number	percent
Total households	**109,297**	**35,705**	**32.7%**
Under age 30	14,803	5,815	39.3
Aged 15 to 19	907	173	19.1
Aged 20 to 24	5,484	1,853	33.8
Aged 25 to 29	8,412	3,789	45.0
Aged 30 to 34	10,576	6,201	58.6
Aged 35 to 54	46,239	22,587	48.8
Aged 55 or older	37,679	1,103	2.9
Married couples	**56,747**	**25,792**	**45.5**
Under age 30	5,155	3,252	63.1
Aged 15 to 19	91	53	58.2
Aged 20 to 24	1,444	834	57.8
Aged 25 to 29	3,620	2,365	65.3
Aged 30 to 34	5,765	4,430	76.8
Aged 35 to 54	27,315	17,224	63.1
Aged 55 or older	18,513	885	4.8
Female householder, no spouse present	**13,143**	**8,010**	**60.9**
Under age 30	2,672	2,144	80.2
Aged 15 to 19	265	106	40.0
Aged 20 to 24	1,094	858	78.4
Aged 25 to 29	1,313	1,180	89.9
Aged 30 to 34	1,541	1,447	93.9
Aged 35 to 54	6,126	4,285	69.9
Aged 55 or older	2,804	134	4.8
Male householder, no spouse present	**4,438**	**1,903**	**42.9**
Under age 30	1,213	420	34.6
Aged 15 to 19	208	14	6.7
Aged 20 to 24	516	161	31.2
Aged 25 to 29	489	245	50.1
Aged 30 to 34	487	324	66.5
Aged 35 to 54	1,918	1,077	56.2
Aged 55 or older	820	84	10.2

Source: Bureau of the Census, Children's Living Arrangements and Characteristics: March 2002, *Detailed Tables, Internet site http://www.census.gov/population/www/socdemo/hh-fam/cps2002.html; calculations by New Strategist*

Table 7.9 Households by Type, Age of Householder, and Presence of Children, 2002: Asian Households

(total number of Asian households and number and percent with own children under age 18 at home, by household type and age of householder, 2002; numbers in thousands)

	total	with own children under age 18 number	with own children under age 18 percent
Total Asian households	**4,071**	**1,582**	**38.9%**
Under age 30	753	132	17.5
Aged 15 to 19	49	1	2.0
Aged 20 to 24	278	36	12.9
Aged 25 to 29	426	95	22.3
Aged 30 to 34	573	274	47.8
Aged 35 to 54	1,890	1,118	59.2
Aged 55 or older	855	59	6.9
Married couples	**2,378**	**1,362**	**57.3**
Under age 30	199	103	51.8
Aged 15 to 19	2	1	50.0
Aged 20 to 24	56	21	37.5
Aged 25 to 29	141	81	57.4
Aged 30 to 34	352	240	68.2
Aged 35 to 54	1,312	967	73.7
Aged 55 or older	515	53	10.3
Female householder, no spouse present	**415**	**190**	**45.8**
Under age 30	93	26	28.0
Aged 15 to 19	15	–	–
Aged 20 to 24	38	14	36.8
Aged 25 to 29	40	12	30.0
Aged 30 to 34	38	28	73.7
Aged 35 to 54	193	130	67.4
Aged 55 or older	92	4	4.3
Male householder, no spouse present	**187**	**30**	**16.0**
Under age 30	82	4	4.9
Aged 15 to 19	13	–	–
Aged 20 to 24	31	1	3.2
Aged 25 to 29	38	3	7.9
Aged 30 to 34	20	6	30.0
Aged 35 to 54	64	20	31.2
Aged 55 or older	22	1	4.5

Note: (–) means number is less than 500 or sample is too small to make a reliable estimate.
Source: Bureau of the Census, Children's Living Arrangements and Characteristics: March 2002, Detailed Tables, Internet site http://www.census.gov/population/www/socdemo/hh-fam/cps2002.html; calculations by New Strategist

Table 7.10 Households by Type, Age of Householder, and Presence of Children, 2002: Black Households

(total number of black households and number and percent with own children under age 18 at home, by household type and age of householder, 2002; numbers in thousands)

	total	with own children under age 18	
		number	percent
Total black households	**13,315**	**5,065**	**38.0%**
Under age 30	2,294	1,274	55.5
Aged 15 to 19	150	53	35.3
Aged 20 to 24	959	487	50.8
Aged 25 to 29	1,185	734	61.9
Aged 30 to 34	1,470	940	63.9
Aged 35 to 54	5,925	2,705	45.7
Aged 55 or older	3,624	146	4.0
Married couples	**4,233**	**2,148**	**50.7**
Under age 30	419	316	75.4
Aged 15 to 19	12	8	66.7
Aged 20 to 24	129	83	64.3
Aged 25 to 29	278	225	80.9
Aged 30 to 34	491	385	78.4
Aged 35 to 54	2,141	1,361	63.6
Aged 55 or older	1,183	86	7.3
Female householder, no spouse present	**3,838**	**2,593**	**67.6**
Under age 30	991	868	87.6
Aged 15 to 19	79	42	53.2
Aged 20 to 24	419	367	87.6
Aged 25 to 29	493	459	93.1
Aged 30 to 34	536	511	95.3
Aged 35 to 54	1,690	1,171	69.3
Aged 55 or older	622	43	6.9
Male householder, no spouse present	**773**	**324**	**41.9**
Under age 30	216	90	41.7
Aged 15 to 19	33	3	9.1
Aged 20 to 24	96	37	38.5
Aged 25 to 29	87	50	57.5
Aged 30 to 34	71	44	62.0
Aged 35 to 54	338	173	51.2
Aged 55 or older	148	17	11.5

Source: Bureau of the Census, Children's Living Arrangements and Characteristics: March 2002, *Detailed Tables, Internet site http://www.census.gov/population/www/socdemo/hh-fam/cps2002.html; calculations by New Strategist*

Table 7.11 Households by Type, Age of Householder, and Presence of Children, 2002: Hispanic Households

(total number of Hispanic households and number and percent with own children under age 18 at home, by household type and age of householder, 2002; numbers in thousands)

	total	with own children under age 18	
		number	percent
Total Hispanic households	**10,499**	**5,343**	**50.9%**
Under age 30	2,389	1,347	56.4
Aged 15 to 19	184	50	27.2
Aged 20 to 24	852	437	51.3
Aged 25 to 29	1,353	860	63.6
Aged 30 to 34	1,604	1,167	72.8
Aged 35 to 54	4,423	2,688	60.8
Aged 55 or older	2,082	140	6.7
Married couples	**5,778**	**3,754**	**65.0**
Under age 30	1,042	841	80.7
Aged 15 to 19	30	27	90.0
Aged 20 to 24	323	240	74.3
Aged 25 to 29	689	574	83.3
Aged 30 to 34	973	849	87.3
Aged 35 to 54	2,676	1,958	73.2
Aged 55 or older	1,087	106	9.8
Female householder, no spouse present	**1,922**	**1,259**	**65.5**
Under age 30	488	389	79.7
Aged 15 to 19	61	17	27.9
Aged 20 to 24	190	158	83.2
Aged 25 to 29	237	214	90.3
Aged 30 to 34	269	243	90.3
Aged 35 to 54	861	603	70.0
Aged 55 or older	304	23	7.6
Male householder, no spouse present	**817**	**330**	**40.4**
Under age 30	368	116	31.5
Aged 15 to 19	51	5	9.8
Aged 20 to 24	156	39	25.0
Aged 25 to 29	161	72	44.7
Aged 30 to 34	122	76	62.3
Aged 35 to 54	257	127	49.4
Aged 55 or older	70	9	12.9

Source: Bureau of the Census, Children's Living Arrangements and Characteristics: March 2002, Detailed Tables, Internet site http://www.census.gov/population/www/socdemo/hh-fam/cps2002.html; calculations by New Strategist

Table 7.12 Households by Type, Age of Householder, and Presence of Children, 2002: Non-Hispanic White Households

(total number of non-Hispanic white households and number and percent with own children under age 18 at home, by household type and age of householder, 2002; numbers in thousands)

	total	with own children under age 18	
		number	percent
Total non-Hispanic white households	**80,818**	**23,532**	**29.1%**
Under age 30	9,306	3,038	32.6
Aged 15 to 19	508	61	12.0
Aged 20 to 24	3,377	893	26.4
Aged 25 to 29	5,421	2,084	38.4
Aged 30 to 34	6,900	3,805	55.1
Aged 35 to 54	33,677	15,940	47.3
Aged 55 or older	30,935	751	2.4
Married couples	**44,117**	**18,415**	**41.7**
Under age 30	3,472	1,978	57.0
Aged 15 to 19	47	16	34.0
Aged 20 to 24	931	487	52.3
Aged 25 to 29	2,494	1,475	59.1
Aged 30 to 34	3,937	2,947	74.9
Aged 35 to 54	21,042	12,856	61.1
Aged 55 or older	15,666	635	4.1
Female householder, no spouse present	**6,884**	**3,927**	**57.1**
Under age 30	1,097	857	78.1
Aged 15 to 19	104	40	38.5
Aged 20 to 24	454	325	71.6
Aged 25 to 29	539	492	91.3
Aged 30 to 34	702	666	94.9
Aged 35 to 54	3,333	2,344	70.3
Aged 55 or older	1,752	61	3.5
Male householder, no spouse present	**2,618**	**1,190**	**45.5**
Under age 30	547	202	36.9
Aged 15 to 19	107	5	4.7
Aged 20 to 24	235	80	34.0
Aged 25 to 29	205	117	57.1
Aged 30 to 34	267	191	71.5
Aged 35 to 54	1,234	740	60.0
Aged 55 or older	568	56	9.9

Source: Bureau of the Census, Children's Living Arrangements and Characteristics: March 2002, *Detailed Tables, Internet site http://www.census.gov/population/www/socdemo/hh-fam/cps2002.html; calculations by New Strategist*

One-Third of Young Adult Households include Preschoolers

The proportion with toddlers is well above average.

The majority of young adults go to college after high school, postponing marriage and family until their mid-twenties. Consequently, a 39 percent minority of householders under age 30 has children under age 18 at home.

But young-adult households are more likely to include preschoolers than is the average household. While 14 percent of all households include children under age 6, the proportion is 34 percent among householders under age 30. Similarly, while only 8 percent of all households include children under age 3, the figure is a much higher 24 percent among young adults. Nine percent of householders under age 30 have infants at home.

■ While most young adults postpone childbearing, others establish independent households because they have children.

Young adult households are more likely than average to include preschoolers

(percent of total households and households headed by people under age 30 with children under age 6 at home, 2002)

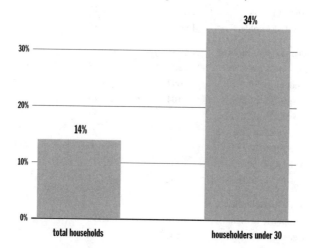

Table 7.13 Households by Presence and Age of Children and Age of Householder, 2002

(number and percent distribution of total households and households with children at home, by age of children and age of householder, 2002; numbers in thousands)

	total	under age 30 total	15 to 19	20 to 24	25 to 29	30 to 34	35 or older
Total households	**109,297**	**14,803**	**907**	**5,484**	**8,412**	**10,576**	**83,918**
With children of any age	45,812	5,863	184	1,863	3,816	6,232	33,716
Under age 25	40,967	5,851	184	1,861	3,806	6,225	28,891
Under age 18	35,705	5,815	173	1,853	3,789	6,201	23,690
Under age 12	26,376	5,751	168	1,842	3,741	5,874	14,753
Under age 6	15,376	4,980	162	1,760	3,058	4,120	6,275
Under age 3	8,909	3,493	143	1,303	2,047	2,528	2,888
Under age 1	2,958	1,311	76	452	783	825	820
Aged 6 to 17	27,438	2,230	14	342	1,874	4,000	21,210

PERCENT DISTRIBUTION BY AGE OF CHILD

	total	under age 30 total	15 to 19	20 to 24	25 to 29	30 to 34	35 or older
Total households	**100.0%**	**100.0%**	**100.0%**	**100.0%**	**100.0%**	**100.0%**	**100.0%**
With children of any age	41.9	39.6	20.3	34.0	45.4	58.9	40.2
Under age 25	37.5	39.5	20.3	33.9	45.2	58.9	34.4
Under age 18	32.7	39.3	19.1	33.8	45.0	58.6	28.2
Under age 12	24.1	38.9	18.5	33.6	44.5	55.5	17.6
Under age 6	14.1	33.6	17.9	32.1	36.4	39.0	7.5
Under age 3	8.2	23.6	15.8	23.8	24.3	23.9	3.4
Under age 1	2.7	8.9	8.4	8.2	9.3	7.8	1.0
Aged 6 to 17	25.1	15.1	1.5	6.2	22.3	37.8	25.3

PERCENT DISTRIBUTION BY AGE OF HOUSEHOLDER

	total	under age 30 total	15 to 19	20 to 24	25 to 29	30 to 34	35 or older
Total households	**100.0%**	**13.5%**	**0.8%**	**5.0%**	**7.7%**	**9.7%**	**76.8%**
With children of any age	100.0	12.8	0.4	4.1	8.3	13.6	73.6
Under age 25	100.0	14.3	0.4	4.5	9.3	15.2	70.5
Under age 18	100.0	16.3	0.5	5.2	10.6	17.4	66.3
Under age 12	100.0	21.8	0.6	7.0	14.2	22.3	55.9
Under age 6	100.0	32.4	1.1	11.4	19.9	26.8	40.8
Under age 3	100.0	39.2	1.6	14.6	23.0	28.4	32.4
Under age 1	100.0	44.3	2.6	15.3	26.5	27.9	27.7
Aged 6 to 17	100.0	8.1	0.1	1.2	6.8	14.6	77.3

Source: Bureau of the Census, Children's Living Arrangements and Characteristics: March 2002, *Detailed Tables, Internet site http://www.census.gov/population/www/socdemo/hh-fam/cps2002.html; calculations by New Strategist*

Most Young Couples Have One or Two Children

Eleven percent have three or more.

Smaller families have been growing in popularity for decades. Most Americans now consider two children the ideal number. Among couples under age 30, the 52 percent majority has one or two children. But a substantial 11 percent have three or more. Among female-headed families in the age group, an even larger 15 percent have three or more children.

Among couples aged 20 to 24, the largest share (42 percent) do not yet have children. Thirty-two percent have one child under age 18 at home, 19 percent have two, and 7 percent have three or more. Among couples aged 25 to 29, a still substantial 35 percent do not yet have children in the household, 27 percent have one child, 25 percent have two children, and 13 percent have three or more.

■ The percentage of couples with three or more children in the household reaches 21 percent in the 35-to-44 age group.

Among couples under age 30, only 37 percent do not have children

(percent of married couples under age 30 by number of children under age 18 at home, 2002)

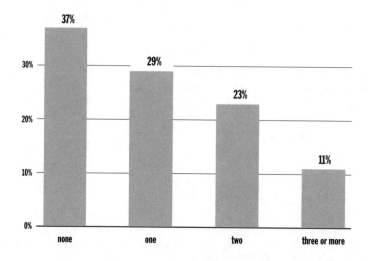

Table 7.14 Married Couples by Presence and Number of Children and Age of Householder, 2002

(number and percent distribution of married couples by presence and number of own children under age 18 at home, by age of householder, 2002; numbers in thousands)

| | total | under age 30 | | | | 30 to 34 | 35 to 44 | 45 to 54 | 55 or older |
		total	15 to 19	20 to 24	25 to 29				
Total married couples	**56,747**	**5,155**	**91**	**1,444**	**3,620**	**5,765**	**14,178**	**13,137**	**18,513**
Without children under18	30,955	1,903	38	610	1,255	1,335	2,791	7,298	17,627
With children under 18	25,792	3,252	53	834	2,365	4,430	11,385	5,839	885
One	9,832	1,494	44	458	992	1,423	3,168	3,122	624
Two	10,440	1,197	8	274	915	1,872	5,205	1,969	197
Three	4,058	415	1	73	341	842	2,174	582	46
Four or more	1,461	146	–	29	117	293	838	166	19

PERCENT DISTRIBUTION BY NUMBER OF CHILDREN

	total	total	15 to 19	20 to 24	25 to 29	30 to 34	35 to 44	45 to 54	55 or older
Total married couples	**100.0%**	**100.0%**	**100.0%**	**100.0%**	**100.0%**	**100.0%**	**100.0%**	**100.0%**	**100.0%**
Without children under18	54.5	36.9	41.8	42.2	34.7	23.2	19.7	55.6	95.2
With children under 18	45.5	63.1	58.2	57.8	65.3	76.8	80.3	44.4	4.8
One	17.3	29.0	48.4	31.7	27.4	24.7	22.3	23.8	3.4
Two	18.4	23.2	8.8	19.0	25.3	32.5	36.7	15.0	1.1
Three	7.2	8.1	1.1	5.1	9.4	14.6	15.3	4.4	0.2
Four or more	2.6	2.8	–	2.0	3.2	5.1	5.9	1.3	0.1

Note: (–) means number is less than 500 or sample is too small to make a reliable estimate.
Source: Bureau of the Census, Children's Living Arrangements and Characteristics: March 2002, *Detailed Tables, Internet site http://www.census.gov/population/www/socdemo/hh-fam/cps2002.html; calculations by New Strategist*

Table 7.15 Female-Headed Families by Presence and Number of Children and Age of Householder, 2002

(number and percent distribution of female-headed families by presence and number of own children under age 18 at home, by age of householder, 2002; numbers in thousands)

	total	under age 30 total	15 to 19	20 to 24	25 to 29	30 to 34	35 to 44	45 to 54	55 or older
Total female-headed families	**13,143**	**2,672**	**265**	**1,094**	**1,313**	**1,541**	**3,596**	**2,530**	**2,805**
Without children under18	5,133	528	159	236	133	94	529	1,312	2,671
With children under 18	8,010	2,144	106	858	1,180	1,447	3,067	1,218	134
One	3,967	1,073	72	525	476	536	1,446	803	109
Two	2,580	667	27	214	426	505	1,065	326	17
Three	1,085	301	7	105	189	281	419	78	7
Four or more	378	103	–	13	90	125	138	12	2
PERCENT DISTRIBUTION BY NUMBER OF CHILDREN									
Total female-headed families	**100.0%**	**100.0%**	**100.0%**	**100.0%**	**100.0%**	**100.0%**	**100.0%**	**100.0%**	**100.0%**
Without children under18	39.1	19.8	60.0	21.6	10.1	6.1	14.7	51.9	95.2
With children under 18	60.9	80.2	40.0	78.4	89.9	93.9	85.3	48.1	4.8
One	30.2	40.2	27.2	48.0	36.3	34.8	40.2	31.7	3.9
Two	19.6	25.0	10.2	19.6	32.4	32.8	29.6	12.9	0.6
Three	8.3	11.3	2.6	9.6	14.4	18.2	11.7	3.1	0.2
Four or more	2.9	3.9	–	1.2	6.9	8.1	3.8	0.5	0.1

Note: (–) means number is less than 500 or sample is too small to make a reliable estimate.
Source: Bureau of the Census, Children's Living Arrangements and Characteristics: March 2002, *Detailed Tables, Internet site http://www.census.gov/population/www/socdemo/hh-fam/cps2002.html; calculations by New Strategist*

Table 7.16 Male-Headed Families by Presence and Number of Children and Age of Householder, 2002

(number and percent distribution of male-headed families by presence and number of own children under age 18 at home, by age of householder, 2002; numbers in thousands)

	total	under age 30 total	15 to 19	20 to 24	25 to 29	30 to 34	35 to 44	45 to 54	55 or older
Total male-headed families	**4,438**	**1,213**	**208**	**516**	**489**	**487**	**1,045**	**873**	**820**
Without children under18	2,535	792	193	355	244	163	349	493	738
With children under 18	1,903	420	14	161	245	324	696	381	84
One	1,162	291	9	119	163	184	356	271	61
Two	538	97	5	27	65	107	228	91	15
Three	157	28	1	11	16	26	82	13	8
Four or more	45	5	–	3	2	6	29	5	–

PERCENT DISTRIBUTION BY NUMBER OF CHILDREN

	total	under age 30 total	15 to 19	20 to 24	25 to 29	30 to 34	35 to 44	45 to 54	55 or older
Total male-headed families	**100.0%**	**100.0%**	**100.0%**	**100.0%**	**100.0%**	**100.0%**	**100.0%**	**100.0%**	**100.0%**
Without children under18	57.1	65.3	92.8	68.8	49.9	33.5	33.4	56.5	90.0
With children under 18	42.9	34.6	6.7	31.2	50.1	66.5	66.6	43.6	10.2
One	26.2	24.0	4.3	23.1	33.3	37.8	34.1	31.0	7.4
Two	12.1	8.0	2.4	5.2	13.3	22.0	21.8	10.4	1.8
Three	3.5	2.3	0.5	2.1	3.3	5.3	7.8	1.5	1.0
Four or more	1.0	0.4	–	0.6	0.4	1.2	2.8	0.6	–

Note: (–) means number is less than 500 or sample is too small to make a reliable estimate.
Source: Bureau of the Census, Children's Living Arrangements and Characteristics: March 2002, *Detailed Tables, Internet site http://www.census.gov/population/www/socdemo/hh-fam/cps2002.html; calculations by New Strategist*

Nearly Half of Black Children Live with Mother Only

Only 13 percent of Asian children live only with mom.

Among the nation's 72 million children, 69 percent live with both parents. The proportion living with both parents stands at a high of 82 percent among Asian children. The figure is a lower 77 percent among non-Hispanic white children and 65 percent among Hispanic children. Only 38 percent of black children live with both parents.

The percentage of children who live only with their mother ranges from a low of 13 percent among Asians to a high of 48 percent among blacks. Only 2 to 5 percent of children live with their father only. A substantial 8 percent of black children live with neither parent. Among them, slightly more than half live with a grandparent.

■ Children who live with only one parent have higher poverty rates than those living with both parents

Asian children are most likely to live with two parents

(percent of children under age 18 who live with both parents, by race and Hispanic origin, 2002)

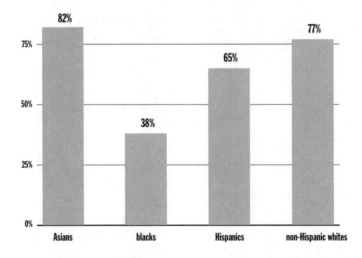

Table 7.17 Living Arrangements of Children by Race and Hispanic Origin, 2002

(number and percent distribution of children under age 18 by living arrangement and race and Hispanic origin of child, 2002; numbers in thousands)

	total	Asian	black	Hispanic	non-Hispanic white
Total children	**72,321**	**3,223**	**11,646**	**12,817**	**44,235**
Both parents	49,666	2,637	4,481	8,338	34,011
Mother only	16,473	419	5,605	3,212	7,124
Father only	3,297	65	605	641	1,926
Neither parent	2,885	102	956	626	1,174
Grandchild of householder	1,273	23	500	196	541
Other relative of householder	802	39	279	257	230
Foster child	235	2	96	32	101
Other nonrelative of householder	575	37	80	141	301
PERCENT DISTRIBUTION BY LIVING ARRANGEMENT					
Both parents	100.0%	100.0%	100.0%	100.0%	100.0%
Two parents	68.7	81.8	38.5	65.1	76.9
Mother only	22.8	13.0	48.1	25.1	16.1
Father only	4.6	2.0	5.2	5.0	4.4
Neither parent	4.0	3.2	8.2	4.9	2.7
Grandchild of householder	1.8	0.7	4.3	1.5	1.2
Other relative of householder	1.1	1.2	2.4	2.0	0.5
Foster child	0.3	0.1	0.8	0.2	0.2
Other nonrelative of householder	0.8	1.1	0.7	1.1	0.7
PERCENT DISTRIBUTION BY RACE AND HISPANIC ORIGIN					
Both parents	100.0%	4.5%	16.1%	17.7%	61.2%
Two parents	100.0	5.3	9.0	16.8	68.5
Mother only	100.0	2.5	34.0	19.5	43.2
Father only	100.0	2.0	18.4	19.4	58.4
Neither parent	100.0	3.5	33.1	21.7	40.7
Grandchild of householder	100.0	1.8	39.3	15.4	42.5
Other relative of householder	100.0	4.9	34.8	32.0	28.7
Foster child	100.0	0.9	40.9	13.6	43.0
Other nonrelative of householder	100.0	6.4	13.9	24.5	52.3

Note: Numbers will not add to total because Hispanics may be of any race and not all races are shown.
Source: Bureau of the Census, 2002 Current Population Survey Annual Demographic Supplement, Internet site http://www.census.gov/population/www/socdemo/hh-fam/cps2002.html

Most Children Share Their Home with Siblings

Most also have a parent with college experience.

Among the nation's 72 million children under age 18, the 80 percent majority share their home with a sibling. Thirty-two percent have a parent with a college degree, and 60 percent have a parent with college experience. Sixty-one percent of children have parents in the 30-to-44 age group.

The characteristics of children's families differ depending on the type of family in which the child lives. Children living in married-couple families tend to have older parents than those living with their mother only, and they have more siblings in the household. Married parents are better educated than single-parents, which leads to higher incomes and more homeownership.

Among children under age 15 in two-parent families, 69 percent have a working mother. Twenty-eight percent have a mom who was not in the labor force during the past year because she was caring for her family. Stay-at-home dads are much less common. Fewer than 1 percent of children under age 15 (or 336,000 children) have a father who was not in the labor force during the past year because he was caring for the family.

■ Perhaps no characteristic distinguishes today's children from those in the past more than working parents. With both mother and father in the labor force, family life has become much more stressful.

Most children have parents in the 30-to-44 age group

(percent distribution of children under age 18 by age of parent, 2002)

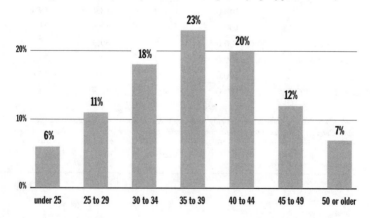

Table 7.18   Children under Age 18 by Selected Characteristics and Type of Family, 2002

(number and percent distribution of children under age 18 by selected characteristics and type of family, 2003; numbers in thousands)

| | number of children | | | | | percent distribution | | | | |
	total	living with both parents	living with mother only	living with father only	living with neither parent	total	living with both parents	living with mother only	living with father only	living with neither parent
Total children under age 18	72,321	49,665	16,473	3,297	2,885	100.0%	100.0%	100.0%	100.0%	100.0%
Sex										
Female	35,257	24,232	8,232	1,403	1,390	48.8	48.8	50.0	42.6	48.2
Male	37,064	25,434	8,240	1,894	1,495	51.2	51.2	50.0	57.4	51.8
Age of child										
Under age 1	3,917	2,778	831	233	75	5.4	5.6	5.0	7.1	2.6
Aged 1 to 2	7,917	5,552	1,723	402	240	10.9	11.2	10.5	12.2	8.3
Aged 3 to 5	11,528	8,028	2,584	506	410	15.9	16.2	15.7	15.3	14.2
Aged 6 to 8	11,954	8,307	2,722	463	460	16.5	16.7	16.5	14.0	15.9
Aged 9 to 11	12,669	8,614	3,031	543	479	17.5	17.3	18.4	16.5	16.6
Aged 12 to 14	12,492	8,521	2,865	551	555	17.3	17.2	17.4	16.7	19.2
Aged 15 to 17	11,842	7,865	2,713	597	667	16.4	15.8	16.5	18.1	23.1
Number of siblings in household										
None	14,693	7,937	4,668	1,270	818	20.3	16.0	28.3	38.5	28.4
One	28,498	20,931	5,916	1,177	475	39.4	42.1	35.9	35.7	16.5
Two	18,436	13,208	3,772	592	864	25.5	26.6	22.9	18.0	29.9
Three or more	10,693	7,589	2,119	258	728	14.8	15.3	12.9	7.8	25.2
Age of parent										
Aged 15 to 19	471	78	356	36	–	0.7	0.2	2.2	1.1	–
Aged 20 to 24	3,507	1,417	1,825	265	–	4.8	2.9	11.1	8.0	–
Aged 25 to 29	7,632	4,448	2,760	425	–	10.6	9.0	16.8	12.9	–
Aged 30 to 34	13,125	9,177	3,375	573	–	18.1	18.5	20.5	17.4	–
Aged 35 to 39	16,647	12,463	3,528	658	–	23.0	25.1	21.4	20.0	–
Aged 40 to 44	14,592	11,426	2,515	651	–	20.2	23.0	15.3	19.7	–
Aged 45 to 49	8,577	6,757	1,437	380	–	11.9	13.6	8.7	11.5	–
Aged 50 to 54	3,340	2,678	478	184	–	4.6	5.4	2.9	5.6	–
Aged 55 to 59	945	746	135	64	–	1.3	1.5	0.8	1.9	–
Aged 60 to 64	329	267	20	44	–	0.5	0.5	0.1	1.3	–
Aged 65 to 74	218	169	35	14	–	0.3	0.3	0.2	0.4	–
Aged 75 or older	54	41	11	2	–	0.1	0.1	0.1	0.1	–
No parents present	2,885	–	–	–	2,885	4.0	–	–	–	100.0

	number of children					percent distribution			
	total	living with both parents	living with mother only	living with father only	living with neither parent	total	living with both parents	living with mother only	living with father only	living with neither parent

Education of parent

Not a high school graduate	10,899	6,526	3,642	733	–	15.1	13.1	22.1	22.2	–
High school graduate	20,871	13,573	5,969	1,330	–	28.9	27.3	36.2	40.3	–
Some college or associate's degree	19,315	13,552	4,924	838	–	26.7	27.3	29.9	25.4	–
Bachelor's degree	12,148	10,460	1,398	290	–	16.8	21.1	8.5	8.8	–
Professional or graduate degree	6,203	5,556	539	108	–	8.6	11.2	3.3	3.3	–
No parents present	2,885	–	–	–	2,885	4.0	–	–	–	100.0

Marital status of parent

Married, spouse present	49,666	49,665	–	–	–	68.7	100.0	–	–	–
Married, spouse absent	951	–	788	164	–	1.3	–	4.8	5.0	–
Widowed	857	–	720	138	–	1.2	–	4.4	4.2	–
Divorced	6,932	–	5,592	1,338	–	9.6	–	33.9	40.6	–
Separated	2,918	–	2,500	418	–	4.0	–	15.2	12.7	–
Never married	8,111	–	6,872	1,239	–	11.2	–	41.7	37.6	–
No parents present	2,885	–	–	–	2,885	4.0	–	–	–	100.0

Homeownership status

Owner	48,542	38,362	6,547	1,808	1,825	67.1	77.2	39.7	54.8	63.3
Renter	22,512	10,366	9,689	1,445	1,012	31.1	20.9	58.8	43.8	35.1

Note: (–) means not applicable.
Source: Bureau of the Census, 2002 Current Population Survey Annual Demographic Supplement, Internet site http://www.census.gov/population/www/socdemo/hh-fam/cps2002.html; calculations by New Strategist

Table 7.19 Children under Age 15 with a Stay-at-Home Parent, 2002

(number and percent distribution of children under age 15 in two-parent families by labor force status of parents, 2003; numbers in thousands)

	number of children	percent distribution
STAY-AT-HOME MOM		
Total children under age 15 in two-parent families	**41,802**	**100.0%**
Mother in labor force for one or more weeks in past year	28,791	68.9
Mother not in labor force for 52 weeks in past year because caring for family, father in labor force for 52 weeks	10,573	25.3
Mother not in labor force for 52 weeks in past year because caring for family, father not in labor force for one or more weeks	1,235	3.0
Mother not in labor force for 52 weeks in past year for other reason	1,203	2.9
STAY-AT-HOME DAD		
Total children under age 15 in two-parent families	**41,802**	**100.0**
Father in labor force for one or more weeks in past year	40,314	96.4
Fother not in labor force for 52 weeks in past year because caring for family, mother in labor force for 52 weeks	189	0.5
Father not in labor force for 52 weeks in past year because caring for family, mother not in labor force for one or more weeks	147	0.4
Father not in labor force for 52 weeks in past year for other reason	1,151	2.8

Source: Bureau of the Census, 2002 Current Population Survey Annual Demographic Supplement, Internet site http://www.census.gov/population/www/socdemo/hh-fam/cps2002.html; calculations by New Strategist

Many Households Have Step or Adopted Children

Householders with adopted children are better educated and have higher incomes.

Among the nation's 45 million households with children of the householder present, 89 percent include only biological children. A substantial 11 percent include step or adopted children—7 percent include stepchildren and 4 percent include adopted children.

Adopted children are less likely to be white than are biological or stepchildren. While 71 percent of biological children are white, the figure is just 64 percent among adopted children. Seventeen percent of adopted children are of a different race than the householder.

Adopted children live in households with higher incomes than biological or stepchildren. Similarly, the educational level of the parents of adopted children is significantly higher than those of other children—33 percent of their parents have at least a college degree.

Adopted children are more likely to be disabled than biological or stepchildren. Among children aged 5 to 17, 12 percent of adopted children have at least one disability versus only 5 percent of biological children and 7 percent of stepchildren. The 53 percent majority of adopted children are female, but among those with disabilities, the 59 percent majority are males.

Thirteen percent of adopted children are foreign born. Among foreign-born adopted children, the most common country of birth is Korea, which accounts for 24 percent of the total. Russia accounts for another 10 percent.

■ The high divorce rate and fertility problems caused by delayed childbearing is creating more diverse families with step and adopted children.

More than one in ten households includes step or adopted children

(percent distribution of households with children under age 18 by relationship of child to householder, 2000)

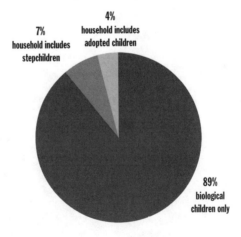

7%
household includes
stepchildren

4%
household includes
adopted children

89%
biological
children only

Table 7.20 Households by Relationship of Children in Household to Householder, 2000 Census

(number and percent distribution of households by presence of biological, step, and adopted children of any age, 2000; numbers in thousands)

	number	percent
Total households with children of householder present	**45,490**	**100.0%**
HOUSEHOLDS BY TYPE OF CHILDREN PRESENT		
Total households with children of householder	**45,490**	**100.0**
Biological children only	40,658	89.4
Other relationships	4,832	10.6
Biological children and stepchildren	1,660	3.6
Stepchildren only	1,485	3.3
Adopted children only	817	1.8
Adopted and biological children	808	1.8
Biological children, adopted children, and stepchildren	32	0.1
Adopted and stepchildren	30	0.1
HOUSEHOLDS BY NUMBER OF ADOPTED CHILDREN PRESENT		
Total households with adopted children	**1,687**	**100.0**
One adopted child	1,383	82.0
Two adopted children	248	14.7
Three or more adopted children	56	3.3

Source: Bureau of the Census, Adopted Children and Stepchildren: 2000, *Census 2000 Special Reports, CENSR-GRV, 2003*

Table 7.21 Biological, Step, and Adopted Children by Race and Hispanic Origin of the Householder, 2000 Census

(number and percent distribution of biological, step, and adopted children of the householder by race and Hispanic origin, 2000; numbers in thousands)

	total	biological	step	adopted
RACE OF CHILD				
Total children under age 18	**64,652**	**59,774**	**3,292**	**1,586**
White alone	45,859	42,359	2,482	1,018
Black alone	8,568	7,911	403	254
American Indian alone	663	598	40	26
Asian alone	2,225	2,069	39	117
Native Hawaiian and				
Other Pacific Islander alone	97	88	4	4
Some other race alone	4,669	4,374	205	90
Two or more races	2,571	2,375	119	78
HISPANIC ORIGIN OF CHILD				
Total children under age 18	**64,652**	**59,774**	**3,292**	**1,586**
Hispanic	9,814	9,720	479	216
Non-Hispanic white	42,413	37,958	2,262	918
CHILD AND HOUSEHOLDER RACE/HISPANIC DIFFERENCE				
Total children under age 18	**64,652**	**59,774**	**3,292**	**1,586**
Child is different race than householder	4,638	4,011	356	271
Child is different Hispanic origin				
than householder	1,708	1,385	218	105
PERCENT DISTRIBUTION BY RELATIONSHIP TO HOUSEHOLDER				
RACE OF CHILD				
Total children under age 18	**100.0%**	**92.5%**	**5.1%**	**2.5%**
White alone	100.0	92.4	5.4	2.2
Black alone	100.0	92.3	4.7	3.0
American Indian alone	100.0	90.1	6.0	3.9
Asian alone	100.0	93.0	1.7	5.3
Native Hawaiian and				
Other Pacific Islander alone	100.0	91.2	4.4	4.3
Some other race alone	100.0	93.7	4.4	1.9
Two or more races	100.0	92.4	4.6	3.0
HISPANIC ORIGIN OF CHILD				
Total children under age 18	**100.0**	**92.5**	**5.1**	**2.5**
Hispanic	100.0	99.0	4.9	2.2
Non-Hispanic white	100.0	89.5	5.3	2.2
CHILD AND HOUSEHOLDER RACE/HISPANIC DIFFERENCE				
Total children under age 18	**100.0**	**92.5**	**5.1**	**2.5**
Child is different race than householder	100.0	86.5	7.7	5.8
Child is different Hispanic origin				
than householder	100.0	81.1	12.8	6.1

PERCENT DISTRIBUTION BY RACE/HISPANIC	total	biological	step	adopted
RACE OF CHILD				
Total children under age 18	**100.0%**	**100.0%**	**100.0%**	**100.0%**
White alone	70.9	70.9	75.4	64.2
Black alone	13.3	13.2	12.2	16.0
American Indian alone	1.0	1.0	1.2	1.6
Asian alone	3.4	3.5	1.2	7.4
Native Hawaiian and Other Pacific Islander alone	0.1	0.1	0.1	0.3
Some other race alone	7.2	7.3	6.2	5.7
Two or more races	4.0	4.0	3.6	4.9
HISPANIC ORIGIN OF CHILD				
Total children under age 18	**100.0**	**100.0**	**100.0**	**100.0**
Hispanic	15.2	16.3	14.6	13.6
Non-Hispanic white	65.6	63.5	68.7	57.9
CHILD AND HOUSEHOLDER RACE/HISPANIC DIFFERENCE				
Total children under age 18	**100.0**	**100.0**	**100.0**	**100.0**
Child is different race than householder	7.2	6.7	10.8	17.1
Child is different Hispanic origin than householder	2.6	2.3	6.6	6.6

Source: Bureau of the Census, Adopted Children and Stepchildren: 2000, *Census 2000 Special Reports, CENSR-GRV, 2003; calculations by New Strategist*

Table 7.22 Biological, Step, and Adopted Children by Household Income, 2000 Census

(number and percent distribution of biological, step, and adopted children of the householder by household income in 1999, 2000; children in thousands as of 2000)

	total	biological	step	adopted
Total children under 18	**64,652**	**59,774**	**3,292**	**1,586**
$0 or less	692	662	15	15
$1 to $9,999	3,774	3,625	78	71
$10,000 to $14,999	2,907	2,768	88	52
$15,000 to $24,999	6,786	6,366	290	129
$25,000 to $34,999	7,509	6,935	418	156
$35,000 to $49,999	11,006	10,062	690	254
$50,000 to $74,999	14,693	13,413	905	376
$75,000 to $99,000	7,905	7,255	426	224
$100,000 to $149,999	5,795	5,351	262	183
$150,000 to $199,999	1,657	1,538	63	56
$200,000 or more	1,929	1,799	59	71
Median household income	$49,528	$48,200	$50,900	$56,138

PERCENT DISTRIBUTION BY RELATIONSHIP TO HOUSEHOLDER

Total children under age 18	**100.0%**	**92.5%**	**5.1%**	**2.5%**
$0 or less	100.0	95.7	2.1	2.1
$1 to $9,999	100.0	96.1	2.1	1.9
$10,000 to $14,999	100.0	95.2	3.0	1.8
$15,000 to $24,999	100.0	93.8	4.3	1.9
$25,000 to $34,999	100.0	92.4	5.6	2.1
$35,000 to $49,999	100.0	91.4	6.3	2.3
$50,000 to $74,999	100.0	91.3	6.2	2.6
$75,000 to $99,000	100.0	91.8	5.4	2.8
$100,000 to $149,999	100.0	92.3	4.5	3.2
$150,000 to $199,999	100.0	92.8	3.8	3.4
$200,000 or more	100.0	93.3	3.1	3.7

PERCENT DISTRIBUTION BY HOUSEHOLD INCOME

Total children under age 18	**100.0%**	**100.0%**	**100.0%**	**100.0%**
$0 or less	1.1	1.1	0.5	0.9
$1 to $9,999	5.8	6.1	2.4	4.5
$10,000 to $14,999	4.5	4.6	2.7	3.2
$15,000 to $24,999	10.5	10.7	8.8	8.1
$25,000 to $34,999	11.6	11.6	12.7	9.8
$35,000 to $49,999	17.0	16.8	21.0	16.0
$50,000 to $74,999	22.7	22.4	27.5	23.7
$75,000 to $99,000	12.2	12.1	12.9	14.1
$100,000 to $149,999	9.0	9.0	7.9	11.5
$150,000 to $199,999	2.6	2.6	1.9	3.5
$200,000 or more	3.0	3.0	1.8	4.5

Source: Bureau of the Census, Adopted Children and Stepchildren: 2000, *Census 2000 Special Reports, CENSR-GRV, 2003; calculations by New Strategist*

Table 7.23 Biological, Step, and Adopted Children by Education of Householder, 2000 Census

(number and percent distribution of biological, step, and adopted children of the householder by educational attainment of householder, 2000; numbers in thousands)

	total	biological	step	adopted
Total children under 18	**64,652**	**59,774**	**3,292**	**1,586**
Less than high school	11,536	10,742	568	227
High school graduate	17,300	15,808	1,133	359
Some college	19,315	17,769	1,075	471
Bachelor's degree or more	16,501	15,455	517	530
Bachelor's degree	10,274	9,631	355	288
Graduate or professional school degree	6,227	5,824	162	241

PERCENT DISTRIBUTION BY RELATIONSHIP TO HOUSEHOLDER

Total children under 18	**100.0%**	**92.5%**	**5.1%**	**2.5%**
Less than high school	100.0	93.1	4.9	2.0
High school graduate	100.0	91.4	6.5	2.1
Some college	100.0	92.0	5.6	2.4
Bachelor's degree or more	100.0	93.7	3.1	3.2
Bachelor's degree	100.0	93.7	3.5	2.8
Graduate or professional school degree	100.0	93.5	2.6	3.9

PERCENT DISTRIBUTION BY EDUCATIONAL ATTAINMENT OF HOUSEHOLDER

Total children under 18	**100.0%**	**100.0%**	**100.0%**	**100.0%**
Less than high school	17.8	18.0	17.3	14.3
High school graduate	26.8	26.4	34.4	22.6
Some college	29.9	29.7	32.6	29.7
Bachelor's degree or more	25.5	25.9	15.7	33.4
Bachelor's degree	15.9	16.1	10.8	18.2
Graduate or professional school degree	9.6	9.7	4.9	15.2

Source: Bureau of the Census, Adopted Children and Stepchildren: 2000, Census 2000 Special Reports, CENSR-GRV, 2003; calculations by New Strategist

Table 7.24 Biological, Step, and Adopted Children by Disability Status, 2000 Census

(number and percent distribution of biological, step, and adopted children of the householder by disability status, 2000; numbers in thousands)

	total	biological	step	adopted
Total children aged 5 to 17	**48,098**	**43,740**	**3,078**	**1,279**
At least one disability	2,643	2,279	214	151
Sensory disability	458	405	35	19
Physical disability	402	361	22	20
Mental disability	2,076	1,768	175	133
Self-care disability	469	418	31	21
Multiple disabilities	525	463	34	28
PERCENT DISTRIBUTION BY RELATIONSHIP TO HOUSEHOLDER				
Total children aged 5 to 17	**100.0%**	**90.9%**	**6.4%**	**2.7%**
At least one disability	100.0	86.2	8.1	5.7
Sensory disability	100.0	88.3	7.5	4.1
Physical disability	100.0	89.7	5.4	4.9
Mental disability	100.0	85.2	8.4	6.4
Self-care disability	100.0	89.1	6.5	4.4
Multiple disabilities	100.0	88.3	6.5	5.2
PERCENT DISTRIBUTION BY DISABILITY STATUS				
Total children aged 5 to 17	**100.0%**	**100.0%**	**100.0%**	**100.0%**
At least one disability	5.5	5.2	6.9	11.8
Sensory disability	1.0	0.9	1.1	1.5
Physical disability	0.8	0.8	0.7	1.5
Mental disability	4.3	4.0	5.7	10.4
Self-care disability	1.0	1.0	1.0	1.6
Multiple disabilities	1.1	1.1	1.1	2.1

Source: Bureau of the Census, Adopted Children and Stepchildren: 2000, *Census 2000 Special Reports, CENSR-GRV, 2003; calculations by New Strategist*

Table 7.25 Biological, Step, and Adopted Children by Nativity and Ability to Speak English, 2000 Census

(number and percent distribution of biological, step, and adopted children of the householder by nativity and ability to speak English, 2000; numbers in thousands)

	total	biological	step	adopted
Total children under age 18	**64,652**	**59,774**	**3,292**	**1,586**
Native	62,007	57,461	3,160	1,387
Foreign born	2,645	2,313	133	199
Foreign born aged 5 to 17	2,351	2,076	128	147
Speaks non-English language at home	1,989	1,836	107	45
Does not speak English very well	907	836	49	20
PERCENT DISTRIBUTION BY RELATIONSHIP TO HOUSEHOLDER				
Total children under age 18	**100.0%**	**92.5%**	**5.1%**	**2.5%**
Native	100.0	92.7	5.1	2.2
Foreign born	100.0	87.5	5.0	7.5
Foreign born aged 5 to 17	100.0	88.3	5.4	6.3
Speaks non-English language at home	100.0	92.3	5.4	2.3
Does not speak English very well	100.0	92.2	5.4	2.2
PERCENT DISTRIBUTION BY NATIVITY AND ENGLISH-SPEAKING ABILITY				
Total children under age 18	**100.0%**	**100.0%**	**100.0%**	**100.0%**
Native	95.9	96.1	96.0	87.4
Foreign born	4.1	3.9	4.0	12.6
Foreign born aged 5 to 17	100.0	100.0	100.0	100.0
Speaks non-English language at home	84.6	88.4	84.0	30.8
Does not speak English very well	38.6	40.3	38.3	13.6

Source: Bureau of the Census, Adopted Children and Stepchildren: 2000, *Census 2000 Special Reports, CENSR-GRV, 2003; calculations by New Strategist*

Table 7.26 Adopted Children under Age 18 by Race, Hispanic Origin, Disability Status, and Sex, 2000

(number and percent distribution of adopted children under age 18 by race, Hispanic origin, disability status, and sex, 2000; numbers in thousands)

	number			percent distribution		
	total	female	male	total	female	male
Total adopted children of householder	**1,586**	**836**	**751**	**100.0%**	**52.7%**	**47.3%**
Race of child						
White alone	1,018	528	490	100.0	51.9	48.1
Black alone	254	132	122	100.0	51.9	48.1
American Indian alone	26	13	13	100.0	50.9	49.1
Asian alone	117	74	43	100.0	63.0	37.0
Native Hawaiian and Other Pacific Islander alone	4	2	2	100.0	51.4	48.6
Some other race alone	90	47	43	100.0	52.7	47.3
Two or more races	78	40	38	100.0	51.1	48.9
Hispanic origin of child						
Hispanic	216	113	103	100.0	52.5	47.5
Non-Hispanic white	918	476	442	100.0	51.8	48.2
Disability status						
Children aged 5 to 17	1,279	668	611	100.0	52.2	47.8
At least one disability	151	62	89	100.0	40.9	59.1
Sensory disability	19	9	10	100.0	48.7	51.3
Physical disability	20	9	11	100.0	45.0	55.0
Mental disability	133	52	81	100.0	39.2	60.8
Self-care disability	21	10	11	100.0	49.2	50.8
Multiple disabilities	28	12	15	100.0	44.2	55.8

Source: Bureau of the Census, Adopted Children and Stepchildren: 2000, Census 2000 Special Reports, CENSR-GRV, 2003; calculations by New Strategist

Table 7.27 Adopted Children by Place of Birth, 2000 Census

(number and percent distribution of adopted children under age 18 by place of birth, 2000; numbers in thousands)

	number	percent
Total adopted children of householder	**1,586**	**100.0%**
Native born	1,387	87.4
Foreign born	199	12.6
Foreign born	**199**	**100.0**
Europe	37	18.5
Russia	20	9.9
Romania	6	3.1
Ukraine	2	1.2
Asia	98	49.4
China	21	10.6
India	8	3.9
Korea	48	23.9
Phillippines	6	3.2
Vietnam	4	2.2
Africa	3	1.6
Latin America	58	29.2
Central America	33	16.3
Guatemala	7	3.7
Mexico	18	9.1
El Salvador	2	1.1
South America	20	10.2
Colombia	7	3.5
North America	2	0.8

Source: Bureau of the Census, Adopted Children and Stepchildren: 2000, *Census 2000 Special Reports, CENSR-GRV, 2003*

Most Young Adults Live with Their Parents

Few head their own households.

Among people under age 30, 51 percent of men and 44 percent of women live with their parents. This figure includes college students living in dormitories because they are considered dependents. Not surprisingly, the proportion of young adults who live with their parents falls with age—more slowly for men than for women. Among men aged 20 to 24, 46 percent still live with their parents, a figure that drops to 18 percent in the 25-to-29 age group. Among women aged 20 to 24, 36 percent live with their parents, as do 11 percent of those aged 25 to 29.

Living with nonrelatives, either roommates or romantic partners, is almost as common as living with a spouse for men under age 30. Among men in the age group, 16 percent live with a spouse and 15 percent live with nonrelatives.

■ With more young adults pursuing a college degree, the dependency of childhood has stretched well into the twentysomething years.

Young men are more likely to live with their parents

(percent of people aged 18 to 29 who live with their parents, by sex and age, 2002)

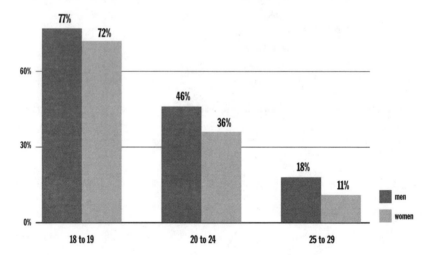

Table 7.28 Living Arrangements of Men under Age 30, 2002

(number and percent distribution of total men and men under age 30 by living arrangement, 2002; numbers in thousands)

	total	aged 15 to 29				
		total	15 to 17	18 to 19	20 to 24	25 to 29
Total men	**106,819**	**29,046**	**6,209**	**4,026**	**9,670**	**9,141**
In family household	84,724	22,951	6,085	3,645	7,045	6,176
Living with spouse	56,747	4,519	7	51	1,087	3,374
Other family householder	4,439	1,213	64	144	516	489
Living with parents	18,077	14,757	5,533	3,096	4,479	1,649
Other family member	5,461	2,462	481	354	963	664
In nonfamily household	22,096	6,097	125	381	2,625	2,966
Living alone	12,004	1,689	6	42	553	1,088
Living with nonrelatives	10,092	4,408	119	339	2,072	1,878
PERCENT DISTRIBUTION BY LIVING ARRANGEMENT						
Total men	**100.0%**	**100.0%**	**100.0%**	**100.0%**	**100.0%**	**100.0%**
In family household	79.3	79.0	9.8	90.5	72.9	67.6
Living with spouse	53.1	15.6	0.1	1.3	11.2	36.9
Other family householder	4.2	4.2	1.0	3.6	5.3	5.3
Living with parents	16.9	50.8	89.1	76.9	46.3	18.0
Other family member	5.1	8.5	7.7	8.8	10.0	7.3
In nonfamily household	20.7	21.0	2.0	9.5	27.1	32.4
Living alone	11.2	5.8	0.1	1.0	5.7	11.9
Living with nonrelatives	9.4	15.2	1.9	8.4	21.4	20.5
PERCENT DISTRIBUTION BY AGE						
Total men	**100.0%**	**27.2%**	**5.8%**	**3.8%**	**9.1%**	**8.6%**
In family household	100.0	27.1	7.2	4.3	8.3	7.3
Living with spouse	100.0	8.0	0.0	0.1	1.9	5.9
Other family householder	100.0	27.3	1.4	3.2	11.6	11.0
Living with parents	100.0	81.6	30.6	17.1	24.8	9.1
Other family member	100.0	45.1	8.8	6.5	17.6	12.2
In nonfamily household	100.0	27.6	0.6	1.7	11.9	13.4
Living alone	100.0	14.1	0.1	0.3	4.6	9.1
Living with nonrelatives	100.0	43.7	1.2	3.4	20.5	18.6

Source: Bureau of the Census, 2002 Current Population Survey Annual Demographic Supplement, Internet site http://www.census.gov/population/www/socdemo/hh-fam/cps2002.html; calculations by New Strategist

Table 7.29 Living Arrangements of Women under Age 30, 2002

(number and percent distribution of total women and women under age 30 by living arrangement, 2002; numbers in thousands)

	total	aged 15 to 29 total	15 to 17	18 to 19	20 to 24	25 to 29
Total women	**114,639**	**28,687**	**5,927**	**3,880**	**9,722**	**9,158**
In family household	90,451	23,532	5,801	3,429	7,186	7,116
Living with spouse	56,747	6,449	21	150	1,983	4,295
Other family householder	13,143	2,671	73	191	1,094	1,313
Living with parents	14,475	12,572	5,274	2,776	3,476	1,046
Other family member	6,086	1,840	433	312	633	462
In nonfamily household	24,188	5,150	124	450	2,535	2,041
Living alone	16,771	1,517	9	80	602	826
Living with nonrelatives	7,417	3,633	115	370	1,933	1,215
PERCENT DISTRIBUTION						
Total women	**100.0%**	**100.0%**	**100.0%**	**100.0%**	**100.0%**	**100.0%**
In family household	78.9	82.0	97.9	88.4	73.9	77.7
Living with spouse	49.5	22.5	0.4	3.9	20.4	46.9
Other family householder	11.5	9.3	1.2	4.9	11.3	14.3
Living with parents	12.6	43.8	89.0	71.5	35.8	11.4
Other family member	5.3	6.4	7.3	8.0	6.5	5.0
In nonfamily household	21.1	18.0	2.1	11.6	26.1	22.3
Living alone	14.6	5.3	0.2	2.1	6.2	9.0
Living with nonrelatives	6.5	12.7	1.9	9.5	19.9	13.3
PERCENT DISTRIBUTION BY AGE						
Total women	**100.0%**	**25.0%**	**5.2%**	**3.4%**	**8.5%**	**8.0%**
In family household	100.0	26.0	6.4	3.8	7.9	7.9
Living with spouse	100.0	11.4	0.0	0.3	3.5	7.6
Other family householder	100.0	20.3	0.6	1.5	8.3	10.0
Living with parents	100.0	86.9	36.4	19.2	24.0	7.2
Other family member	100.0	30.2	7.1	5.1	10.4	7.6
In nonfamily household	100.0	21.3	0.5	1.9	10.5	8.4
Living alone	100.0	9.0	0.1	0.5	3.6	4.9
Living with nonrelatives	100.0	49.0	1.6	5.0	26.1	16.4

Source: Bureau of the Census, 2002 Current Population Survey Annual Demographic Supplement, Internet site http://www.census.gov/population/www/socdemo/hh-fam/cps2002.html; calculations by New Strategist

A Minority of Young Adults Are Married

Most women are single until their late twenties, men until their early thirties.

The majority of men and women under age 25 have never married. Among men aged 20 to 24, fully 85 percent are single. The figure is 74 percent among their female counterparts. The percentage of women who have never married drops sharply in the 25-to-29 age group, to just 40 percent. But the 54 percent majority of men aged 25 to 29 are still single. Among men, the proportion who are single drops to just 34 percent in the 30-to-34 age group.

This pattern does not vary much by race and Hispanic origin. The percentage of women who have never married falls below 50 percent in the 25-to-29 age group for Asians, Hispanics, and non-Hispanic whites. It falls below the 50 percent mark for black women in the 30-to-34 age group. The percentage of men who have never married falls below the majority in the 30-to-34 age group in every racial and ethnic group.

■ The great diversity in the living arrangements of young adults is the consequence of postponed marriages.

Most men under age 30 have never married

(percent of people aged 18 to 29 who have never married, by sex and age, 2002)

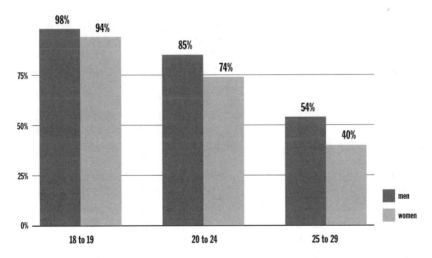

Table 7.30 Marital Status by Sex and Age, 2002: Total People

(number and percent distribution of people aged 15 or older by sex, age, and current marital status, 2002; numbers in thousands)

	total	never married	married, spouse present	married, spouse absent	separated	divorced	widowed
Total people	**221,459**	**63,090**	**115,838**	**2,926**	**4,606**	**20,955**	**14,044**
Under age 30	57,732	43,590	11,552	600	746	1,182	61
Aged 15 to 17	12,136	11,947	42	20	59	59	8
Aged 18 to 19	7,906	7,583	249	22	27	23	2
Aged 20 to 24	19,391	15,456	3,316	187	201	220	11
Aged 25 to 29	18,299	8,604	7,945	371	459	880	40
Aged 30 to 34	20,349	5,791	12,045	301	554	1,569	89
Aged 35 to 44	44,256	7,039	29,328	640	1,377	5,456	415
Aged 45 to 54	39,511	3,913	26,749	568	1,075	6,320	887
Aged 55 to 64	25,859	1,533	17,796	343	542	3,921	1,725
Aged 65 or older	33,750	1,224	18,368	474	311	2,506	10,867
Total women	**114,639**	**28,861**	**57,919**	**1,376**	**2,808**	**12,268**	**11,408**
Under age 30	28,687	20,361	6,759	322	462	736	47
Aged 15 to 17	5,927	5,826	32	6	28	32	4
Aged 18 to 19	3,880	3,640	181	19	22	16	2
Aged 20 to 24	9,722	7,195	2,115	115	124	164	8
Aged 25 to 29	9,158	3,700	4,431	182	288	524	33
Aged 30 to 34	10,270	2,362	6,421	120	347	946	75
Aged 35 to 44	22,453	2,933	14,984	270	872	3,079	317
Aged 45 to 54	20,209	1,799	13,261	257	654	3,566	672
Aged 55 to 64	13,497	715	8,530	157	305	2,384	1,407
Aged 65 or older	19,523	693	7,964	250	167	1,559	8,890
Total men	**106,819**	**34,229**	**57,919**	**1,551**	**1,798**	**8,686**	**2,636**
Under age 30	29,046	23,230	4,793	280	283	447	14
Aged 15 to 17	6,209	6,122	11	14	31	28	4
Aged 18 to 19	4,026	3,943	68	3	5	7	–
Aged 20 to 24	9,670	8,261	1,200	73	77	56	3
Aged 25 to 29	9,141	4,904	3,514	190	170	356	7
Aged 30 to 34	10,079	3,429	5,624	181	207	623	15
Aged 35 to 44	21,802	4,107	14,345	370	506	2,378	98
Aged 45 to 54	19,302	2,113	13,488	310	421	2,755	215
Aged 55 to 64	12,363	818	9,265	186	237	1,538	318
Aged 65 or older	14,227	532	10,404	223	144	947	1,977

	total	never married	married, spouse present	married, spouse absent	separated	divorced	widowed
PERCENT DISTRIBUTION							
Total people	**100.0%**	**28.5%**	**52.3%**	**1.3%**	**2.1%**	**9.5%**	**6.3%**
Under age 30	100.0	75.5	20.0	1.0	1.3	2.1	0.1
Aged 15 to 17	100.0	98.4	0.3	0.2	0.5	0.5	0.1
Aged 18 to 19	100.0	95.9	3.1	0.3	0.3	0.3	0.0
Aged 20 to 24	100.0	79.7	17.1	1.0	1.0	1.1	0.1
Aged 25 to 29	100.0	47.0	43.4	2.0	2.5	4.8	0.2
Aged 30 to 34	100.0	28.5	59.2	1.5	2.7	7.7	0.4
Aged 35 to 44	100.0	15.9	66.3	1.4	3.1	12.3	0.9
Aged 45 to 54	100.0	9.9	67.7	1.4	2.7	16.0	2.2
Aged 55 to 64	100.0	5.9	68.8	1.3	2.1	15.2	6.7
Aged 65 or older	100.0	3.6	54.4	1.4	0.9	7.4	32.2
Total women	**100.0**	**25.2**	**50.5**	**1.2**	**2.4**	**10.7**	**10.0**
Under age 30	100.0	71.0	23.6	1.1	1.6	2.6	0.2
Aged 15 to 17	100.0	98.3	0.5	0.1	0.5	0.5	0.1
Aged 18 to 19	100.0	93.8	4.7	0.5	0.6	0.4	0.1
Aged 20 to 24	100.0	74.0	21.8	1.2	1.3	1.7	0.1
Aged 25 to 29	100.0	40.4	48.4	2.0	3.1	5.7	0.4
Aged 30 to 34	100.0	23.0	62.5	1.2	3.4	9.2	0.7
Aged 35 to 44	100.0	13.1	66.7	1.2	3.9	13.7	1.4
Aged 45 to 54	100.0	8.9	65.6	1.3	3.2	17.6	3.3
Aged 55 to 64	100.0	5.3	63.2	1.2	2.3	17.7	10.4
Aged 65 or older	100.0	3.5	40.8	1.3	0.9	8.0	45.5
Total men	**100.0**	**32.0**	**54.2**	**1.5**	**1.7**	**8.1**	**2.5**
Under age 30	100.0	80.0	16.5	1.0	1.0	1.5	0.1
Aged 15 to 17	100.0	98.6	0.2	0.2	0.5	0.5	0.1
Aged 18 to 19	100.0	97.9	1.7	0.1	0.1	0.2	–
Aged 20 to 24	100.0	85.4	12.4	0.8	0.8	0.6	0.0
Aged 25 to 29	100.0	53.6	38.4	2.1	1.9	3.9	0.1
Aged 30 to 34	100.0	34.0	55.8	1.8	2.1	6.2	0.1
Aged 35 to 44	100.0	18.8	65.8	1.7	2.3	10.9	0.4
Aged 45 to 54	100.0	10.9	69.9	1.6	2.2	14.3	1.1
Aged 55 to 64	100.0	6.6	74.9	1.5	1.9	12.4	2.6
Aged 65 or older	100.0	3.7	73.1	1.6	1.0	6.7	13.9

Note: (–) means number is less than 500 or sample is too small to make a reliable estimate.
Source: Bureau of the Census, 2002 Current Population Survey Annual Demographic Supplement, Internet site http://www.census.gov/population/www/socdemo/hh-fam/cps2002.html

Table 7.31 Marital Status by Sex and Age, 2002: Asians

(number and percent distribution of Asians aged 15 or older by sex, age, and current marital status, 2002; numbers in thousands)

	total	never married	married, spouse present	married, spouse absent	separated	divorced	widowed
Total Asians	**9,837**	**3,229**	**5,246**	**318**	**137**	**488**	**418**
Under age 30	3,039	2,406	516	53	23	39	2
Aged 15 to 17	591	582	5	2	1	–	1
Aged 18 to 19	376	364	6	3	3	–	–
Aged 20 to 24	1,008	863	125	6	7	8	–
Aged 25 to 29	1,064	597	380	42	12	31	1
Aged 30 to 34	1,168	352	726	35	13	41	1
Aged 35 to 44	2,071	267	1,538	71	45	135	13
Aged 45 to 54	1,723	124	1,321	73	26	139	40
Aged 55 to 64	938	53	664	41	18	77	85
Aged 65 or older	899	27	480	44	12	58	277
Total Asian women	**5,079**	**1,363**	**2,822**	**139**	**93**	**316**	**346**
Under age 30	1,481	1,048	367	28	13	23	1
Aged 15 to 17	276	271	3	–	1	–	–
Aged 18 to 19	173	164	4	3	1	–	–
Aged 20 to 24	507	408	91	6	2	–	–
Aged 25 to 29	525	205	269	19	9	23	1
Aged 30 to 34	610	124	426	18	10	30	1
Aged 35 to 44	1,063	98	806	28	30	91	10
Aged 45 to 54	908	48	692	26	18	89	34
Aged 55 to 64	510	27	324	22	13	52	73
Aged 65 or older	507	20	206	17	8	30	226
Total Asian men	**4,758**	**1,866**	**2,423**	**180**	**44**	**172**	**72**
Under age 30	1,557	1,357	148	26	10	16	1
Aged 15 to 17	315	311	2	2	–	–	1
Aged 18 to 19	203	200	1	–	2	–	–
Aged 20 to 24	501	454	34	1	5	8	–
Aged 25 to 29	538	392	111	23	3	8	–
Aged 30 to 34	558	228	300	18	3	10	–
Aged 35 to 44	1,008	169	733	44	15	44	3
Aged 45 to 54	815	76	629	47	7	50	6
Aged 55 to 64	428	27	340	19	5	25	12
Aged 65 or older	392	9	274	27	5	26	51

PERCENT DISTRIBUTION	total	never married	married, spouse present	married, spouse absent	separated	divorced	widowed
Total Asians	100.0%	32.8%	53.3%	3.2%	1.4%	5.0%	4.2%
Under age 30	100.0	79.2	17.0	1.7	0.8	1.3	0.1
Aged 15 to 17	100.0	98.5	0.8	0.3	0.2	–	0.2
Aged 18 to 19	100.0	96.8	1.6	0.8	0.8	–	–
Aged 20 to 24	100.0	85.6	12.4	0.6	0.7	0.8	–
Aged 25 to 29	100.0	56.1	35.7	3.9	1.1	2.9	0.1
Aged 30 to 34	100.0	30.1	62.2	3.0	1.1	3.5	0.1
Aged 35 to 44	100.0	12.9	74.3	3.4	2.2	6.5	0.6
Aged 45 to 54	100.0	7.2	76.7	4.2	1.5	8.1	2.3
Aged 55 to 64	100.0	5.7	70.8	4.4	1.9	8.2	9.1
Aged 65 or older	100.0	3.0	53.4	4.9	1.3	6.5	30.8
Total Asian women	100.0	26.8	55.6	2.7	1.8	6.2	6.8
Under age 30	100.0	70.8	24.8	1.9	0.9	1.6	0.1
Aged 15 to 17	100.0	98.2	1.1	–	0.4	–	–
Aged 18 to 19	100.0	94.8	2.3	1.7	0.6	–	–
Aged 20 to 24	100.0	80.5	17.9	1.2	0.4	–	–
Aged 25 to 29	100.0	39.1	51.2	3.6	1.7	4.4	0.2
Aged 30 to 34	100.0	20.3	69.8	3.0	1.6	4.9	0.2
Aged 35 to 44	100.0	9.2	75.8	2.6	2.8	8.6	0.9
Aged 45 to 54	100.0	5.3	76.2	2.9	2.0	9.8	3.7
Aged 55 to 64	100.0	5.3	63.5	4.3	2.5	10.2	14.3
Aged 65 or older	100.0	3.9	40.6	3.4	1.6	5.9	44.6
Total Asian men	100.0	39.2	50.9	3.8	0.9	3.6	1.5
Under age 30	100.0	87.2	9.5	1.7	0.6	1.0	0.1
Aged 15 to 17	100.0	98.7	0.6	0.6	–	–	0.3
Aged 18 to 19	100.0	98.5	0.5	–	1.0	–	–
Aged 20 to 24	100.0	90.6	6.8	0.2	1.0	1.6	–
Aged 25 to 29	100.0	72.9	20.6	4.3	0.6	1.5	–
Aged 30 to 34	100.0	40.9	53.8	3.2	0.5	1.8	–
Aged 35 to 44	100.0	16.8	72.7	4.4	1.5	4.4	0.3
Aged 45 to 54	100.0	9.3	77.2	5.8	0.9	6.1	0.7
Aged 55 to 64	100.0	6.3	79.4	4.4	1.2	5.8	2.8
Aged 65 or older	100.0	2.3	69.9	6.9	1.3	6.6	13.0

Note: (–) means number is less than 500 or sample is too small to make a reliable estimate.
Source: Bureau of the Census, 2002 Current Population Survey Annual Demographic Supplement, Internet site http://www.census.gov/population/www/socdemo/hh-fam/cps2002.html

Table 7.32 Marital Status by Sex and Age, 2002: Blacks

(number and percent distribution of blacks aged 15 or older by sex, age, and current marital status, 2002; numbers in thousands)

	total	never married	married, spouse present	married, spouse absent	separated	divorced	widowed
Total blacks	**26,137**	**11,334**	**8,640**	**522**	**1,241**	**2,727**	**1,673**
Under age 30	8,241	6,938	924	116	130	131	4
Aged 15 to 17	1,856	1,815	7	6	9	19	–
Aged 18 to 19	1,181	1,151	23	4	–	4	–
Aged 20 to 24	2,772	2,432	254	28	34	24	–
Aged 25 to 29	2,432	1,540	640	78	87	84	4
Aged 30 to 34	2,598	1,192	1,036	53	140	164	13
Aged 35 to 44	5,491	1,781	2,461	136	343	696	72
Aged 45 to 54	4,462	957	1,931	120	341	914	199
Aged 55 to 64	2,495	305	1,137	59	182	504	308
Aged 65 or older	2,852	161	1,152	39	103	319	1,077
Total black women	**14,442**	**6,068**	**4,216**	**272**	**772**	**1,758**	**1,354**
Under age 30	4,374	3,602	536	73	93	68	4
Aged 15 to 17	928	901	5	4	7	10	–
Aged 18 to 19	601	580	15	4	–	2	–
Aged 20 to 24	1,492	1,292	150	17	22	12	–
Aged 25 to 29	1,353	829	366	48	64	44	4
Aged 30 to 34	1,441	652	536	33	95	111	13
Aged 35 to 44	3,027	981	1,228	60	229	474	54
Aged 45 to 54	2,448	547	922	56	196	576	151
Aged 55 to 64	1,421	188	536	26	99	324	248
Aged 65 or older	1,730	97	457	25	60	207	884
Total black men	**11,695**	**5,266**	**4,423**	**249**	**469**	**968**	**319**
Under age 30	3,866	3,337	387	44	37	62	–
Aged 15 to 17	928	914	2	2	2	8	–
Aged 18 to 19	580	571	7	–	–	2	–
Aged 20 to 24	1,279	1,140	104	12	12	12	–
Aged 25 to 29	1,079	712	274	30	23	40	–
Aged 30 to 34	1,157	540	499	19	46	53	–
Aged 35 to 44	2,463	800	1,233	76	114	223	18
Aged 45 to 54	2,013	409	1,009	64	145	338	48
Aged 55 to 64	1,074	118	600	33	83	180	59
Aged 65 or older	1,120	63	694	13	44	112	193

	total	never married	married, spouse present	married, spouse absent	separated	divorced	widowed
PERCENT DISTRIBUTION							
Total blacks	**100.0%**	**43.4%**	**33.1%**	**2.0%**	**4.7%**	**10.4%**	**6.4%**
Under age 30	100.0	84.2	11.2	1.4	1.6	1.6	0.1
Aged 15 to 17	100.0	97.8	0.4	0.3	0.5	1.0	–
Aged 18 to 19	100.0	97.5	1.9	0.3	–	0.3	–
Aged 20 to 24	100.0	87.7	9.2	1.0	1.2	0.9	–
Aged 25 to 29	100.0	63.3	26.3	3.2	3.6	3.5	0.2
Aged 30 to 34	100.0	45.9	39.9	2.0	5.4	6.3	0.5
Aged 35 to 44	100.0	32.4	44.8	2.5	6.2	12.7	1.3
Aged 45 to 54	100.0	21.4	43.3	2.7	7.6	20.5	4.5
Aged 55 to 64	100.0	12.2	45.6	2.4	7.3	20.2	12.3
Aged 65 or older	100.0	5.6	40.4	1.4	3.6	11.2	37.8
Total black women							
Under age 30	100.0	82.4	12.3	1.7	2.1	1.6	0.1
Aged 15 to 17	100.0	97.1	0.5	0.4	0.8	1.1	–
Aged 18 to 19	100.0	96.5	2.5	0.7	–	0.3	–
Aged 20 to 24	100.0	86.6	10.1	1.1	1.5	0.8	–
Aged 25 to 29	100.0	61.3	27.1	3.5	4.7	3.3	0.3
Aged 30 to 34	100.0	45.2	37.2	2.3	6.6	7.7	0.9
Aged 35 to 44	100.0	32.4	40.6	2.0	7.6	15.7	1.8
Aged 45 to 54	100.0	22.3	37.7	2.3	8.0	23.5	6.2
Aged 55 to 64	100.0	13.2	37.7	1.8	7.0	22.8	17.5
Aged 65 or older	100.0	5.6	26.4	1.4	3.5	12.0	51.1
Total black men							
Under age 30	100.0	86.3	10.0	1.1	1.0	1.6	–
Aged 15 to 17	100.0	98.5	0.2	0.2	0.2	0.9	–
Aged 18 to 19	100.0	98.4	1.2	–	–	0.3	–
Aged 20 to 24	100.0	89.1	8.1	0.9	0.9	0.9	–
Aged 25 to 29	100.0	66.0	25.4	2.8	2.1	3.7	–
Aged 30 to 34	100.0	46.7	43.1	1.6	4.0	4.6	–
Aged 35 to 44	100.0	32.5	50.1	3.1	4.6	9.1	0.7
Aged 45 to 54	100.0	20.3	50.1	3.2	7.2	16.8	2.4
Aged 55 to 64	100.0	11.0	55.9	3.1	7.7	16.8	5.5
Aged 65 or older	100.0	5.6	62.0	1.2	3.9	10.0	17.2

Note: (–) means number is less than 500 or sample is too small to make a reliable estimate.
Source: Bureau of the Census, 2002 Current Population Survey Annual Demographic Supplement, Internet site http:// www.census.gov/population/www/socdemo/hh-fam/cps2002.html

Table 7.33 Marital Status by Sex and Age, 2002: Hispanics

(number and percent distribution of Hispanics aged 15 or older by sex, age, and current marital status, 2002; numbers in thousands)

	total	never married	married, spouse present	married, spouse absent	separated	divorced	widowed
Total Hispanics	**26,332**	**9,557**	**12,432**	**846**	**889**	**1,734**	**875**
Under age 30	10,214	7,103	2,521	254	178	150	10
Aged 15 to 17	1,801	1,764	13	4	16	4	–
Aged 18 to 19	1,321	1,205	90	9	13	4	–
Aged 20 to 24	3,557	2,570	801	95	54	30	8
Aged 25 to 29	3,535	1,564	1,617	146	95	112	2
Aged 30 to 34	2,598	1,192	1,036	53	140	164	13
Aged 35 to 44	5,491	1,781	2,461	136	343	696	72
Aged 45 to 54	4,462	957	1,931	120	341	914	199
Aged 55 to 64	2,495	305	1,137	59	182	504	308
Aged 65 or older	2,852	161	1,152	39	103	319	1,077
Total Hispanic women	**12,900**	**3,936**	**6,316**	**289**	**604**	**1,026**	**727**
Under age 30	4,749	2,982	1,457	101	118	82	7
Aged 15 to 17	851	829	10	–	9	2	–
Aged 18 to 19	646	558	66	6	12	4	–
Aged 20 to 24	1,648	1,027	512	50	32	21	5
Aged 25 to 29	1,604	568	869	45	65	55	2
Aged 30 to 34	1,441	652	536	33	95	111	13
Aged 35 to 44	3,027	981	1,228	60	229	474	54
Aged 45 to 54	2,448	547	922	56	196	576	151
Aged 55 to 64	1,421	188	536	26	99	324	248
Aged 65 or older	1,730	97	457	25	60	207	884
Total Hispanic men	**13,432**	**5,621**	**6,116**	**556**	**284**	**707**	**147**
Under age 30	5,466	4,120	1,064	151	61	67	3
Aged 15 to 17	950	934	3	3	7	2	–
Aged 18 to 19	675	647	25	3	1	–	–
Aged 20 to 24	1,910	1,543	288	44	23	8	3
Aged 25 to 29	1,931	996	748	101	30	57	–
Aged 30 to 34	1,157	540	499	19	46	53	–
Aged 35 to 44	2,463	800	1,233	76	114	223	18
Aged 45 to 54	2,013	409	1,009	64	145	338	48
Aged 55 to 64	1,074	118	600	33	83	180	59
Aged 65 or older	1,120	63	694	13	44	112	193

	total	never married	married, spouse present	married, spouse absent	separated	divorced	widowed
PERCENT DISTRIBUTION							
Total Hispanics	**100.0%**	**36.3%**	**47.2%**	**3.2%**	**3.4%**	**6.6%**	**3.3%**
Under age 30	100.0	69.5	24.7	2.5	1.7	1.5	0.1
Aged 15 to 17	100.0	97.9	0.7	0.2	0.9	0.2	–
Aged 18 to 19	100.0	91.2	6.8	0.7	1.0	0.3	–
Aged 20 to 24	100.0	72.3	22.5	2.7	1.5	0.8	0.2
Aged 25 to 29	100.0	44.2	45.7	4.1	2.7	3.2	0.1
Aged 30 to 34	100.0	45.9	39.9	2.0	5.4	6.3	0.5
Aged 35 to 44	100.0	32.4	44.8	2.5	6.2	12.7	1.3
Aged 45 to 54	100.0	21.4	43.3	2.7	7.6	20.5	4.5
Aged 55 to 64	100.0	12.2	45.6	2.4	7.3	20.2	12.3
Aged 65 or older	100.0	5.6	40.4	1.4	3.6	11.2	37.8
Total Hispanic women	**100.0**	**30.5**	**49.0**	**2.2**	**4.7**	**8.0**	**5.6**
Under age 30	100.0	62.8	30.7	2.1	2.5	1.7	0.1
Aged 15 to 17	100.0	97.4	1.2	–	1.1	0.2	–
Aged 18 to 19	100.0	86.4	10.2	0.9	1.9	0.6	–
Aged 20 to 24	100.0	62.3	31.1	3.0	1.9	1.3	0.3
Aged 25 to 29	100.0	35.4	54.2	2.8	4.1	3.4	0.1
Aged 30 to 34	100.0	45.2	37.2	2.3	6.6	7.7	0.9
Aged 35 to 44	100.0	32.4	40.6	2.0	7.6	15.7	1.8
Aged 45 to 54	100.0	22.3	37.7	2.3	0.8	23.5	6.2
Aged 55 to 64	100.0	13.2	37.7	1.8	7.0	22.8	17.5
Aged 65 or older	100.0	5.6	26.4	1.4	3.5	12.0	51.1
Total Hispanic men	**100.0**	**41.8**	**45.5**	**4.1**	**2.1**	**5.3**	**1.1**
Under age 30	100.0	75.4	19.5	2.8	1.1	1.2	0.1
Aged 15 to 17	100.0	98.3	0.3	0.3	0.7	0.2	–
Aged 18 to 19	100.0	95.9	3.7	0.4	0.1	–	–
Aged 20 to 24	100.0	80.8	15.1	2.3	1.2	0.4	0.2
Aged 25 to 29	100.0	51.6	38.7	5.2	1.6	3.0	–
Aged 30 to 34	100.0	46.7	43.1	1.6	4.0	4.6	–
Aged 35 to 44	100.0	32.5	50.1	3.1	4.6	9.1	0.7
Aged 45 to 54	100.0	20.3	50.1	3.2	7.2	16.8	2.4
Aged 55 to 64	100.0	11.0	55.9	3.1	7.7	16.8	5.5
Aged 65 or older	100.0	5.6	62.0	1.2	3.9	10.0	17.2

Note: ( ) means number is less than 500 or sample is too small to make a r eliable estimate.
Source: Bureau of the Census, 2002 Current Population Survey Annual Demographic Supplement, Internet site http://www.census.gov/population/www/socdemo/hh-fam/cps2002.html

Table 7.34 Marital Status by Sex and Age, 2002: Non-Hispanic Whites

(number and percent distribution of non-Hispanic whites aged 15 or older by sex, age, and current marital status, 2002; numbers in thousands)

	total	never married	married, spouse present	married, spouse absent	separated	divorced	widowed
Total non-Hispanic whites	**158,188**	**38,770**	**89,082**	**1,250**	**2,327**	**15,778**	**10,981**
Under age 30	36,085	27,011	7,582	187	418	844	42
Aged 15 to 17	7,815	7,713	19	9	32	35	7
Aged 18 to 19	4,985	4,823	128	7	10	15	2
Aged 20 to 24	12,033	9,566	2,129	63	114	157	3
Aged 25 to 29	11,252	4,909	5,306	108	262	637	30
Aged 30 to 34	13,061	3,315	8,200	83	274	1,132	57
Aged 35 to 44	31,015	4,052	21,748	223	716	4,011	265
Aged 45 to 54	29,719	2,461	21,187	242	532	4,760	538
Aged 55 to 64	20,353	994	14,676	171	259	3,070	1,184
Aged 65 or older	27,956	938	15,690	344	129	1,962	8,894
Total non-Hispanic white women	**81,625**	**17,373**	**44,303**	**667**	**1,332**	**9,045**	**8,904**
Under age 30	17,980	12,635	4,394	123	243	548	36
Aged 15 to 17	3,842	3,793	13	2	10	19	4
Aged 18 to 19	2,432	2,310	94	7	9	10	2
Aged 20 to 24	6,045	4,443	1,354	44	72	129	3
Aged 25 to 29	5,661	2,089	2,933	70	152	390	27
Aged 30 to 34	6,513	1,254	4,357	38	153	664	46
Aged 35 to 44	15,608	1,508	11,188	122	422	2,168	201
Aged 45 to 54	14,964	1,035	10,485	120	318	2,607	398
Aged 55 to 64	10,465	420	7,025	79	140	1,842	959
Aged 65 or older	16,096	520	6,854	185	55	1,215	7,265
Total non-Hispanic white men	**76,564**	**21,397**	**44,779**	**583**	**995**	**6,733**	**2,077**
Under age 30	18,105	14,375	3,189	64	175	296	8
Aged 15 to 17	3,973	3,919	6	7	22	16	4
Aged 18 to 19	2,553	2,513	34	–	1	5	–
Aged 20 to 24	5,988	5,123	776	19	42	28	–
Aged 25 to 29	5,591	2,820	2,373	38	110	247	4
Aged 30 to 34	6,548	2,062	3,842	45	120	468	12
Aged 35 to 44	15,407	2,543	10,560	101	294	1,843	64
Aged 45 to 54	14,755	1,426	10,702	122	213	2,152	140
Aged 55 to 64	9,888	573	7,651	92	119	1,228	225
Aged 65 or older	11,860	418	8,834	159	72	746	1,629

	total	never married	married, spouse present	married, spouse absent	separated	divorced	widowed
PERCENT DISTRIBUTION							
Total non-Hispanic							
whites	**100.0%**	**24.5%**	**56.3%**	**0.8%**	**1.5%**	**10.0%**	**6.9%**
Under age 30	100.0	74.9	21.0	0.5	1.2	2.3	0.1
Aged 15 to 17	100.0	98.7	0.2	0.1	0.4	0.4	0.1
Aged 18 to 19	100.0	96.8	2.6	0.1	0.2	0.3	0.0
Aged 20 to 24	100.0	79.5	17.7	0.5	0.9	1.3	0.0
Aged 25 to 29	100.0	43.6	47.2	1.0	2.3	5.7	0.3
Aged 30 to 34	100.0	25.4	62.8	0.6	2.1	8.7	0.4
Aged 35 to 44	100.0	13.1	70.1	0.7	2.3	12.9	0.9
Aged 45 to 54	100.0	8.3	71.3	0.8	1.8	16.0	1.8
Aged 55 to 64	100.0	4.9	72.1	0.8	1.3	15.1	5.8
Aged 65 or older	100.0	3.4	56.1	1.2	0.5	7.0	31.8
Total non-Hispanic							
white women	**100.0**	**21.3**	**54.3**	**0.8**	**1.6**	**11.1**	**10.9**
Under age 30	100.0	70.3	24.4	0.7	1.4	3.1	0.2
Aged 15 to 17	100.0	98.7	0.3	0.1	0.3	0.5	0.1
Aged 18 to 19	100.0	95.0	3.9	0.3	0.4	0.4	0.1
Aged 20 to 24	100.0	73.5	22.4	0.7	1.2	2.1	0.1
Aged 25 to 29	100.0	36.9	51.8	1.2	2.7	6.9	0.5
Aged 30 to 34	100.0	19.3	66.9	0.6	2.3	10.2	0.7
Aged 35 to 44	100.0	9.7	71.7	0.8	2.7	13.9	1.3
Aged 45 to 54	100.0	6.9	70.1	0.8	2.1	17.4	2.7
Aged 55 to 64	100.0	4.0	67.1	0.8	1.3	17.6	9.2
Aged 65 or older	100.0	3.2	42.6	1.1	0.3	7.5	45.1
Total non-Hispanic							
white men	**100.0**	**27.9**	**58.5**	**0.8**	**1.3**	**8.8**	**2.7**
Under age 30	100.0	79.4	17.6	0.4	1.0	1.6	0.0
Aged 15 to 17	100.0	98.6	0.2	0.2	0.6	0.4	0.1
Aged 18 to 19	100.0	98.4	1.3	–	0.0	0.2	–
Aged 20 to 24	100.0	85.6	13.0	0.3	0.7	0.5	–
Aged 25 to 29	100.0	50.4	42.4	0.7	2.0	4.4	0.1
Aged 30 to 34	100.0	31.5	58.7	0.7	1.8	7.1	0.2
Aged 35 to 44	100.0	16.5	68.5	0.7	1.9	12.0	0.4
Aged 45 to 54	100.0	9.7	72.5	0.8	1.4	14.6	0.9
Aged 55 to 64	100.0	5.8	77.4	0.9	1.2	12.4	2.3
Aged 65 or older	100.0	3.5	74.5	1.3	0.6	6.3	13.7

Note: (–) means number is less than 500 or sample is too small to make a reliable estimate.
Source: Bureau of the Census, 2002 Current Population Survey Annual Demographic Supplement, Internet site http://www.census.gov/population/www/socdemo/hh-fam/cps2002.html

8

Population

■ The 2000 census counted 73 million members of the Millennial generation in the U.S., a figure that includes everyone born between 1977 and 1994. Millennials account for 26 percent of the total population.

■ America's children and young adults are much more diverse than middle-aged or older people. Non-Hispanic whites account for 69 percent of all Americans and for a smaller 62 percent of Millennials, aged 6 to 23 in 2000.

■ While 12 percent of all Americans are foreign born, the proportion is a far lower 7 percent among people under age 25. The figure climbs to an above-average 15 percent only among those aged 20 to 24.

■ More than 1 million immigrants were admitted to the U.S. in 2002, more than 350,000 of them under age 25. Behind this number is the fact that many people who immigrate do so as teens and young adults, looking for job opportunities.

■ Because of immigration and higher fertility rates, Hispanics outnumber blacks among people under age 25 in nearly half (23) of the 50 states. In California, 43 percent of the population under age 25 is Hispanic, a greater share than the 35 percent of whom are non-Hispanic whites.

Millennials Are the Second-Largest Generation

They are not far behind the Baby-Boom generation in size.

The 2000 census counted 73 million members of the Millennial generation (aged 6 to 23 in that year) in the United States, a figure that includes everyone born between 1977 and 1994. Millennials account for 26 percent of the total population, making them the second-largest generation. Boomers, the parents of many Millennials, are in first place. They numbered 78 million in 2000 and accounted for 28 percent of the population.

Between 2000 and 2002, Millennials entirely filled the 20-to-24 age group. During those two years, the number of 20-to-24-year-olds grew 6 percent, more than twice as fast as the 2.5 percent gain for the overall population. In contrast, as the small Generation X filled the 25-to-29 age group, it shrank by 2 percent.

In the ten years between 2000 and 2010, Millennials will fill the 15-to-34 age group. At the same time, Generation X will fill the 35-to-44 age group. As these two generations—one large and one small—fill the broad 20-to-44 age group, the consequence will be virtually no change in the number of 20-to-44-year-olds in the U.S. during this decade.

■ Millennials are bringing renewed attention to the youth market, but businesses will miss an opportunity if they abandon aging Boomers in favor of young adults.

The number of people aged 20 to 44 will not grow during this decade

(percent change in number of people by age, 2000–10)

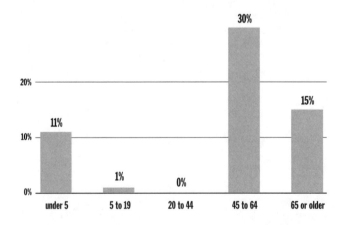

Table 8.1 Population by Age and Generation, 2000 Census

(number and percent distribution of people by age and generation, 2000; numbers in thousands)

	number	percent distribution
TOTAL PEOPLE	**281,422**	**100.0%**
Under age 25	99,437	35.3
Under age 5	19,176	6.8
Aged 5 to 9	20,550	7.3
Aged 10 to 14	20,528	7.3
Aged 15 to 19	20,220	7.2
Aged 20 to 24	18,964	6.7
Aged 25 to 29	19,381	6.9
Aged 30 to 34	20,510	7.3
Aged 35 to 39	22,707	8.1
Aged 40 to 44	22,442	8.0
Aged 45 to 49	20,092	7.1
Aged 50 to 54	17,586	6.2
Aged 55 to 59	13,469	4.8
Aged 60 to 64	10,805	3.8
Aged 65 to 69	9,534	3.4
Aged 70 to 74	8,857	3.1
Aged 75 to 79	7,416	2.6
Aged 80 to 84	4,945	1.8
Aged 85 or older	4,240	1.5
TOTAL PEOPLE	**281,422**	**100.0**
Post-Millennial (under age 6)	23,141	8.2
Millennial (aged 6 to 23)	**72,655**	**25.8**
Generation X (aged 24 to 35)	48,049	17.1
Baby Boom (aged 36 to 54)	78,310	27.8
Swing (aged 55 to 67)	30,061	10.7
World War II (aged 68 or older)	29,205	10.4

Source: Bureau of the Census, Census 2000 Summary File 1, Internet site http://factfinder.census.gov/servlet/BasicFactsServlet; calculations by New Strategist

Table 8.2 Population by Age and Sex, 2000 Census

(number of people by age and sex, and sex ratio by age, 2000; numbers in thousands)

	total	female	male	sex ratio
Total people	**281,422**	**143,368**	**138,054**	**96**
Under age 25	99,437	48,504	50,933	105
Under age 5	19,176	9,365	9,811	105
Aged 5 to 9	20,550	10,026	10,523	105
Aged 10 to 14	20,528	10,008	10,520	105
Aged 15 to 19	20,220	9,829	10,391	106
Aged 20 to 24	18,964	9,276	9,688	104
Aged 25 to 29	19,381	9,583	9,799	102
Aged 30 to 34	20,510	10,189	10,322	101
Aged 35 to 39	22,707	11,388	11,319	99
Aged 40 to 44	22,442	11,313	11,129	98
Aged 45 to 49	20,092	10,203	9,890	97
Aged 50 to 54	17,586	8,978	8,608	96
Aged 55 to 59	13,469	6,961	6,509	94
Aged 60 to 64	10,805	5,669	5,137	91
Aged 65 to 69	9,534	5,133	4,400	86
Aged 70 to 74	8,857	4,955	3,903	79
Aged 75 to 79	7,416	4,371	3,044	70
Aged 80 to 84	4,945	3,110	1,835	59
Aged 85 or older	4,240	3,013	1,227	41

Note: The sex ratio is the number of men per 100 women.
Source: Bureau of the Census, Census 2000 Summary File 1, Internet site http://factfinder.census.gov/servlet/BasicFactsServlet; calculations by New Strategist

Table 8.3 Population by Age, 2000 and 2002

(number of people by age, April 1, 2000, and July 1, 2002; percent change 2000–02; numbers in thousands)

	2000	2002	percent change 2000–02
Total people	**281,422**	**288,369**	**2.5%**
Under age 25	99,437	101,236	1.8
Under age 5	19,176	19,609	2.3
Aged 5 to 9	20,550	19,901	–3.2
Aged 10 to 14	20,528	21,136	3.0
Aged 15 to 19	20,220	20,376	0.8
Aged 20 to 24	18,964	20,214	6.6
Aged 25 to 29	19,381	18,972	–2.1
Aged 30 to 34	20,510	20,956	2.2
Aged 35 to 39	22,707	21,915	–3.5
Aged 40 to 44	22,442	23,002	2.5
Aged 45 to 49	20,092	21,302	6.0
Aged 50 to 54	17,586	18,782	6.8
Aged 55 to 59	13,469	14,991	11.3
Aged 60 to 64	10,805	11,611	7.5
Aged 65 to 69	9,534	9,581	0.5
Aged 70 to 74	8,857	8,693	–1.9
Aged 75 to 79	7,416	7,420	0.1
Aged 80 to 84	4,945	5,314	7.5
Aged 85 to 89	2,790	2,943	5.5
Aged 90 to 94	1,113	1,250	12.4
Aged 95 to 99	287	342	19.2
Aged 100 or older	50	59	16.3

Source: Bureau of the Census, National Population Estimates, Internet site http://eire.census.gov/popest/data/national/tables/ asro/NA-EST2002-ASRO-01.php; calculations by New Strategist

Table 8.4 Population by Age, 2000 to 2020

(number and percent distribution of people by age, 2000 to 2020; percent and percentage point change, 2000–2010 and 2010–20; numbers in thousands)

	2000	2010	2020	percent change 2000–10	percent change 2010–20
Total people	**282,125**	**308,936**	**335,805**	**9.5%**	**8.7%**
Under age 5	19,218	21,426	22,932	11.5	7.0
Aged 5 to 19	61,331	61,810	65,955	0.8	6.7
Aged 20 to 44	104,075	104,444	108,632	0.4	4.0
Aged 45 to 64	62,440	81,012	83,653	29.7	3.3
Aged 65 to 84	30,794	34,120	47,363	10.8	38.8
Aged 85 or older	4,267	6,123	7,269	43.5	18.7

	2000	2010	2020	percentage point change 2000–10	percentage point change 2010–20
Percent distribution by age					
Total people	**100.0%**	**100.0%**	**100.0%**	–	–
Under age 5	6.8	6.9	6.8	0.1	–0.1
Aged 5 to 19	21.7	20.0	19.6	–1.7	–0.4
Aged 20 to 44	36.9	33.8	32.3	–3.1	–1.5
Aged 45 to 64	22.1	26.2	24.9	4.1	–1.3
Aged 65 to 84	10.9	11.0	14.1	0.1	3.1
Aged 85 or older	1.5	2.0	2.2	0.5	0.2

Source: Bureau of the Census, U.S. Interim Projections by Age, Sex, Race, and Hispanic Origin, 2004, Internet site http://www.census.gov/ipc/www/usinterimproj/; calculations by New Strategist

The Nation's Children and Young Adults Are Diverse

Hispanics outnumber non-Hispanic blacks among the under-25 population.

America's children and young adults are much more diverse than middle-aged or older people. While non-Hispanic whites account for 69 percent of all Americans, their share is a smaller 62 percent among Millennials, aged 6 to 23 in 2000. Among children under age 5, non-Hispanic whites account for only 58 percent of the population.

Among Millennials, 16.4 percent are Hispanic, slightly surpassing the 15.8 percent who are black. Among children under age 5, Hispanics outnumber blacks by more than 600,000. Hispanics in the Millennial generation outnumber those in any other generation, accounting for 34 percent of the nation's total Hispanic population.

Among the 7 million multiracial Americans, 36 percent are members of the Millennial generation, far surpassing the share accounted for by any other generation. Three percent of Millennials are multiracial.

■ Racial and ethnic differences between young and old may divide the nation in the years ahead as older non-Hispanic whites attempt to govern young Hispanics, Asians, and blacks.

Minorities account for a large share of children and young adults

(percent distribution of people under age 25, by race and Hispanic origin, 2000)

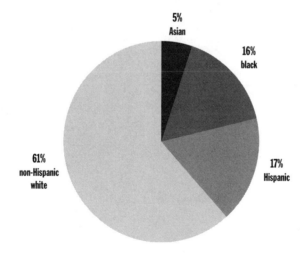

Table 8.5 Population by Age, Race, and Hispanic Origin, 2000 Census

(number and percent distribution of people by age, race, and Hispanic origin, 2000; numbers in thousands)

	total	American Indian	Asian	black	Native Hawaiian	white total	white non-Hispanic	other race	multiracial	Hispanic
Total people	**281,422**	**4,119**	**11,899**	**36,419**	**874**	**216,931**	**194,553**	**18,521**	**6,826**	**35,306**
Under age 25	99,437	1,846	4,568	15,843	431	71,353	60,736	9,355	3,655	17,086
Under age 5	19,176	359	919	3,167	88	13,656	11,194	2,017	948	3,718
Aged 5 to 14	41,078	791	1,771	6,823	175	29,533	25,186	3,648	1,533	6,787
Aged 15 to 24	39,184	697	1,878	5,853	168	28,164	24,355	3,690	1,174	6,581
Aged 25 to 34	39,892	588	2,179	5,374	140	29,096	25,356	3,578	997	6,510
Aged 35 to 44	45,149	644	1,953	5,699	126	34,984	31,801	2,693	891	5,129
Aged 45 to 54	37,678	501	1,499	4,194	86	30,494	28,387	1,553	607	3,136
Aged 55 to 64	24,275	281	839	2,429	47	20,316	19,028	718	332	1,710
Aged 65 or older	34,992	260	862	2,881	44	30,688	29,245	625	344	1,734

PERCENT DISTRIBUTION BY RACE AND HISPANIC ORIGIN

	total	American Indian	Asian	black	Native Hawaiian	white total	white non-Hispanic	other race	multiracial	Hispanic
Total people	**100.0%**	**1.5%**	**4.2%**	**12.9%**	**0.3%**	**77.1%**	**69.1%**	**6.6%**	**2.4%**	**12.5%**
Under age 25	100.0	1.9	4.6	15.9	0.4	71.8	61.1	9.4	3.7	17.2
Under age 5	100.0	1.9	4.8	16.5	0.5	71.2	58.4	10.5	4.9	19.4
Aged 5 to 14	100.0	1.9	4.3	16.6	0.4	71.9	61.3	8.9	3.7	16.5
Aged 15 to 24	100.0	1.8	4.8	14.9	0.4	71.9	62.2	9.4	3.0	16.8
Aged 25 to 34	100.0	1.5	5.5	13.5	0.4	72.9	63.6	9.0	2.5	16.3
Aged 35 to 44	100.0	1.4	4.3	12.6	0.3	77.5	70.4	6.0	2.0	11.4
Aged 45 to 54	100.0	1.3	4.0	11.1	0.2	80.9	75.3	4.1	1.6	8.3
Aged 55 to 64	100.0	1.2	3.5	10.0	0.2	83.7	78.4	3.0	1.4	7.1
Aged 65 or older	100.0	0.7	2.5	8.2	0.1	87.7	83.6	1.8	1.0	5.0

Note: Numbers will not add to total because each racial category includes those who identified themselves as being of the race alone and those who identified themselves as being of the race in combination with one or more other races, because the multiracial are shown, and because Hispanics may be of any race. Non-Hispanic whites include only those who identified themselves as "white alone" and non-Hispanic.
Source: Bureau of the Census, Census 2000 Summary File 1; Internet site http://factfinder.census.gov/servlet/BasicFactsServlet; calculations by New Strategist

Table 8.6 Population by Generation, Race, and Hispanic Origin, 2000 Census

(number and percent distribution of people by generation, race, and Hispanic origin, 2000; numbers in thousands)

	total	American Indian	Asian	black	Native Hawaiian	white total	white non-Hispanic	other race	Hispanic
TOTAL PEOPLE	**281,422**	**4,119**	**11,899**	**36,419**	**874**	**216,931**	**194,553**	**18,521**	**35,306**
Post-Millennial (under age 6)	23,141	432	1,100	3,833	106	16,475	13,539	2,414	4,451
Millennial (aged 6 to 23)	**72,655**	**1,356**	**3,266**	**11,498**	**311**	**52,303**	**45,002**	**6,551**	**11,948**
Generation X (aged 24 to 35)	48,049	711	2,592	6,486	169	35,076	30,585	4,295	7,812
Baby Boom (aged 36 to 54)	78,310	1,080	3,240	9,293	198	62,074	57,154	3,919	7,652
Swing (aged 55 to 67)	30,061	337	1,024	2,999	57	25,214	23,629	859	2,085
World War II (aged 68+)	29,205	203	676	2,310	34	25,790	24,644	484	1,360

PERCENT DISTRIBUTION BY RACE AND HISPANIC ORIGIN

	total	American Indian	Asian	black	Native Hawaiian	white total	white non-Hispanic	other race	Hispanic
TOTAL PEOPLE	**100.0%**	**100.0%**	**100.0%**	**100.0%**	**100.0%**	**100.0%**	**100.0%**	**100.0%**	**100.0%**
Post-Millennial (under age 6)	8.2	10.5	9.2	10.5	12.2	7.6	7.0	13.0	12.6
Millennial (aged 6 to 23)	**25.8**	**32.9**	**27.5**	**31.6**	**35.5**	**24.1**	**23.1**	**35.4**	**33.8**
Generation X (aged 24 to 35)	17.1	17.3	21.8	17.8	19.3	16.2	15.7	23.2	22.1
Baby Boom (aged 36 to 54)	27.8	26.2	27.2	25.5	22.6	28.6	29.4	21.2	21.7
Swing (aged 55 to 67)	10.7	8.2	8.6	8.2	6.5	11.6	12.1	4.6	5.9
World War II (aged 68+)	10.4	4.9	5.7	6.3	3.9	11.9	12.7	2.6	3.9

PERCENT DISTRIBUTION BY GENERATION

	total	American Indian	Asian	black	Native Hawaiian	white total	white non-Hispanic	other race	Hispanic
TOTAL PEOPLE	**100.0%**	**1.5%**	**4.2%**	**12.9%**	**0.3%**	**77.1%**	**69.1%**	**6.6%**	**12.5%**
Post-Millennial (under age 6)	100.0	1.9	4.8	16.6	0.5	71.2	58.5	10.4	19.2
Millennial (aged 6 to 23)	**100.0**	**1.9**	**4.5**	**15.8**	**0.4**	**72.0**	**61.9**	**9.0**	**16.4**
Generation X (aged 24 to 35)	100.0	1.5	5.4	13.5	0.4	73.0	63.7	8.9	16.3
Baby Boom (aged 36 to 54)	100.0	1.4	4.1	11.9	0.3	79.3	73.0	5.0	9.8
Swing (aged 55 to 67)	100.0	1.1	3.4	10.0	0.2	83.9	78.6	2.9	6.9
World War II (aged 68+)	100.0	0.7	2.3	7.9	0.1	88.3	84.4	1.7	4.7

Note: Numbers will not add to total because each racial category includes those who identified themselves as being of the race alone and those who identified themselves as being of the race in combination with one or more other races, and because Hispanics may be of any race. Non-Hispanic whites include only those who identified themselves as "white alone" and non-Hispanic. Source: Bureau of the Census, Census 2000 Summary File 2, Internet site http://factfinder.census.gov/servlet/BasicFactsServlet; calculations by New Strategist

Table 8.7 Multiracial Population by Age and Generation, 2000 Census

(number of total people and number and percent distribution of the multiracial population, by age and generation, 2000; numbers in thousands)

	total	multiracial number	multiracial percent distribution	multiracial share of total
TOTAL PEOPLE	281,422	6,826	100.0%	2.4%
Under age 5	19,176	948	13.9	4.9
Aged 5 to 9	20,550	830	12.2	4.0
Aged 10 to 14	20,528	703	10.3	3.4
Aged 15 to 19	20,220	622	9.1	3.1
Aged 20 to 24	18,964	552	8.1	2.9
Aged 25 to 29	19,381	512	7.5	2.6
Aged 30 to 34	20,510	484	7.1	2.4
Aged 35 to 39	22,707	471	6.9	2.1
Aged 40 to 44	22,442	421	6.2	1.9
Aged 45 to 49	20,092	338	5.0	1.7
Aged 50 to 54	17,586	269	3.9	1.5
Aged 55 to 59	13,469	189	2.8	1.4
Aged 60 to 64	10,805	143	2.1	1.3
Aged 65 to 69	9,534	112	1.6	1.2
Aged 70 to 74	8,857	91	1.3	1.0
Aged 75 to 79	7,416	67	1.0	0.9
Aged 80 to 84	4,945	41	0.6	0.8
Aged 85 or older	4,240	34	0.5	0.8
TOTAL PEOPLE	**281,422**	**6,826**	**100.0**	**2.4**
Post-Millennial (under 6)	23,141	1,122	16.4	4.8
Millennial (aged 6 to 23)	**72,655**	**2,429**	**35.6**	**3.3**
Generation X (24 to 35)	48,049	1,200	17.6	2.5
Baby Boom (aged 36 to 54)	78,310	1,399	20.5	1.8
Swing (aged 55 to 67)	30,061	402	5.9	1.3
World War II (68+)	29,205	274	4.0	0.9

Source: Bureau of the Census, Census 2000 Summary File 2, Internet site http://factfinder.census.gov/servlet/BasicFactsServlet; calculations by New Strategist

Few Children Are Foreign Born

But many young adults were born in another country.

While 12 percent of all Americans are foreign born, the proportion is a far lower 7 percent among people under age 25. The figure climbs to an above-average 15 percent only among those aged 20 to 24. A larger share of 20-to-24-year-olds are foreign born because young adults migrate to the United States in search of job opportunities. Among the nearly 3 million 20-to-24-year-olds who were born in a foreign country, only 15 percent are naturalized citizens.

Among the foreign born in the 20-to-24 age group, fully 50 percent were born in Central America (which includes Mexico in these statistics), while 21 percent were born in Asia. Only 8 percent were born in Europe.

■ The foreign-born population adds to the diversity of young adults. Because most are not citizens, however, they lack political power.

Among foreign-born young adults, most are from Central America

(percent distribution of foreign-born people aged 20 to 24 by region of birth, 2002)

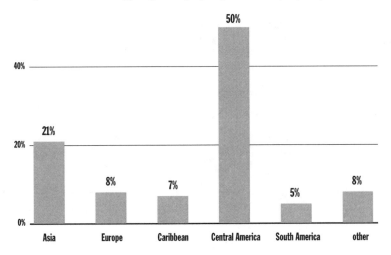

Table 8.8 Population under Age 25 by Citizenship Status, 2002

(number and percent distribution of total people and people under age 25 by citizenship status, 2002; numbers in thousands)

	total	native born	foreign born total	foreign born naturalized citizen	foreign born not a citizen
TOTAL PEOPLE	282,082	249,629	32,453	11,962	20,491
Total under age 25	99,940	93,278	6,661	966	5,695
Under age 5	19,428	19,107	320	55	265
Aged 5 to 9	20,026	19,332	694	89	605
Aged 10 to 14	21,037	19,937	1,100	144	956
Aged 15 to 19	20,045	18,339	1,706	247	1,459
Aged 20 to 24	19,404	16,563	2,841	431	2,410
PERCENT DISTRIBUTION BY CITIZENSHIP STATUS					
TOTAL PEOPLE	100.0%	88.5%	11.5%	4.2%	7.3%
Total under age 25	100.0	93.3	6.7	1.0	5.7
Under age 5	100.0	98.3	1.6	0.3	1.4
Aged 5 to 9	100.0	96.5	3.5	0.4	3.0
Aged 10 to 14	100.0	94.8	5.2	0.7	4.5
Aged 15 to 19	100.0	91.5	8.5	1.2	7.3
Aged 20 to 24	100.0	85.4	14.6	2.2	12.4
PERCENT DISTRIBUTION BY AGE					
TOTAL PEOPLE	100.0%	100.0%	100.0%	100.0%	100.0%
Total under age 25	35.4	37.4	20.5	8.1	27.8
Under age 5	6.9	7.7	1.0	0.5	1.3
Aged 5 to 9	7.1	7.7	2.1	0.7	3.0
Aged 10 to 14	7.5	8.0	3.4	1.2	4.7
Aged 15 to 19	7.1	7.3	5.3	2.1	7.1
Aged 20 to 24	6.9	6.6	8.8	3.6	11.8

Source: Bureau of the Census, Foreign-Born Population of the United States, Current Population Survey, March 2002, *Internet site http://www.census.gov/population/www/socdemo/foreign/ppl-162.html; calculations by New Strategist*

Table 8.9 Foreign-Born Population under Age 25, 2002

(number and percent distribution of total people and people under age 25 by foreign-born status and region of birth, 2002; numbers in thousands)

		foreign born							
					Latin America				
	total	total	Asia	Europe	total	Caribbean	Central America	South America	other
TOTAL PEOPLE	282,082	32,453	8,281	4,548	16,943	3,102	11,819	2,022	2,680
Total under age 25	99,940	6,661	1,402	579	4,108	507	3,185	416	574
Under age 5	19,428	320	84	41	165	12	139	14	30
Aged 5 to 9	20,026	694	142	71	415	51	324	40	67
Aged 10 to 14	21,037	1,100	215	95	679	81	508	90	111
Aged 15 to 19	20,045	1,706	370	148	1,055	153	783	120	133
Aged 20 to 24	19,404	2,841	591	224	1,794	210	1,431	152	233
PERCENT DISTRIBUTION OF FOREIGN-BORN BY REGION OF BIRTH									
TOTAL PEOPLE	–	100.0%	25.5%	14.0%	52.2%	9.6%	36.4%	6.2%	8.3%
Total under age 25	–	100.0	21.1	8.7	61.7	7.6	47.8	6.2	8.6
Under age 5	–	100.0	26.2	12.8	51.6	3.8	43.4	4.4	9.4
Aged 5 to 9	–	100.0	20.5	10.2	59.8	7.3	46.7	5.8	9.7
Aged 10 to 14	–	100.0	19.5	8.6	61.7	7.4	46.2	8.2	10.1
Aged 15 to 19	–	100.0	21.7	8.7	61.8	9.0	45.9	7.0	7.8
Aged 20 to 24	–	100.0	20.8	7.9	63.1	7.4	50.4	5.4	8.2
PERCENT DISTRIBUTION BY AGE									
TOTAL PEOPLE	100.0%	100.0%	100.0%	100.0%	100.0%	100.0%	100.0%	100.0%	100.0%
Total under age 25	35.4	20.5	16.9	12.7	24.2	16.3	26.9	20.6	21.4
Under age 5	6.9	1.0	1.0	0.9	1.0	0.4	1.2	0.7	1.1
Aged 5 to 9	7.1	2.1	1.7	1.6	2.4	1.6	2.7	2.0	2.5
Aged 10 to 14	7.5	3.4	2.6	2.1	4.0	2.6	4.3	4.5	4.1
Aged 15 to 19	7.1	5.3	4.5	3.3	6.2	4.9	6.6	5.9	5.0
Aged 20 to 24	6.9	8.8	7.1	4.9	10.6	6.8	12.1	7.5	8.7

Note: Central America includes Mexico in these statistics; (–) means not applicable.
Source: Bureau of the Census, Foreign-Born Population of the United States, Current Population Survey, March 2002, *Internet site http://www.census.gov/population/www/socdemo/foreign/ppl-162.html; calculations by New Strategist*

Among Immigrants, the Young Count

One-third of immigrants are under age 25.

More than 1 million immigrants were admitted to the U.S. in 2002, with more than 350,000 of them under age 25. Behind this substantial number is the fact that many people who immigrate do so as teens and young adults, looking for job opportunities.

Seventeen percent of immigrants to the United States in 2002 were aged 15 to 24. The figure rises to 29 percent in the next 10-year age group, 25 to 34. It then declines steadily with age. Just 11 percent of immigrants are aged 55 or older.

■ Because most immigrants are children and young adults, immigration has a much greater impact on the diversity of young Americans than on the middle-aged or older populations.

Immigrants under age 25 account for 33 percent of the total

(percent distribution of immigrants by age, 2002)

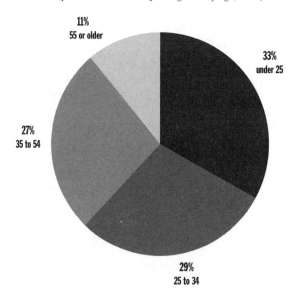

11%
55 or older

33%
under 25

27%
35 to 54

29%
25 to 34

Table 8.10 Immigrants by Age, 2002

(number and percent distribution of immigrants by age, 2002)

	number	percent distribution
Total immigrants	**1,063,732**	**100.0%**
Under age 25	354,515	33.3
Under age 1	11,673	1.1
Aged 1 to 4	31,791	3.0
Aged 5 to 9	54,493	5.1
Aged 10 to 14	70,860	6.7
Aged 15 to 19	92,566	8.7
Aged 20 to 24	93,132	8.8
Aged 25 to 29	152,476	14.3
Aged 30 to 34	160,962	15.1
Aged 35 to 39	112,247	10.6
Aged 40 to 44	75,743	7.1
Aged 45 to 49	54,811	5.2
Aged 50 to 54	40,319	3.8
Aged 55 to 59	31,694	3.0
Aged 60 to 64	29,201	2.7
Aged 65 to 74	39,014	3.7
Aged 75 or older	12,541	1.2

Source: U.S. Citizenship and Immigration Services, 2002 Yearbook of Immigration Statistics, Internet site http://uscis.gov/graphics/shared/aboutus/statistics/IMM02yrbk/IMM2002list.htm

The Largest Share of Millennials Lives in the South

Millennials account for fully 46 percent of the population of Utah.

The South is home to the largest share of the population, and consequently to the largest share of Millennials. The 2000 census found 36 percent of Millennials living in the South, where they accounted for 26 percent of the population.

The diversity of Millennials varies greatly by state. In Maine, New Hampshire, Vermont, and West Virginia at least 90 percent of people under age 25 are non-Hispanic white. But in California, the most populous state, the figure is just 35 percent. In Texas, only 43 percent of people under age 25 are non-Hispanic white. Hawaii, New Mexico, and the District of Columbia also have minority majorities in the under-25 age group.

Because of immigration and higher fertility rates, Hispanics outnumber blacks among people under age 25 in nearly half (23) of the 50 states. In California, 43 percent of the population under age 25 is Hispanic (a greater share than the 35 percent that is non-Hispanic white), 12 percent are Asian, and 9 percent are black. In other states with large Hispanic populations, such as Texas and Florida, Hispanics also greatly outnumber blacks in the under-25 population.

■ Although Millennials are more diverse in some states than others, the cultural influence of racial and ethnic diversity is shared by children and young adults everywhere.

In California, diversity is the rule among children and young adults

(percent distribution of people under age 25 in California by race and Hispanic origin, 2000)

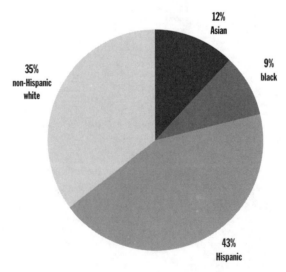

12%
Asian

9%
black

35%
non-Hispanic
white

43%
Hispanic

Table 8.11 Population under Age 25 by Region, 2000 Census

(number and percent distribution of total people and people under age 25 by age and region, 2000; numbers in thousands)

	total	Northeast	Midwest	South	West
TOTAL PEOPLE	**281,422**	**53,594**	**64,393**	**100,237**	**63,198**
Total under age 25	**99,437**	**17,805**	**22,888**	**35,393**	**23,350**
Under age 5	19,176	3,396	4,353	6,848	4,579
Aged 5 to 9	20,550	3,744	4,688	7,214	4,904
Aged 10 to 14	20,528	3,762	4,764	7,234	4,768
Aged 15 to 19	20,220	3,593	4,767	7,217	4,643
Aged 20 to 24	18,964	3,310	4,316	6,881	4,457
PERCENT DISTRIBUTION BY AGE					
TOTAL PEOPLE	**100.0%**	**100.0%**	**100.0%**	**100.0%**	**100.0%**
Total under age 25	**35.3**	**33.2**	**35.5**	**35.3**	**36.9**
Under age 5	6.8	6.3	6.8	6.8	7.2
Aged 5 to 9	7.3	7.0	7.3	7.2	7.8
Aged 10 to 14	7.3	7.0	7.4	7.2	7.5
Aged 15 to 19	7.2	6.7	7.4	7.2	7.3
Aged 20 to 24	6.7	6.2	6.7	6.9	7.1
PERCENT DISTRIBUTION BY REGION					
TOTAL PEOPLE	**100.0%**	**19.0%**	**22.9%**	**35.6%**	**22.5%**
Total under age 25	**100.0**	**17.9**	**23.0**	**35.6**	**23.5**
Under age 5	100.0	17.7	22.7	35.7	23.9
Aged 5 to 9	100.0	18.2	22.8	35.1	23.9
Aged 10 to 14	100.0	18.3	23.2	35.2	23.2
Aged 15 to 19	100.0	17.8	23.6	35.7	23.0
Aged 20 to 24	100.0	17.5	22.8	36.3	23.5

Source: Bureau of the Census, Census 2000 Summary File 2, Internet site http://factfinder.census.gov/servlet/BasicFactsServlet; calculations by New Strategist

Table 8.12 Regional Populations by Generation, 2000 Census

(number and percent distribution of people by generation and region, 2000; numbers in thousands)

	total	Northeast	Midwest	South	West
TOTAL PEOPLE	281,422	53,594	64,393	100,237	63,198
Post-Millennial (under age 6)	23,141	4,115	5,255	8,238	5,532
Millennial (aged 6 to 23)	**72,655**	**13,059**	**16,826**	**25,834**	**16,936**
Generation X (aged 24 to 35)	48,049	8,938	10,547	17,248	11,315
Baby Boom (aged 36 to 54)	78,310	15,303	17,958	27,635	17,415
Swing (aged 55 to 67)	30,061	5,957	6,863	10,995	6,246
World War II (aged 68 or older)	29,205	6,222	6,944	10,286	5,753
PERCENT DISTRIBUTION BY GENERATION					
TOTAL PEOPLE	100.0%	100.0%	100.0%	100.0%	100.0%
Post-Millennial (under age 6)	8.2	7.7	8.2	8.2	8.8
Millennial (aged 6 to 23)	**25.8**	**24.4**	**26.1**	**25.8**	**26.8**
Generation X (aged 24 to 35)	17.1	16.7	16.4	17.2	17.9
Baby Boom (aged 36 to 54)	27.8	28.6	27.9	27.6	27.6
Swing (aged 55 to 67)	10.7	11.1	10.7	11.0	9.9
World War II (aged 68 or older)	10.4	11.6	10.8	10.3	9.1
PERCENT DISTRIBUTION BY REGION					
TOTAL PEOPLE	100.0%	19.0%	22.9%	35.6%	22.5%
Post-Millennial (under age 6)	100.0	17.8	22.7	35.6	23.9
Millennial (aged 6 to 23)	**100.0**	**18.0**	**23.2**	**35.6**	**23.3**
Generation X (aged 24 to 35)	100.0	18.6	22.0	35.9	23.5
Baby Boom (aged 36 to 54)	100.0	19.5	22.9	35.3	22.2
Swing (aged 55 to 67)	100.0	19.8	22.8	36.6	20.8
World War II (aged 68 or older)	100.0	21.3	23.8	35.2	19.7

Source: Bureau of the Census, Census 2000 Summary File 2, Internet site http://factfinder.census.gov/servlet/BasicFactsServlet; calculations by New Strategist

Table 8.13   Population under Age 25 by State, 2000 Census

(number and percent distribution of total people and people under age 25 by state, 2000; numbers in thousands)

| | number | | | | | percent distribution | | | |
| | total | under age 25 | | | total | total | under age 25 | | |
		total	< 5	5–14	15–24			< 5	5–14	15–24
United States	**281,422**	**99,438**	**19,176**	**41,078**	**39,184**	**100.0%**	**35.3%**	**6.8%**	**14.6%**	**13.9%**
Alabama	4,447	1,563	296	636	631	100.0	35.1	6.7	14.3	14.2
Alaska	627	248	48	110	90	100.0	39.6	7.6	17.6	14.4
Arizona	5,131	1,881	382	768	731	100.0	36.7	7.5	15.0	14.2
Arkansas	2,673	942	182	380	380	100.0	35.2	6.8	14.2	14.2
California	33,872	12,616	2,487	5,297	4,832	100.0	37.2	7.3	15.6	14.3
Colorado	4,301	1,531	298	620	614	100.0	35.6	6.9	14.4	14.3
Connecticut	3,406	1,113	223	486	404	100.0	32.7	6.6	14.3	11.9
Delaware	784	270	52	111	107	100.0	34.4	6.6	14.2	13.7
District of Columbia	572	188	33	65	90	100.0	32.8	5.7	11.4	15.7
Florida	15,982	4,977	946	2,089	1,942	100.0	31.1	5.9	13.1	12.2
Georgia	8,186	3,007	595	1,223	1,189	100.0	36.7	7.3	14.9	14.5
Hawaii	1,212	411	78	168	164	100.0	33.9	6.5	13.9	13.6
Idaho	1,294	508	98	205	205	100.0	39.2	7.5	15.9	15.8
Illinois	12,419	4,456	877	1,835	1,745	100.0	35.9	7.1	14.8	14.1
Indiana	6,080	2,189	423	887	879	100.0	36.0	7.0	14.6	14.5
Iowa	2,926	1,032	188	413	430	100.0	35.3	6.4	14.1	14.7
Kansas	2,688	989	189	400	400	100.0	36.8	7.0	14.9	14.9
Kentucky	4,042	1,397	266	559	572	100.0	34.6	6.6	13.8	14.2
Louisiana	4,469	1,694	317	685	692	100.0	37.9	7.1	15.3	15.5
Maine	1,275	405	71	175	159	100.0	31.8	5.5	13.7	12.5
Maryland	5,296	1,807	353	784	670	100.0	34.1	6.7	14.8	12.7
Massachusetts	6,349	2,079	397	862	820	100.0	32.8	6.3	13.6	12.9
Michigan	9,938	3,528	672	1,492	1,364	100.0	35.5	6.8	15.0	13.7
Minnesota	4,919	1,757	330	731	697	100.0	35.7	6.7	14.9	14.2
Mississippi	2,845	1,086	204	436	446	100.0	38.2	7.2	15.3	15.7
Missouri	5,595	1,964	370	811	783	100.0	35.1	6.6	14.5	14.0
Montana	902	316	55	131	130	100.0	35.0	6.1	14.5	14.4
Nebraska	1,711	625	117	252	255	100.0	36.5	6.8	14.7	14.9
Nevada	1,998	692	146	289	257	100.0	34.6	7.3	14.4	12.9
New Hampshire	1,236	413	76	182	156	100.0	33.4	6.1	14.7	12.6
New Jersey	8,414	2,764	564	1,195	1,005	100.0	32.9	6.7	14.2	11.9
New Mexico	1,819	686	131	289	267	100.0	37.7	7.2	15.9	14.7
New York	18,976	6,456	1,239	2,684	2,532	100.0	34.0	6.5	14.1	13.3
North Carolina	8,049	2,771	540	1,114	1,117	100.0	34.4	6.7	13.8	13.9
North Dakota	642	234	39	90	104	100.0	36.4	6.1	14.1	16.2
Ohio	11,353	3,945	755	1,644	1,546	100.0	34.7	6.6	14.5	13.6
Oklahoma	3,451	1,249	236	497	517	100.0	36.2	6.8	14.4	15.0
Oregon	3,421	1,174	223	477	475	100.0	34.3	6.5	13.9	13.9
Pennsylvania	12,281	4,017	728	1,692	1,597	100.0	32.7	5.9	13.8	13.0
Rhode Island	1,048	354	64	143	147	100.0	33.8	6.1	13.7	14.1
South Carolina	4,012	1,418	265	576	577	100.0	35.3	6.6	14.3	14.4

	number					percent distribution			
		under age 25					under age 25		
	total	total	< 5	5–14	15–24	total	total	< 5	5–14	15–24
South Dakota	755	280	51	114	115	100.0	37.1	6.8	15.1	15.3
Tennessee	5,689	1,947	375	791	782	100.0	34.2	6.6	13.9	13.7
Texas	20,852	8,086	1,625	3,285	3,176	100.0	38.8	7.8	15.8	15.2
Utah	2,233	1,036	209	385	441	100.0	46.4	9.4	17.3	19.8
Vermont	609	204	34	87	84	100.0	33.5	5.6	14.2	13.7
Virginia	7,079	2,418	462	991	965	100.0	34.2	6.5	14.0	13.6
Washington	5,894	2,073	394	861	818	100.0	35.2	6.7	14.6	13.9
West Virginia	1,808	575	102	227	246	100.0	31.8	5.6	12.6	13.6
Wisconsin	5,364	1,889	342	783	765	100.0	35.2	6.4	14.6	14.3
Wyoming	494	179	31	73	75	100.0	36.2	6.3	14.7	15.3

Source: Bureau of the Census, Census 2000 Summary File 2, Internet site http://factfinder.census.gov/servlet/BasicFactsServlet

Table 8.14 Population under Age 25 by State, Race, and Hispanic Origin, 2000 Census

(total number of people, number under age 25, and percent distribution by race and Hispanic origin, by state, 2000)

	total number	total percent	American Indian	Asian	black	Native Hawaiian	white total	white non-Hispanic	other	Hispanic
ALABAMA										
State total	4,447,100	100.0%	1.0%	0.9%	26.3%	0.1%	72.0%	70.3%	0.9%	1.7%
Total under 25	1,563,034	100.0	1.1	1.0	32.4	0.1	65.6	63.3	1.3	2.4
Under age 5	295,992	100.0	0.9	1.1	32.2	0.1	66.1	63.0	1.7	2.9
Aged 5 to 9	315,345	100.0	1.0	0.9	33.4	0.1	65.0	62.7	1.2	2.2
Aged 10 to 14	320,252	100.0	1.1	0.9	32.6	0.1	65.7	63.9	0.9	1.7
Aged 15 to 19	324,580	100.0	1.2	1.0	32.8	0.1	65.0	63.1	1.1	2.2
Aged 20 to 24	306,865	100.0	1.0	1.3	31.0	0.1	66.0	63.7	1.8	3.2
ALASKA										
State total	626,932	100.0	19.0	5.2	4.3	0.9	74.0	67.6	2.4	4.1
Total under 25	248,009	100.0	24.6	5.7	5.8	1.3	69.2	59.6	3.0	5.4
Under age 5	47,591	100.0	25.5	6.4	7.4	1.5	68.8	56.1	3.5	6.7
Aged 5 to 9	53,771	100.0	25.8	5.6	6.0	1.3	68.8	58.2	3.0	5.6
Aged 10 to 14	56,661	100.0	25.8	5.5	5.1	1.2	69.0	59.7	2.5	4.6
Aged 15 to 19	50,094	100.0	24.0	5.5	4.6	1.2	70.2	61.8	2.5	4.6
Aged 20 to 24	39,892	100.0	20.7	5.5	5.8	1.2	69.6	62.5	3.4	5.8
ARIZONA										
State total	5,130,632	100.0	5.7	2.3	3.6	0.3	77.9	63.8	13.2	25.3
Total under 25	1,881,048	100.0	8.0	2.6	4.7	0.4	70.0	50.4	19.2	35.7
Under age 5	382,386	100.0	7.7	2.7	5.3	0.4	69.1	46.1	21.2	40.1
Aged 5 to 9	389,869	100.0	8.5	2.5	5.1	0.4	69.6	48.6	19.4	36.9
Aged 10 to 14	378,211	100.0	9.0	2.3	4.8	0.3	70.7	52.2	17.5	33.1
Aged 15 to 19	367,722	100.0	8.1	2.5	4.4	0.4	70.8	53.2	17.9	33.1
Aged 20 to 24	362,860	100.0	6.4	2.8	4.1	0.4	70.0	52.2	19.9	35.3
ARKANSAS										
State total	2,673,400	100.0	1.4	1.0	16.0	0.1	81.2	78.6	1.8	3.2
Total under 25	942,107	100.0	1.5	1.1	21.0	0.2	75.3	71.6	2.8	4.9
Under age 5	181,585	100.0	1.4	1.2	21.7	0.2	74.8	69.7	3.5	6.2
Aged 5 to 9	187,224	100.0	1.6	1.0	21.9	0.1	74.9	70.9	2.7	4.8
Aged 10 to 14	192,935	100.0	1.7	1.0	21.2	0.1	75.8	72.6	2.1	3.8
Aged 15 to 19	198,765	100.0	1.6	1.1	20.9	0.2	75.5	72.4	2.4	4.2
Aged 20 to 24	181,598	100.0	1.3	1.4	19.5	0.2	75.7	72.1	3.4	5.8
CALIFORNIA										
State total	33,871,648	100.0	1.9	12.3	7.4	0.7	63.4	46.7	19.4	32.4
Total under 25	12,615,859	100.0	2.2	12.2	8.6	0.9	56.9	35.1	26.6	43.4
Under age 5	2,486,981	100.0	2.1	11.8	8.8	0.9	57.0	31.7	28.5	47.8
Aged 5 to 9	2,725,880	100.0	2.2	11.4	9.2	0.9	57.3	33.7	27.1	45.4
Aged 10 to 14	2,570,822	100.0	2.3	11.9	9.2	0.8	58.3	37.4	24.6	40.6
Aged 15 to 19	2,450,888	100.0	2.3	13.0	8.2	0.9	56.7	37.3	25.4	40.4
Aged 20 to 24	2,381,288	100.0	2.0	13.1	7.4	0.8	54.9	35.4	27.5	42.9

	total		American			Native	white			
	number	percent	Indian	Asian	black	Hawaiian	total	non-Hispanic	other	Hispanic
COLORADO										
State total	4,301,261	100.0%	1.9%	2.8%	4.4%	0.2%	85.2%	74.5%	8.5%	17.1%
Total under 25	1,530,906	100.0	2.3	3.3	5.7	0.3	81.1	66.3	12.2	23.6
Under age 5	297,505	100.0	2.3	3.8	6.5	0.4	79.8	62.0	13.9	27.2
Aged 5 to 9	308,428	100.0	2.3	3.1	6.4	0.3	81.0	65.6	12.4	24.0
Aged 10 to 14	311,497	100.0	2.3	3.0	5.7	0.3	82.5	69.0	10.7	21.0
Aged 15 to 19	307,238	100.0	2.4	3.3	5.1	0.3	82.1	68.7	11.1	21.7
Aged 20 to 24	306,238	100.0	2.2	3.5	4.7	0.4	80.1	66.2	12.9	24.2
CONNECTICUT										
State total	3,405,565	100.0	0.7	2.8	10.0	0.1	83.3	77.5	5.5	9.4
Total under 25	1,113,273	100.0	0.9	3.4	13.6	0.2	77.3	68.8	8.4	14.2
Under age 5	223,344	100.0	0.9	4.0	14.2	0.2	77.0	67.2	8.7	15.1
Aged 5 to 9	244,144	100.0	0.9	3.1	13.8	0.1	78.0	69.5	8.0	13.8
Aged 10 to 14	241,587	100.0	0.9	2.8	13.2	0.1	78.7	71.1	7.5	12.9
Aged 15 to 19	216,627	100.0	1.0	3.2	13.2	0.2	77.6	69.9	8.1	13.5
Aged 20 to 24	187,571	100.0	1.0	4.2	13.5	0.3	74.7	65.8	9.9	16.0
DELAWARE										
State total	783,600	100.0	0.8	2.4	20.1	0.1	75.9	72.5	2.6	4.8
Total under 25	269,915	100.0	0.9	2.6	25.3	0.1	70.2	64.8	4.0	7.2
Under age 5	51,531	100.0	0.9	3.2	26.6	0.1	69.2	61.7	4.9	8.8
Aged 5 to 9	55,813	100.0	0.9	2.6	26.6	0.1	69.3	63.8	4.0	7.1
Aged 10 to 14	55,274	100.0	0.9	2.4	26.0	0.1	70.1	65.8	3.3	5.7
Aged 15 to 19	55,632	100.0	1.0	2.3	24.7	0.1	70.9	66.5	3.4	6.3
Aged 20 to 24	51,665	100.0	0.9	2.7	22.5	0.1	71.4	66.3	4.4	8.2
DISTRICT OF COLUMBIA										
District total	572,059	100.0	0.8	3.1	61.3	0.1	32.2	27.8	5.0	7.9
Total under 25	187,629	100.0	0.8	3.3	65.3	0.2	26.8	21.8	6.7	10.0
Under age 5	32,536	100.0	0.9	2.9	71.1	0.2	21.1	14.9	7.9	11.8
Aged 5 to 9	35,385	100.0	0.7	1.9	79.2	0.1	14.7	10.1	6.2	9.5
Aged 10 to 14	30,018	100.0	0.8	1.9	79.0	0.1	15.0	11.1	5.8	8.7
Aged 15 to 19	37,867	100.0	0.7	3.2	62.1	0.2	30.1	25.8	6.0	9.0
Aged 20 to 24	51,823	100.0	0.8	5.3	46.4	0.3	43.2	37.5	7.2	10.6
FLORIDA										
State total	15,982,378	100.0	0.7	2.1	15.5	0.2	79.7	65.4	4.4	16.8
Total under 25	4,976,942	100.0	0.9	2.5	22.4	0.2	71.2	55.0	6.5	20.0
Under age 5	945,823	100.0	0.8	2.6	22.9	0.2	71.4	54.1	6.7	20.5
Aged 5 to 9	1,031,718	100.0	0.8	2.3	23.2	0.2	71.2	55.2	6.1	19.1
Aged 10 to 14	1,057,024	100.0	0.9	2.3	22.7	0.2	71.6	56.4	5.7	18.4
Aged 15 to 19	1,014,067	100.0	0.9	2.5	22.3	0.2	70.8	55.3	6.5	19.6
Aged 20 to 24	928,310	100.0	0.9	2.8	20.6	0.3	71.0	53.6	7.8	22.8
GEORGIA										
State total	8,186,453	100.0	0.6	2.4	29.2	0.1	66.1	62.6	2.9	5.3
Total under 25	3,006,966	100.0	0.7	2.6	34.7	0.2	59.8	55.1	4.3	7.4
Under age 5	595,150	100.0	0.6	2.8	34.6	0.2	60.2	54.3	4.8	8.2
Aged 5 to 9	615,584	100.0	0.6	2.5	36.5	0.1	59.0	54.5	3.6	6.2
Aged 10 to 14	607,759	100.0	0.7	2.3	35.9	0.1	60.2	56.8	2.7	4.7
Aged 15 to 19	596,277	100.0	0.7	2.6	34.3	0.2	60.0	55.8	4.0	7.0
Aged 20 to 24	592,196	100.0	0.7	2.9	32.0	0.2	59.8	53.9	6.2	11.0

	total		American			Native	white			
	number	percent	Indian	Asian	black	Hawaiian	total	non-Hispanic	other	Hispanic
HAWAII										
State total	**1,211,537**	**100.0%**	**2.1%**	**58.0%**	**2.8%**	**23.3%**	**39.3%**	**22.9%**	**3.9%**	**7.2%**
Total under 25	**410,660**	**100.0**	**3.0**	**58.0**	**4.3**	**34.5**	**43.8**	**17.3**	**5.5**	**11.5**
Under age 5	78,163	100.0	3.5	58.6	5.6	37.8	47.0	15.8	6.5	14.0
Aged 5 to 9	84,980	100.0	3.2	60.0	4.5	37.3	44.4	15.0	5.7	12.0
Aged 10 to 14	83,106	100.0	3.1	60.6	3.4	36.5	43.2	15.0	5.0	10.7
Aged 15 to 19	81,002	100.0	2.9	60.2	3.2	34.5	41.0	15.7	5.0	10.4
Aged 20 to 24	83,409	100.0	2.5	50.5	4.7	26.5	43.7	24.8	5.5	10.3
IDAHO										
State total	**1,293,953**	**100.0**	**2.1**	**1.3**	**0.6**	**0.2**	**92.8**	**88.1**	**5.0**	**7.9**
Total under 25	**507,859**	**100.0**	**2.5**	**1.6**	**1.0**	**0.3**	**90.6**	**83.7**	**7.2**	**11.3**
Under age 5	97,643	100.0	2.7	1.8	1.4	0.3	89.6	80.7	8.6	13.8
Aged 5 to 9	100,756	100.0	2.7	1.5	1.1	0.3	90.4	82.4	7.7	12.5
Aged 10 to 14	104,608	100.0	2.7	1.4	0.8	0.3	91.6	85.2	6.3	10.0
Aged 15 to 19	110,858	100.0	2.3	1.4	0.7	0.3	91.5	86.0	6.2	9.6
Aged 20 to 24	93,994	100.0	2.2	1.6	1.0	0.4	89.9	84.0	7.3	11.1
ILLINOIS										
State total	**12,419,293**	**100.0**	**0.6**	**3.8**	**15.6**	**0.1**	**75.1**	**67.8**	**6.8**	**12.3**
Total under 25	**4,456,349**	**100.0**	**0.7**	**4.0**	**19.1**	**0.1**	**69.4**	**59.2**	**9.7**	**17.5**
Under age 5	876,549	100.0	0.7	4.3	19.6	0.1	68.6	55.9	10.9	20.1
Aged 5 to 9	929,858	100.0	0.7	3.5	20.9	0.1	68.6	58.0	9.5	17.4
Aged 10 to 14	905,097	100.0	0.7	3.5	19.7	0.1	70.4	61.7	8.3	14.8
Aged 15 to 19	894,002	100.0	0.7	3.9	18.3	0.1	70.3	61.5	9.1	15.8
Aged 20 to 24	850,843	100.0	0.7	4.8	16.7	0.2	69.0	58.7	11.1	19.4
INDIANA										
State total	**6,080,485**	**100.0**	**0.6**	**1.2**	**8.8**	**0.1**	**88.6**	**85.8**	**2.0**	**3.5**
Total under 25	**2,189,117**	**100.0**	**0.7**	**1.4**	**11.2**	**0.1**	**85.9**	**81.7**	**3.0**	**5.1**
Under age 5	423,215	100.0	0.7	1.6	12.6	0.1	84.9	79.1	3.7	6.2
Aged 5 to 9	443,273	100.0	0.7	1.2	12.2	0.1	85.6	81.1	2.8	4.9
Aged 10 to 14	443,416	100.0	0.7	1.2	11.1	0.1	86.7	83.1	2.2	3.9
Aged 15 to 19	453,482	100.0	0.7	1.4	10.1	0.1	86.8	83.4	2.5	4.4
Aged 20 to 24	425,731	100.0	0.7	1.9	9.9	0.1	85.3	81.4	3.7	6.3
IOWA										
State total	**2,926,324**	**100.0**	**0.6**	**1.5**	**2.5**	**0.1**	**94.9**	**92.6**	**1.6**	**2.8**
Total under 25	**1,031,646**	**100.0**	**0.9**	**2.0**	**3.8**	**0.1**	**92.8**	**89.0**	**2.6**	**4.4**
Under age 5	188,413	100.0	0.9	2.3	5.1	0.1	91.7	85.8	3.5	6.0
Aged 5 to 9	202,603	100.0	0.9	1.8	4.5	0.1	92.7	88.2	2.7	4.7
Aged 10 to 14	210,547	100.0	0.9	1.7	3.5	0.1	93.7	90.4	2.0	3.6
Aged 15 to 19	226,420	100.0	0.8	1.8	3.0	0.1	93.8	91.0	2.0	3.5
Aged 20 to 24	203,663	100.0	0.7	2.4	3.3	0.2	92.0	89.0	2.8	4.6
KANSAS										
State total	**2,688,418**	**100.0**	**1.8**	**2.1**	**6.3**	**0.1**	**87.9**	**83.1**	**4.0**	**7.0**
Total under 25	**988,585**	**100.0**	**2.2**	**2.5**	**8.3**	**0.2**	**84.6**	**77.2**	**6.0**	**10.3**
Under age 5	188,708	100.0	2.2	2.8	9.5	0.2	83.4	73.2	7.5	13.1
Aged 5 to 9	195,574	100.0	2.2	2.3	9.2	0.2	84.3	76.1	6.2	10.8
Aged 10 to 14	204,018	100.0	2.3	2.1	8.1	0.1	85.7	79.3	5.1	8.7
Aged 15 to 19	210,118	100.0	2.2	2.3	7.4	0.2	85.8	79.9	5.1	8.6
Aged 20 to 24	190,167	100.0	2.1	3.0	7.4	0.2	83.4	77.2	6.4	10.7

	total		American			Native	white			
	number	percent	Indian	Asian	black	Hawaiian	total	non-Hispanic	other	Hispanic
KENTUCKY										
State total	4,041,769	100.0%	0.6%	0.9%	7.7%	0.1%	91.0%	89.3%	0.8%	1.5%
Total under 25	1,396,676	100.0	0.6	1.1	9.9	0.1	88.9	86.3	1.3	2.1
Under age 5	265,901	100.0	0.5	1.2	10.9	0.1	88.5	84.6	1.7	2.5
Aged 5 to 9	279,258	100.0	0.6	1.0	10.5	0.1	88.8	86.0	1.2	1.9
Aged 10 to 14	279,481	100.0	0.6	1.0	9.6	0.1	89.5	87.3	0.9	1.5
Aged 15 to 19	289,004	100.0	0.7	0.9	9.3	0.1	89.3	87.2	1.0	1.9
Aged 20 to 24	283,032	100.0	0.6	1.2	9.2	0.1	88.4	86.1	1.6	3.0
LOUISIANA										
State total	4,468,976	100.0	1.0	1.4	32.9	0.1	64.8	62.5	1.1	2.4
Total under 25	1,693,600	100.0	1.1	1.6	39.7	0.1	57.8	55.2	1.3	2.7
Under age 5	317,392	100.0	1.1	1.6	40.7	0.1	57.3	54.1	1.4	2.8
Aged 5 to 9	336,780	100.0	1.1	1.5	41.7	0.1	56.1	53.5	1.2	2.5
Aged 10 to 14	347,912	100.0	1.1	1.5	40.3	0.1	57.4	55.1	1.0	2.3
Aged 15 to 19	365,945	100.0	1.1	1.6	38.9	0.1	58.4	56.2	1.1	2.5
Aged 20 to 24	325,571	100.0	1.0	1.9	37.0	0.1	59.7	57.1	1.6	3.2
MAINE										
State total	1,274,923	100.0	1.0	0.9	0.7	0.1	97.9	96.5	0.4	0.7
Total under 25	405,141	100.0	1.4	1.4	1.4	0.1	96.8	94.6	0.7	1.2
Under age 5	70,726	100.0	1.5	1.7	1.9	0.1	96.6	93.5	0.8	1.4
Aged 5 to 9	83,022	100.0	1.4	1.4	1.6	0.1	97.0	94.5	0.6	1.2
Aged 10 to 14	92,252	100.0	1.4	1.2	1.3	0.1	97.1	95.1	0.6	1.1
Aged 15 to 19	89,485	100.0	1.4	1.4	1.2	0.1	96.8	94.9	0.7	1.1
Aged 20 to 24	69,656	100.0	1.4	1.5	1.3	0.1	96.5	94.6	0.7	1.2
MARYLAND										
State total	5,296,486	100.0	0.7	4.5	28.8	0.1	65.4	62.1	2.5	4.3
Total under 25	1,807,094	100.0	0.9	4.9	33.7	0.1	60.3	55.5	3.5	5.7
Under age 5	353,393	100.0	0.8	5.1	34.2	0.1	60.4	54.1	4.0	6.5
Aged 5 to 9	391,318	100.0	0.8	4.4	34.8	0.1	60.1	55.2	3.2	5.4
Aged 10 to 14	392,135	100.0	0.9	4.3	33.6	0.1	61.2	57.2	2.8	4.6
Aged 15 to 19	356,119	100.0	0.9	4.8	33.0	0.2	60.7	56.7	3.2	5.3
Aged 20 to 24	314,129	100.0	0.9	5.8	32.5	0.2	58.8	54.1	4.5	7.4
MASSACHUSETTS										
State total	6,349,097	100.0	0.6	4.2	6.3	0.1	86.2	81.9	5.1	6.8
Total under 25	2,079,392	100.0	0.8	5.3	8.6	0.2	81.2	74.7	7.8	10.5
Under age 5	397,268	100.0	0.7	5.4	8.9	0.2	81.5	73.8	8.0	11.3
Aged 5 to 9	430,861	100.0	0.8	4.6	9.2	0.2	81.5	74.6	7.7	10.9
Aged 10 to 14	431,247	100.0	0.8	4.3	8.7	0.2	82.3	76.3	7.1	9.9
Aged 15 to 19	415,737	100.0	0.8	5.4	8.1	0.2	81.2	75.3	7.7	9.8
Aged 20 to 24	404,279	100.0	0.7	6.8	7.9	0.2	79.5	73.1	8.3	10.6
MICHIGAN										
State total	9,938,444	100.0	1.3	2.1	14.8	0.1	81.8	78.6	2.0	3.3
Total under 25	3,527,904	100.0	1.6	2.5	18.3	0.1	78.0	72.9	2.9	4.8
Under age 5	672,005	100.0	1.6	3.0	19.4	0.1	77.2	70.3	3.6	5.9
Aged 5 to 9	745,181	100.0	1.6	2.3	20.8	0.1	76.2	70.7	2.9	4.8
Aged 10 to 14	747,012	100.0	1.6	2.1	18.3	0.1	78.5	74.0	2.4	4.1
Aged 15 to 19	719,867	100.0	1.6	2.3	16.1	0.1	80.0	75.7	2.6	4.3
Aged 20 to 24	643,839	100.0	1.4	2.9	16.5	0.1	78.3	73.9	3.3	5.2

	total		American			Native	white			
	number	percent	Indian	Asian	black	Hawaiian	total	non-Hispanic	other	Hispanic
MINNESOTA										
State total	4,919,479	100.0%	1.6%	3.3%	4.1%	0.1%	90.8%	88.2%	1.8%	2.9%
Total under 25	1,757,328	100.0	2.4	4.9	6.2	0.2	86.8	82.4	2.8	4.5
Under age 5	329,594	100.0	2.6	5.4	7.8	0.2	85.4	79.1	3.7	5.9
Aged 5 to 9	355,894	100.0	2.5	5.1	7.1	0.2	86.2	81.3	2.7	4.5
Aged 10 to 14	374,995	100.0	2.5	5.0	5.9	0.2	87.3	83.6	2.1	3.4
Aged 15 to 19	374,362	100.0	2.2	4.6	4.9	0.2	88.3	84.9	2.3	3.6
Aged 20 to 24	322,483	100.0	2.0	4.5	5.5	0.2	86.7	82.9	3.4	5.3
MISSISSIPPI										
State total	2,844,658	100.0	0.7	0.8	36.6	0.1	61.9	60.7	0.7	1.4
Total under 25	1,086,161	100.0	0.8	0.9	44.7	0.1	53.7	52.2	0.9	1.7
Under age 5	204,364	100.0	0.8	1.0	45.2	0.1	53.5	51.5	0.1	1.9
Aged 5 to 9	216,920	100.0	0.7	0.9	46.6	0.1	52.1	50.6	0.7	1.5
Aged 10 to 14	218,742	100.0	0.8	0.9	45.0	0.1	53.6	52.4	0.6	1.3
Aged 15 to 19	233,188	100.0	0.8	0.9	44.6	0.1	53.7	52.5	0.8	1.6
Aged 20 to 24	212,947	100.0	0.7	1.0	42.1	0.1	55.7	54.2	1.2	2.2
MISSOURI										
State total	5,595,211	100.0	1.1	1.4	11.7	0.1	86.1	83.8	1.2	2.1
Total under 25	1,963,670	100.0	1.2	1.6	14.9	0.2	82.9	79.3	1.8	3.1
Under age 5	369,898	100.0	1.1	1.8	15.7	0.2	82.6	77.8	2.2	3.7
Aged 5 to 9	398,898	100.0	1.2	1.4	16.7	0.1	81.6	77.8	1.7	3.0
Aged 10 to 14	412,080	100.0	1.2	1.3	15.2	0.1	83.0	79.9	1.4	2.6
Aged 15 to 19	413,296	100.0	1.3	1.5	13.7	0.2	83.8	80.9	1.5	2.7
Aged 20 to 24	369,498	100.0	1.1	2.0	13.1	0.2	83.2	80.2	2.1	3.5
MONTANA										
State total	902,195	100.0	7.4	0.8	0.5	0.1	92.2	89.5	0.9	2.0
Total under 25	315,819	100.0	10.7	1.1	0.9	0.2	88.8	84.7	1.2	3.1
Under age 5	54,869	100.0	12.3	1.2	1.3	0.2	87.5	82.1	1.5	3.9
Aged 5 to 9	61,963	100.0	11.8	1.1	1.0	0.2	88.2	83.6	1.2	3.2
Aged 10 to 14	69,298	100.0	11.2	1.1	0.7	0.1	88.6	84.6	1.1	2.9
Aged 15 to 19	71,310	100.0	10.0	1.0	0.7	0.2	89.7	86.0	1.1	2.8
Aged 20 to 24	58,379	100.0	8.4	1.3	0.8	0.2	90.0	86.8	1.3	2.8
NEBRASKA										
State total	1,711,263	100.0	1.3	1.6	4.4	0.1	90.8	87.3	3.3	5.5
Total under 25	624,667	100.0	1.9	2.0	6.1	0.1	87.7	82.2	4.9	8.2
Under age 5	117,048	100.0	2.1	2.3	7.2	0.1	85.9	78.0	6.5	11.0
Aged 5 to 9	123,445	100.0	2.1	1.8	7.0	0.1	87.0	80.7	5.1	8.9
Aged 10 to 14	128,934	100.0	1.9	1.6	6.1	0.1	88.8	84.1	3.9	6.5
Aged 15 to 19	134,909	100.0	1.7	1.7	5.3	0.2	89.1	84.9	3.9	6.5
Aged 20 to 24	120,331	100.0	1.5	2.4	5.1	0.2	87.3	82.7	5.3	8.5
NEVADA										
State total	1,998,257	100.0	2.1	5.6	7.5	0.8	78.4	65.2	9.7	19.7
Total under 25	691,507	100.0	2.6	6.0	9.6	1.1	72.9	53.8	14.4	28.9
Under age 5	145,817	100.0	2.5	6.0	10.1	1.2	72.9	49.7	15.9	33.2
Aged 5 to 9	149,322	100.0	2.5	5.6	10.6	1.1	72.9	52.8	14.4	29.6
Aged 10 to 14	139,193	100.0	2.8	5.6	10.1	1.1	74.2	57.4	12.6	24.9
Aged 15 to 19	127,169	100.0	2.7	6.0	9.1	1.1	73.5	57.0	13.2	25.8
Aged 20 to 24	130,006	100.0	2.3	6.6	8.0	1.2	71.1	52.7	15.7	30.5

| | total | | American | | | Native | white | | | |
	number	percent	Indian	Asian	black	Hawaiian	total	non-Hispanic	other	Hispanic
NEW HAMPSHIRE										
State total	1,235,786	100.0%	0.6%	1.6%	1.0%	0.1%	97.0%	95.1%	0.9%	1.7%
Total under 25	412,931	100.0	0.7	1.9	1.5	0.1	96.2	93.2	1.3	2.5
Under age 5	75,685	100.0	0.7	2.5	2.0	0.1	95.7	91.7	1.6	3.1
Aged 5 to 9	88,537	100.0	0.7	1.7	1.5	0.1	96.6	93.5	1.3	2.6
Aged 10 to 14	93,255	100.0	0.7	1.5	1.3	0.1	96.9	94.2	1.1	2.1
Aged 15 to 19	86,688	100.0	0.8	1.7	1.3	0.1	96.3	93.8	1.2	2.3
Aged 20 to 24	68,766	100.0	0.8	2.5	1.5	0.1	95.2	92.4	1.5	2.7
NEW JERSEY										
State total	8,414,350	100.0	0.6	6.2	14.4	0.1	74.4	66.0	6.9	13.3
Total under 25	2,764,186	100.0	0.7	6.9	17.9	0.2	68.7	58.1	9.5	17.4
Under age 5	563,785	100.0	0.7	7.7	17.6	0.1	69.2	57.6	9.4	17.6
Aged 5 to 9	604,529	100.0	0.7	6.7	18.3	0.1	69.5	59.3	8.5	16.1
Aged 10 to 14	590,577	100.0	0.7	6.3	17.8	0.1	70.3	60.9	8.2	15.2
Aged 15 to 19	525,216	100.0	0.7	6.5	17.9	0.2	68.4	58.4	9.7	17.3
Aged 20 to 24	480,079	100.0	0.8	7.2	17.8	0.2	65.6	53.7	12.1	21.5
NEW MEXICO										
State total	1,819,046	100.0	10.5	1.5	2.3	0.2	69.9	44.7	19.4	42.1
Total under 25	686,150	100.0	13.8	1.6	3.0	0.2	62.1	33.2	24.7	50.4
Under age 5	130,628	100.0	13.8	1.9	3.7	0.3	61.2	29.6	26.4	54.1
Aged 5 to 9	141,171	100.0	14.9	1.5	3.1	0.2	61.7	31.7	24.6	51.3
Aged 10 to 14	147,309	100.0	14.5	1.5	2.8	0.2	62.6	34.1	23.7	49.0
Aged 15 to 19	145,751	100.0	13.1	1.5	2.7	0.2	63.4	35.3	23.7	48.9
Aged 20 to 24	121,291	100.0	12.4	1.8	2.9	0.2	61.5	35.1	25.3	49.0
NEW YORK										
State total	18,976,457	100.0	0.9	6.2	17.0	0.2	70.0	62.0	9.1	15.1
Total under 25	6,455,560	100.0	1.1	6.4	20.5	0.2	64.1	54.4	11.9	19.4
Under age 5	1,239,417	100.0	1.2	6.5	21.0	0.2	64.0	52.9	12.6	20.5
Aged 5 to 9	1,351,857	100.0	1.2	5.8	21.6	0.2	63.9	53.9	11.8	19.5
Aged 10 to 14	1,332,433	100.0	1.1	5.7	21.0	0.2	65.2	56.1	10.8	17.8
Aged 15 to 19	1,287,544	100.0	1.1	6.3	20.2	0.2	64.7	55.7	11.4	18.4
Aged 20 to 24	1,244,309	100.0	1.1	7.9	18.9	0.2	62.8	53.0	13.1	20.7
NORTH CAROLINA										
State total	8,049,313	100.0	1.6	1.7	22.1	0.1	73.1	70.2	2.8	4.7
Total under 25	2,770,868	100.0	2.0	2.1	26.6	0.2	67.0	62.4	4.4	7.3
Under age 5	539,509	100.0	2.1	2.4	26.6	0.2	67.2	61.0	5.1	8.5
Aged 5 to 9	562,553	100.0	2.0	2.1	28.4	0.1	66.3	62.0	3.6	5.9
Aged 10 to 14	551,367	100.0	2.0	1.9	28.0	0.1	67.1	63.9	2.7	4.4
Aged 15 to 19	539,931	100.0	2.0	2.1	26.5	0.2	67.0	63.2	4.0	6.6
Aged 20 to 24	577,508	100.0	1.9	2.2	23.7	0.2	67.4	61.9	6.4	10.8
NORTH DAKOTA										
State total	642,200	100.0	5.5	0.8	0.8	0.1	93.4	91.7	0.6	1.2
Total under 25	233,967	100.0	8.3	1.0	1.5	0.1	90.4	87.6	1.0	2.0
Under age 5	39,400	100.0	10.0	1.3	2.3	0.1	88.7	84.3	1.3	2.7
Aged 5 to 9	42,982	100.0	9.9	1.1	1.5	0.1	89.0	85.9	1.0	2.1
Aged 10 to 14	47,464	100.0	9.0	0.9	1.1	0.1	90.2	87.5	0.8	1.6
Aged 15 to 19	53,618	100.0	7.2	0.7	1.1	0.1	91.6	89.5	0.8	1.6
Aged 20 to 24	50,503	100.0	5.9	1.0	1.6	0.1	91.5	89.5	1.1	2.0

	total		American			Native	white			
	number	percent	Indian	Asian	black	Hawaiian	total	non-Hispanic	other	Hispanic
OHIO										
State total	**11,353,140**	**100.0%**	**0.7%**	**1.4%**	**12.1%**	**0.1%**	**86.1%**	**84.0%**	**1.1%**	**1.9%**
Total under 25	**3,944,883**	**100.0**	**0.8**	**1.6**	**15.2**	**0.1**	**83.1**	**79.7**	**1.7**	**2.8**
Under age 5	754,930	100.0	0.7	1.9	16.8	0.1	82.3	77.5	2.2	3.3
Aged 5 to 9	816,346	100.0	0.7	1.5	16.9	0.1	81.9	78.2	1.8	2.8
Aged 10 to 14	827,811	100.0	0.8	1.3	15.3	0.1	83.3	80.3	1.5	2.4
Aged 15 to 19	816,868	100.0	0.8	1.4	13.8	0.1	84.3	81.6	1.5	2.5
Aged 20 to 24	728,928	100.0	0.8	2.1	13.3	0.1	83.7	81.1	1.8	2.9
OKLAHOMA										
State total	**3,450,654**	**100.0**	**11.4**	**1.7**	**8.3**	**0.1**	**80.3**	**74.1**	**3.0**	**5.2**
Total under 25	**1,249,445**	**100.0**	**14.9**	**2.1**	**10.9**	**0.2**	**74.3**	**65.5**	**4.5**	**7.9**
Under age 5	236,353	100.0	16.1	2.1	12.0	0.3	73.1	62.0	5.4	9.7
Aged 5 to 9	244,525	100.0	16.1	1.8	11.8	0.2	73.4	63.9	4.4	7.9
Aged 10 to 14	252,029	100.0	15.8	1.7	10.6	0.2	74.8	66.2	3.7	6.8
Aged 15 to 19	269,373	100.0	14.7	1.9	10.1	0.2	75.3	67.2	4.0	7.0
Aged 20 to 24	247,165	100.0	11.9	2.8	10.0	0.2	74.8	67.5	5.1	8.4
OREGON										
State total	**3,421,399**	**100.0**	**2.5**	**3.7**	**2.1**	**0.5**	**89.3**	**83.5**	**5.2**	**8.1**
Total under 25	**1,174,410**	**100.0**	**3.2**	**4.6**	**3.1**	**0.7**	**85.6**	**76.3**	**8.3**	**12.9**
Under age 5	223,005	100.0	3.2	5.2	3.9	0.8	84.0	71.6	10.2	16.6
Aged 5 to 9	234,474	100.0	3.3	4.5	3.5	0.7	85.6	75.5	8.4	13.5
Aged 10 to 14	242,098	100.0	3.6	4.1	3.0	0.7	87.6	79.3	6.5	10.2
Aged 15 to 19	244,427	100.0	3.2	4.4	2.6	0.7	86.7	79.1	7.0	10.7
Aged 20 to 24	230,406	100.0	2.8	5.0	2.6	0.8	83.6	75.5	9.4	14.1
PENNSYLVANIA										
State total	**12,281,054**	**100.0**	**0.4**	**2.0**	**10.5**	**0.1**	**86.3**	**84.1**	**1.9**	**3.2**
Total under 25	**4,016,670**	**100.0**	**0.5**	**2.6**	**13.7**	**0.1**	**82.2**	**78.6**	**3.1**	**5.0**
Under age 5	727,804	100.0	0.5	2.8	15.0	0.1	81.3	76.3	3.7	5.9
Aged 5 to 9	827,945	100.0	0.5	2.2	15.1	0.1	81.3	77.4	3.3	5.2
Aged 10 to 14	863,849	100.0	0.5	2.1	14.0	0.1	82.4	79.2	2.8	4.6
Aged 15 to 19	850,986	100.0	0.5	2.6	12.3	0.1	83.4	80.5	2.7	4.5
Aged 20 to 24	746,086	100.0	0.5	3.3	12.3	0.1	82.2	79.1	3.2	5.1
RHODE ISLAND										
State total	**1,048,319**	**100.0**	**1.0**	**2.7**	**5.5**	**0.2**	**86.9**	**81.9**	**6.6**	**8.7**
Total under 25	**354,429**	**100.0**	**1.5**	**3.9**	**8.2**	**0.2**	**80.8**	**73.1**	**10.0**	**13.5**
Under age 5	63,896	100.0	1.6	3.7	9.1	0.3	79.9	69.9	11.6	16.3
Aged 5 to 9	71,905	100.0	1.6	3.5	8.7	0.2	80.6	71.7	10.5	14.9
Aged 10 to 14	71,370	100.0	1.5	3.4	8.2	0.2	81.5	74.4	9.6	12.7
Aged 15 to 19	75,445	100.0	1.4	4.4	7.5	0.2	81.4	75.3	8.9	11.5
Aged 20 to 24	71,813	100.0	1.1	4.7	7.5	0.3	80.6	74.0	9.5	12.5
SOUTH CAROLINA										
State total	**4,012,012**	**100.0**	**0.7**	**1.1**	**29.9**	**0.1**	**68.0**	**66.1**	**1.3**	**2.4**
Total under 25	**1,417,492**	**100.0**	**0.8**	**1.3**	**36.3**	**0.1**	**61.3**	**58.6**	**1.9**	**3.4**
Under age 5	264,679	100.0	0.8	1.4	35.8	0.1	62.4	58.7	2.1	3.6
Aged 5 to 9	285,243	100.0	0.7	1.2	38.2	0.1	60.2	57.6	1.5	2.7
Aged 10 to 14	290,479	100.0	0.8	1.1	38.3	0.1	60.0	58.0	1.2	2.2
Aged 15 to 19	295,377	100.0	0.8	1.3	36.5	0.1	60.8	58.5	1.8	3.3
Aged 20 to 24	281,714	100.0	0.8	1.5	32.6	0.2	63.3	60.3	3.0	5.2

	total		American			Native	white			
	number	percent	Indian	Asian	black	Hawaiian	total	non-Hispanic	other	Hispanic
SOUTH DAKOTA										
State total	754,844	100.0%	9.1%	0.8%	0.9%	0.1%	89.9%	88.0%	0.7%	1.4%
Total under 25	280,283	100.0	13.8	1.1	1.4	0.1	85.0	82.0	0.1	2.2
Under age 5	51,069	100.0	16.0	1.3	2.2	0.2	82.8	78.4	1.4	2.9
Aged 5 to 9	54,486	100.0	15.9	1.1	1.6	0.1	83.3	79.7	1.0	2.3
Aged 10 to 14	59,463	100.0	15.0	1.0	1.2	0.1	84.4	81.5	0.8	1.9
Aged 15 to 19	62,463	100.0	12.4	0.8	1.1	0.1	86.7	84.4	0.7	1.7
Aged 20 to 24	52,802	100.0	9.9	1.3	1.3	0.1	87.8	85.6	1.1	2.1
TENNESSEE										
State total	5,689,283	100.0	0.7	1.2	16.8	0.1	81.2	79.2	1.3	2.2
Total under 25	1,947,377	100.0	0.7	1.5	21.5	0.1	76.1	73.2	2.0	3.2
Under age 5	374,880	100.0	0.6	1.6	22.4	0.1	75.7	71.6	2.4	3.8
Aged 5 to 9	395,813	100.0	0.6	1.3	23.1	0.1	75.2	72.3	1.7	2.6
Aged 10 to 14	395,155	100.0	0.7	1.3	21.9	0.1	76.4	74.0	1.3	2.1
Aged 15 to 19	395,184	100.0	0.7	1.4	20.6	0.1	76.7	74.3	1.8	3.0
Aged 20 to 24	386,345	100.0	0.7	1.6	19.5	0.1	76.5	73.7	2.8	4.6
TEXAS										
State total	20,851,820	100.0	1.0	3.1	12.0	0.1	73.1	52.4	13.3	32.0
Total under 25	8,085,640	100.0	1.1	3.1	13.4	0.2	68.2	42.8	17.6	40.4
Under age 5	1,624,628	100.0	1.0	3.3	13.4	0.2	67.5	39.5	19.3	44.0
Aged 5 to 9	1,654,184	100.0	1.1	2.9	14.0	0.2	68.1	41.6	17.5	41.3
Aged 10 to 14	1,631,192	100.0	1.1	2.9	13.8	0.2	69.3	45.0	16.0	38.0
Aged 15 to 19	1,636,232	100.0	1.1	3.0	13.2	0.2	68.9	45.0	16.5	38.4
Aged 20 to 24	1,539,404	100.0	1.1	3.5	12.5	0.2	67.0	43.1	18.6	40.5
UTAH										
State total	2,233,169	100.0	1.8	2.2	1.1	1.0	91.1	85.3	5.1	9.0
Total under 25	1,036,129	100.0	2.2	2.2	1.4	1.3	90.2	82.9	6.0	10.6
Under age 5	209,378	100.0	2.2	2.4	1.8	1.5	89.6	80.1	7.1	12.8
Aged 5 to 9	193,033	100.0	2.4	2.2	1.7	1.4	89.8	81.5	6.4	11.5
Aged 10 to 14	192,288	100.0	2.4	2.0	1.3	1.3	90.7	83.9	5.3	9.5
Aged 15 to 19	216,278	100.0	2.1	2.1	1.1	1.2	90.9	84.9	5.2	9.1
Aged 20 to 24	225,152	100.0	1.7	2.3	1.0	1.0	90.0	83.9	6.0	10.3
VERMONT										
State total	608,827	100.0	1.1	1.1	0.7	0.1	97.9	96.2	0.4	0.9
Total under 25	204,109	100.0	1.2	1.6	1.3	0.1	97.1	94.5	0.7	1.4
Under age 5	33,989	100.0	1.1	2.1	1.7	0.1	96.9	93.9	0.7	1.3
Aged 5 to 9	41,101	100.0	1.3	1.4	1.4	0.1	97.3	94.6	0.7	1.3
Aged 10 to 14	45,397	100.0	1.2	1.3	1.1	0.1	97.5	95.1	0.6	1.2
Aged 15 to 19	45,770	100.0	1.3	1.5	1.2	0.1	97.1	94.7	0.7	1.4
Aged 20 to 24	37,852	100.0	1.1	1.9	1.1	0.1	96.4	94.1	0.8	1.6
VIRGINIA										
State total	7,078,515	100.0	0.7	4.3	20.4	0.1	73.9	70.2	2.7	4.7
Total under 25	2,417,660	100.0	0.8	4.8	24.4	0.2	69.4	63.9	3.9	6.4
Under age 5	461,982	100.0	0.8	5.2	24.6	0.2	69.9	62.6	4.5	7.3
Aged 5 to 9	495,084	100.0	0.8	4.5	25.7	0.2	69.2	63.5	3.5	6.0
Aged 10 to 14	495,955	100.0	0.8	4.3	25.2	0.2	69.7	65.1	2.9	5.0
Aged 15 to 19	484,065	100.0	0.9	4.6	24.3	0.2	69.4	64.8	3.4	5.7
Aged 20 to 24	480,574	100.0	0.9	5.2	22.3	0.3	69.0	63.7	5.1	8.2

	total		American			Native	white			
	number	percent	Indian	Asian	black	Hawaiian	total	non-Hispanic	other	Hispanic
WASHINGTON										
State total	5,894,121	100.0%	2.7%	6.7%	4.0%	0.7%	84.9%	78.9%	4.9%	7.5%
Total under 25	2,073,204	100.0	3.5	7.8	5.6	1.1	81.2	71.5	7.6	11.7
Under age 5	394,306	100.0	3.7	8.2	6.8	1.2	80.4	67.5	9.3	14.7
Aged 5 to 9	425,909	100.0	3.6	7.4	6.2	1.1	81.5	70.9	7.8	12.3
Aged 10 to 14	434,836	100.0	3.7	7.2	5.4	1.0	82.6	73.9	6.4	9.9
Aged 15 to 19	427,968	100.0	3.5	7.9	4.9	1.1	81.7	73.7	6.6	9.9
Aged 20 to 24	390,185	100.0	3.1	8.4	4.8	1.1	79.4	71.3	8.1	12.1
WEST VIRGINIA										
State total	1,808,344	100.0	0.6	0.7	3.5	0.1	95.9	94.6	0.3	0.7
Total under 25	574,824	100.0	0.6	0.9	4.6	0.1	94.9	92.9	0.5	1.0
Under age 5	101,805	100.0	0.5	0.9	5.4	0.1	94.9	91.9	0.7	1.1
Aged 5 to 9	111,150	100.0	0.5	0.7	4.8	0.1	95.1	92.8	0.6	1.0
Aged 10 to 14	116,182	100.0	0.6	0.7	4.2	0.1	95.3	93.5	0.4	0.9
Aged 15 to 19	125,578	100.0	0.7	0.7	4.3	0.1	95.0	93.3	0.4	0.9
Aged 20 to 24	120,109	100.0	0.5	1.2	4.5	0.1	94.1	92.8	0.5	0.9
WISCONSIN										
State total	5,363,675	100.0	1.3	1.9	6.1	0.1	90.0	87.3	2.0	3.6
Total under 25	1,889,385	100.0	1.8	3.0	8.9	0.1	85.5	81.1	3.1	5.6
Under age 5	342,340	100.0	1.9	3.3	10.6	0.1	84.0	77.6	3.9	7.2
Aged 5 to 9	379,484	100.0	1.9	3.2	10.4	0.1	84.2	79.4	3.1	5.6
Aged 10 to 14	403,074	100.0	1.9	3.1	8.9	0.1	85.8	82.0	2.4	4.5
Aged 15 to 19	407,195	100.0	1.7	2.8	7.6	0.1	86.9	83.3	2.6	4.8
Aged 20 to 24	357,292	100.0	1.5	2.7	7.2	0.1	86.5	82.6	3.6	6.2
WYOMING										
State total	493,782	100.0	3.0	0.8	1.0	0.1	93.7	88.9	3.2	6.4
Total under 25	178,801	100.0	4.1	1.0	1.5	0.2	91.8	85.0	4.4	8.9
Under age 5	30,940	100.0	4.6	1.2	2.0	0.2	90.9	81.8	5.5	11.3
Aged 5 to 9	34,127	100.0	4.5	1.0	1.5	0.2	91.5	84.1	4.5	9.4
Aged 10 to 14	38,376	100.0	4.3	0.9	1.3	0.2	92.4	85.9	3.8	8.0
Aged 15 to 19	41,903	100.0	3.6	0.9	1.2	0.2	92.7	86.8	3.8	7.8
Aged 20 to 24	33,455	100.0	3.3	1.3	1.6	0.2	91.0	85.5	4.6	8.6

Note: Percentages will not add to 100 because each race includes those who identified themselves as being of the race alone and those who identified themselves as being of the race in combination with one or more other races, and because Hispanics may be of any race. Non-Hispanic whites include only those who identified themselves as being "white alone" and non-Hispanic. American Indians include Alaska natives. Native Hawaiians include other Pacific Islanders.
Source: Bureau of the Census, Census 2000 Summary File 2, Internet site http://factfinder.census.gov/servlet/BasicFactsServlet; calculations by New Strategist

Spending

■ Households headed by people under age 25 spent fully 18 percent more in 2002 than in 1997 as the economic boom of the late 1990s boosted their incomes.

■ The incomes of young adults are well below average, and so is their spending. Householders under age 25 spend just 60 percent as much as the average household.

■ Many Millennials are young children and their economic well-being depends on that of their parents. Those living with two parents are faring much better than those in single-parent families.

■ Married couples with school-aged children rank among the most affluent households in the nation. Their incomes grew a substantial 15 percent between 1997 and 2002, and their spending rose 10 percent, after adjusting for inflation.

■ Single parents with children under age 18 at home spent 3 percent more in 2002 than in 1997, after adjusting for inflation. But this household type spent $3,000 more than it made in 2002.

■ Overall, couples with preschoolers spent 30 percent more than the average household in 2002. Couples with school-aged children spent 43 percent more, while those with grown children at home spent 50 percent more.

Millennials Are Spending Much More

Spending by the youngest householders grew faster than that of any other age group between 1997 and 2002

The average household boosted its spending by 5 percent between 1997 and 2002, after adjusting for inflation. Households headed by people under age 25, members of the Millennial generation (also know as Generation Y), spent fully 18 percent more as the economic boom of the late 1990s boosted their incomes.

Householders under age 25 spent 19 percent more on food away from home in 2002 than in 1997. They spent 39 percent more on alcoholic beverages. They were one of the few age groups to spend more on women's clothes—up 15 percent during those years. As homeownership rates rose among young adults, Millennials spent 95 percent more on owned dwellings in 2002 than in 1997. They also spent more on transportation, health care, and entertainment.

Many householders under age 25 are in college, and their spending on education rose 34 percent between 1997 and 2002 thanks to rising tuition costs. Despite their education, young adults are not big on reading. Their spending on reading material fell 20 percent between 1997 and 2002—a troubling trend for the print media.

■ Householders under age 25 are a diverse mix of single parents, people living alone, and friends living together. Their spending patterns reflect this diversity.

Young adults are spending more on many items

(percent change in spending by householders under age 25, 1997 to 2002; in 2002 dollars)

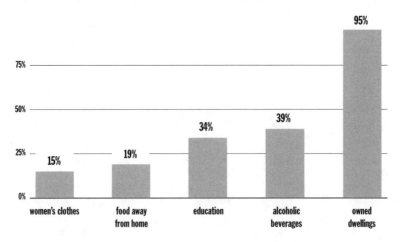

Table 9.1 Average Spending of Householders under Age 25, 1997 and 2002

(average annual spending of total consumer units and consumer units headed by people under age 25, 1997 and 2002; percent change, 1997–2002; in 2002 dollars)

	total consumer units			under age 25		
	2002	1997	percent change 1997–02	2002	1997	percent change 1997–02
Number of consumer units (in 000s)	112,108	105,576	6.2%	8,737	7,501	16.5%
Average before-tax income	$49,430	$44,610	10.8	$20,773	$17,504	18.7
Average annual spending	40,677	38,904	4.6	24,229	20,615	17.5
FOOD	**$5,375**	**$5,364**	**0.2%**	**$3,621**	**$3,171**	**14.2%**
Food at home	**3,099**	**3,218**	**−3.7**	**1,926**	**1,750**	**10.1**
Cereals and bakery products	450	506	−11.1	287	278	3.2
Cereals and cereal products	154	180	−14.4	113	108	4.3
Bakery products	296	326	−9.3	174	169	3.1
Meats, poultry, fish, and eggs	798	830	−3.9	460	430	6.9
Beef	231	250	−7.7	131	140	−6.2
Pork	167	175	−4.8	95	84	13.4
Other meats	101	107	−5.8	52	57	−8.7
Poultry	144	162	−11.1	96	87	10.2
Fish and seafood	121	99	21.7	61	41	47.6
Eggs	34	37	−7.8	24	22	7.4
Dairy products	328	351	−6.5	200	189	5.9
Fresh milk and cream	127	143	−11.2	87	88	−1.4
Other dairy products	201	208	−3.3	113	101	12.4
Fruits and vegetables	552	532	3.8	338	270	2.5
Fresh fruits	178	168	6.2	105	86	22.1
Fresh vegetables	175	160	9.5	100	72	39.8
Processed fruits	116	114	1.8	81	62	31.8
Processed vegetables	83	89	−7.1	53	51	3.1
Other food at home	970	1,000	−3.0	640	581	10.2
Sugar and other sweets	117	127	−8.1	64	59	8.1
Fats and oils	85	91	−6.1	47	44	7.9
Miscellaneous foods	472	450	4.8	344	268	28.3
Nonalcoholic beverages	254	274	−7.2	160	179	−10.5
Food prepared by household on trips	41	58	−29.4	25	31	−20.1
Food away from home	**2,276**	**2,146**	**6.0**	**1,696**	**1,421**	**19.3**
ALCOHOLIC BEVERAGES	**376**	**345**	**8.9**	**394**	**283**	**39.4**
HOUSING	**13,283**	**12,594**	**5.5**	**7,436**	**6,548**	**13.6**
Shelter	**7,829**	**7,088**	**10.4**	**4,851**	**4,085**	**18.8**
Owned dwellings	5,165	4,397	17.5	830	426	95.0
Mortgage interest and charges	2,962	2,486	19.1	443	250	7.7
Property taxes	1,242	1,085	14.5	281	113	14.9
Maintenance, repairs, insurance, other expenses	960	825	16.4	106	64	66.4
Rented dwellings	2,160	2,216	−2.5	3,644	3,354	8.6
Other lodging	505	476	6.1	377	305	23.6

	total consumer units			under age 25		
	2002	1997	percent change 1997–02	2002	1997	percent change 1997–02
Utilities, fuels, public services	**$2,684**	**$2,695**	**–0.4%**	**$1,348**	**$1,220**	**10.5%**
Natural gas	330	336	–1.9	108	98	9.8
Electricity	981	1,016	–3.4	471	436	8.1
Fuel oil and other fuels	88	121	–27.1	21	12	70.9
Telephone services	957	904	5.9	641	615	4.3
Water and other public services	328	320	2.6	108	62	75.7
Household services	**706**	**612**	**15.3**	**198**	**213**	**–7.2**
Personal services	331	294	12.6	99	148	–32.9
Other household services	375	318	17.8	99	65	52.8
Housekeeping supplies	**545**	**508**	**7.2**	**226**	**182**	**24.1**
Laundry and cleaning supplies	131	130	1.1	77	63	23.1
Other household products	283	235	20.6	95	67	41.7
Postage and stationery	131	144	–9.1	54	53	2.8
Household furnishings, equipment	**1,518**	**1,689**	**–10.1**	**812**	**848**	**–4.3**
Household textiles	136	88	54.1	93	50	85.0
Furniture	401	432	–7.3	170	287	–40.8
Floor coverings	40	87	–54.1	8	20	–60.2
Major appliances	188	189	–0.4	88	85	3.6
Small appliances, misc. housewares	100	103	–2.7	76	51	47.9
Miscellaneous household equipment	652	790	–17.5	377	354	6.4
APPAREL AND SERVICES	**1,749**	**1,932**	**–9.5**	**1,365**	**1,393**	**–2.0**
Men and boys	**409**	**455**	**–10.1**	**266**	**301**	**–11.5**
Men, aged 16 or older	319	361	–11.6	230	276	–16.7
Boys, aged 2 to 15	90	94	–4.1	36	25	46.5
Women and girls	**704**	**760**	**–7.3**	**609**	**521**	**17.0**
Women, aged 16 or older	587	641	–8.5	559	485	15.3
Girls, aged 2 to 15	117	118	–1.2	50	37	35.6
Children under age 2	**83**	**86**	**–3.5**	**102**	**124**	**–17.8**
Footwear	**313**	**352**	**–11.1**	**246**	**279**	**–11.9**
Other apparel products and services	**240**	**279**	**–14.1**	**142**	**169**	**–15.8**
TRANSPORTATION	**7,759**	**7,215**	**7.5**	**5,102**	**4,172**	**22.3**
Vehicle purchases	**3,665**	**3,057**	**19.9**	**2,635**	**1,941**	**35.8**
Cars and trucks, new	1,753	1,373	27.7	664	573	15.8
Cars and trucks, used	1,842	1,636	12.6	1,917	1,336	43.5
Other vehicles	70	48	45.7	–	30	–
Gasoline and motor oil	**1,235**	**1,227**	**0.7**	**903**	**774**	**16.6**
Other vehicle expenses	**2,471**	**2,492**	**–0.8**	**1,339**	**1,215**	**10.2**
Vehicle finance charges	397	327	21.3	217	181	19.9
Maintenance and repairs	697	762	–8.5	394	362	8.8
Vehicle insurance	894	844	6.0	479	381	25.7
Vehicle rental, leases, licenses, other charges	483	560	–13.7	249	291	–14.3
Public transportation	**389**	**439**	**–11.4**	**225**	**243**	**–7.2**

	total consumer units			under age 25		
	2002	**1997**	**percent change 1997–02**	**2002**	**1997**	**percent change 1997–02**
HEALTH CARE	**$2,350**	**$2,057**	**14.2%**	**$640**	**$475**	**34.8%**
Health insurance	1,168	984	18.7	285	224	27.5
Medical services	590	593	–0.6	196	143	37.1
Drugs	487	358	36.2	130	73	79.0
Medical supplies	105	121	–13.0	30	35	–13.4
ENTERTAINMENT	**2,079**	**2,026**	**2.6**	**1,212**	**1,174**	**3.2**
Fees and admissions	542	526	3.0	313	294	6.5
Television, radio, sound equipment	692	645	7.3	457	488	–6.4
Pets, toys, and playground equipment	369	365	1.0	193	210	–8.1
Other entertainment supplies, services	476	491	–3.0	249	181	37.6
PERSONAL CARE PRODUCTS AND SERVICES	**526**	**590**	**–10.8**	**329**	**326**	**0.8**
READING	**139**	**183**	**–24.1**	**57**	**72**	**–20.3**
EDUCATION	**752**	**638**	**17.9**	**1,664**	**1,245**	**33.7**
TOBACCO PRODUCTS AND SMOKING SUPPLIES	**320**	**295**	**8.5**	**286**	**224**	**28.0**
MISCELLANEOUS	**792**	**946**	**–16.3**	**422**	**307**	**37.3**
CASH CONTRIBUTIONS	**1,277**	**1,118**	**14.2**	**319**	**175**	**81.9**
PERSONAL INSURANCE AND PENSIONS	**3,899**	**3,601**	**8.3**	**1,382**	**1,050**	**31.6**
Life and other personal insurance	406	424	–4.1	51	53	–2.9
Pensions and Social Security	3,493	3,178	9.9	1,331	998	33.4
PERSONAL TAXES	**2,496**	**3,621**	**–31.1**	**567**	**737**	**–23.1**
Federal income taxes	1,843	2,758	–33.2	402	577	–30.3
State and local income taxes	506	721	–29.8	149	160	–6.7
Other taxes	147	144	2.0	16	–	–
GIFTS FOR NON-HOUSEHOLD MEMBERS	**1,036**	**1,183**	**–12.4**	**437**	**703**	**–37.8**
Food	**82**	**76**	**7.9**	**27**	**54**	**–49.7**
Alcoholic beverages	**13**	**–**	**–**	**15**	**–**	**–**
Housing	**259**	**305**	**–15.1**	**104**	**201**	**–48.3**
Housekeeping supplies	42	41	1.6	24	15	65.2
Household textiles	14	9	56.6	–	3	–
Appliances and miscellaneous housewares	24	30	–20.4	13	13	–3.0
Major appliances	8	7	19.3	–	3	–
Small appliances and misc. housewares	16	24	–31.8	13	10	29.3
Miscellaneous household equipment	65	74	–11.9	24	35	–30.7
Other housing	114	151	–24.4	42	135	–68.9
Apparel and services	**237**	**282**	**–15.8**	**170**	**151**	**12.7**
Males, aged 2 or older	64	68	–6.1	55	17	228.2
Females, aged 2 or older	82	91	–9.4	37	57	35.1
Children under age 2	40	37	8.5	34	25	38.3
Other apparel products and services	52	86	–39.6	44	54	–18.0
Jewelry and watches	24	55	–56.2	13	47	–72.3
All other apparel products and services	28	32	–13.6	32	6	472.8

	total consumer units			under age 25		
	2002	1997	percent change 1997–02	2002	1997	percent change 1997–02
Transportation	$44	$64	−30.9%	$15	$47	−68.0%
Health care	33	34	−1.6	–	8	–
Entertainment	78	111	−29.5	30	41	−27.4
Toys, games, hobbies, and tricycles	30	46	−34.5	11	11	−1.6
Other entertainment	48	65	−25.9	19	31	−39.3
Personal care products, services	21	–	–	13	–	–
Reading	1	–	–	–	–	–
Education	184	173	6.2	43	159	−72.9
All other gifts	84	140	−39.9	18	41	−56.5

Note: The Bureau of Labor Statistics uses consumer units rather than households as the sampling unit in the Consumer Expenditure Survey. For the definition of consumer unit, see the glossary. Spending on gifts is included in the preceding product and service categories. (–) means sample is too small to make a reliable estimate or data are not available.
Source: Bureau of Labor Statistics, 1997 and 2002 Consumer Expenditure Surveys, Internet site http://www.bls.gov/cex/; calculations by New Strategist

Young Adults Spend Less than Average on Most Things

Householders under age 25 spend just 60 percent as much as the average household.

The incomes of young adults are well below average, and so is their spending. On some things, however, Millennials spend more. They spend 11 percent more than the average household on alcoholic beverages away from home—such as at restaurants and bars. They spend 70 percent more on rent. Because many young householders are single parents, they spend 23 percent more than the average household on clothes for children under age 2. They spend 9 percent more on used cars and 28 percent more than average on towing charges. Millennial householders spend more than twice as much as the average household on education. Many are students paying for college tuition at least partly out of their own pocket.

On most items, Millennials spend far less than the average household. They spend only 16 percent as much as the average household on owned dwellings, for example, because most are renters. They spend only 27 percent of the average on health care since most are in good health and have few medical needs. Their spending on reading material is just 41 percent of the average.

■ As Millennial householders complete their education and embark on careers, their spending will rise with their income.

The youngest householders are big spenders on beer, rent, and college tuition

(indexed spending by householders under age 25 on selected items, 2002)

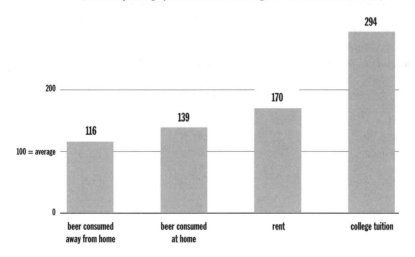

Table 9.2 Average and Indexed Spending of Householders under Age 25, 2002

(average annual spending of total consumer units (CUs) and average annual and indexed spending of consumer units headed by people under age 25, 2002)

	total consumer units	CUs headed by people under age 25	
		average spending	indexed spending
Number of consumer units (in 000s)	112,108	8,737	–
Average before-tax income	$49,430.00	$20,773.00	42
Average annual spending	40,676.60	24,229.46	60
FOOD	**$5,374.80**	**$3,621.39**	**67**
FOOD AT HOME	3,098.52	1,925.70	62
Cereals and bakery products	**450.13**	**287.26**	**64**
Cereals and cereal products	154.07	112.99	73
Flour	8.65	5.83	67
Prepared flour mixes	12.40	7.27	59
Ready-to-eat and cooked cereals	87.66	69.04	79
Rice	17.82	11.47	64
Pasta, cornmeal, and other cereal products	27.54	19.38	70
Bakery products	296.06	174.27	59
Bread	83.83	53.84	64
White bread	35.21	24.88	71
Bread, other than white	48.62	28.96	60
Crackers and cookies	70.67	41.94	59
Cookies	46.31	29.89	65
Crackers	24.36	12.05	49
Frozen and refrigerated bakery products	25.64	12.78	50
Other bakery products	115.92	65.72	57
Biscuits and rolls	41.04	23.25	57
Cakes and cupcakes	35.73	21.69	61
Bread and cracker products	3.50	2.04	58
Sweetrolls, coffee cakes, doughnuts	25.84	12.03	47
Pies, tarts, turnovers	9.82	6.70	68
Meats, poultry, fish, and eggs	**798.42**	**460.36**	**58**
Beef	231.17	130.85	57
Ground beef	86.29	54.18	63
Roast	40.99	18.55	45
Chuck roast	11.71	5.09	43
Round roast	10.23	7.68	75
Other roast	19.05	5.77	30
Steak	84.47	46.96	56
Round steak	13.29	10.09	76
Sirloin steak	26.62	15.12	57
Other steak	44.56	21.74	49
Pork	167.34	95.36	57
Bacon	28.45	17.75	62
Pork chops	38.43	24.70	64
Ham	37.16	21.17	57
Ham, not canned	35.66	20.23	57
Canned ham	1.50	0.94	63

		CUs headed by people under age 25	
	total consumer units	average spending	indexed spending
Sausage	$26.17	$13.13	50
Other pork	37.13	18.61	50
Other meats	101.08	52.49	52
Frankfurters	20.95	10.39	50
Lunch meats (cold cuts)	68.99	36.11	52
Bologna, liverwurst, salami	21.11	9.92	47
Lamb, organ meats, and others	11.14	5.98	54
Lamb and organ meats	7.99	5.25	66
Mutton, goat, and game	3.15	0.73	23
Poultry	144.13	96.39	67
Fresh and frozen chicken	113.25	74.71	66
Fresh and frozen whole chicken	32.08	21.73	68
Fresh and frozen chicken parts	81.17	52.98	65
Other poultry	30.88	21.68	70
Fish and seafood	120.97	61.49	51
Canned fish and seafood	16.13	8.94	55
Fresh fish and shellfish	69.31	36.68	53
Frozen fish and shellfish	35.53	15.86	45
Eggs	33.75	23.79	70
Dairy products	**328.34**	**199.73**	**61**
Fresh milk and cream	127.15	86.53	68
Fresh milk, all types	114.63	79.42	69
Cream	12.52	7.11	57
Other dairy products	201.19	113.20	56
Butter	18.48	9.10	49
Cheese	95.64	50.60	53
Ice cream and related products	58.74	32.84	56
Miscellaneous dairy products	28.33	20.66	73
Fruits and vegetables	**552.01**	**337.94**	**61**
Fresh fruits	178.20	104.78	59
Apples	32.59	21.65	66
Bananas	31.24	20.39	65
Oranges	20.34	14.22	70
Citrus fruits, excl. oranges	14.29	8.70	61
Other fresh fruits	79.74	39.82	50
Fresh vegetables	174.88	99.97	57
Potatoes	33.35	18.91	57
Lettuce	22.22	12.53	56
Tomatoes	33.71	24.27	72
Other fresh vegetables	85.60	44.26	52
Processed fruits	115.50	80.55	70
Frozen fruits and fruit juices	12.45	13.24	106
Frozen orange juice	6.31	6.72	106
Frozen fruits	2.79	1.36	49
Frozen fruit juices, excl. orange	3.35	5.15	154
Canned fruits	15.06	8.71	58
Dried fruits	6.06	3.10	51
Fresh fruit juice	22.20	9.60	43
Canned and bottled fruit juice	59.74	45.91	77

	total consumer units	CUs headed by people under age 25	
		average spending	indexed spending
Processed vegetables	$83.43	$52.64	63
Frozen vegetables	27.85	18.77	67
Canned and dried vegetables and juices	55.58	33.87	61
Canned beans	12.47	7.19	58
Canned corn	7.34	4.00	54
Canned miscellaneous vegetables	17.85	9.23	52
Dried peas	0.36	0.34	94
Dried beans	2.55	2.51	98
Dried miscellaneous vegetables	7.38	6.83	93
Dried processed vegetables	0.34	0.14	41
Frozen vegetable juices	0.06	0.09	150
Fresh and canned vegetable juices	7.23	3.54	49
Sugar and other sweets	**117.39**	**64.28**	**55**
Candy and chewing gum	75.44	40.61	54
Sugar	15.56	10.14	65
Artificial sweeteners	4.33	1.70	39
Jams, preserves, other sweets	22.06	11.83	54
Fats and oils	**85.16**	**47.46**	**56**
Margarine	9.86	4.23	43
Fats and oils	26.08	15.43	59
Salad dressings	27.01	15.52	57
Nondairy cream and imitation milk	9.33	3.43	37
Peanut butter	12.89	8.85	69
Miscellaneous foods	**471.92**	**344.32**	**73**
Frozen prepared foods	98.09	65.01	66
Frozen meals	29.88	21.29	71
Other frozen prepared foods	68.22	43.72	64
Canned and packaged soups	35.82	21.18	59
Potato chips, nuts, and other snacks	100.53	60.15	60
Potato chips and other snacks	76.37	51.89	68
Nuts	24.16	8.26	34
Condiments and seasonings	86.81	56.60	65
Salt, spices, and other seasonings	21.14	14.39	68
Olives, pickles, relishes	9.70	4.95	51
Sauces and gravies	37.78	28.14	74
Baking needs and miscellaneous products	18.19	9.12	50
Other canned/packaged prepared foods	150.67	141.38	94
Prepared salads	21.46	9.20	43
Prepared desserts	10.32	4.76	46
Baby food	31.57	56.69	180
Miscellaneous prepared foods	87.24	70.74	81
Nonalcoholic beverages	253.94	159.59	63
Cola	81.11	54.00	67
Other carbonated drinks	43.93	33.93	77
Coffee	41.59	12.74	31
Roasted coffee	27.38	8.64	32
Instant and freeze-dried coffee	14.21	4.09	29
Noncarbonated fruit-flavored drinks	18.95	14.05	74

		CUs headed by people under age 25	
	total consumer units	average spending	indexed spending
Tea	$15.86	$7.88	50
Nonalcoholic beer	0.64	–	–
Other nonalcoholic beverages and ice	51.85	36.99	71
Food prepared by CU on trips	41.20	24.76	60
FOOD AWAY FROM HOME	**2,276.29**	**1,695.69**	**74**
Meals at restaurants, carry-outs, other	**1,866.42**	**1,390.49**	**75**
Lunch	685.79	511.07	75
• At fast food, take-out, delivery, concession stands, buffet, and cafeteria (other than employer and school cafeteria)	377.71	338.28	90
• At full-service restaurants	224.82	118.97	53
• At vending machines, mobile vendors	5.50	4.85	88
• At employer and school cafeterias	77.76	48.97	63
Dinner	736.54	460.76	63
• At fast food, take-out, delivery, concession stands, buffet, and cafeteria (other than employer and school cafeteria)	213.33	193.43	91
• At full-service restaurants	518.02	252.60	49
• At vending machines, mobile vendors	1.87	0.46	25
• At employer and school cafeterias	3.32	14.27	430
Snacks and nonalcoholic beverages	262.67	252.11	96
• At fast food, take-out, delivery, concession stands, buffet, and cafeteria (other than employer and school cafeteria)	185.69	175.82	95
• At full-service restaurants	30.17	21.77	72
• At vending machines, mobile vendors	36.71	43.68	119
• At employer and school cafeterias	10.11	10.84	107
Breakfast and brunch	181.42	166.55	92
• At fast food, take-out, delivery, concession stands, buffet, and cafeteria (other than employer and school cafeteria)	87.83	97.87	111
• At full-service restaurants	87.08	56.03	64
• At vending machines, mobile vendors	1.40	1.86	133
• At employer and school cafeterias	5.11	10.79	211
Board (including at school)	**46.54**	**108.35**	**233**
Catered affairs	**69.00**	**39.50**	**57**
Food on trips	**211.49**	**117.19**	**55**
School lunches	**60.00**	**6.67**	**11**
Meals as pay	**22.86**	**33.49**	**147**
ALCOHOLIC BEVERAGES	**$375.95**	**$394.21**	**105**
At home	**228.08**	**230.11**	**101**
Beer and ale	112.34	156.18	139
Whiskey	13.90	13.17	95
Wine	77.75	28.08	36
Other alcoholic beverages	24.09	32.68	136

	total consumer units	CUs headed by people under age 25	
		average spending	indexed spending
Away from home	$147.87	$164.10	111
Beer and ale	52.86	61.51	116
• At fast food, take-out, delivery, concession stands, buffet, and cafeteria	7.99	14.70	184
• At full-service restaurants	41.95	45.90	109
• At vending machines, mobile vendors	0.32	0.63	197
• At catered affairs	2.59	0.29	11
Wine	25.85	27.17	105
• At fast food, take-out, delivery, concession stands, buffet and cafeteria	4.41	5.24	119
• At full-service restaurants	20.36	21.90	108
• At catered affairs	1.09	0.03	3
Other alcoholic beverages	69.16	75.42	109
• At fast food, take-out, delivery, concession stands, buffet, and cafeteria	3.50	7.73	221
• At full-service restaurants	28.94	29.24	101
• At catered affairs	3.94	0.13	3
Alcoholic beverages purchased on trips	32.78	38.31	117
HOUSING	**$13,283.08**	**$7,436.31**	**56**
SHELTER	**7,829.41**	**4,851.44**	**62**
Owned dwellings*	**5,164.96**	**830.26**	**16**
Mortgage interest and charges	2,962.16	443.10	15
Mortgage interest	2,811.49	418.60	15
Interest paid, home equity loan	88.61	22.25	25
Interest paid, home equity line of credit	61.88	2.25	4
Property taxes	1,242.36	280.75	23
Maintenance, repairs, insurance, other expenses	960.43	106.41	11
Homeowner's insurance	283.30	33.42	12
Ground rent	40.96	11.36	28
Maintenance and repair services	519.60	43.43	8
Painting and papering	55.58	10.89	20
Plumbing and water heating	46.63	5.76	12
Heat, air conditioning, electrical work	86.28	4.02	5
Roofing and gutters	71.20	2.46	3
Other repair and maintenance services	214.77	18.56	9
Repair, replacement of hard-surface flooring	43.54	1.67	4
Repair of built-in appliances	1.62	0.08	5
Maintenance and repair materials	83.75	12.58	15
Paints, wallpaper, and supplies	14.71	2.85	19
Tools, equipment for painting, wallpapering	1.58	0.31	20
Plumbing supplies and equipment	5.62	0.22	4
Electrical supplies, heating, cooling equip.	3.46	0.16	5
Hard-surface flooring, repair and replacement	8.72	0.95	11
Roofing and gutters	5.29	0.67	13
Plaster, paneling, siding, windows, doors, screens, awnings	13.92	0.94	7
Patio, walk, fence, driveway, masonry, brick, and stucco materials	1.29	0.15	12

	total consumer units	CUs headed by people under age 25	
		average spending	indexed spending
Landscape maintenance	$4.73	$0.05	1
Miscellaneous supplies and equipment	24.43	6.29	26
Insulation, other maintenance, repair	13.15	2.91	22
Finish basement, remodel rooms, build patios, walks, etc.	11.28	3.39	30
Property management and security	27.64	4.00	14
Property management	21.94	3.69	17
Management and upkeep services for security	5.71	0.31	5
Parking	5.17	1.61	31
Rented dwellings	**2,159.89**	**3,644.35**	**169**
Rent	2,104.66	3,568.54	170
Rent as pay	27.17	47.52	175
Maintenance, insurance, and other expenses	28.06	28.28	101
Tenant's insurance	8.90	5.26	59
Maintenance and repair services	11.16	7.14	64
Repair and maintenance services	10.58	7.13	67
Repair, replacement of hard-surface flooring	0.51	–	–
Repair of built-in appliances	0.07	0.01	14
Maintenance and repair materials	8.00	15.88	199
Paint, wallpaper, and supplies	1.01	1.61	159
Painting and wallpapering tools	0.11	0.17	155
Plastering, paneling, roofing, gutters, etc.	0.90	0.98	109
Plumbing supplies and equipment	0.80	2.43	304
Electrical supplies, heating, cooling equip.	0.30	–	–
Miscellaneous supplies and equipment	3.67	7.43	202
Insulation, other maintenance and repair	1.09	2.84	261
Materials for additions, finishing basements, remodeling rooms	2.43	4.58	188
Construction materials for jobs not started	0.15	–	–
Hard-surface flooring	0.73	2.63	360
Landscape maintenance	0.49	0.63	129
Other lodging	**504.56**	**376.84**	**75**
Owned vacation homes	171.55	26.58	15
Mortgage interest and charges	71.98	10.48	15
Property taxes	63.76	9.42	15
Maintenance, insurance and other expenses	35.81	6.68	19
Homeowner's insurance	9.70	1.96	20
Ground rent	2.93	–	–
Maintenance and repair services	16.76	1.12	7
Maintenance and repair materials	2.07	–	–
Property management and security	3.60	3.35	93
Property management	2.50	2.88	115
Management, upkeep services for security	1.10	0.48	44
Parking	0.76	0.25	33
Housing while attending school	80.14	257.06	321
Lodging on trips	252.87	93.20	37

	total consumer units	CUs headed by people under age 25	
		average spending	indexed spending
UTILITIES, FUELS, PUBLIC SERVICES	$2,684.32	$1,348.26	50
Natural gas	329.75	107.80	33
Natural gas (renter)	60.32	68.43	113
Natural gas (owner)	266.79	39.21	15
Natural gas (vacation)	2.54	0.09	4
Electricity	981.09	470.64	48
Electricity (renter)	223.26	343.12	154
Electricity (owner)	750.48	127.15	17
Electricity (vacation)	6.32	0.28	4
Fuel oil and other fuels	88.41	21.36	24
Fuel oil	45.98	7.58	16
Fuel oil (renter)	4.64	5.82	125
Fuel oil (owner)	40.98	1.77	4
Fuel oil (vacation)	0.36	–	–
Coal	0.07	–	–
Bottled/tank gas	35.27	11.60	33
Gas (renter)	5.09	5.13	101
Gas (owner)	27.19	2.76	10
Gas (vacation)	2.98	3.71	124
Wood and other fuels	7.09	2.18	31
Wood and other fuels (renter)	1.32	2.07	157
Wood and other fuels (owner)	5.68	0.10	2
Telephone services	956.74	640.94	67
Residential telephone and pay phones	641.00	345.92	54
Cellular phone service	293.76	258.73	88
Pager service	1.71	0.30	18
Phone cards	20.28	35.99	177
Water and other public services	328.33	107.52	33
Water and sewerage maintenance	237.16	78.73	33
Water and sewerage maintenance (renter)	32.76	45.36	138
Water and sewerage maintenance (owner)	201.79	33.01	16
Water and sewerage maintenance (vacation)	2.36	0.36	15
Trash and garbage collection	89.05	28.36	32
Trash and garbage collection (renter)	9.89	14.50	147
Trash and garbage collection (owner)	76.61	12.33	16
Trash and garbage collection (vacation)	2.53	1.53	60
Septic tank cleaning	2.12	0.43	20
HOUSEHOLD SERVICES	705.71	198.20	28
Personal services	331.02	98.89	30
Babysitting, child care in your own home	35.91	6.44	18
Babysitting, child care in someone else's home	27.48	19.07	69
Care for elderly, invalids, handicapped, etc.	50.07	1.55	3
Adult day care centers	6.81	–	–
Day care centers, nurseries, and preschools	210.74	71.83	34
Other household services	374.70	99.31	27
Housekeeping services	79.90	2.44	3
Gardening, lawn care service	72.38	6.96	10
Water softening service	3.15	0.19	6

	total consumer units	CUs headed by people under age 25	
		average spending	indexed spending
Nonclothing laundry, dry cleaning, sent out	$1.72	$0.73	42
Nonclothing laundry, dry cleaning, coin-operated	4.13	5.86	142
Termite/pest control services	13.25	1.17	9
Home security system service fee	17.40	4.35	25
Other home services	15.06	2.17	14
Termite/pest control products	0.68	0.20	29
Moving, storage, and freight express	33.13	16.71	50
Appliance repair, including service center	10.86	0.72	7
Reupholstering and furniture repair	7.40	1.06	14
Repairs/rentals of lawn/garden equipment, hand/power tools, etc.	3.62	0.45	12
Appliance rental	1.07	1.27	119
Rental of office equip., nonbusiness use	0.41	0.50	122
Repair of misc. household equip., furnishings	0.62	–	–
Repair of computer systems, nonbusiness use	2.53	0.68	27
Computer information services	107.29	53.88	50
HOUSEKEEPING SUPPLIES	**545.28**	**225.96**	**41**
Laundry and cleaning supplies	**130.57**	**77.18**	**59**
Soaps and detergents	72.89	48.58	67
Other laundry cleaning products	57.68	28.60	50
Other household products	**283.28**	**94.78**	**33**
Cleansing and toilet tissue, paper towels, and napkins	76.46	38.04	50
Miscellaneous household products	96.81	48.49	50
Lawn and garden supplies	110.01	8.25	7
Postage and stationery	**131.44**	**54.01**	**41**
Stationery, stationery supplies, giftwrap	60.20	25.71	43
Postage	69.12	27.56	40
Delivery services	2.12	0.74	35
HOUSEHOLD FURNISHINGS, EQUIPMENT	**1,518.36**	**812.45**	**54**
Household textiles	**135.52**	**93.31**	**69**
Bathroom linens	22.35	17.56	79
Bedroom linens	65.98	67.37	102
Kitchen and dining room linens	10.11	1.42	14
Curtains and draperies	16.65	4.28	26
Slipcovers and decorative pillows	7.40	0.29	4
Sewing materials for household items	11.44	2.01	18
Other linens	1.59	0.37	23
Furniture	**401.28**	**170.35**	**42**
Mattresses and springs	52.91	33.54	63
Other bedroom furniture	68.33	27.17	40
Sofas	85.33	38.60	45
Living room chairs	39.21	11.17	28
Living room tables	18.03	10.12	56
Kitchen and dining room furniture	61.28	17.50	29
Infants' furniture	6.46	5.30	82
Outdoor furniture	16.79	2.61	16
Wall units, cabinets, and other furniture	52.94	24.35	46

	total consumer units	CUs headed by people under age 25 average spending	indexed spending
Floor coverings	**$40.49**	**$8.05**	**20**
Wall-to-wall carpeting (renter)	0.65	0.73	112
Wall-to-wall carpet (replacement) (owner)	21.04	2.42	12
Floor coverings, nonpermanent	18.79	4.89	26
Major appliances	**188.47**	**87.72**	**47**
Dishwashers (built-in), garbage disposals, range hoods (renter)	1.24	0.79	64
Dishwashers (built-in), garbage disposals, range hoods (owner)	15.28	1.63	11
Refrigerators and freezers (renter)	5.58	10.97	197
Refrigerators and freezers (owner)	46.50	14.18	30
Washing machines (renter)	4.42	8.66	196
Washing machines (owner)	17.88	0.89	5
Clothes dryers (renter)	3.17	6.86	216
Clothes dryers (owner)	13.88	3.33	24
Cooking stoves, ovens (renter)	2.86	3.58	125
Cooking stoves, ovens (owner)	28.09	6.30	22
Microwave ovens (renter)	2.14	4.33	202
Microwave ovens (owner)	8.36	2.03	24
Portable dishwasher (renter)	0.25	0.26	104
Portable dishwasher (owner)	0.51	–	–
Window air conditioners (renter)	1.83	3.92	214
Window air conditioners (owner)	6.07	1.99	33
Electric floor-cleaning equipment	22.80	7.19	32
Sewing machines	4.79	1.18	25
Miscellaneous household appliances	**2.81**	**9.63**	**343**
Small appliances and misc. housewares	100.43	75.67	75
Housewares	77.55	60.73	78
Plastic dinnerware	1.57	1.70	108
China and other dinnerware	14.51	24.48	169
Flatware	3.79	2.41	64
Glassware	6.51	2.23	34
Silver serving pieces	4.05	0.82	20
Other serving pieces	1.44	1.80	125
Nonelectric cookware	24.25	16.18	67
Tableware, nonelectric kitchenware	21.44	11.11	52
Small appliances	22.89	14.95	65
Small electric kitchen appliances	17.18	10.96	64
Portable heating and cooling equipment	5.70	3.98	70
Miscellaneous household equipment	**652.17**	**377.35**	**58**
Window coverings	13.91	2.22	16
Infants' equipment	12.96	4.28	33
Laundry and cleaning equipment	15.15	6.87	45
Outdoor equipment	31.52	2.09	7
Clocks	5.87	3.11	53
Lamps and lighting fixtures	11.74	5.38	46
Other household decorative items	144.94	77.12	53
Telephones and accessories	32.73	17.37	53
Lawn and garden equipment	48.16	7.68	16

	total consumer units	CUs headed by people under age 25	
		average spending	indexed spending
Power tools	$33.27	$46.15	139
Office furniture for home use	10.57	6.05	57
Hand tools	8.05	3.63	45
Indoor plants and fresh flowers	49.78	21.24	43
Closet and storage items	9.98	2.40	24
Rental of furniture	4.60	5.81	126
Luggage	5.98	3.25	54
Computers and computer hardware, nonbusiness use	138.58	125.33	90
Computer software and accessories, nonbusiness use	17.67	15.56	88
Telephone answering devices	1.08	1.00	93
Calculators	1.44	2.37	165
Business equipment for home use	0.97	0.91	94
Other hardware	12.85	3.36	26
Smoke alarms (owner)	1.10	0.05	5
Smoke alarms (renter)	0.39	0.11	28
Other household appliances (owner)	8.00	0.31	4
Other household appliances (renter)	1.23	2.21	180
Misc. household equipment and parts	29.62	11.50	39
APPAREL AND SERVICES	**$1,749.22**	**$1,364.87**	**78**
Men's apparel	**319.48**	**229.89**	**72**
Suits	32.96	20.73	63
Sport coats and tailored jackets	10.65	3.46	32
Coats and jackets	33.86	24.32	72
Underwear	15.27	7.25	47
Hosiery	12.22	9.79	80
Nightwear	2.98	1.60	54
Accessories	22.41	14.16	63
Sweaters and vests	15.68	14.82	95
Active sportswear	15.13	8.39	55
Shirts	78.89	55.67	71
Pants	57.64	57.94	101
Shorts and shorts sets	12.22	4.22	35
Uniforms	3.21	3.69	115
Costumes	6.35	3.84	60
Boys' (aged 2 to 15) apparel	**89.98**	**36.21**	**40**
Coats and jackets	6.38	1.48	23
Sweaters	3.65	0.94	26
Shirts	19.50	11.61	60
Underwear	5.02	1.74	35
Nightwear	2.59	4.07	157
Hosiery	4.21	1.48	35
Accessories	4.12	2.87	70
Suits, sport coats, and vests	2.37	0.92	39
Pants	22.58	6.49	29
Shorts and shorts sets	8.66	1.86	21
Uniforms	3.35	0.68	20
Active sportswear	3.84	1.05	27
Costumes	3.72	1.03	28

	total consumer units	CUs headed by people under age 25 average spending	CUs headed by people under age 25 indexed spending
Women's apparel	**$586.91**	**$558.81**	**95**
Coats and jackets	50.06	58.15	116
Dresses	56.40	39.90	71
Sport coats and tailored jackets	6.48	2.70	42
Sweaters and vests	50.47	44.92	89
Shirts, blouses, and tops	103.24	111.72	108
Skirts	17.48	16.60	95
Pants	96.29	138.15	143
Shorts and shorts sets	16.09	21.08	131
Active sportswear	30.07	21.07	70
Nightwear	27.63	16.96	61
Undergarments	33.55	32.51	97
Hosiery	21.22	13.04	61
Suits	29.01	17.88	62
Accessories	33.37	16.60	50
Uniforms	6.12	3.70	60
Costumes	9.42	3.83	41
Girls' (aged 2 to 15) apparel	**117.21**	**50.15**	**43**
Coats and jackets	6.49	1.92	30
Dresses and suits	12.41	1.96	16
Shirts, blouses, and sweaters	29.33	12.77	44
Skirts and pants	24.07	6.62	28
Shorts and shorts sets	8.28	2.10	25
Active sportswear	9.32	12.68	136
Underwear and nightwear	7.63	2.39	31
Hosiery	4.30	3.10	72
Accessories	5.81	2.07	36
Uniforms	4.77	1.79	38
Costumes	4.80	2.75	57
Children under age 2	**82.60**	**101.63**	**123**
Coats, jackets, and snowsuits	2.43	2.26	93
Outerwear including dresses	23.71	28.55	120
Underwear	43.60	61.52	141
Nightwear and loungewear	4.07	3.01	74
Accessories	8.79	6.29	72
Footwear	**313.17**	**246.34**	**79**
Men's	102.90	88.10	86
Boys'	36.87	16.36	44
Women's	141.64	130.00	92
Girls'	31.76	11.88	37
Other apparel products and services	**239.87**	**141.82**	**59**
Material for making clothes	5.11	0.85	17
Sewing patterns and notions	8.20	3.74	46
Watches	13.62	6.98	51
Jewelry	89.65	36.56	41
Shoe repair and other shoe services	1.44	0.35	24
Coin-operated apparel laundry and dry cleaning	37.58	62.85	167
Apparel alteration, repair, and tailoring services	5.86	2.59	44
Clothing rental	2.66	3.10	117
Watch and jewelry repair	5.49	0.79	14
Professional laundry, dry cleaning	69.69	23.61	34
Clothing storage	0.55	0.40	73

	total consumer units	CUs headed by people under age 25	
		average spending	indexed spending
TRANSPORTATION	**$7,759.29**	**$5,101.90**	**66**
VEHICLE PURCHASES	**3,664.93**	**2,635.02**	**72**
Cars and trucks, new	**1,752.96**	**663.94**	**38**
New cars	883.08	532.32	60
New trucks	869.88	131.61	15
Cars and trucks, used	**1,842.29**	**1,917.15**	**104**
Used cars	1,113.46	1,215.74	109
Used trucks	728.82	701.42	96
Other vehicles	**69.68**	**53.93**	**77**
New motorcycles	36.26	33.30	92
Used motorcycles	33.42	20.63	62
GASOLINE AND MOTOR OIL	**1,235.06**	**903.03**	**73**
Gasoline	1,125.01	803.85	71
Diesel fuel	10.86	2.00	18
Gasoline on trips	88.24	86.71	98
Motor oil	10.05	9.60	96
Motor oil on trips	0.89	0.88	99
OTHER VEHICLE EXPENSES	**2,470.55**	**1,339.31**	**54**
Vehicle finance charges	**397.04**	**216.66**	**55**
Automobile finance charges	193.12	138.60	72
Truck finance charges	182.89	73.43	40
Motorcycle and plane finance charges	2.36	1.53	65
Other vehicle finance charges	18.67	3.09	17
Maintenance and repairs	**697.30**	**394.44**	**57**
Coolant, additives, brake, transmission fluids	3.82	3.71	97
Tires—purchased, replaced, installed	89.93	55.95	62
Parts, equipment, and accessories	41.70	34.72	83
Vehicle audio equipment, excl. labor	12.32	2.02	16
Vehicle products	4.92	1.78	36
Miscellaneous auto repair, servicing	43.69	20.97	48
Body work and painting	31.24	19.87	64
Clutch, transmission repair	48.68	26.71	55
Drive shaft and rear-end repair	6.51	1.57	24
Brake work	57.73	32.01	55
Repair to steering or front-end	16.91	16.41	97
Repair to engine cooling system	21.68	5.17	24
Motor tune-up	49.69	30.32	61
Lube, oil change, and oil filters	65.07	38.59	59
Front-end alignment, wheel balance, rotation	11.90	11.13	94
Shock absorber replacement	4.82	1.77	37
Gas tank repair, replacement	4.32	–	–
Tire repair and other repair work	39.83	14.72	37
Vehicle air conditioning repair	17.00	4.47	26
Exhaust system repair	12.56	13.76	110
Electrical system repair	28.42	11.74	41
Motor repair, replacement	76.62	45.20	59
Auto repair service policy	7.93	1.86	23

	total consumer units	CUs headed by people under age 25 average spending	indexed spending
Vehicle insurance	$893.50	$478.79	54
Vehicle rental, leases, licenses, other charges	482.71	249.41	52
Leased and rented vehicles	324.48	142.27	44
Rented vehicles	41.33	15.02	36
Auto rental	6.76	2.85	42
Auto rental on trips	28.28	5.53	20
Truck rental	2.21	4.84	219
Truck rental on trips	3.55	0.80	23
Leased vehicles	283.15	127.24	45
Car lease payments	149.63	70.41	47
Cash down payment (car lease)	11.13	9.16	82
Termination fee (car lease)	1.28	0.51	40
Truck lease payments	114.24	46.72	41
Cash down payment (truck lease)	4.92	–	–
Termination fee (truck lease)	1.94	0.45	23
Vehicle registration, state	72.82	39.06	54
Vehicle registration, local	7.76	4.26	55
Driver's license	6.26	6.02	96
Vehicle inspection	9.26	4.80	52
Parking fees	29.25	34.37	118
Parking fees in home city, excluding residence	24.24	30.99	128
Parking fees on trips	5.01	3.38	67
Tolls	10.59	5.38	51
Tolls on trips	3.94	3.08	78
Towing charges	5.60	7.19	128
Automobile service clubs	12.75	2.99	23
PUBLIC TRANSPORTATION	388.75	224.54	58
Airline fares	243.57	138.30	57
Intercity bus fares	11.48	7.38	64
Intracity mass transit fares	49.97	48.49	97
Local transportation on trips	10.91	5.81	53
Taxi fares and limousine service on trips	6.41	3.41	53
Taxi fares and limousine service	18.95	10.04	53
Intercity train fares	16.09	8.23	51
Ship fares	29.74	2.83	10
School bus	1.64	0.05	3
HEALTH CARE	$2,350.32	$640.23	27
HEALTH INSURANCE	1,167.71	284.87	24
Commercial health insurance	217.53	71.55	33
Traditional fee-for-service health plan (not BCBS)	68.27	21.90	32
Preferred-provider health plan (not BCBS)	149.26	49.65	33
Blue Cross, Blue Shield	315.67	82.12	26
Traditional fee-for-service health plan	53.76	13.92	26
Preferred-provider health plan	106.99	28.53	27
Health maintenance organization	101.53	29.06	29
Commercial Medicare supplement	47.35	9.47	20
Other BCBS health insurance	6.05	1.15	19

	total consumer units	CUs headed by people under age 25	
		average spending	indexed spending
Health maintenance plans (HMOs)	$280.47	$81.95	29
Medicare payments	186.87	13.91	7
Commercial Medicare supplements/ other health insurance	167.18	35.33	21
Commercial Medicare supplement (not BCBS)	106.32	19.14	18
Other health insurance (not BCBS)	60.86	16.19	27
MEDICAL SERVICES	589.87	195.61	33
Physician's services	147.53	45.22	31
Dental services	226.99	40.58	18
Eye care services	34.20	11.44	33
Service by professionals other than physician	42.76	7.13	17
Lab tests, X-rays	26.79	20.53	77
Hospital room	36.57	31.34	86
Hospital services other than room	51.51	25.70	50
Care in convalescent or nursing home	12.46	–	–
Other medical services	9.46	13.67	145
DRUGS	487.43	130.13	27
Nonprescription drugs	64.45	41.84	65
Nonprescription vitamins	49.15	16.85	34
Prescription drugs	373.83	71.45	19
MEDICAL SUPPLIES	105.31	29.61	28
Eyeglasses and contact lenses	52.26	20.42	39
Hearing aids	14.98	0.12	1
Topicals and dressings	27.56	8.57	31
Medical equipment for general use	2.69	0.34	13
Supportive, convalescent medical equipment	5.21	0.10	2
Rental of medical equipment	1.06	–	–
Rental of supportive, convalescent medical equipment	1.55	0.06	4
ENTERTAINMENT	$2,078.99	$1,211.84	58
FEES AND ADMISSIONS	541.67	313.15	58
Recreation expenses on trips	25.64	14.91	58
Social, recreation, civic club membership	107.92	59.72	55
Fees for participant sports	75.05	35.77	48
Participant sports on trips	29.50	19.40	66
Movie, theater, opera, ballet	98.30	98.98	101
Movie, other admissions on trips	45.57	21.07	46
Admission to sports events	36.18	26.13	72
Admission to sports events on trips	15.19	7.02	46
Fees for recreational lessons	82.69	15.23	18
Other entertainment services on trips	25.64	14.91	58
TELEVISION, RADIO, SOUND EQUIPMENT	691.90	456.96	66
Television	543.66	305.98	56
Cable service and community antenna	382.28	169.76	44
Black-and-white TV	0.80	–	–
Color TV, console	38.63	17.47	45
Color TV, portable, table model	39.14	33.53	86

	total consumer units	CUs headed by people under age 25	
		average spending	indexed spending
VCRs and video disc players	$23.25	$16.93	73
Video cassettes, tapes, and discs	33.13	41.06	124
Video game hardware and software	23.46	26.03	111
Repair of TV, radio, and sound equipment	2.50	0.15	6
Rental of television sets	0.46	1.05	228
Radio and sound equipment	**148.25**	**150.97**	**102**
Radios	3.98	–	–
Tape recorders and players	5.31	3.78	71
Sound components and component systems	20.19	17.03	84
Miscellaneous sound equipment	3.18	0.09	3
Sound equipment accessories	5.97	3.46	58
Satellite dishes	1.00	1.19	119
Compact disc, tape, record, video mail order clubs	6.53	6.94	106
Records, CDs, audio tapes, needles	36.47	50.20	138
Rental of VCR, radio, sound equipment	0.25	0.26	104
Musical instruments and accessories	24.82	20.05	81
Rental and repair of musical instruments	1.22	0.03	2
Rental of video cassettes, tapes, discs, films	39.33	47.94	122
PETS, TOYS, PLAYGROUND EQUIPMENT	**369.12**	**192.62**	**52**
Pets	**248.25**	**119.31**	**48**
Pet food	102.56	36.50	36
Pet purchase, supplies, and medicines	52.29	60.87	116
Pet services	21.95	5.45	25
Veterinarian services	71.44	16.49	23
Toys, games, hobbies, and tricycles	**117.34**	**72.83**	**62**
Playground equipment	**3.54**	**0.48**	**14**
OTHER ENTERTAINMENT SUPPLIES, EQUIPMENT, SERVICES	**476.30**	**249.11**	**52**
Unmotored recreational vehicles	**47.14**	**40.27**	**85**
Boat without motor and boat trailers	16.15	0.61	4
Trailer and other attachable campers	30.99	39.66	128
Motorized recreational vehicles	**170.19**	**68.57**	**40**
Motorized camper	40.05	–	–
Other vehicle	35.47	27.61	78
Motorboats	94.67	40.96	43
Rental of recreational vehicles	**1.99**	**0.81**	**41**
Outboard motors	**0.71**	**0.31**	**44**
Docking and landing fees	**6.66**	**1.27**	**19**
Sports, recreation, exercise equipment	**150.33**	**79.80**	**53**
Athletic gear, game tables, exercise equipment	60.51	36.71	61
Bicycles	13.45	7.59	56
Camping equipment	9.59	8.40	88
Hunting and fishing equipment	35.68	8.80	25
Winter sports equipment	5.45	7.56	139
Water sports equipment	8.95	1.65	18
Other sports equipment	14.62	8.32	57
Rental and repair of misc. sports equipment	2.07	0.76	37

	total consumer units	CUs headed by people under age 25	
		average spending	indexed spending
Photographic equipment and supplies	**$90.48**	**$55.54**	**61**
Film	17.74	13.63	77
Other photographic supplies	2.27	–	–
Film processing	26.60	20.11	76
Repair and rental of photographic equipment	0.12	0.03	25
Photographic equipment	23.34	13.35	57
Photographer fees	20.42	8.41	41
Fireworks	**1.52**	**–**	**–**
Souvenirs	**1.25**	**–**	**–**
Visual goods	**1.19**	**–**	**–**
Pinball, electronic video games	**4.84**	**2.55**	**53**
PERSONAL CARE PRODUCTS AND SERVICES	**$525.80**	**$329.38**	**63**
Personal care products	**276.65**	**199.15**	**72**
Hair care products	53.57	41.15	77
Hair accessories	6.57	6.53	99
Wigs and hairpieces	1.32	1.57	119
Oral hygiene products	27.33	15.89	58
Shaving products	15.09	7.50	50
Cosmetics, perfume, and bath products	129.13	90.08	70
Deodorants, feminine hygiene, misc. products	30.29	32.27	107
Electric personal care appliances	13.34	4.17	31
Personal care services	**249.15**	**130.23**	**52**
READING	**$138.57**	**$56.68**	**41**
Newspaper subscriptions	43.88	5.60	13
Newspaper, nonsubscription	11.30	5.92	52
Magazine subscriptions	16.59	6.82	41
Magazines, nonsubscription	9.35	8.82	94
Books purchased through book clubs	6.62	1.67	25
Books not purchased through book clubs	50.38	27.78	55
Encyclopedia and other reference book sets	0.33	0.05	15
EDUCATION	**$751.95**	**$1,663.52**	**221**
College tuition	444.45	1,304.63	294
Elementary and high school tuition	128.94	4.32	3
Other school tuition	25.53	9.93	39
Other school expenses including rentals	25.77	26.99	105
Books, supplies for college	57.93	265.85	459
Books, supplies for elementary, high school	16.14	4.57	28
Books, supplies for day care, nursery school	3.39	1.78	53
Miscellaneous school expenses and supplies	49.80	45.46	91

	total consumer units	CUs headed by people under age 25	
		average spending	indexed spending
TOBACCO PRODUCTS AND SMOKING SUPPLIES	**$320.49**	**$285.68**	**89**
Cigarettes	291.89	259.31	89
Other tobacco products	26.27	21.99	84
Smoking accessories	2.33	4.38	188
FINANCIAL PRODUCTS, SERVICES	**$788.12**	**$422.38**	**54**
Miscellaneous fees	2.25	–	–
Lottery and gambling losses	46.94	8.15	17
Legal fees	132.99	50.82	38
Funeral expenses	77.91	26.65	34
Safe deposit box rental	3.84	1.14	30
Checking accounts, other bank service charges	25.91	27.85	107
Cemetery lots, vaults, and maintenance fees	16.05	0.39	2
Accounting fees	57.85	11.33	20
Miscellaneous personal services	39.77	73.51	185
Finance charges, except mortgage and vehicles	271.37	199.07	73
Occupational expenses	38.46	14.05	37
Expenses for other properties	65.99	6.72	10
Credit card memberships	2.82	1.25	44
Shopping club membership fees	5.97	1.45	24
CASH CONTRIBUTIONS	**$1,277.10**	**$318.97**	**25**
Support for college students	75.94	5.11	7
Alimony expenditures	21.18	0.60	3
Child support expenditures	190.75	60.96	32
Gifts to non-CU members of stocks, bonds, and mutual funds	24.23	6.38	26
Cash contributions to charities and other organizations	137.62	20.24	15
Cash contributions to church, religious organizations	557.29	142.53	26
Cash contributions to educational institutions	33.42	1.75	5
Cash contributions to political organizations	10.90	1.28	12
Other cash gifts	225.76	80.13	35
PERSONAL INSURANCE, PENSIONS	**$3,898.62**	**$1,382.11**	**35**
Life and other personal insurance	**406.11**	**51.26**	**13**
Life, endowment, annuity, other personal insurance	391.65	49.29	13
Other nonhealth insurance	14.46	1.97	14
Pensions and Social Security	**3,492.51**	**1,330.85**	**38**
Deductions for government retirement	69.48	6.03	9
Deductions for railroad retirement	2.21	–	–
Deductions for private pensions	390.38	46.63	12
Nonpayroll deposit to retirement plans	426.12	57.22	13
Deductions for Social Security	2,604.32	1,220.97	47

	total consumer units	CUs headed by people under age 25	
		average spending	indexed spending
PERSONAL TAXES	$2,496.26	$566.64	23
Federal income taxes	1,842.57	401.66	22
State and local income taxes	506.45	148.58	29
Other taxes	147.24	16.41	11
GIFTS FOR NON-HOUSEHOLD MEMBERS**	$1,036.24	$436.63	42
FOOD	82.18	26.83	33
Cakes and cupcakes	2.41	0.53	22
Other fresh fruits (excl. apples, bananas, citrus)	2.26	2.26	100
Candy and chewing gum	11.69	3.22	28
Board (including at school)	21.90	2.43	11
Catered affairs	26.19	12.22	47
ALCOHOLIC BEVERAGES	13.42	14.93	111
Beer and ale	4.73	11.50	243
Wine	5.84	1.55	27
HOUSING	258.69	104.49	40
Housekeeping supplies	42.48	24.34	57
Laundry and cleaning supplies	2.93	5.70	195
Other household products	11.69	6.36	54
Miscellaneous household products	5.85	5.22	89
Lawn and garden supplies	4.20	0.01	0
Postage and stationery	27.86	12.28	44
Stationery, stationery supplies, giftwrap	21.13	8.97	42
Postage	6.14	2.91	47
Household textiles	13.72	1.55	11
Bathroom linens	2.59	0.50	19
Bedroom linens	6.10	0.88	14
Appliances and miscellaneous housewares	23.98	12.75	53
Major appliances	8.41	0.23	3
Electric floor cleaning equipment	2.77	–	–
Small appliances and miscellaneous housewares	15.57	12.52	80
China and other dinnerware	2.46	1.18	48
Nonelectric cookware	3.53	8.50	241
Tableware, nonelectric kitchenware	2.63	0.61	23
Small electric kitchen appliances	2.71	1.45	54
Miscellaneous household equipment	64.70	23.55	36
Infants' equipment	3.82	0.15	4
Outdoor equipment	2.07	–	–
Other household decorative items	25.76	8.86	34
Power tools	2.80	–	–
Indoor plants, fresh flowers	13.43	8.71	65
Computers and computer hardware	6.59	0.18	3
Miscellaneous household equipment	2.19	2.11	96
Other housing	113.80	42.31	37
Repair or maintenance services	4.51	1.47	33
Housing while attending school	39.93	3.42	9

	total consumer units	CUs headed by people under age 25	
		average spending	indexed spending
Natural gas (renter)	$3.62	$1.13	31
Electricity (renter)	14.67	13.95	95
Water, sewer maintenance (renter)	3.04	2.11	69
Daycare centers, nurseries, and preschools	23.81	5.69	24
APPAREL AND SERVICES	**237.13**	**169.74**	**72**
Men and boys, aged 2 or older	**63.74**	**55.08**	**86**
Men's coats and jackets	5.09	3.65	72
Men's accessories	4.45	3.27	73
Men's sweaters and vests	3.06	2.45	80
Men's active sportswear	2.76	–	–
Men's shirts	16.79	24.70	147
Men's pants	6.93	9.53	138
Boys' shirts	3.71	1.09	29
Boys' pants	3.76	0.70	19
Women and girls, aged 2 or older	**81.76**	**36.73**	**45**
Women's coats and jackets	5.62	1.11	20
Women's dresses	7.66	1.95	25
Women's vests and sweaters	8.50	3.87	46
Women's shirts, tops, blouses	9.06	10.48	116
Women's pants	6.62	3.82	58
Women's active sportswear	4.33	0.60	14
Women's sleepwear	6.45	1.75	27
Women's accessories	5.71	1.49	26
Girls' dresses and suits	2.98	0.05	2
Girls' shirts, blouses, sweaters	4.48	0.37	8
Girls' skirts and pants	3.32	1.12	34
Girls' accessories	2.38	0.25	11
Children under age 2	**39.99**	**33.56**	**84**
Infant dresses, outerwear	15.28	11.38	74
Infant underwear	16.91	19.22	114
Infant nightwear, loungewear	2.55	1.06	42
Infant accessories	3.93	1.48	38
Other apparel products and services	**51.63**	**44.37**	**86**
Jewelry and watches	24.01	12.79	53
Watches	2.16	1.45	67
Jewelry	21.85	11.33	52
Men's footwear	8.37	18.78	224
Boys' footwear	4.46	2.30	52
Women's footwear	8.82	7.39	84
Girls' footwear	3.30	1.23	37
TRANSPORTATION	**43.87**	**15.09**	**34**
New cars	7.09	–	–
Used cars	12.21	8.81	72
Airline fares	6.78	1.81	27
Ship fares	2.74	0.88	32

	total consumer units	CUs headed by people under age 25	
		average spending	indexed spending
HEALTH CARE	**$32.59**	**$1.12**	**3**
Physician's services	3.07	–	–
Dental services	4.03	–	–
Care in convalescent or nursing home	5.19	–	–
Nonprescription vitamins	3.93	–	–
Prescription drugs	2.38	–	–
ENTERTAINMENT	**78.24**	**29.87**	**38**
Toys, games, hobbies, and tricycles	29.98	10.55	35
Other entertainment	48.26	19.33	40
Fees for recreational lessons	7.88	1.05	13
Community antenna or cable TV	6.37	7.18	113
VCRs and videodisc players	2.26	1.11	49
Video game hardware and software	2.13	1.18	55
Athletic gear, game tables, exercise equipment	6.60	0.87	13
Hunting and fishing equipment	3.06	1.40	46
Photographer fees	3.19	–	–
PERSONAL CARE PRODUCTS, SERVICES	**21.15**	**13.16**	**62**
Cosmetics, perfume, bath preparation	12.53	11.50	92
Electric personal care appliances	3.31	–	–
EDUCATION	**183.88**	**43.25**	**24**
College tuition	127.83	23.90	19
Elementary and high school tuition	25.95	0.20	1
Other school tuition	4.44	0.49	11
Other school expenses including rentals	3.99	1.06	27
College books and supplies	11.93	15.29	128
Miscellaneous school supplies	7.38	1.81	25
ALL OTHER GIFTS	**83.76**	**17.94**	**21**
Gifts of trip expenses	44.40	11.39	26
Lottery and gambling losses	2.86	0.46	16
Legal fees	5.82	1.75	30
Funeral expenses	25.25	2.10	8
Miscellaneous personal services	2.16	1.55	72

This figure does not include the amount paid for mortgage principle, which is considered an asset.

** *Expenditures on gifts are also included in the preceding product and service categories. Food spending, for example, includes the amount spent on food gifts. Only gift categories with spending of $2.00 or more by the average consumer unit are shown.*

Note: The Bureau of Labor Statistics uses consumer unit rather than household as the sampling unit in the Consumer Expenditure Survey. For the definition of consumer unit, see the glossary. (–) means not applicable or the sample is too small to make a reliable estimate.

Source: Bureau of Labor Statistics, unpublished data from the 2002 Consumer Expenditure Survey; calculations by New Strategist

Parents of Preschoolers Spend Cautiously

The spending of married couples with preschoolers rose more slowly than their incomes between 1997 and 2002.

The incomes of married couples with preschoolers rose 6 percent between 1997 and 2002, after adjusting for inflation. Their spending increased a smaller 3 percent as they reined in their purchases.

Couples with preschoolers cut their spending on groceries (food at home) by 4 percent between 1997 and 2002. But they spent 10 percent more on food away from home. They spent 12 percent more on alcoholic beverages, but 7 percent less on furniture and 11 percent less on major appliances. As homeownership rates rose, they spent more on owned dwellings and less on rent. They spent 6 percent more on women's clothes and 28 percent more on shoes. Their spending on new cars and trucks rose 9 percent. Health insurance spending rose 30 percent. Couples with preschoolers spent 6 percent more on entertainment, but 10 percent less on pets, toys, and playground equipment.

■ The spending patterns of couples with preschoolers is a mixed bag, revealing the diversity of their economic status.

Married couples with preschoolers spent more on some things, less on others

(percent change in spending by married couples with children under age 6 at home, 1997 to 2002; in 2002 dollars)

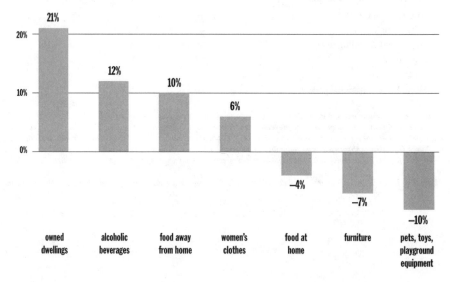

Table 9.3 Average Spending of Married Couples with Children under Age 6, 1997 and 2002

(average annual spending of married-couple consumer units with children under age 6, 1997 and 2002; percent change, 1997–2002; in 2002 dollars)

	2002	1997	percent change 1997–02
Number of consumer units (in 000s)	5,547	5,431	2.1%
Average before-tax income	$67,587	$63,758	6.0
Average annual spending	52,779	51,087	3.3
FOOD	**$6,348**	**$6,273**	**1.2%**
Food at home	**3,940**	**4,089**	**–3.7**
Cereals and bakery products	560	607	–7.7
Cereals and cereal products	206	230	–10.5
Bakery products	354	377	–6.0
Meats, poultry, fish, and eggs	942	969	–2.8
Beef	275	268	2.6
Pork	193	219	–11.9
Other meats	112	139	–19.2
Poultry	180	197	–8.5
Fish and seafood	143	106	34.7
Eggs	39	40	–3.0
Dairy products	454	477	–4.8
Fresh milk and cream	182	196	–6.9
Other dairy products	272	282	–3.4
Fruits and vegetables	711	636	11.8
Fresh fruits	211	189	11.7
Fresh vegetables	216	181	19.3
Processed fruits	172	161	6.9
Processed vegetables	112	104	7.8
Other food at home	1,274	1,402	–9.1
Sugar and other sweets	132	146	–9.8
Fats and oils	92	96	–4.3
Miscellaneous foods	729	787	–7.3
Nonalcoholic beverages	276	310	–10.8
Food prepared by household on trips	45	64	–29.3
Food away from home	**2,408**	**2,183**	**10.3**
ALCOHOLIC BEVERAGES	**340**	**304**	**11.9**
HOUSING	**19,141**	**17,827**	**7.4**
Shelter	**11,269**	**9,782**	**15.2**
Owned dwellings	8,506	7,037	20.9
Mortgage interest and charges	5,950	4,902	21.4
Property taxes	1,545	1,369	12.9
Maintenance, repairs, insurance, other expenses	1,011	767	31.9
Rented dwellings	2,384	2,457	–3.0
Other lodging	379	288	31.5

	2002	1997	percent change 1997–02
Utilities, fuels, public services	**$2,979**	**$2,881**	**3.4%**
Natural gas	351	353	–0.6
Electricity	1,041	1,020	2.1
Fuel oil and other fuels	78	114	–31.6
Telephone services	1,128	1,050	7.4
Water and other public services	381	343	11.1
Household services	**2,320**	**2,401**	**–3.4**
Personal services	1,912	2,028	–5.7
Other household services	408	373	9.3
Housekeeping supplies	**552**	**705**	**–21.7**
Laundry and cleaning supplies	156	159	–1.7
Other household products	252	340	–25.8
Postage and stationery	145	207	–29.9
Household furnishings, equipment	**2,021**	**2,058**	**–1.8**
Household textiles	147	104	41.5
Furniture	540	581	–7.1
Floor coverings	41	113	–63.7
Major appliances	228	255	–10.5
Small appliances, miscellaneous housewares	158	121	30.9
Miscellaneous household equipment	907	884	2.6
APPAREL AND SERVICES	**2,630**	**2,485**	**5.8**
Men and boys	**579**	**558**	**3.8**
Men, aged 16 or older	452	454	–0.4
Boys, aged 2 to 15	127	105	20.9
Women and girls	**758**	**722**	**5.0**
Women, aged 16 or older	594	561	5.9
Girls, aged 2 to 15	163	161	1.3
Children under age 2	**535**	**577**	**–7.2**
Footwear	**471**	**368**	**28.1**
Other apparel products and services	**288**	**262**	**10.2**
TRANSPORTATION	**10,467**	**10,525**	**–0.6**
Vehicle purchases	**5,391**	**5,196**	**3.8**
Cars and trucks, new	2,668	2,448	9.0
Cars and trucks, used	2,531	2,721	–7.0
Gasoline and motor oil	**1,494**	**1,479**	**1.0**
Other vehicle expenses	**3,176**	**3,378**	**–6.0**
Vehicle finance charges	622	543	14.5
Maintenance and repairs	827	906	–8.7
Vehicle insurance	993	1,008	–1.5
Vehicle rental, leases, licenses, other charges	733	918	–20.2
Public transportation	**406**	**473**	**–14.1**
HEALTH CARE	**2,233**	**1,882**	**18.7**
Health insurance	1,253	962	30.2
Medical services	633	589	7.5
Drugs	274	213	28.4
Medical supplies	73	116	–37.2

	2002	1997	percent change 1997–02
ENTERTAINMENT	**$2,425**	**$2,277**	**6.5%**
Fees and admissions	558	597	–6.5
Television, radio, sound equipment	783	705	11.1
Pets, toys, and playground equipment	486	539	–9.8
Other entertainment supplies, services	598	437	36.9
PERSONAL CARE PRODUCTS, SERVICES	**549**	**687**	**–20.1**
READING	**132**	**184**	**–28.4**
EDUCATION	**336**	**330**	**1.9**
TOBACCO PRODUCTS AND SMOKING SUPPLIES	**275**	**273**	**0.9**
MISCELLANEOUS	**913**	**1,153**	**–20.8**
CASH CONTRIBUTIONS	**1,037**	**1,188**	**–12.7**
PERSONAL INSURANCE, PENSIONS	**5,952**	**5,701**	**4.4**
Life and other personal insurance	424	512	–17.1
Pensions and Social Security	5,528	5,189	6.5
PERSONAL TAXES	**3,738**	**5,908**	**–36.7**
Federal income taxes	2,766	4,489	–38.4
State and local income taxes	837	1,291	–35.1
Other taxes	135	130	4.2
GIFTS FOR NON-HOUSEHOLD MEMBERS	**773**	**1,017**	**–24.0**

Note: The Bureau of Labor Statistics uses consumer unit rather than household as the sampling unit in the Consumer Expenditure Survey. For the definition of consumer unit, see the glossary. Spending on gifts is included in the preceding product and service categories.
Source: Bureau of Labor Statistics, 1997 and 2002 Consumer Expenditure Surveys, Internet site http://www.bls.gov/cex/; calculations by New Strategist

Couples with School-Aged Children Are Spending More

Many categories saw spending increases between 1997 and 2002.

Married couples with school-aged children rank among the most affluent households in the nation. Their incomes grew a substantial 15 percent between 1997 and 2002, and their spending rose 10 percent, after adjusting for inflation.

Couples with school-aged children boosted their spending on food away from home by 16 percent between 1997 and 2002, although they spent only 0.4 percent more on groceries. They spent fully 29 percent more on alcoholic beverages. Their spending on owned dwellings rose 19 percent as more became homeowners. They also spent more on household furnishings and equipment as they outfitted their homes. They spent fully 49 percent more on new cars and trucks.

Couples with school-aged children spent 26 percent more on health insurance in 2002 than in 1997, and fully 51 percent more on prescription drugs. Despite these increase in nondiscretionary expenses, they also spent a substantial amount more on entertainment—up 20 percent between 1997 and 2002.

■ With gains in income outstripping those in spending, parents with school-aged children are making sure their kids have everything they need.

Couples with school-aged children are spending more on many items

(percent change in spending by married couples with children aged 6 to 17 at home on selected items, 1997 to 2002; in 2002 dollars)

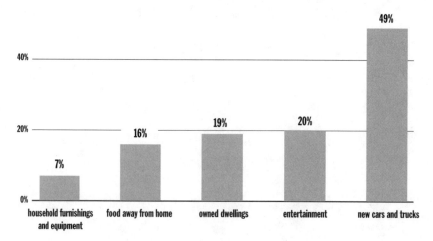

Table 9.4 Average Spending of Married Couples with Children Aged 6 to 17, 1997 and 2002

(average annual spending of married-couple consumer units with children aged 6 to 17, 1997 and 2002; percent change, 1997–2002; in 2002 dollars)

	2002	1997	percent change 1997–02
Number of consumer units (in 000s)	15,206	15,360	–0.1%
Average before-tax income	$72,720	$63,322	14.8
Average annual spending	58,104	52,653	10.4
FOOD	**$8,041**	**$7,565**	**6.3%**
Food at home	**4,664**	**4,646**	**0.4**
Cereals and bakery products	708	761	–7.0
Cereals and cereal products	248	278	–10.9
Bakery products	460	484	–4.9
Meats, poultry, fish, and eggs	1,163	1,170	–0.6
Beef	355	380	–6.6
Pork	240	228	5.3
Other meats	155	148	5.1
Poultry	214	234	–8.4
Fish and seafood	156	135	15.4
Eggs	43	45	–3.8
Dairy products	517	534	–3.2
Fresh milk and cream	199	222	–10.5
Other dairy products	319	312	2.3
Fruits and vegetables	789	706	11.7
Fresh fruits	259	216	20.1
Fresh vegetables	242	190	27.4
Processed fruits	172	165	4.0
Processed vegetables	116	134	–13.5
Other food at home	1,487	1,475	0.8
Sugar and other sweets	190	199	–4.5
Fats and oils	119	121	–1.4
Miscellaneous foods	728	676	7.7
Nonalcoholic beverages	381	398	–4.2
Food prepared by household on trips	69	82	–15.4
Food away from home	**3,376**	**2,920**	**15.6**
ALCOHOLIC BEVERAGES	**436**	**337**	**29.2**
HOUSING	**18,619**	**16,848**	**10.5**
Shelter	**10,912**	**9,684**	**12.7**
Owned dwellings	8,728	7,361	18.6
Mortgage interest and charges	5,739	4,752	20.8
Property taxes	1,822	1,552	17.4
Maintenance, repairs, insurance, other expenses	1,166	1,057	10.3
Rented dwellings	1,600	1,668	–4.1
Other lodging	584	656	–11.0

	2002	1997	percent change 1997–02
Utilities, fuels, public services	**$3,491**	**$3,441**	**1.4%**
Natural gas	442	424	4.4
Electricity	1,285	1,323	–2.9
Fuel oil and other fuels	106	160	–33.7
Telephone services	1,204	1,092	10.3
Water and other public services	455	445	2.3
Household services	**1,221**	**926**	**31.8**
Personal services	705	548	28.8
Other household services	515	379	36.0
Housekeeping supplies	**724**	**682**	**6.2**
Laundry and cleaning supplies	195	199	–2.0
Other household products	378	327	15.5
Postage and stationery	151	154	–2.1
Household furnishings, equipment	**2,271**	**2,115**	**7.4**
Household textiles	164	102	61.3
Furniture	620	561	10.5
Floor coverings	67	62	9.0
Major appliances	248	217	14.4
Small appliances, miscellaneous housewares	128	148	–13.2
Miscellaneous household equipment	1,044	1,027	1.7
APPAREL AND SERVICES	**2,689**	**2,993**	**–10.2**
Men and boys	**769**	**834**	**–7.7**
Men, aged 16 or older	469	537	–12.7
Boys, aged 2 to 15	300	296	1.3
Women and girls	**1,020**	**1,142**	**–10.7**
Women, aged 16 or older	627	732	–14.3
Girls, aged 2 to 15	392	410	–4.4
Children under age 2	**100**	**86**	**16.2**
Footwear	**508**	**589**	**–13.7**
Other apparel products and services	**292**	**343**	**–14.9**
TRANSPORTATION	**11,203**	**9,412**	**19.0**
Vehicle purchases	**5,512**	**3,818**	**44.4**
Cars and trucks, new	2,556	1,718	48.7
Cars and trucks, used	2,831	2,059	37.5
Gasoline and motor oil	**1,761**	**1,699**	**3.6**
Other vehicle expenses	**3,491**	**3,416**	**2.2**
Vehicle finance charges	641	487	31.6
Maintenance and repairs	974	1,112	–12.4
Vehicle insurance	1,140	1,039	9.7
Vehicle rental, leases, licenses, other charges	736	778	–5.4
Public transportation	**439**	**480**	**–8.6**
HEALTH CARE	**2,676**	**2,256**	**18.6**
Health insurance	1,343	1,066	26.0
Medical services	815	784	3.9
Drugs	400	265	51.1
Medical supplies	118	140	–15.5

	2002	1997	percent change 1997–02
ENTERTAINMENT	**$3,593**	**$2,987**	**20.3%**
Fees and admissions	1,087	901	20.7
Television, radio, sound equipment	964	865	11.5
Pets, toys, and playground equipment	605	521	16.2
Other entertainment supplies, services	937	701	33.8
PERSONAL CARE PRODUCTS, SERVICES	**757**	**760**	**–0.4**
READING	**169**	**218**	**–22.4**
EDUCATION	**1,246**	**959**	**30.0**
TOBACCO PRODUCTS AND SMOKING SUPPLIES	**318**	**331**	**–3.8**
MISCELLANEOUS	**827**	**1,006**	**–17.8**
CASH CONTRIBUTIONS	**1,399**	**1,236**	**13.2**
PERSONAL INSURANCE, PENSIONS	**6,129**	**5,744**	**6.7**
Life and other personal insurance	609	662	–7.9
Pensions and Social Security	5,520	5,083	8.6
PERSONAL TAXES	**3,710**	**4,783**	**–22.4**
Federal income taxes	2,742	3,559	–22.9
State and local income taxes	782	1,017	–23.1
Other taxes	186	208	–10.5
GIFTS FOR NON-HOUSEHOLD MEMBERS	**1,253**	**1,232**	**1.7**

Note: The Bureau of Labor Statistics uses consumer unit rather than household as the sampling unit in the Consumer Expenditure Survey. For the definition of consumer unit, see the glossary. Spending on gifts is included in the preceding product and service categories.
Source: Bureau of Labor Statistics, 1997 and 2002 Consumer Expenditure Surveys, Internet site http://www.bls.gov/cex/; calculations by New Strategist

Couples with Adult Children at Home Are Spending More

But their incomes grew much faster than spending.

Married couples with grown children (aged 18 or older) at home are the most affluent household type. That's because these households have the most earners—2.6 versus 1.7 earners in the average household. The incomes of couples with adult children at home rose 21 percent between 1997 and 2002, after adjusting for inflation. Their spending rose a much more modest 8 percent.

Married couples with adult children at home are spending less on some items—such as a 3 percent decline in spending on groceries between 1997 and 2002. But they spent 14 percent more on food away from home, and fully 45 percent more on alcoholic beverages. Spending on owned homes increased 29 percent as homeownership rates rose, and consequently spending on furniture rose 16 percent. But spending on other lodging (mostly hotels and motels) was down slightly, and spending on apparel fell 10 percent.

Spending on new vehicles rose 48 percent among couples with grown children at home. But spending on public transportation fell 23 percent. Spending on health insurance was up 19 percent, and spending on education rose fully 34 percent. Perhaps as a consequence, spending on entertainment fell 5 percent.

■ Many couples with adult children at home are paying college tuition, tempering their discretionary purchases.

Couples with adult children at home boosted their spending on food away from home, alcoholic beverages, and education

(percent change in spending by married couples with children aged 18 or older at home, 1997 and 2002: in 2002 dollars)

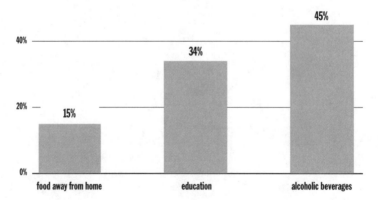

Table 9.5   **Average Spending of Married Couples with Children Aged 18 or Older at Home,**
1997 and 2002

(average annual spending of married-couple consumer units with children aged 18 or older at home, 1997 and
2002; percent change, 1997–2002; in 2002 dollars)

	2002	1997	percent change 1997–02
Number of consumer units (in 000s)	8,036	7,591	5.9%
Average before-tax income	$81,042	$66,970	21.0
Average annual spending	60,860	56,408	7.9
FOOD	**$8,324**	**$8,019**	**3.8%**
Food at home	**4,690**	**4,854**	**–3.4**
Cereals and bakery products	697	800	–12.9
Cereals and cereal products	229	284	–19.3
Bakery products	468	516	–9.3
Meats, poultry, fish, and eggs	1,263	1,305	–3.2
Beef	397	387	2.7
Pork	234	268	–12.7
Other meats	175	182	–3.9
Poultry	233	262	–10.9
Fish and seafood	174	153	13.7
Eggs	49	54	–8.6
Dairy products	487	529	–7.9
Fresh milk and cream	193	211	–8.6
Other dairy products	294	317	–7.3
Fruits and vegetables	808	762	6.0
Fresh fruits	270	243	11.4
Fresh vegetables	254	241	5.2
Processed fruits	166	153	8.4
Processed vegetables	118	125	–5.7
Other food at home	1,434	1,457	–1.6
Sugar and other sweets	164	181	–9.4
Fats and oils	140	136	2.7
Miscellaneous foods	684	629	8.7
Nonalcoholic beverages	391	417	–6.2
Food prepared by household on trips	55	94	–41.4
Food away from home	**3,634**	**3,165**	**14.8**
ALCOHOLIC BEVERAGES	**490**	**339**	**44.7**
HOUSING	**17,697**	**15,339**	**15.4**
Shelter	10,247	8,241	24.3
Owned dwellings	8,196	6,345	29.2
Mortgage interest and charges	4,635	3,568	29.9
Property taxes	1,883	1,657	13.6
Maintenance, repairs, insurance, other expenses	1,677	1,121	49.6
Rented dwellings	1,097	936	17.2
Other lodging	954	960	–0.6

	2002	1997	percent change 1997–02
Utilities, fuels, public services	**$3,797**	**$3,786**	**0.3%**
Natural gas	451	456	–1.1
Electricity	1,371	1,437	–4.6
Fuel oil and other fuels	131	203	–35.6
Telephone services	1,365	1,205	13.3
Water and other public services	480	485	–1.0
Household services	**615**	**378**	**62.8**
Personal services	125	30	314.4
Other household services	490	348	41.0
Housekeeping supplies	**804**	**787**	**2.2**
Laundry and cleaning supplies	213	186	14.8
Other household products	392	394	–0.6
Postage and stationery	199	207	–3.7
Household furnishings, equipment	**2,234**	**2,146**	**4.1**
Household textiles	212	122	74.1
Furniture	526	453	16.2
Floor coverings	54	74	–26.8
Major appliances	272	225	21.1
Small appliances, miscellaneous housewares	153	136	12.2
Miscellaneous household equipment	1,017	1,137	–10.6
APPAREL AND SERVICES	**2,565**	**2,846**	**–9.9**
Men and boys	**702**	**687**	**2.2**
Men, aged 16 or older	634	607	4.5
Boys, aged 2 to 15	68	80	–15.5
Women and girls	**961**	**1,125**	**–14.6**
Women, aged 16 or older	866	1,015	–14.6
Girls, aged 2 to 15	95	111	–14.1
Children under age 2	**58**	**41**	**40.3**
Footwear	**507**	**498**	**1.7**
Other apparel products and services	**337**	**495**	**–31.9**
TRANSPORTATION	**12,506**	**12,352**	**1.2**
Vehicle purchases	**5,600**	**5,050**	**10.9**
Cars and trucks, new	2,791	1,887	47.9
Cars and trucks, used	2,661	3,140	–15.2
Gasoline and motor oil	**2,112**	**2,165**	**–2.5**
Other vehicle expenses	**4,274**	**4,460**	**–4.2**
Vehicle finance charges	684	596	14.9
Maintenance and repairs	1,141	1,199	–4.8
Vehicle insurance	1,623	1,629	–0.4
Vehicle rental, leases, licenses, other charges	825	1,037	–20.4
Public transportation	**521**	**676**	**–22.9**
HEALTH CARE	**3,127**	**2,837**	**10.2**
Health insurance	1,473	1,236	19.2
Medical services	909	1,000	–9.1
Drugs	604	409	47.7
Medical supplies	140	192	–27.2

	2002	1997	percent change 1997–02
ENTERTAINMENT	**$3,037**	**$3,188**	**–4.7%**
Fees and admissions	756	771	–1.9
Television, radio, sound equipment	952	912	4.4
Pets, toys, and playground equipment	475	529	–10.1
Other entertainment supplies, services	854	977	–12.5
PERSONAL CARE PRODUCTS, SERVICES	**736**	**824**	**–10.6**
READING	**184**	**236**	**–22.0**
EDUCATION	**2,303**	**1,717**	**34.1**
TOBACCO PRODUCTS AND SMOKING SUPPLIES	**440**	**408**	**7.9**
MISCELLANEOUS	**1,205**	**1,360**	**–11.4**
CASH CONTRIBUTIONS	**1,941**	**1,296**	**49.8**
PERSONAL INSURANCE, PENSIONS	**6,304**	**5,650**	**11.6**
Life and other personal insurance	675	669	0.9
Pensions and Social Security	5,629	4,981	1.3
PERSONAL TAXES	**3,672**	**4,535**	**–19.0**
Federal income taxes	2,748	3,330	–17.5
State and local income taxes	710	1,021	–30.5
Other taxes	215	184	16.6
GIFTS FOR NON-HOUSEHOLD MEMBERS	**1,710**	**1,761**	**–2.9**

Note: The Bureau of Labor Statistics uses consumer unit rather than household as the sampling unit in the Consumer Expenditure Survey. For the definition of consumer unit, see the glossary. Spending on gifts is included in the preceding product and service categories.
Source: Bureau of Labor Statistics, 1997 and 2002 Consumer Expenditure Surveys, Internet site <www.bls.gov/csxhome.htm>; calculations by New Strategist

Spending of Single Parents Rises Faster than Income

Single parents spend more than they make, a troubling trend for the nation's poorest households.

Single parents with children under age 18 at home spent 3 percent more in 2002 than in 1997, after adjusting for inflation. Their incomes rose a much smaller 0.2 percent during those years. This household type spent $3,000 more than it made in 2002.

Spending trends for single-parent families are a mixed bag of ups and downs. Single parents spent fully 17 percent more on food away from home in 2002 than in 1997. Like most other household types, they spent more on owned dwellings as homeownership rates increased. As they outfitted those homes, their spending on major appliances rose 28 percent. They spent 52 percent more on new cars and trucks, and 16 percent more on women's clothes.

Single parents cut their spending in a number of categories between 1997 and 2002. Spending on food at home fell 1 percent, while spending on alcoholic beverages fell 0.3 percent. Furniture spending was down 29 percent. Single parents spent 20 percent less on personal care products and services and 2 percent less on entertainment.

■ The spending of single-parent families reveals pent-up demand for many products and services. But their incomes are not keeping pace with their spending, which could spell trouble down the road.

The income of single parents was less than their spending in 2002

(average household income and average annual spending of single-parent families with cildren under age 18 at home, 2002)

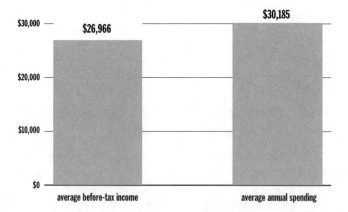

Table 9.6 Average Spending of Single Parents with Children under Age 18 at Home, 1997 and 2002

(average annual spending of single-parent consumer units with children under age 18 at home, 1997 and 2002; percent change, 1997–2002; in 2002 dollars)

	2002	1997	percent change 1997–02
Number of consumer units (in 000s)	6,730	6,626	1.6%
Average before-tax income	$26,966	$27,022	–0.2
Average annual spending	30,185	29,444	2.5
FOOD	**$4,745**	**$4,531**	**4.7%**
Food at home	**3,057**	**3,089**	**–1.1**
Cereals and bakery products	461	460	0.1
Cereals and cereal products	180	196	–7.9
Bakery products	281	265	6.1
Meats, poultry, fish, and eggs	832	863	–3.5
Beef	225	265	–15.0
Pork	195	169	15.6
Other meats	111	104	6.8
Poultry	146	191	–23.6
Fish and seafood	117	94	24.7
Eggs	38	40	–5.5
Dairy products	318	335	–5.1
Fresh milk and cream	135	148	–8.5
Other dairy products	183	187	–1.9
Fruits and vegetables	498	511	–2.5
Fresh fruits	152	146	3.8
Fresh vegetables	146	182	–19.8
Processed fruits	116	101	15.4
Processed vegetables	84	80	4.4
Other food at home	948	922	2.8
Sugar and other sweets	106	115	–7.9
Fats and oils	87	84	3.8
Miscellaneous foods	493	415	18.9
Nonalcoholic beverages	244	277	–11.9
Food prepared by household on trips	19	31	–39.3
Food away from home	**1,688**	**1,443**	**17.0**
ALCOHOLIC BEVERAGES	**146**	**146**	**–0.3**
HOUSING	**11,022**	**10,987**	**0.3**
Shelter	**6,513**	**6,161**	**5.7**
Owned dwellings	3,102	2,625	18.2
Mortgage interest and charges	1,872	1,713	9.3
Property taxes	623	567	10.0
Maintenance, repairs, insurance, other expenses	607	346	75.2
Rented dwellings	3,280	3,323	–1.3
Other lodging	131	212	–38.3

	2002	1997	percent change 1997–02
Utilities, fuels, public services	**$2,471**	**$2,531**	**−2.4%**
Natural gas	307	311	−1.2
Electricity	961	993	−3.3
Fuel oil and other fuels	50	66	−24.2
Telephone services	913	914	−0.1
Water and other public services	240	247	−2.8
Household services	**814**	**744**	**9.4**
Personal services	571	552	3.5
Other household services	243	192	26.4
Housekeeping supplies	**337**	**372**	**−9.4**
Laundry and cleaning supplies	120	135	−11.2
Other household products	147	155	−5.3
Postage and stationery	70	82	−14.2
Household furnishings, equipment	**886**	**1,180**	**−24.9**
Household textiles	73	63	16.7
Furniture	232	327	−29.1
Floor coverings	15	54	−72.0
Major appliances	140	110	27.9
Small appliances, miscellaneous housewares	56	72	−21.7
Miscellaneous household equipment	371	555	−33.2
APPAREL AND SERVICES	**1,885**	**1,697**	**11.1**
Men and boys	**392**	**327**	**19.7**
Men, aged 16 or older	178	104	71.3
Boys, aged 2 to 15	214	224	−4.2
Women and girls	**878**	**713**	**23.2**
Women, aged 16 or older	566	487	16.2
Girls, aged 2 to 15	312	226	38.2
Children under age 2	**71**	**131**	**−45.7**
Footwear	**391**	**358**	**9.4**
Other apparel products and services	**154**	**168**	**−8.1**
TRANSPORTATION	**5,549**	**4,693**	**18.2**
Vehicle purchases	**2,833**	**1,948**	**45.5**
Cars and trucks, new	1,186	779	52.3
Cars and trucks, used	1,593	1,111	43.4
Gasoline and motor oil	**912**	**849**	**7.4**
Other vehicle expenses	**1,645**	**1,640**	**0.3**
Vehicle finance charges	253	224	13.2
Maintenance and repairs	448	570	−21.4
Vehicle insurance	643	534	20.4
Vehicle rental, leases, licenses, other charges	301	313	−3.8
Public transportation	**159**	**256**	**−37.9**
HEALTH CARE	**1,252**	**1,225**	**2.2**
Health insurance	578	515	12.2
Medical services	411	408	0.8
Drugs	187	202	−7.5
Medical supplies	77	99	−22.6

	2002	1997	percent change 1997–02
ENTERTAINMENT	**$1,362**	**$1,394**	**–2.3%**
Fees and admissions	305	348	–12.2
Television, radio, sound equipment	612	618	–1.0
Pets, toys, and playground equipment	263	225	17.1
Other entertainment supplies, services	182	206	–11.5
PERSONAL CARE PRODUCTS, SERVICES	**428**	**533**	**–19.7**
READING	**72**	**94**	**–23.3**
EDUCATION	**454**	**660**	**–31.2**
TOBACCO PRODUCTS AND SMOKING SUPPLIES	**262**	**210**	**24.7**
MISCELLANEOUS	**569**	**914**	**–37.7**
CASH CONTRIBUTIONS	**374**	**465**	**–19.5**
PERSONAL INSURANCE, PENSIONS	**2,066**	**1,895**	**9.0**
Life and other personal insurance	182	197	–7.4
Pensions and Social Security	1,883	1,698	10.9
PERSONAL TAXES	**483**	**1,713**	**–71.8**
Federal income taxes	195	1,275	–84.7
State and local income taxes	243	362	–32.9
Other taxes	45	76	–40.8
GIFTS FOR NON-HOUSEHOLD MEMBERS	**513**	**672**	**–23.6**

Note: The Bureau of Labor Statistics uses consumer unit rather than household as the sampling unit in the Consumer Expenditure Survey. For the definition of consumer unit, see the glossary. Spending on gifts is included in the preceding product and service categories.
Source: Bureau of Labor Statistics, 1997 and 2002 Consumer Expenditure Surveys, Internet site http://www.bls.gov/cex/; calculations by New Strategist

Married Couples with Children Spend More than Average

Single parents spend much less than average on most products and services.

Because married couples have higher than average incomes, their spending is also above average. Overall, couples with preschoolers spent 30 percent more than the average household in 2002. Couples with school-aged children spent 43 percent more, while those with grown children at home spent 50 percent more. In contrast, single-parent families spent 26 percent less than the average household in 2002.

Couples with preschoolers spend much more than average on items needed by young children—such as household personal services (day care) and clothes for children under age 2. On most other products and services, however, they spend close to or even less than the average household.

Couples with school-aged or older children at home spend much more than average on most products and services. Those with adult children at home spend substantially more on items needed by workers (since their households have more workers than the average household) and by college students (since many have children in college). They spend nearly twice the average on other lodging (which includes college dorm room expenses), and more than three times the average on education.

Single parents spend less than average in all but a few categories. They are above-average spenders on some foods, rent, personal services (mostly day care), and children's clothes.

■ Married couples with children spend more than the average household, but their spending levels are well within their means. Single parents are living closer to the edge.

Married couples with adult children at home spend the most

(indexed average annual spending of households with children by type of household, 2002)

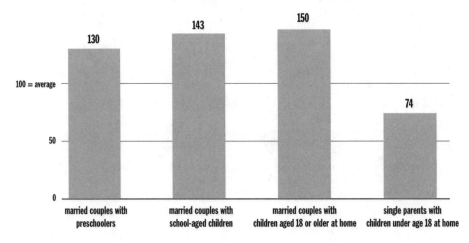

Table 9.7 Indexed Spending of Households with Children, 2002

(indexed spending of total consumer units, married-couple, and single-parent consumer units by age of children at home, 2002)

	total consumer units	married couples			single parents
		with children under age 6	with children aged 6 to 17	with children aged 18 or older	with children under age 18
Average before-tax income	100	137	147	164	55
Average annual spending	100	130	143	150	74
FOOD	100	118	150	155	88
Food at home	100	127	151	151	99
Cereals and bakery products	100	124	157	155	102
Cereals and cereal products	100	134	161	149	117
Bakery products	100	120	155	158	95
Meats, poultry, fish, and eggs	100	118	146	158	104
Beef	100	119	154	172	97
Pork	100	116	144	140	117
Other meats	100	111	154	173	110
Poultry	100	125	149	162	101
Fish and seafood	100	118	129	144	97
Eggs	100	115	127	144	112
Dairy products	100	138	158	149	97
Fresh milk and cream	100	143	157	152	106
Other dairy products	100	135	159	146	91
Fruits and vegetables	100	129	143	146	90
Fresh fruits	100	119	146	152	85
Fresh vegetables	100	123	138	145	83
Processed fruits	100	148	148	143	100
Processed vegetables	100	135	140	142	101
Other food at home	100	131	153	148	98
Sugar and other sweets	100	113	162	140	91
Fats and oils	100	108	140	165	102
Miscellaneous foods	100	154	154	145	104
Nonalcoholic beverages	100	109	150	154	96
Food prepared by household on trips	100	110	168	134	46
Food away from home	100	106	148	160	74
ALCOHOLIC BEVERAGES	100	90	116	130	39
HOUSING	100	144	140	133	83
Shelter	100	144	139	131	83
Owned dwellings	100	165	169	159	60
Mortgage interest and charges	100	201	194	157	63
Property taxes	100	124	147	152	50
Maintenance, repairs, insurance, other expenses	100	105	122	175	63
Rented dwellings	100	110	74	51	152
Other lodging	100	75	116	189	26

	total consumer units	married couples with children under age 6	married couples with children aged 6 to 17	married couples with children aged 18 or older	single parents with children under age 18
Utilities, fuels, public services	**100**	**111**	**130**	**142**	**92**
Natural gas	100	106	134	137	93
Electricity	100	106	131	140	98
Fuel oil and other fuels	100	89	121	149	57
Telephone services	100	118	126	143	95
Water and other public services	100	116	139	146	73
Household services	**100**	**329**	**173**	**87**	**115**
Personal services	100	578	213	38	173
Other household services	100	109	137	131	65
Housekeeping supplies	**100**	**101**	**133**	**148**	**62**
Laundry and cleaning supplies	100	119	149	163	92
Other household products	100	89	134	139	52
Postage and stationery	100	111	115	152	53
Household furnishings, equipment	**100**	**133**	**150**	**147**	**58**
Household textiles	100	108	121	156	54
Furniture	100	135	155	131	58
Floor coverings	100	103	168	135	38
Major appliances	100	121	132	145	75
Small appliances, miscellaneous housewares	100	158	128	153	56
Miscellaneous household equipment	100	139	160	156	57
APPAREL AND SERVICES	**100**	**150**	**154**	**147**	**108**
Men and boys	**100**	**142**	**188**	**172**	**96**
Men, aged 16 or older	100	142	147	199	56
Boys, aged 2 to 15	100	141	333	76	238
Women and girls	**100**	**108**	**145**	**137**	**125**
Women, aged 16 or older	100	101	107	148	96
Girls, aged 2 to 15	100	139	335	81	267
Children under age 2	**100**	**645**	**121**	**70**	**86**
Footwear	**100**	**151**	**162**	**162**	**125**
Other apparel products and services	**100**	**120**	**122**	**140**	**64**
TRANSPORTATION	**100**	**135**	**144**	**161**	**72**
Vehicle purchases	**100**	**147**	**150**	**153**	**77**
Cars and trucks, new	100	152	146	159	68
Cars and trucks, used	100	137	154	145	87
Gasoline and motor oil	**100**	**121**	**143**	**171**	**74**
Other vehicle expenses	**100**	**129**	**141**	**173**	**67**
Vehicle finance charges	100	157	162	172	64
Maintenance and repairs	100	119	140	164	64
Vehicle insurance	100	111	128	182	72
Vehicle rental, leases, licenses, other charges	100	152	152	171	62
Public transportation	**100**	**104**	**113**	**134**	**41**
HEALTH CARE	**100**	**95**	**114**	**133**	**53**
Health insurance	100	107	115	126	50
Medical services	100	107	138	154	70
Drugs	100	56	82	124	38
Medical supplies	100	70	112	133	73

	total consumer units	married couples with children under age 6	married couples with children aged 6 to 17	married couples with children aged 18 or older	single parents with children under age 18
ENTERTAINMENT	**100**	**117**	**173**	**146**	**66**
Fees and admissions	100	103	201	140	56
Television, radio, sound equipment	100	113	139	138	88
Pets, toys, and playground equipment	100	132	164	129	71
Other entertainment supplies, services	100	126	197	179	38
PERSONAL CARE PRODUCTS, SERVICES	**100**	**104**	**144**	**140**	**81**
READING	**100**	**95**	**122**	**132**	**52**
EDUCATION	**100**	**45**	**166**	**306**	**60**
TOBACCO PRODUCTS AND SMOKING SUPPLIES	**100**	**86**	**99**	**138**	**82**
MISCELLANEOUS	**100**	**115**	**104**	**152**	**72**
CASH CONTRIBUTIONS	**100**	**81**	**110**	**152**	**29**
PERSONAL INSURANCE, PENSIONS	**100**	**153**	**157**	**162**	**53**
Life and other personal insurance	100	104	150	166	45
Pensions and Social Security	100	158	158	161	54
PERSONAL TAXES	**100**	**150**	**149**	**147**	**19**
Federal income taxes	100	150	149	149	11
State and local income taxes	100	165	155	140	48
Other taxes	100	92	127	146	31
GIFTS FOR NON-HOUSEHOLD MEMBERS	**100**	**75**	**121**	**165**	**50**

Note: The index compares the spending of consumer units with children with the spending of the average consumer unit by dividing the spending of consumer units with children by average spending in each category and multiplying by 100. An index of 100 means the spending of consumer units with children in the category equals average spending. An index of 130 means the spending of consumer units with children is 30 percent above average, while an index of 70 means the spending of consumer units with children is 30 percent below average. The Bureau of Labor Statistics uses consumer unit rather than household as the sampling unit in the Consumer Expenditure Survey. For the definition of consumer unit, see the glossary.
Source: Bureau of Labor Statistics, 1997 and 2002 Consumer Expenditure Surveys, Internet site http://www.bls.gov/cex/; calculations by New Strategist

For More Information

The federal government is a rich source of data on almost every aspect of American life. Below are the Internet addresses of federal and other agencies collecting the demographic data analyzed in this book. Also shown are phone numbers of the agencies and of the subject specialists at the Census Bureau and the Bureau of Labor Statistics, organized alphabetically by name of agency or specialty topic. A list of State Data Centers and Small Business Development Centers is also below to help you track down demographic and economic information for your state or local area. E-mail addresses are shown when available. Note: Telephone numbers at the Census Bureau change regularly. If the numbers below do not allow you to reach the specialists you need, go to http://www.census.gov/contacts/www/contacts.html for the most up-to-date lists.

Internet Addresses

- AARP, http://www.aarp.org
- Agency for Healthcare Research and Quality, www.meps.ahrq.gov/Data_Public.htm
- Behavioral Risk Factor Surveillance System, http://apps.nccd.cdc.gov/brfss/index.asp
- Bureau of the Census, www.census.gov
- Bureau of Labor Statistics, www.bls.gov
- Centers for Disease Control and Prevention,www.cdc.gov
- Consumer Expenditure Survey, www.bls.gov/cex/
- Current Population Survey, www.bls.census.gov/cps/cpsmain.htm
- Employee Benefit Research Institute, www.ebri.org
- Federal Interagency Forum on Child and Family Statistics, http://childstats.gov/
- Higher Education Research Institute, www.gseis.ucla.edu/heri/heri.html
- Institute for Social Research, University of Michigan, http://monitoringthefuture.org
- Investment Company Institute, http://www.ici.org
- National Center for Education Statistics, http://nces.ed.gov
- National Center for Health Statistics, www.cdc.gov/nchs
- National Sporting Goods Association, www.nsga.org
- Securities Industry Association, www.sia.com
- Sourcebook of Criminal Justice Statistics,www.albany.edu/sourcebook/

- Sporting Goods Manufacturers Association, www.sgma.com
- Survey of Consumer Finances, www.federalreserve.gov/pubs/oss/oss2/scfindex.html
- U.S. Substance Abuse and Mental Health Services Administrations, www.samhsa.gov
- U.S. Citizenship and Immigration Services, http://uscis.gov/graphics/shared/aboutus/statistics/index.htm
- Youth Risk Behavior Surveillance System, www.cdc.gov/nccdphp/dash/yrbs/results.htm

Subject Specialists

Absences from work, Staff 202-691-6378
Aging population, Staff 301-763-2378
American Community Survey/C2SS Results, Larry McGinn 301-763-8050
Ancestry, Staff 301-763-2403
Apportionment, Edwin Byerly 301-763-2381
Apportionment and redistricting, Cathy McCully 301-763-4039
Business expenditures, Sheldon Ziman 301-763-3315
Business investment, Charles Funk 301-763-3324
Business owners, characteristics of, Valerie Strang 301-763-3316
Census 1990 and earlier, Staff 301-763-2422
Census 2000
- American Factfinder, Staff 301-763-INFO (4636)
- Annexations/boundary changes, Joe Marinucci 301-763-1099
- Apportionment, Edwin Byerly 301-763-2381
- Census 2000 Briefs, Staff 301-763-2437
- Census 2000 tabulations, Staff 301-763-2422
- Census 2010, Ed Gore 301-763-3998
- Census history, Dave Pemberton 301-763-1167
- Citizenship, Staff 301-763-2411
- Commuting and place of work, Clara Reschovsky/ Celia Boertlein 301-763-2454
- Confidentiality and privacy, Jerry Gates 301-763-2515
- Count question resolution, Staff 866-546-0527
- Count review, Paul Campbell 301-763-2381
- Data dissemination, Staff 301-763-INFO (4636)
- Disability, Staff 301-763-3242
- Education, Staff 301-763-2464
- Employment/unemployment, Staff 301-763-3230
- Foreign born, Staff 301-763-2411
- Geographic entities, Staff 301-763-1099

- Grandparents as caregivers, Staff 301-763-2416
- Group quarters population, Denise Smith 301-763-2378
- Hispanic origin, ethnicity, ancestry, Staff 301-763-2403
- Homeless, Annetta Clark 301-763-2378
- Housing, Staff 301-763-3237
- Immigration/emigration, Staff 301-763-2411
- Income, Staff 301-763-3243
- Island areas, Idabelle Hovland 301-763-8443
- Labor force status/work experience, Staff 301-763-3230
- Language spoken in home, Staff 301-763-2464
- Living arrangements, Staff 301-763-2416
- Maps, customer services 301-763-INFO (4636)
- Marital status, Staff 301-763-2416
- Metropolitan areas, concepts and standards,
  Michael Ratcliffe 301-763-2419
- Microdata files, Amanda Shields 301-763-1326
- Migration, Carol Faber 301-763-2454
- Occupation/industry, Staff 301-763-3239
- Place of birth/native born, Carol Faber 301-763-2454
- Population (general information), Staff 301-763-2422
- Poverty, Alemayehu Bishaw 301-763-3213
- Race, Staff 301-763-2402
- Redistricting, Cathy McCully 301-763-4039
- Residence rules, Karen Mills 301-763-2381
- Small area income and poverty estimates,
  David Waddington 301-763-3195
- Special censuses, Mike Stump 301-763-3577
- Special populations, Staff 301-763-2378
- Special tabulations, Linda Showalter 301-763-2429
- Undercount, Phil Gbur 301-763-4206
  - Demographic analysis, Greg Robinson 301-763-2110
- Unmarried partners, Staff 301-763-2416
- Urban/rural, Ryan Short 301-763-1099
- U.S. citizens abroad, Staff 301-763-2422
- Veteran status, Staff 301-763-3230
- Voting districts, John Byle 301-763-1099
- Women, Renee Spraggins 301-763-2378
- ZIP codes, Staff 301-763-2422
Census Bureau customer service,
  Staff 301-763-INFO (4636)
Child care, Martin O'Connell/Kristin Smith
  301-763-2416
Children, Staff 301-763-2416
Citizenship status, Staff 301-763-2411
Communications and Utilities
- Current programs, Ruth Bramblett 301-763-2787
- Economic census, Jim Barron 301-763-2786
Commuting, means of transportation, and place of work,
  Clara Reschovsky/Celia Boertlein 301-763-2454

Construction
- Building permits, Staff 301-763-5160
- Economic census, Susan Bucci, Staff 301-763-4680
- Housing starts and completions, Staff 301-763-5160
- Manufactured housing, Lisa Feldman 301-763-1605
- Residential characteristics, price index, and sales,
  Staff 301-763-5160
- Residential improvements and repairs,
  Joe Huesman 301-763-1605
- Value of new construction, Mike Davis 301-763-1605
Consumer Expenditure Survey, Staff
  202-691-6900, cexinfo@bls.gov
Contingent workers, Staff 202-691-6378
County Business Patterns, Phillip Thompson
  301-763-2580
County populations, Staff 301-763-2422
Crime, Marilyn Monahan 301-763-5315
Current Population Survey, general information,
  Staff, 301-763-3806
Demographic surveys, demographic statistics,
  Staff 301-763-2422
Disability, Staff 301-763-3242
Discouraged workers, Staff 202-691-6378
Displaced workers, Staff 202-691-6378
Economic census 1997
- Accommodations and food services,
  Fay Dorsett 301-763-2687
- Construction, Staff 301-763-4680
- Finance and insurance, Faye Jacobs 301-763-2824
- General information, Robert Marske 301-763-2547
- Internet dissemination, Paul Zeisset 301-763-4151
- Manufacturing:
  - Consumer goods industries, Robert Reinard
    301-763-4810
  - Investment goods industries, Kenneth Hansen
    301-763-4755
  - Primary goods industries, Nat Shelton 301-763-6614
- Mining, Susan Bocci 301-763-4680
- Minority/women-owned businesses, Valerie Strang
  301-763-3316
- North American Industry Class. System,
  Wanda Dougherty 301-763-2790
- Puerto Rico and the Island Areas, Irma Harahush
  301-763-3319
- Real estate and rental/leasing, Pam Palmer
  301-763-2824
- Retail trade, Fay Dorsett 301-763-2687
- Services:
  - Administrative, waste management, remediation,
    Dan Wellwood 301-763-5181

- Arts, entertainment, and recreation, Tara Dryden 301-763-5181
- Educational services, Kim Casey 301-763-5181
- Health care and social assistance, Laurie Davis 301-763-5181
- Information, Joyce Kiessling/Joy Pierson/ Steve Cornell 301-763-5181
- Management of companies and enterprises, Julie Ishman 301-763-5181
- Other services (except public administration), Patrice Norman 301-763-5181
- Professional, scientific, and technical services, Karen Dennison/John Goodenough 301-763-5181
- Transportation and utilities:
  - Commodity Flow Survey, John Fowler 301-763-2108
  - Establishments, James Barron 301-763-2786
  - Vehicle Inventory and Use Survey, Thomas Zabelsky 301-763-5175
- Wholesale trade, Donna Hambric 301-763-2725
- Zip codes:
  - Accommodation and food services, Fay Dorsett 301-763-5180
  - Retail trade, Fay Dorsett 301-763-5180
Economic studies, Arnold Reznek 301-763-1856
Education surveys, Steve Tourkin 301-763-3791
Educational attainment, Staff 301-763-2464
Emigration, Staff 301-763-2422
Employee Benefits Survey, Staff 202-691-6199; ocltinfo@bls.gov
Employment and Earnings periodical, John Stinson 202-691-6373
Employment and unemployment trends, Staff 202-691-6378
Employment projections, demographics, Mitra Toosi 202-691-5721
Enterprise statistics, Melvin Cole 301-763-3321
Equal employment opportunity data, Staff 301-763-3242
Fertility, Barbara Downs 301-763-2416
Finance and insurance, Faye Jacobs 301-763-2824
Flexitime and shift work, Staff 202-691-6378
Foreign born:
- General information, Staff 301-763-2422
- Concepts and analysis, Staff 301-763-2411
Geographic concepts:
- American Indian and Alaska Native areas, Vince Osier 301-763-1099
- Annexations and boundary changes, Dorothy Stroz 301-763-1099
- Area measurement:
  - Land, Jim Davis 301-763-1099
  - Water, Dave Aultman 301-763-1099

- Census blocks, Barbara Saville 301-763-1099
- Census county divisions, Pat Ream 301-763-1099
- Census designated places, Pat Ream 301-763-1099
- Census geographic concepts, Staff 301-763-1099
- Census maps, 1990 and 2000, Staff 301-763-INFO (4636)
- Census tracts, Dan Flynn 301-763-1099
- Centers of population, Staff 301-763-1128
- Congressional districts, boundaries, Donna Zorn 301-763-1099
- Island areas, Jim Davis 301-763-1099
- Metropolitan areas, Michael Ratcliffe 301-763-2419
- Postal geography, Dan Sweeney 301-763-1106
- School districts, Dave Aultman 301-763-1099
- Traffic analysis zones, Carrie Saunders 301-763-1099
- Urban/rural concepts, Ryan Short 301-763-1099
- Urban areas, Ryan Short 301-763-1099
- Voting districts, John Byle 301-763-1099
- Zip code tabulation areas, Andy Flora 301-763-1100
- Zip codes:
  - Demographic data, Staff 301-763-INFO (4636)
  - Economic data, Andy Hait 301-763-6747
  - Geography, Andy Flora 301-763-1100
Governments
- Census of governments, Donna Hirsch 301-763-5154
- Criminal and juvenile justice, Charlene Sebold 301-763-1591
- Education
  - Education and library statistics, Johnny Monaco 301-763-2584
  - Elementary and secondary, Staff 301-763-1563
- Employment, Ellen Thompson 301-763-1531
- Federal expenditure data, Gerard Keffer 301-763-1522
- Government finance, Stephen Poyta/David Kellerman 301-763-1580/7242
- Government information, Staff 301-763-1580
- Governmental organization, Stephen Owens 301-763-5149
- Public retirement systems, Sandra Reading 301-763-7248
Group quarters population, Denise Smith 301-763-2378
Health insurance statistics, Staff 301-763-3242
Health surveys, Adrienne Oneto 301-763-3891
Hispanic statistics
- General information, Staff 301-763-2422
- Concepts and analysis, Staff 301-763-2403
Home-based work, Staff 202-691-6378
Homeless, Annetta Clark 301-763-2378
Household wealth, Staff 301-763-3242
Households and families, Staff 301-763-2416

Housing
- American Housing Survey data, Paul Harble
  301-763-3235
- Census, Staff 301-763-3237
- Homeownership, vacancy data, Linda Cavanaugh/
  Robert Callis 301-763-3199
- Housing affordability, Howard Savage 301-763-3199
- Market absorption, Alan Friedman/Mary Schwartz
  301-763-3199
- New York City Housing and Vacancy Survey,
  Alan Friedman/Robert Callis 301-763-3199
- Residential finance, Howard Savage 301-763-3199
Immigration and Emigration
- General information, Staff 301-763-2422
- Concepts and analysis, Staff 301-763-2411
Income statistics, Staff 301-763-3243
Industry and commodity classification, James Kristoff
  301-763-5179
International Statistics:
- Africa, Asia, Latin Am., North Am., and Oceania,
  Staff 301-763-1358
- Aging population, Staff 301-763-1371
- China, People's Republic, Staff 301-763-1360
- Europe, former Soviet Union, Staff 301-763-1360
- Health, Staff 301-763-1433
- International data base, Pat Dickerson/Peter Johnson
  301-763-1351/1410
- Technical assistance and training, Staff 301-763-1444
- Women in development, Victoria Velkoff
  301-763-1371
Job tenure, Staff 202-691-6378
Journey to work, Phil Salopek/Celia Boertlein
  301-763-2454
Labor force concepts, Staff 202-691-6378
Language, Staff 301-763-2464
Longitudinal surveys, Ron Dopkowski 301-763-3801
Manufacturing and mining:
- Concentration, Patrick Duck 301-763-4699
- Exports from manufacturing establishments, John Gates
  301-763-4589
- Financial statistics (Quarterly Financial Report),
  Yolando St. George 301-763-3343
- Foreign direct investment, Julius Smith 301-763-4683
- Fuels, electric energy consumed and prod. index,
  Susan Bucci 301-763-4680
- General information and data requests, Nishea Quash
  301-763-4673
- Industries:
  - Electrical and trans. equip., instruments, machinery,
    Kenneth Hansen 301-763-4755

- Food, textiles, and apparel, Robert Reinard
  301-763-4810
- Furniture, printing, and misc., Robert Reinard
  301-763-4810
- Metals, Nat Shelton 301-763-6614
- Wood, paper, chemicals, petroleum prod., rubber,
  plastics, Nat Shelton 301-763-6614
- Mining, Susan Bucci 301-763-4680
- Monthly shipments, inventories, and orders,
  Dan Sansbury 301-763-4832
- Plant capacity utilization, Julius Smith 301-763-4683
- Research and development, Julius Smith 301-763-4683
Marital and family characteristics of workers,
  Staff 202-691-6378
Metropolitan areas, Staff 301-763-2422
Metropolitan standards, Michael Ratcliffe 301-763-2419
Migration
- General information, Staff 301-763-2422
- Domestic/internal, Carol Faber 301-763-2454
- International, Staff 301-763-2411
Minimum wage data, Steven Haugen 202-691-6378
Minority/women-owned businesses, Valerie Strang
  301-763-3316
Minority workers, Staff 202-691-6378
Multiple jobholders, Staff 202-691-6373
National Center for Education Statistics,
  Staff 202-502-7300
National Center for Health Statistics, Staff 301-458-4000
National Compensation Survey, Staff 202-691-6199;
  ocltinfo@bls.gov
National Opinion Research Center, Staff 773-256-6000;
  norcinfo@norcmail.uchicago.edu
Nonemployer statistics, Staff 301-763-5184
North Am. Industry Class. System (NAICS),
  Wanda Dougherty 301-763-2790
Occupational and industrial statistics, Staff 301-763-3239
Occupational data, Staff 202-691-6378
Occupational employment statistics, Staff 202-691-6569;
  oesinfo@bls.gov
Occupational Outlook Quarterly, Kathleen Green
  202-691-5717
Occupational projections:
- College graduate outlook, Arlene Dohm/Ian Wyatt
  202-691-5727/5690
- Education and training, Chet Levine/Jon Sargent
  202-691-5715/5722
- General information, Chet Levine/Jon Sargent
  202-691-5715/5722
- Industry-occupation matrix, David Frank 202-691-5708

- Projections:
  - Computer, Chet Levine/Roer Moncarz 202-691-5715/5694
  - Construction, Doug Braddock/William Lawhorn 202-691-5695/5093
  - Education, Arlene Dohm 202-691-5727
  - Engineering, Doug Braddock 202-691-5695
  - Food and lodging, Theresa Cosca/Jon Kelinson 202-691-5712/5688
  - Health, Theresa Cosca/Alan Lacey/Terry Schau 202-601-5712/5731/5720
  - Legal, Tamara Dillon 202-691-5733
  - Mechanics and repairers, Theresa Cosca 202-691-5712
  - Sales, Doug Braddock/Andrew Alpert 202-691-5695/5754
  - Scientific, Henry Kasper 292-691-5696
- Replacement and separation rates, Alan Lacey/ Lynn Shniper 202-691-5731/5732

Older workers, Staff 202-691-6378

Outlying areas, Michael Levin 301-763-1444

Part-time workers, Staff 202-691-6378

Place of birth, Staff 301-763-2422

Population estimates and projections, Staff 301-763-2422

Population information, Staff 301-763-2422

Poverty statistics, Staff 301-763-3242

Prisoner surveys, Marilyn Monahan 301-763-5315

Puerto Rico, Idabelle Hovland 301-763-8443

Quarterly Financial Report, Yolando St. George 301-763-3343

Race, concepts and interpretation, Staff 301-763-2402

Race statistics, Staff 301-763-2422

Retail trade
- Advance monthly, Scott Scheleur 301-763-2713; svsd@census.gov
- Annual retail, Scott Scheleur 301-763-2713; svsd@census.gov
- Economic census, Fay Dorsett 301-763-5180; rcb@census.gov
- Monthly sales and inventory, Nancy Piesto 301-763-2747; retail.trade@census.gov
- Quarterly Financial Report, Yolando St. George 301-763-3343; cad@census.gov

School enrollment, Staff 301-763-2464

Seasonal adjustment methodology, Richard Tiller/Thomas Evans 202-691-6370/6354

Services
- Current Reports, Ruth Bramblett 301-763-2787; svsd@census.gov
- Economic census, Jack Moody 301-763-5181; scb@census.gov

- General information, Staff 1-800-541-8345; scb@census.gov

Small area income and poverty estimates, Staff 301-763-3193

Special censuses, Mike Stump 301-763-3577

Special surveys, Ron Dopkowski 301-763-3801

Special tabulations, Linda Showalter 301-763-2429

State population estimates, Staff 301-763-2422

Statistics of U.S. businesses, Melvin Cole 301-763-3321

Survey of Income and Program Participation (SIPP), Staff 301-763-3242

Transportation
- Commodity Flow Survey, John Fowler 301-763-2108; svsd@census.gov
- Establishments, James Barron 301-763-2786; ucb@census.gov
- Vehicle inventory and use survey, Thomas Zabelsky 301-763-5175; vius@census.gov
- Wholesale trade, Donna Hambric 301-763-2725; svsd@census.gov

Undercount, demographic analysis, Gregg Robinson 301-763-2110

Union membership, Staff 202-691-6378

Urban/rural population, Michael Ratcliff 301-763-2419

Veterans in labor force, Staff 202-691-6378

Veterans' status, Staff 301-763-3230

Voters, characteristics, Staff 301-763-2464

Voting age population, Staff 301-763-2464

Weekly earnings, Staff 202-691-6378

Wholesale trade
- Annual wholesale, Scott Scheleur 301-763-2713; svsd@census.gov
- Current sales and inventories, Scott Scheleur 301-763-2713; svsd@census.gov
- Economic census, Donna Hambric 301-763-2725; wcb@census.gov
- Quarterly Financial Report, Yolando St. George 301-763-3343; csd@census.gov

Women, Renee Spraggins 301-763-2378

Women in the labor force, Staff 202-691-6378

Work experience, Staff 202-691-6378

Working poor, Staff 202-691-6378

Youth, students, and dropouts in labor force, Staff 202-691-6378

Census Regional Offices

Information specialists in the Census Bureau's 12 regional offices answer thousands of questions each year. If you have questions about the Census Bureau's products and services, contact the regional office serving your state. The states served by each regional office are listed in parentheses.

- Atlanta (AL, FL, GA) 404-730-3833
  www.census.gov/atlanta
- Boston, MA (CT, MA, ME, NH, NY, RI, VT)
  617-424-0510; www.census.gov/boston
- Charlotte (KY, NC, SC, TN, VA) 704-424-6430
  www.census.gov/charlotte
- Chicago (IL, IN, WI) 708-562-1350
  www.census.gov/chicago
- Dallas (LA, MS, TX) 214-253-4481
  www.census.gov/dallas
- Denver (AZ, CO, MT, NE, ND, NM, NV, SD, UT, WY)
  303-969-7750; www.census.gov/denver
- Detroit (MI, OH, WV) 313-259-1875
  www.census.gov/detroit
- Kansas City (AR, IA, KS, MN, MO, OK)
  913-551-6711; www.census.gov/kansascity
- Los Angeles (southern CA, HI) 818-904-6339
  www.census.gov/losangeles
- New York (NY, NJ-selected counties) 212-264-4730
  www.census.gov/newyork
- Philadelphia (DE, DC, MD, NJ-selected counties, PA)
  215-656-7578; www.census.gov/philadelphia
- Seattle (northern CA, AK, ID, OR, WA) 206-553-5835
  www.census.gov/seattle
- Puerto Rico and the U.S. Virgin Islands are serviced by the Boston regional office. All other outlying areas are serviced by the Los Angeles regional office.

State Data Centers and Business and Industry Data Centers

For demographic and economic information about states and local areas, contact your State Data Center (SDC) or Business and Industry Data Center (BIDC). Every state has a State Data Center. Below are listed the leading centers for each state-usually a state government agency, university, or library that heads a network of affiliate centers. Asterisks (*) identify states that also have BIDCs. In some states, one agency serves as the lead for both the SDC and the BIDC. The BIDC is listed separately if a separate agency serves as the lead.

- Alabama, Annette Watters, University of Alabama
  205-348-6191; awatters@cba.ua.edu
- Alaska, Kathryn Lizik, Department of Labor
  907-465-2437; kathryn_lizik@labor.state.ak.us
- American Samoa, Vaitoelau Filiga, Department of Commerce 684-633-5155; vfiliga@doc.asg.as
- Arizona*, Betty Jeffries, Dept of Economic Security
  602-542-5984; betty.jeffries@de.state.az.us

- Arkansas, Sarah Breshears, University of Arkansas/ Little Rock 501-569-8530; sgbreshears@ualr.edu
- California, Julie Hoang, Department of Finance
  916-323-4086; fijhoang@dof.ca.gov
- Colorado, Rebecca Picaso, Department of Local Affairs
  303-866-3120; rebecca.picaso@state.co.us
- Connecticut, Bill Kraynak, Office of Policy and Mgmt., 860-418-6230; william.kraynak@po.state.ct.us
- Delaware*, Mike Helmer, Economic Development Office 302-672-6848; michael.helmer@state.de.us
- District of Columbia, Herb Bixhorn, Mayor's Office of Planning 202-442-7603; herb.bixhorn@dc.gov
- Florida*, Pam Schenker, Florida Agency for Workforce Innovation 850-488-1048;
  pamela.schenker@awi.state.fl.us
- Georgia, Robert Giacomini, Office of Planning and Budget 404-656-6505;
  girt@mail.opb.state.ga.us
- Guam, Isabel Lujan, Bureau of Statistics and Plans
  671-472-4201; idlujan@mail.gov.gu
- Hawaii, Jan Nakamoto, Dept. of Business, Ec. Dev., and Tourism 808-586-2493;
  jnakamot@dbedt.hawaii.gov
- Idaho, Alan Porter, Department of Commerce
  208-334-2470; aporter@idoc.state.id.us
- Illinois*, Suzanne Ebetsch, Dept. of Commerce and Community Affairs
  217-782-1381; sue_ebetsch@commerce.state.il.us
- Illinois BIDC, Ed Taft, Dept. of Commerce and Community Affairs
  217-785-7545; ed_taft@commerce.state.il.us
- Indiana*, Roberta Brooker, State Library
  317-232-3733; rbrooker@statelib.lib.in.us
- Indiana BIDC, Carol Rogers, Business Research Center
  317-274-2205; rogersc@iupui.edu
- Iowa, Beth Henning, State Library 515-281-4350;
  beth.henning@lib.state.ia.us
- Kansas, Marc Galbraith, State Library 785-296-3296;
  marcg@kslib.info
- Kentucky*, Ron Crouch, University of Louisville
  502-852-7990; rtcrou01@gwise.louisville.edu
- Louisiana, Karen Paterson, Office of Planning and Budget 225-219-5987; kpaters@doa.state.la.us
- Maine*, Eric VonMagnus, State Planning Office
  207-287-3261; eric.vonmagnus@state.me.us
- Maryland*, Jane Traynham, Office of Planning
  410-767-4450; jtraynham@mdp.state.md.us
- Massachusetts*, John Gaviglio, Institute for Social and Econ. Research 413-545-3460; miser@miser.umass.edu

- Michigan, Daarren Warner, Library of Michigan 517-373-2548; warnerd@michigan.gov
- Minnesota*, Dona Ronningen, State Demographer's Office 651-296-4886; barbara.ronningen@state.mn.us
- Mississippi*, Rachel McNeely, University of Mississippi 662-915-7288; rmcneely@olemiss.edu
- Mississippi BIDC, Deloise Tate, Dept. of Ec. and Comm. Dev. 601-359-3593; dtate@mississippi.org
- Missouri*, Debra Pitts, State Library 573-526-7648; pittsd@sosmail.state.mo.us
- Missouri BIDC, Cathy Frank, Small Business Research Information Center 573-341-6484; cfrank@umr.edu
- Montana*, Pam Harris, Department of Commerce 406-841-2740; paharris@state.mt.us
- Nebraska, Jerome Deichert, University of Nebraska at Omaha 402-554-2134; jerome_deichert@unomaha.edu
- Nevada, Ramona Reno, State Library and Archives 775-684-3326; rlreno@clan.lib.nv.us
- New Hampshire, Thomas Duffy, Office of State Planning 603-271-2155; t_duffy@osp.state.nh.us
- New Jersey*, David Joye, Department of Labor 609-984-2595; djoye@dol.state.nj.us
- New Mexico*, Kevin Kargacin, University of New Mexico 505-277-6626; kargacin@unm.edu
- New Mexico BIDC, Beth Davis, Economic Development Dept. 505-827-0264; edavis@edd.state.nm.us
- New York*, Staff, Department of Economic Development 518-292-5300; rscardamalia@empire.state.ny.us
- North Carolina*, Staff, State Library 919-733-3270; francine.stephenson@ncmail.net
- North Dakota, Richard Rathge, North Dakota State University 701-231-8621; richard.rathge@ndsu.nodak.edu
- Northern Mariana Islands, Diego A. Sasamoto, Dept. of Commerce 670-664-3033; csd@itecnmi.com
- Ohio*, Steve Kelley, Department of Development 614-466-2116; skelley@odod.state.oh.us
- Oklahoma*, Jeff Wallace, Department of Commerce 405-815-5184; jeff_wallace@odoc.state.ok.us
- Oregon, George Hough, Portland State University. 503-725-5159; houghg@mail.pdx.edu
- Pennsylvania*, Sue Copella, Pennsylvania State Univ./ Harrisburg 717-948-6336; sdc3@psu.edu
- Puerto Rico, Lillian Torres Aguirre, Planning Bd. 787-727-4444; torres_l@jp.gobierno.pr
- Rhode Island, Mark Brown, Department of Administration 401-222-6183; mbrown@planning.state.ri.us
- South Carolina, Mike MacFarlane, Budget and Control Board 803-734-3780; mmacfarl@drss.state.sc.us
- South Dakota, Nancy Nelson, University of South Dakota 605-677-5287; nnelson@usd.edu
- Tennessee, Betty Vickers, University of Tennessee, Knoxville 865-974-5441; bvickers@utk.edu
- Texas*, Steve Murdock, Texas A&M University 979-845-5115/5332; smurdock@rsocsun.tamu.edu
- Texas BIDC, Ann Griffith, Dept. of Economic Dev. 512-936-0550; bidc@txed.state.tx.us
- Utah*, Sophia DiCaro, Governor's Office of Planning and Budget 801-537-9013; sdicaro@utah.gov
- Vermont, William Sawyer, Center for Rural Studies 802-656-3021; william.sawyer@uvm.edu
- Virgin Islands, Frank Mills, University of the Virgin Islands 340-693-1027; fmills@uvi.edu
- Virginia*, Don Lillywhite, Virginia Employment Commission 804-786-7496; dlillywhite@vec.state.va.us
- Washington*, Yi Zhao, Office of Financial Management 360-902-0592; yi.zhao@ofm.wa.gov
- West Virginia*, Delphine Coffey, West Virginia Dev. Office 304-558-4010; dcoffey@wvdo.org
- West Virginia BIDC, Randy Childs, Bureau of Business & Economic Research 304-293-7832; randy.childs@mail.wvu.edu
- Wisconsin*, Robert Naylor, Demographic Services Center 608-266-1927; bob.naylor@doa.state.wi.us
- Wisconsin BIDC, Dan Veroff, University of Wisconsin 608-265-9545; dlveroff@facstaff.wisc.edu
- Wyoming, Wenlin Liu, Dept. of Administration and Information 307-777-7504; wliu@missc.state.wy.us

Glossary

adjusted for inflation Income or a change in income that has been adjusted for the rise in the cost of living, or the consumer price index (CPI-U-RS).

American Housing Survey (AHS) The AHS collects national and metropolitan-level data on the nation's housing, including apartments, single-family homes, and mobile homes. The nationally representative survey, with a sample of 55,000 homes, is conducted by the Census Bureau for the Department of Housing and Urban Development every other year.

American Indians In this book, American Indians include Alaska Natives (Eskimos and Aleuts). In tables showing 2000 census data, the term "American Indian" may include those who identified themselves as American Indian and no other race (called "American Indian alone") or those who identified themselves as American Indian and some other race (called "American Indian in combination").

Asian The term "Asian" is defined differently depending on whether census or survey data are shown. In tables showing 2000 census data, Asians do not include Native Hawaiians or other Pacific Islanders unless noted. The term "Asian" may include those who identified themselves as Asian and no other race (called "Asian alone") or those who identified themselves as Asian and some other race (called "Asian in combination"). Asian estimates from the 2003 Current Population Survey include both those who identified themselves as Asian alone and those who identified themselves as Asian in combination. Asian estimates in earlier survey data do not include the multiracial option. Also, in surveys and other noncensus data collections, Asian figures include Native Hawaiians and other Pacific Islanders.

Baby Boom Americans born between 1946 and 1964.

Baby Bust Americans born between 1965 and 1976, also known as Generation X.

Behavioral Risk Factor Surveillance System (BRFSS) The BRFSS is a collaborative project of the Centers for Disease Control and Prevention and U.S. states and territories. It is an ongoing data collection program designed to measure behavioral risk factors in the adult population aged 18 or older. All 50 states, three territories, and the District of Columbia take part in the survey, making the BRFSS the primary source of information on the health-related behaviors of Americans.

black The black racial category includes those who identified themselves as "black or African American." The term "black" is defined differently depending on whether census or survey data are shown. In tables showing 2000 census data, the term "black" may include those who identified themselves as black and no other race (called "black alone") or those who identified themselves as black and some other race (called "black in combination"). Black estimates from the 2003 Current Population Survey include both those who identified themselves as black alone and those who identified themselves as black in combination. Black estimates in earlier survey data do not include the multiracial option.

central cities The largest city in a metropolitan area is called the central city. The balance of the metropolitan area outside the central city is regarded as the "suburbs."

Consumer Expenditure Survey (CEX) The Consumer Expenditure Survey is an ongoing study of the day-to-day spending of American households administered by the Bureau of Labor Statistics. The survey is used to update prices for the Consumer Price Index. The CEX includes an interview survey and a diary survey. The average spending figures shown in this book are the integrated data from both the diary and interview components of the survey. Two separate, nationally representative samples are used for the interview and diary surveys. For the interview survey, about 7,500 consumer units are interviewed on a rotating panel basis each quarter for five consecutive quarters. For the diary survey, 7,500 consumer units keep weekly diaries of spending for two consecutive weeks.

consumer unit *(on spending tables only)* For convenience, the term consumer unit and households are used interchangeably in the spending section of this book, although consumer units are somewhat different from the Census Bureau's households. Consumer units are all related members of a household, or financially independent members of a household. A household may include more than one consumer unit.

disability *(1997 Current Population Survey data)* People aged 15 or older were identified as having a disability if they met any of the following criteria: 1) used a wheelchair, cane, crutches, or walker; 2) had difficulty performing one or more functional activities (seeing, hearing, speaking, lifting/carrying, climbing stairs, walking, or grasping small objects); 3) had difficulty with one or more activities of daily living (or ADL, which include getting around inside the home, getting in or out of bed or a chair, bathing, dressing, eating, and toileting); 4) had difficulty with one or more instrumental activities of daily living (or IADL, which include going outside the home, keeping track of money and bills, preparing meals, doing light housework, taking prescription medicines, and using the telephone); 5) had one or more specified conditions such as a learning disability, mental retardation, or another developmental disability, Alzheimer's disease, or some other type of mental or emotional condition; 6) had any other mental or emotional condition that seriously interfered with everyday activities (frequently depressed or anxious, trouble getting along with others, trouble concentrating, or trouble coping with day-to-day stress); 7) had a condition that limited the ability to work around the house; 8) if age 16 to 67, had a condition that made it difficult to work at a job or business; or 9) received federal benefits based on an inability to work. People were considered to have a severe disability if they met criteria 1, 6, or 9, or had Alzheimer's disease, mental retardation, or another developmental disability, or were unable to perform or needed help to perform one or more activities in criteria 2, 3, 4, 7, or 8. Children under age 5 were identified as disabled if they had a developmental delay or a condition that limited the ability to use arms or legs or a condition that limited walking, running, or playing. Children aged 6 to 14 were identified as severely disabled if they met any of the following criteria: 1) had a mental retardation or some other developmental disability; 2) had a developmental condition for which they had received therapy or diagnostic services; 3) used an ambulatory aid; 4) had a severe limitation in the ability to see, hear, or speak; or 5) needed personal assistance for an activity of daily living.

disability *(2000 Census data)* The 2000 Census defined the disabled as those who were blind, deaf, or had severe vision or hearing impairments, and/or had a condition that substantially limited one or more basic physical activities such as walking, climbing stairs, reaching, lifting, or carrying. It also included people who, because of a physical, mental, or emotional condition lasting six months or more, have difficulty learning, remembering, concentrating, dressing, bathing, getting around inside the home, going outside the home alone to shop or visit a doctor's office, or working at a job or business.

disability *(2001 National Health Interview Survey data)* This survey estimated the number of people aged 18 or older who had difficulty in physical and/or social functioning, probing whether respondents could perform 12 activities by themselves without using special equipment. Physical functioning questions were grouped in two categories: mobility, and flexibility/strength. The mobility category comprised difficulties in performing the following activities: walking a quarter of a mile, standing for two hours, or walking up 10 steps without resting. The flexibility/strength category comprised difficulties in performing the following activities: stooping, bending, kneeling, reaching over one's head, grasping or handling small objects, carrying a 10-pound object, or pushing/pulling a large object. Social functioning questions probed the following: difficulty in sitting for two hours, going shopping, going to movies, attending sporting events, visiting friends, attending clubs or meetings, going to parties, reading, watching television, sewing, or listening to music. Adults who indicated that the activities were "only a little difficult" or "somewhat difficult" were considered to have a moderate difficulty, and those who indicated that the activities were "very difficult" or "can't do this activity" were considered to have severe difficulty.

disability, work *(2003 Current Population Survey data)* A work disability is a specific physical or mental condition that prevents an individual from working. The disability must be so severe that it completely incapacitates the individual and prevents him/her from doing any kind of work for at least the next six months.

Current Population Survey (CPS) The CPS is a nationally representative survey of the civilian noninstitutional population aged 15 or older. It is taken monthly by the Census Bureau for the Bureau of Labor Statistics, collecting information from more than 50,000 households on employment and unemployment. In March of each year, the survey includes the Annual Social and Economic Supplement (formerly called the Annual Demographic Survey), which is the source of most national data on the characteristics of Americans, such as educational attainment, living arrangements, and incomes.

dual-earner couple A married couple in which both the householder and the householder's spouse are in the labor force.

earnings A type of income, earnings is the amount of money a person receives from his or her job. *See also* Income.

employed All civilians who did any work as a paid employee or farmer/self-employed worker, or who worked 15 hours or more as an unpaid farm worker or in a family-owned business, during the reference period. All those who have jobs but who are temporarily absent from their jobs due to illness, bad weather, vacation, labor management dispute, or personal reasons are considered employed.

expenditure The transaction cost including excise and sales taxes of goods and services acquired during the survey period. The full cost of each purchase is recorded even though full payment may not have been made at the date of purchase. Average expenditure figures may be artificially low for infrequently purchased items such as cars because figures are calculated using all consumer units within a demographic segment rather than just purchasers. Expenditure estimates include money spent on gifts for others.

family A group of two or more people (one of whom is the householder) related by birth, marriage, or adoption and living in the same household.

family household A household maintained by a householder who lives with one or more people related to him or her by blood, marriage, or adoption.

female/male householder A woman or man who maintains a household without a spouse present. May head family or nonfamily households.

foreign-born population People who are not U.S. citizens at birth.

full-time employment Full-time is 35 or more hours of work per week during a majority of the weeks worked.

full-time, year-round Indicates 50 or more weeks of full-time employment during the previous calendar year.

Generation X Americans born between 1965 and 1976, also known as the baby-bust generation.

group quarters population The group quarters population includes all people not living in households. Two general categories of people in group quarters are recognized: 1) the institutionalized population, which includes people under formally authorized, supervised care or custody in institutions at the time of enumeration such as correctional institutions, nursing homes, and juvenile institutions; and 2) the noninstitutionalized population, which includes all people who live in group quarters other than institutions such as college dormitories, military quarters, and group homes.

Hispanic Hispanic origin is self-reported in a question separate from race. Because Hispanic is an ethnic origin rather than a race, Hispanics may be of any race. While most Hispanics are white, there are black, Asian, American Indian, and even Native Hawaiian Hispanics. On the 2000 census, many Hispanics identified their race as "other" rather than white, black, and so on. In fact, 90 percent of people identifying their race as "other" also identified themselves as Hispanic. The 2000 census count of Hispanics differs from estimates in the Current Population Survey and other noncensus data collections in part due to methodological differences.

household All the persons who occupy a housing unit. A household includes the related family members and all the unrelated persons, if any, such as lodgers, foster children, wards, or employees who share the housing unit. A person living alone is counted as a household. A group of unrelated people who share a housing unit as roommates or unmarried partners is also counted as a household. Households do not include group quarters such as college dormitories, prisons, or nursing homes.

household, race/ethnicity of Households are categorized according to the race or ethnicity of the householder only.

householder The householder is the person (or one of the persons) in whose name the housing unit is owned or rented or, if there is no such person, any adult member. With married couples, the householder may be either the husband or wife. The householder is the reference person for the household.

householder, age of The age of the householder is used to categorize households into age groups such as those used in this book. Married couples, for example, are classified according to the age of either the husband or wife, depending on which one identified him or herself as the householder.

housing unit A housing unit is a house, an apartment, a group of rooms, or a single room occupied or intended for occupancy as separate living quarters. Separate living quarters are those in which the occupants do not live and eat with any other persons in the structure and that have direct access from the outside of the building or through a common hall that is used or intended for use by the occupants of another unit or by the general public. The occupants may be a single family, one person living alone, two or more families living together, or any other group of related or unrelated persons who share living arrangements.

Housing Vacancy Survey The AHS is a supplement to the Current Population Survey, providing quarterly and annual data on rental and homeowner vacancy rates, characteristics of units available for occupancy, and homeownership rates by age, household type, region, state, and metropolitan area. The Current Population Survey sample includes 51,000 occupied housing units and 9,000 vacant units.

housing value The respondent's estimate of how much his or her house and lot would sell for if it were for sale.

immigration The relatively permanent movement (change of residence) of people into the country of reference.

in-migration The relatively permanent movement (change of residence) of people into a subnational geographic entity, such as a region, division, state, metropolitan area, or county.

income Money received in the preceding calendar year by each person aged 15 or older from each of the following sources: (1) earnings from longest job (or self-employment); (2) earnings from jobs other than longest job; (3) unemployment compensation; (4) workers' compensation; (5) Social Security; (6) Supplemental Security income; (7) public assistance; (8) veterans' payments; (9) survivor benefits; (10) disability benefits; (11) retirement pensions; (12) interest; (13) dividends; (14) rents and royalties or estates and trusts; (15) educational assistance; (16) alimony; (17) child support; (18) financial assistance from outside the household, and other periodic income. Income is reported in several ways in this book. Household income is the combined income of all household members. Income of persons is all income accruing to a person from all sources. Earnings are the money a person receives from his or her job.

industry Refers to the industry in which a person worked longest in the preceding calendar year.

institutionalized population *See* Group quarters population.

job tenure The length of time a person has been employed continuously by the same employer.

labor force The labor force tables in this book show the civilian labor force only. The labor force includes both the employed and the unemployed (people who are looking for work). People are counted as in the labor force if they were working or looking for work during the reference week in which the Census Bureau fields the Current Population Survey.

labor force participation rate The percent of the civilian noninstitutional population that is in the civilian labor force, which includes both the employed and the unemployed.

married couples with or without children under age 18 Refers to married couples with or without own children under age 18 living in the same household. Couples without children under age 18 may be parents of grown children who live elsewhere, or they could be childless couples.

median The median is the amount that divides the population or households into two equal portions: one below and one above the median. Medians can be calculated for income, age, and many other characteristics.

median income The amount that divides the income distribution into two equal groups, half having incomes above the median, half having incomes below the median. The medians for households or families are based on all households or families. The median for persons are based on all persons aged 15 or older with income.

Medical Expenditure Panel Survey MEPS is a nationally representative survey that collects detailed information on the health status, access to care, health care use and expenses and health insurance coverage of the civilian noninstitutionalized population of the U.S. and nursing home residents. MEPS comprises four component surveys: the Household Component, the Medical Provider Component, the Insurance Component, and the Nursing Home Component. The Household Component is the core survey and is conducted each year, and includes 15,000 households and 37,000 people.

metropolitan statistical area (MSA) To be defined as a metropolitan statistical area (or MSA), an area must include a city with 50,000 or more inhabitants, or a Census Bureau-defined urbanized area of at least 50,000 inhabitants and a total metropolitan population of at least 100,000 (75,000 in New England). The county (or counties) that contains the largest city becomes the "central county" (counties), along with any adjacent counties that have at least 50 percent of their population in the urbanized area surrounding the largest city. Additional "outlying counties" are included in the MSA if they meet specified requirements of commuting to the central counties and other selected requirements of metropolitan character (such as population density and percent urban). In New England, MSAs are defined in terms of cities and towns rather than counties. For this reason, the concept of NECMA is used to define metropolitan areas in the New England division.

Millennial generation Americans born between 1977 and 1994.

mobility status People are classified according to their mobility status on the basis of a comparison between their place of residence at the time of the March Current Population Survey and their place of residence in March of the previous year. Nonmovers are people living in the same house at the end of the period as at the beginning of the period. Movers are people living in a different house at the end of the period than at the beginning of the period. Movers from abroad are either citizens or aliens whose place of residence is outside the United States at the beginning of the period, that is, in an outlying area under the jurisdiction of the United States or in a foreign country. The mobility status for children is fully allocated from the mother if she is in the household; otherwise it is allocated from the householder.

Monitoring the Future Project (MTF) The MTF survey is conducted by the University of Michigan Survey Research Center. The survey is administered to approximately 50,000 students in 420 public and private secondary schools every year. High school seniors have been surveyed annually since 1975. Students in 8th and 10th grade have been surveyed annually since 1991.

National Ambulatory Medical Care Survey (NAMCS) The NAMCS is an annual survey of visits to nonfederally employed office-based physicians who are primarily engaged in direct patient care. Data are collected from physicians rather than patients, with each physician assigned a one-week reporting period. During that week, a systematic random sample of visit characteristics are recorded by the physician or office staff.

National Health Interview Survey (NHIS) The NHIS is a continuing nationwide sample survey of the civilian noninstitutional population of the U.S. conducted by the Census Bureau for the National Center for Health Statistics. Each year, data are collected from more than 100,000 people about their illnesses, injuries, impairments, chronic and acute conditions, activity limitations, and the use of health services.

National Home and Hospice Care Survey These are a series of surveys of a nationally representative sample of home and hospice care agencies in the U.S., sponsored by the National Center for Health Statistics. Data on the characteristics of patients and services provided are collected through personal interviews with administrators and staff.

National Hospital Discharge Survey This survey has been conducted annually since 1965, sponsored by the National Center for Health Statistics, to collect nationally representative information on the characteristics of inpatients discharged from nonfederal, short-stay hospitals in the U.S. The survey collects data from a sample of approximately 270,000 inpatient records acquired from a national sample of about 500 hospitals.

National Household Education Survey (NHES) The NHES, sponsored by the National Center for Education Statistics, provides descriptive data on the educational activities of the U.S. population, including after-school care and adult education. The NHES is a system of telephone surveys of a representative sample of 45,000 to 60,000 households in the U.S. It has been conducted in 1991, 1993, 1995, 1996, 1999, 2001, and 2003.

National Nursing Home Survey This is a series of national sample surveys of nursing homes, their residents, and staff conducted at various intervals since 1973–74 and sponsored by the National Center for Health Statistics. The latest survey was taken in 1999. data for the survey are obtained through personal interviews with administrators and staff, and occasionally with self-administered questionnaires, in a sample of about 1,500 facilities.

National Survey on Drug Use and Health *(formerly called the National Household Survey on Drug Abuse)* This survey, sponsored by the Substance Abuse and Mental Health Services Administration, has been conducted since 1971. It is the primary source of information on the use of illegal drugs by the U.S. population. Each year, a nationally representative sample of about 70,000 individuals aged 12 or older are surveyed in the 50 states and the District of Columbia.

Native Hawaiian and other Pacific Islander The 2000 census, for the first time, identified this group as a separate racial category from Asians. The term "Native Hawaiian and other Pacific Islander" may include those who identified themselves as Native Hawaiian and other Pacific Islander and no other race (called "Native Hawaiian and other Pacific Islander alone") or those who identified themselves as Native Hawaiian and other Pacific Islander and some other race (called "Native Hawaiian and other Pacific Islander in combination").

net migration Net migration is the result of subtracting out-migration from in-migration for an area. Another way to derive net migration is to subtract natural increase (births minus deaths) from total population change in an area.

net worth The amount of money left over after a household's debts are subtracted from its assets.

nonfamily household A household maintained by a householder who lives alone or who lives with people to whom he or she is not related.

nonfamily householder A householder who lives alone or with nonrelatives.

non-Hispanic People who do not identify themselves as Hispanic are classified as non-Hispanic. Non-Hispanics may be of any race.

non-Hispanic white People who identify their race as white and who do not indicate a Hispanic origin. The 2000 census classified people as non-Hispanic white if they identified their race as "white alone" and did not indicate their ethnicity as Hispanic. This definition is close to the one used in the Current Population Survey and other government data collection efforts.

noninstitutionalized population *See* Group quarters population.

nonmetropolitan area Counties that are not classified as metropolitan areas.

occupation Occupational classification is based on the kind of work a person did at his or her job during the previous calendar year. If a person changed jobs during the year, the data refer to the occupation of the job held the longest during that year.

occupied housing units A housing unit is classified as occupied if a person or group of people is living in it or if the occupants are only temporarily absent—on vacation, example. By definition, the count of occupied housing units is the same as the count of households.

other race The 2000 census included "other race" as a racial category. The category was meant to capture the few Americans, such as Creoles, who may not consider themselves as belonging to the other five racial groups. In fact, more than 18 million Americans identified themselves as "other race," including 42 percent of the nation's Hispanics. Among the 18 million people who claim to be of "other" race, 90 percent also identified themselves as Hispanic. The government considers Hispanic to be an ethnic identification rather than a race since there are white, black, American Indian, and Asian Hispanics. But many Hispanics consider their ethnicity to be a separate race.

outside central city The portion of a metropolitan county or counties that falls outside of the central city or cities; generally regarded as the suburbs.

own children Own children are sons and daughters, including stepchildren and adopted children, of the householder. The totals include never-married children living away from home in college dormitories.

owner occupied A housing unit is "owner occupied" if the owner lives in the unit, even if it is mortgaged or not fully paid for. A cooperative or condominium unit is "owner occupied" only if the owner lives in it. All other occupied units are classified as "renter occupied."

part-time employment Part-time is less than 35 hours of work per week in a majority of the weeks worked during the year.

percent change The change (either positive or negative) in a measure that is expressed as a proportion of the starting measure. When median income changes from $20,000 to $25,000, for example, this is a 25 percent increase.

percentage point change The change (either positive or negative) in a value which is already expressed as a percentage. When a labor force participation rate changes from 70 percent of 75 percent, for example, this is a 5 percentage point increase.

poverty level The official income threshold below which families and people are classified as living in poverty. The threshold rises each year with inflation and varies depending on family size and age of householder.

proportion or share The value of a part expressed as a percentage of the whole. If there are 4 million people aged 25 and 3 million of them are white, then the white proportion is 75 percent.

race Race is self-reported and defined differently depending on the data source. On the 2000 census, respondents identified themselves as belonging to one or more of six racial groups: American Indian and Alaska Native, Asian, black, Native Hawaiian and other Pacific Islander, white, and other. In publishing the results, the Census Bureau created three new terms to distinguish one group from another. The "race alone" population is people who identified themselves as only one race. The "race in combination" population is people who identified themselves as more than one race, such as white and black. The "race, alone or in combination" population includes both those who identified themselves as one race and those who identified themselves as more than one race. Other government data collection efforts included the multira-

cial option beginning in 2003. The tables in this book that include race data from government surveys or from censuses prior to 2000 do not include the multiracial option.

regions The four major regions and nine census divisions of the United States are the state groupings as shown below:

Northeast:
—New England: Connecticut, Maine, Massachusetts, New Hampshire, Rhode Island, and Vermont
—Middle Atlantic: New Jersey, New York, and Pennsylvania

Midwest:
—East North Central: Illinois, Indiana, Michigan, Ohio, and Wisconsin
—West North Central: Iowa, Kansas, Minnesota, Missouri, Nebraska, North Dakota, and South Dakota

South:
—South Atlantic: Delaware, District of Columbia, Florida, Georgia, Maryland, North Carolina, South Carolina, Virginia, and West Virginia
—East South Central: Alabama, Kentucky, Mississippi, and Tennessee
—West South Central: Arkansas, Louisiana, Oklahoma, and Texas

West:
—Mountain: Arizona, Colorado, Idaho, Montana, Nevada, New Mexico, Utah, and Wyoming
—Pacific: Alaska, California, Hawaii, Oregon, and Washington

renter occupied *See* Owner occupied.

rounding Percentages are rounded to the nearest tenth of a percent; therefore, the percentages in a distribution do not always add exactly to 100.0 percent. The totals, however, are always shown as 100.0. Moreover, individual figures are rounded to the nearest thousand without being adjusted to group totals, which are independently rounded; percentages are based on the unrounded numbers.

self-employment A person is categorized as self-employed if he or she was self-employed in the job held longest during the reference period. Persons who report self-employment from a second job are excluded, but those who report wage-and-salary income from a second job are included. Unpaid workers in family businesses are excluded. Self-employment statistics include only nonagricultural workers and exclude people who work for themselves in incorporated business.

sex ratio The number of men per 100 women.

suburbs *See* Outside central city.

Survey of Consumer Finances The Survey of Consumer Finances is a triennial survey taken by the Federal Reserve Board. It collects data on the assets, debts, and net worth of American households. For the 2001 survey, the Federal Reserve Board interviewed more than 4,000 households.

Survey of Income and Program Participation (SIPP) SIPP is a longitudinal survey conducted at four-month intervals by the Census Bureau. The main focus of SIPP is information on labor force participation, jobs, income, and participation in federal assistance programs. Information on other topics is collected in topical modules on a rotating basis.

two or more races People who identified themselves as belonging to two or more racial groups on the 2000 Census. *See* Race.

unemployed Unemployed people are those who, during the survey period, had no employment but were available and looking for work. Those who were laid off from their jobs and were waiting to be recalled are also classified as unemployed.

white The term "white" is defined differently depending on whether census or survey data are shown. In tables showing 2000 census data, the term "white" may include those who identified themselves as white and no other race (called "white alone") or those who identified themselves as white and some other race (called "white in combination"). White estimates from the 2003 Current Population Survey include both those who identified themselves as white alone and those who identified themselves as white in combination. White estimates in earlier survey data do not include the multiracial option.

Youth Risk Behavior Surveillance System (YRBSS) The YRBSS was created by the Centers for Disease Control to monitor health risks being taken by young people at the national, state, and local level. The national survey is taken every two years based on a nationally representative sample of 16,000 students in 9th through 12th grade in public and private schools.

Bibliography

Bureau of Justice Statistics

Internet site http://www.albany.edu/sourcebook/

—*Sourcebook of Criminal Justice Statistics, 2002* [online], Kathleen Maguire and Ann L. Pastore, eds.

Bureau of Labor Statistics

Internet site http://www.bls.gov

—1997 and 2002 Consumer Expenditure Surveys, Internet site http://www.bls.gov/cex/

—2002 Consumer Expenditure Survey, unpublished data

—2003 Current Population Survey, unpublished data

—*Characteristics of Minimum Wage Workers, 2002,* Internet site http://www.bls.gov/cps/minwage2002.htm

—*College Enrollment and Work Activity of 2002 High School Graduates,* USDL 03-330, 2003, Internet site http://www.bls.gov/news.release/hsgec.toc.htm

—*Contingent and Alternative Employment Arrangements,* February 2001, USDL 01-153, Internet site http://www.bls.gov/news.release/conemp.toc.htm

—*Employee Tenure in 2002,* Internet site http://www.bls.gov/news.release/tenure.toc.htm

—*Employment Characteristics of Families, 2002,* Internet site http://www.bls.gov/news.release/famee.toc.htm

—Employment Projections, 2002–2012, Internet site http://www.bls.gov/emp/emplab1.htm

—Labor force participation rates, historical, Public Query Data Tool, Internet site http://www.bls.gov/data

—*Workers on Flexible and Shift Schedules in 2001,* USDL 02-225, Internet site http://www.bls.gov/news.release/flex.toc.htm

Bureau of the Census

Internet site http://www.census.gov

—2003 Current Population Survey Annual Social and Economic Supplement, Internet site http://www.census.gov/hhes/income/dinctabs.html

—*Adopted Children and Stepchildren: 2000,* Census 2000 Special Report, CENSR-GRV, 2003

—*Age: 2000,* Census 2000 Brief, 2001

—*American Housing Survey for the United States in 2001,* Internet site http://www.census.gov/hhes/www/ahs.html

—*Americans with Disabilities: 1997,* detailed tables from Current Population Reports, P70-73, Internet site http://www.census.gov/hhes/www/disable/sipp/disable97.html

—Census 2000, Internet site http://factfinder.census.gov/servlet/BasicFactsServlet

—*Children with Health Insurance: 2001,* Current Population Reports, P20-224, 2003

—*Children's Living Arrangements and Characteristics: March 2002,* detailed tables for Current Population Report P20-547, Internet site http://www.census.gov/population/www/socdemo/hh-fam/cps2002.html

—*A Child's Day: 2000 (Selected Indicators of Child Well-Being)*, Current Population Reports, detailed tables for P70-89, 2003, Internet site http://www.census.gov/population/www/socdemo/00p70-89.html

—Current Population Surveys, historical data, Internet site http://www.census.gov/hhes/income/histinc/histinctb.html

—*Disability Status: 2000*, Census 2000 Brief, 2003

—*Educational Attainment in the United States: March 2002*, detailed tables (PPL-169), Internet site http://www.census.gov/population/www/socdemo/education/ppl-169.html

—*Fertility of American Women: June 2002*, detailed tables, Internet site http://www.census.gov/population/www/socdemo/fertility/cps2002.html

—*Foreign-Born Population of the United States, Current Population Survey—March 2002*, detailed tables (PPL-162), Internet site http://www.census.gov/population/www/socdemo/foreign/ppl-162.html

—*Geographic Mobility: 2003*, detailed tables for P20-549, Internet site http://www.census.gov/population/www/socdemo/migrate/p20-549.html

—Housing Vacancy Surveys, Internet site http://www.census.gov/hhes/www/housing/hvs/annual03/ann03ind.html

—National Population Estimates, Internet site http://eire.census.gov/popest

—*School Enrollment—Social and Economic Characteristics of Students: October 2002*, detailed tables; Internet site http://www.census.gov/population/www/socdemo/school/cps2002.html

—*U.S. Interim Projections by Age, Sex, Race, and Hispanic Origin*, Internet site http://www.census.gov/ipc/www/usinterimproj/

Centers for Disease Control and Prevention

Internet site http://www.cdc.gov

—Behavioral Risk Factor Surveillance System Prevalence Data, Internet site http://apps.nccd.cdc.gov/brfss/index.asp

—"Physical Activity Levels Among Children Aged 9–13 Years—United States, 2002," *Mortality and Morbidity Weekly Report*, Vol. 52, No. 33, August 22, 2003

—Youth Risk Behavior Surveillance System, Internet site http://www.cdc.gov/nccdphp/dash/yrbs/results.htm

—"Youth Risk Behavior Surveillance—United States, 2001," *Mortality and Morbidity Weekly Report*, Vol. 51/SS-4, June 28, 2002

Federal Interagency Forum on Child and Family Statistics

Internet site http://www.childstats.gov/americaschildren/

—*America's Children: Key National Indicators of Well-Being, 2003*

Higher Education Research Institute

Internet site http://www.gseis.ucla.edu/heri/heri.html

—*The American Freshman: National Norms for Fall 2003*, L. J. Sax, A. W. Astin, J. A. Lindholm, W. S. Korn, V. B. Saenz, and K. M. Mahoney (UCLA: 2003)

Institute for Social Research, University of Michigan
    Internet site http://monitoringthefuture.org
    —Monitoring the Future Survey, 2002

National Center for Education Statistics
    Internet site http://nces.ed.gov
    —Adult Education and Lifelong Learning Survey of the National Household Education Surveys Program, Internet site http://nces.ed.gov/programs/coe/2003/section1/tables/t08_2.asp
    —*Computer and Internet Use by Children and Adolescents*, NCES 2004-014, 2003, Internet site http://nces.ed.gov/pubsearch/pubsinfo.asp?pubid=2004014
    —*Digest of Education Statistics, 2002*, Internet site http://nces.ed.gov/pubs2003/digest02/index.asp
    —*Projections of Education Statistics to 2013*, Internet site http://nces.ed.gov/programs/projections

National Center for Health Statistics
    Internet site http://www.cdc.gov/nchs
    —Births: Final Data for 2002, *National Vital Statistics Reports*, Vol. 52, No. 10, 2003
    —Deaths: Leading Causes for 2001, *National Vital Statistics Report*, Vol. 52, No. 9, 2003
    —Deaths: Preliminary Data for 2002, *National Vital Statistics Report*, Vol. 52, No. 13, 2004
    —Health Behaviors of Adults: United States, 1999–2001, *Vital and Health Statistics*, Series 10, No. 219, 2004
    —*Health, United States, 2003*, Internet site http://www.cdc.gov/nchs/hus.htm
    —National Ambulatory Medical Care Survey: 2001 Summary, *Advance Data* No. 337, 2003
    —National Hospital Ambulatory Medical Care Survey: 2001 Emergency Department Summary, *Advance Data* No. 335, 2003
    —National Hospital Ambulatory Medical Care Survey: 2001 Outpatient Department Summary, *Advance Data* No. 338, 2003
    —Revised Birth and Fertility Rates for the 1990s and New Rates for the Hispanic Populations 2000 and 2001: United States, *National Vital Statistics Report*, Vol. 51, No. 12, 2003
    —*Summary Health Statistics for U.S. Children: National Health Interview Survey, 2001*, Series 10, No. 216, 2003

National Sporting Goods Association
    Internet site http://www.nsga.org

U.S. Citizenship and Immigration Services
    —*2002 Yearbook of Immigration Statistics*, Internet site http://uscis.gov/graphics/shared/aboutus/statistics/index.htm

U.S. Substance Abuse and Mental Health Services Administration, Office of Applied Studies
    Internet site http://www.samhsa.gov/
    —National Survey on Drug Use and Health, 2002

Index

Black-American men:
  educational attainment, 49–50
  employment status, 203, 208–209
  full-time workers, 185, 188
  income, 185, 188
  living alone, 245, 247
  marital status, 288–289
Black-American women:
  births to, 91, 95–96
  educational attainment, 49, 51
  employment status, 210
  full-time workers, 191, 194
  income, 191, 194
  living alone, 245, 247
  marital status, 283, 288–289
Black Americans:
  attitude toward children, 23–24
  biological, step, and adopted children, 272–273, 278
  by state, 295, 310, 315–323
  changing schools, 18
  children in day care, 239
  college enrollment rate, 64, 66
  educational attainment, 49–51
  expected to go to college, 22
  extracurricular activities, 14–15
  health conditions, 116–117, 119, 121
  health insurance coverage, 113–115
  homeownership, 148–149
  household income, 165, 168, 171
  household types, 241, 244–245, 247
  households with children, 241, 252, 255
  in gifted classes, 17
  in poverty, 200–202
  living arrangements of children, 241, 264–265
  parents of college freshmen, 34–36
  physical activities, 84
  population, 295, 301–303, 310, 315–323
  SAT scores, 60–61
  with school problems, 19–20
  with television rules, 10–12

Caesarean section, 97
cancer, as cause of death, 132, 134–138
cash contributions:
  spending by householders under age 25, 329, 348
  spending by married couples with children, 355, 359, 363, 371
  spending by single parents, 367, 371
cerebrovascular disease, as cause of death, 134–138
child support, as source of income, 198–199
childbearing. See Births.
childless, 88, 90–93

children:
  adopted, 241, 270–279
  average number in household, 250–251
  biological, 241, 270–279
  by age of parent, 266–267
  by education of parent, 266, 268
  by family characteristics, 241, 266–268
  by homeownership status of parent, 266, 268
  by marital status of parent, 266, 268
  by number of siblings, 266–267
  by parent's educational expectations, 21–22
  changing schools, 18
  computer use of, 32–33
  delinquent behavior of, 5, 25–31
  eating meals with parents, 5–8
  in day care, 236, 239
  in extracurricular activities, 13–15
  in gifted classes, 16–17
  in poverty, 200–202
  income of families with, 177–181
  Internet use of, 5, 32–33
  living arrangements of, 241, 264–268
  mobility status by presence of, 158, 161
  number ever born, 88–90
  parent attitude toward, 23–24
  parent interaction with, 6–8
  presence of in households, 241, 252–263, 270–271
  repeating a grade, 16, 19
  step, 241, 270–279
  suspended from school, 16, 20
  with school problems, 5, 16, 19–20
  with stay-at-home parent, 266, 269
  with television rules, 5, 9–12
  with working parents, 236, 239
cigarette smoking, 38, 75, 98–101, 103, 110. See also Tobacco products.
citizens:
  college freshmen, 34, 36
  health insurance coverage, 113–115
  number of, 305–306
climate, as a reason for moving, 162–164
clubs, children participating in, 13–15
cocaine use, 108–110
college: See also Education.
  alcohol consumption by students, 37, 38, 101, 103
  as a reason for moving, 141, 158, 162–164
  attendance status, 45
  attitudes of freshmen, 5, 39–41
  characteristics of freshmen, 5, 34–36
  children expected to go, 21–22
  cigarette smoking by students, 101, 103
  computer use by students, 37–38
  concern about financing, 5, 42–43

females:
  adopted children, 270, 278
  attitudes of college freshmen, 39–41
  births to, 88–97
  by race and Hispanic origin, 91
  by region, 91
  changing schools, 18
  childless, 88, 90–93
  cigarette smoking, 38
  college enrollment, number, 67–72
  college enrollment, rate, 45, 64–65
  computer use, 37–38
  delinquent behavior, 25–31
  depression, 38
  dieting, 75, 78, 80
  disabled, 124–126
  drinking, 25–29
  educational attainment, 45–46, 48–49, 51, 91
  employment status, 91, 206–208, 210
  exercise, participation in, 82, 85
  expected to go to college, 22
  extracurricular activities, 13–15
  full-time workers, 191–196, 221–222, 236, 238
  health conditions, 116–117, 119, 121, 123–126
  in gifted classes, 17
  income, 91, 165, 174–176, 182, 184, 191–197, 199
  Internet use, 37–38
  labor force participation, 203–208, 210–212, 234–235
  labor force projections, 234–235
  life expectancy, 132, 139
  living alone, 242–243, 245–249, 280, 282
  living arrangements, 280, 282
  marijuana use, 107
  marital status, 91, 241, 283–293
  metropolitan status, 91
  objectives of college freshmen, 39, 41
  occupation, 91
  overweight, 75, 78–80
  part-time workers, 203, 221–222, 238
  physical activities, 83–85
  physician visits, 128–129
  population, 267, 298
  religious service attendance, 38
  SAT scores, 60–61
  self-employed, 223–224
  sexually active, 75, 86–87
  sources of income, 197, 199
  unemployed, 206–208, 210
  union membership, 232–233
  volunteering, 37–38
  with AIDS, 123
  with flexible schedules, 227–228
  with school problems, 19–20
  with television rules, 10–12
  working parent, 236–239, 269

fighting, physical, 25–31
financial services, spending on, 348
fishing, 83
food:
  at home, 327, 332–335, 352–353, 356–357, 360–361, 365, 369
  away from home, 326–327, 335, 352–353, 356–357, 360–361, 364–365, 369
  spending by householders under age 25, 326–327, 329, 332–335, 349, 360–361
  spending by married couples with children, 352–353, 356–357, 369
  spending by single parents, 364–365, 369
foreign-born:
  biological, step, and adopted children, 270, 277, 279
  health insurance coverage, 111, 113–115
  parents of college freshmen, 34, 36
  population, 295, 305–307
  women giving birth, 91
full-time workers, 185–196, 221–222, 236, 238
furnishings and equipment:
  spending by householders under age 25, 326, 339–340
  spending by married couples with children, 352, 354, 356, 358, 360, 362, 370
  spending by single parents, 364, 366, 370

geographic mobility:
  rate, 141, 158–161
  reason for, 141, 158, 162–164
gifted classes, children in, 16–17
gifts for non-household members:
  spending by householders under age 25, 329–330, 349–351
  spending by married couples with children, 355, 359, 363, 371
  spending by single parents, 367, 371
golf, 83
grade, school enrollment by, 52, 54
grandparent, children living with, 264–265
gun control, attitudes toward, 39–40

hallucinogens, use of, 108–109
hay fever, 117–122
health, as a reason for moving, 162–164
health care:
  spending by householders under age 25, 326, 329–331, 344–345, 351
  spending by married couples with children, 352, 354, 356, 362, 370
  spending by single parents, 366, 370
health conditions, 116–127